WinSock 2.0

WinSock 2.0

Lewis Napper

IDG Books Worldwide, Inc.
An International Data Group Company

Foster City, CA ◆ Chicago, IL ◆ Indianapolis, IN ◆ Southlake, TX

WinSock 2.0

Published by
IDG Books Worldwide, Inc.
An International Data Group Company
919 E. Hillsdale Blvd., Suite 400
Foster City, CA 94404
www.idgbooks.com (IDG Books Worldwide Web site)

Copyright © 1997 IDG Books Worldwide, Inc. All rights reserved. No part of this book, including interior design, cover design, and icons, may be reproduced or transmitted in any form, by any means (electronic, photocopying, recording, or otherwise) without the prior written permission of the publisher.

Library of Congress Catalog Card No.: 97-76684

ISBN: 0-7645-8049-3

Printed in the United States of America

10 9 8 7 6 5 4 3 2 1

IB/QR/RS/ZX/FC

Distributed in the United States by IDG Books Worldwide, Inc.

Distributed by Macmillan Canada for Canada; by Transworld Publishers Limited in the United Kingdom; by IDG Norge Books for Norway; by IDG Sweden Books for Sweden; by Woodslane Pty. Ltd. for Australia; by Woodslane Enterprises Ltd. for New Zealand; by Longman Singapore Publishers Ltd. for Singapore, Malaysia, Thailand, and Indonesia; by Simron Pty. Ltd. for South Africa; by Toppan Company Ltd. for Japan; by Distribuidora Cuspide for Argentina; by Livraria Cultura for Brazil; by Ediciencia S.A. for Ecuador; by Addison-Wesley Publishing Company for Korea; by Ediciones ZETA S.C.R. Ltda. for Peru; by WS Computer Publishing Corporation, Inc., for the Philippines; by Unalis Corporation for Taiwan; by Contemporanea de Ediciones for Venezuela; by Computer Book & Magazine Store for Puerto Rico; by Express Computer Distributors for the Caribbean and West Indies. Authorized Sales Agent: Anthony Rudkin Associates for the Middle East and North Africa.

For general information on IDG Books Worldwide's books in the U.S., please call our Consumer Customer Service department at 800-762-2974. For reseller information, including discounts and premium sales, please call our Reseller Customer Service department at 800-434-3422.

For information on where to purchase IDG Books Worldwide's books outside the U.S., please contact our International Sales department at 415-655-3200 or fax 415-655-3295.

For information on foreign language translations, please contact our Foreign & Subsidiary Rights department at 415-655-3021 or fax 415-655-3281.

For sales inquiries and special prices for bulk quantities, please contact our Sales department at 415-655-3200 or write to the address above.

For information on using IDG Books Worldwide's books in the classroom or for ordering examination copies, please contact our Educational Sales department at 800-434-2086 or fax 817-251-8174.

For press review copies, author interviews, or other publicity information, please contact our Public Relations department at 415-655-3000 or fax 415-655-3299.

For authorization to photocopy items for corporate, personal, or educational use, please contact Copyright Clearance Center, 222 Rosewood Drive, Danvers, MA 01923, or fax 508-750-4470.

LIMIT OF LIABILITY/DISCLAIMER OF WARRANTY: AUTHOR AND PUBLISHER HAVE USED THEIR BEST EFFORTS IN PREPARING THIS BOOK. IDG BOOKS WORLDWIDE, INC., AND AUTHOR MAKE NO REPRESENTATIONS OR WARRANTIES WITH RESPECT TO THE ACCURACY OR COMPLETENESS OF THE CONTENTS OF THIS BOOK AND SPECIFICALLY DISCLAIM ANY IMPLIED WARRANTIES OF MERCHANTABILITY OR FITNESS FOR A PARTICULAR PURPOSE. THERE ARE NO WARRANTIES WHICH EXTEND BEYOND THE DESCRIPTIONS CONTAINED IN THIS PARAGRAPH. NO WARRANTY MAY BE CREATED OR EXTENDED BY SALES REPRESENTATIVES OR WRITTEN SALES MATERIALS. THE ACCURACY AND COMPLETENESS OF THE INFORMATION PROVIDED HEREIN AND THE OPINIONS STATED HEREIN ARE NOT GUARANTEED OR WARRANTED TO PRODUCE ANY PARTICULAR RESULTS, AND THE ADVICE AND STRATEGIES CONTAINED HEREIN MAY NOT BE SUITABLE FOR EVERY INDIVIDUAL. NEITHER IDG BOOKS WORLDWIDE, INC., NOR AUTHOR SHALL BE LIABLE FOR ANY LOSS OF PROFIT OR ANY OTHER COMMERCIAL DAMAGES, INCLUDING BUT NOT LIMITED TO SPECIAL, INCIDENTAL, CONSEQUENTIAL, OR OTHER DAMAGES.

Trademarks: All brand names and product names used in this book are trade names, service marks, trademarks, or registered trademarks of their respective owners. IDG Books Worldwide is not associated with any product or vendor mentioned in this book.

IDG BOOKS WORLDWIDE™ is a trademark under exclusive license to IDG Books Worldwide, Inc., from International Data Group, Inc.

ABOUT IDG BOOKS WORLDWIDE

Welcome to the world of IDG Books Worldwide.

IDG Books Worldwide, Inc., is a subsidiary of International Data Group, the world's largest publisher of computer-related information and the leading global provider of information services on information technology. IDG was founded more than 25 years ago and now employs more than 8,500 people worldwide. IDG publishes more than 275 computer publications in over 75 countries (see listing below). More than 60 million people read one or more IDG publications each month.

Launched in 1990, IDG Books Worldwide is today the #1 publisher of best-selling computer books in the United States. We are proud to have received eight awards from the Computer Press Association in recognition of editorial excellence and three from *Computer Currents*' First Annual Readers' Choice Awards. Our best-selling ...*For Dummies*® series has more than 30 million copies in print with translations in 30 languages. IDG Books Worldwide, through a joint venture with IDG's Hi-Tech Beijing, became the first U.S. publisher to publish a computer book in the People's Republic of China. In record time, IDG Books Worldwide has become the first choice for millions of readers around the world who want to learn how to better manage their businesses.

Our mission is simple: Every one of our books is designed to bring extra value and skill-building instructions to the reader. Our books are written by experts who understand and care about our readers. The knowledge base of our editorial staff comes from years of experience in publishing, education, and journalism — experience we use to produce books for the '90s. In short, we care about books, so we attract the best people. We devote special attention to details such as audience, interior design, use of icons, and illustrations. And because we use an efficient process of authoring, editing, and desktop publishing our books electronically, we can spend more time ensuring superior content and spend less time on the technicalities of making books.

You can count on our commitment to deliver high-quality books at competitive prices on topics you want to read about. At IDG Books Worldwide, we continue in the IDG tradition of delivering quality for more than 25 years. You'll find no better book on a subject than one from IDG Books Worldwide.

John Kilcullen
CEO
IDG Books Worldwide, Inc.

Steven Berkowitz
President and Publisher
IDG Books Worldwide, Inc.

Eighth Annual Computer Press Awards ≥1992

Ninth Annual Computer Press Awards ≥1993

Tenth Annual Computer Press Awards ≥1994

Eleventh Annual Computer Press Awards ≥1995

IDG Books Worldwide, Inc., is a subsidiary of International Data Group, the world's largest publisher of computer-related information and the leading global provider of information services on information technology. International Data Group publishes over 275 computer publications in over 75 countries. Sixty million people read one or more International Data Group publications each month. International Data Group's publications include: **ARGENTINA:** Buyer's Guide, Computerworld Argentina, PC World Argentina; **AUSTRALIA:** Australian Macworld, Australian PC World, Australian Reseller News, Computerworld, IT Casebook, Network World, Publish, Webmaster; **AUSTRIA:** Computerwelt Osterreich, Networks Austria, PC Tip Austria; **BANGLADESH:** PC World Bangladesh; **BELARUS:** PC World Belarus; **BELGIUM:** Data News; **BRAZIL:** Annuario de Informática, Computerworld, Connections, Macworld, PC Player, PC World, Publish, Reseller News, Supergamepower; **BULGARIA:** Computerworld Bulgaria, Network World Bulgaria, PC & MacWorld Bulgaria; **CANADA:** CIO Canada, Client/Server World, ComputerWorld Canada, InfoWorld Canada, NetworkWorld Canada, WebWorld; **CHILE:** Computerworld Chile, PC World Chile; **COLOMBIA:** Computerworld Colombia, PC World Colombia; **COSTA RICA:** PC World Centro America; **THE CZECH AND SLOVAK REPUBLICS:** Computerworld Czechoslovakia, Macworld Czech Republic, PC World Czechoslovakia; **DENMARK:** Communications World Danmark, Computerworld Danmark, Macworld Danmark, PC World Danmark, Techworld Danmark; **DOMINICAN REPUBLIC:** PC World Republica Dominicana; **ECUADOR:** PC World Ecuador; **EGYPT:** Computerworld Middle East, PC World Middle East; **EL SALVADOR:** PC World Centro America; **FINLAND:** MikroPC, Tietoverkko, Tietoviikko; **FRANCE:** Distributique, Hebdo, Info PC, Le Monde Informatique, Macworld, Reseaux & Telecoms, WebMaster France; **GERMANY:** Computer Partner, Computerwoche, Computerwoche Extra, Computerwoche FOCUS, Global Online, Macwelt, PC Welt; **GREECE:** Amiga Computing, GamePro Greece, Multimedia World, Computer & Communication, Electronic Design China, Electronics Today, Electronics Weekly, Game Software, PC World China, Popular Computer Week, Software Weekly, Software World, Telecom World; **PERU:** Computerworld Peru, PC World Profesional Peru, PC World SoHo Peru; **PHILIPPINES:** Click!, Computerworld Philippines, PC World Philippines, Publish in Asia; **POLAND:** Computerworld Poland, Computerworld Special Report Poland, Cyber, Macworld Poland, Networld Poland, PC World Komputer; **PORTUGAL:** Cerebro/PC World, Computerworld/Correio Informático, Dealer World Portugal, Mac*In/PC*In Portugal, Multimedia World; **PUERTO RICO:** PC World Puerto Rico; **ROMANIA:** Computerworld Romania, PC World Romania, Telecom Romania; **RUSSIA:** Computerworld Russia, Mir PK, Publish, Seti; **SINGAPORE:** Computerworld Singapore, PC World Singapore, Publish in Asia; **SLOVENIA:** Monitor; **SOUTH AFRICA:** Computing SA, Network World SA, Software World SA; **SPAIN:** Communications World España, Computerworld España, Dealer World España, Macworld España, PC World España; **SRI LANKA:** Infolink PC World; **SWEDEN:** CAP&Design, Computer Sweden, Corporate Computing Sweden, Internetworld Sweden, it branschen, Macworld Sweden, MaxiData Sweden, MikroDatorn, Natverk & Kommunikation, PC World Sweden, PCaktiv, Windows World Sweden; **SWITZERLAND:** Computerworld Schweiz, Macworld Schweiz, PCtip; **TAIWAN:** Computerworld Taiwan, Macworld Taiwan, NEW ViSiON/Publish, PC World Taiwan, Windows World Taiwan; **THAILAND:** Publish in Asia, Thai Computerworld; **TURKEY:** Computerworld Turkiye, Macworld Turkiye, Network World Turkiye, PC World Turkiye; **UKRAINE:** Computerworld Kiev, Multimedia World Ukraine, PC World Ukraine; **UNITED KINGDOM:** Acorn User UK, Amiga Action UK, Amiga Computing UK, Apple Talk UK, Computing, Macworld, Parents and Computers UK, PC Advisor, PC Home, PSX Pro, The WEB; **UNITED STATES:** Cable in the Classroom, CIO Magazine, Computerworld, DOS World, Federal Computer Week, GamePro Magazine, InfoWorld, I-Way, Macworld, Network World, PC Games, PC World, Publish, Video Event, THE WEB Magazine, and WebMaster; online webzines: JavaWorld, NetscapeWorld, and SunWorld Online; **URUGUAY:** InfoWorld Uruguay; **VENEZUELA:** Computerworld Venezuela, PC World Venezuela; and **VIETNAM:** PC World Vietnam. 3/24/97

Credits

ACQUISITIONS EDITOR
John Osborn

DEVELOPMENT EDITORS
Carol E. Henry
Barbra Guerra

TECHNICAL EDITOR
Garrett Pease

COPY EDITORS
Carol E. Henry
Marcia Baker

PRODUCTION COORDINATOR
Susan Parini

BOOK DESIGNER
Jim Donohue

GRAPHICS AND PRODUCTION SPECIALIST
Shannon Miller
Maureen Moore
Mark Schumann

QUALITY CONTROL SPECIALIST
Mark Schumann

ILLUSTRATOR
Greg Maxson

PROOFREADERS
Annie Sheldon
Mary C. Barnack

INDEXER
C^2 Editorial Services

About the Author

LEWIS NAPPER refers to himself as an amateur philosopher and a professional geek. He was raised by good, hard-working parents who instilled in him a sense of honesty and the work ethic, but he finally forgave them. He managed to spend more than a decade of his life attending Louisiana Tech University before he was finally forced to graduate.

He has been programming with C and C++ for over ten years. He worked for six of those years as a programming consultant for clients including Philips Electronics, Nissan Motor Company, Bar Code Systems Integrators, Arkla Gas, Petro Truck Stops, assorted financial institutions, and a guy named Ronnie. Currently, Lewis works for Levi Strauss & Co. maintaining PC-controlled warehouse automation systems.

Lewis's amateur philosopher side comes out in the form of a series of articles he refuses to stop writing, called "From DEEP Inside The Binary Bunker." Several of these articles have been published in various magazines and read on popular radio talk shows.

Lewis is married to the most wonderful woman who ever walked the face of the earth and has two step-daughters who are also too good for this world. He was last seen typing somewhere in Mississippi.

To Mom and Dad

Preface

Microsoft Windows clearly dominates the desktop PC market, and the number of people connected to the global Internet continues to grow exponentially. The Windows Sockets (WinSock) API is the point where these two extraordinary technologies connect.

That's enough to make WinSock one of the most important programming interfaces developed in this decade. But now, WinSock is more than that. With the introduction of WinSock 2 and the additional capabilities it provides, WinSock promises to become the de facto standard for developing Windows network applications.

WinSock: Transparent Network Programming under Windows

WinSock is a network API for Microsoft Windows. It is a well-defined, open standard that has been agreed upon by a group of over 30 network providers.

WinSock gives the application programmer a single interface to network functionality. It clearly defines which duties are assigned to the network vendor's software and which ones are left to the application. WinSock resides between your application and the network, and shields you from the details of low-level network protocols. Don't be misled by the book's title – it says *WinSock 2.0*, but because WinSock 2 encompasses almost all of the WinSock 1.1 API, you'll find what you need here to develop applications for either version. More important, the book shows you how to develop applications that work on *both* API sets, so your code runs on as many WinSock implementations as possible.

Even though WinSock 2 is available only for Windows 95 and Windows NT 4, the WinSock 1.1 sample programs developed in this book will run on 16-bit and 32-bit Windows platforms. The WinSock 2 sample programs that are created in the last section of the book require Windows 95 or Windows NT 4.

Who Should Read This Book

This book is for anyone who wants to write any kind of network program for Windows. In the past, WinSock has been restricted to programming for TCP/IP networks. But this isn't your father's WinSock. WinSock 2 enables you to use the familiar socket interface to access any number of installed transport protocols simultaneously. So WinSock ain't just for TCP/IP anymore. It's well on its way to becoming *the* standard API for any type of network access from Windows.

You need not have any prior knowledge at all of WinSock programming to find this book of value. If you're uncertain exactly what WinSock is, you won't be overly challenged by the text and examples, as long as you are familiar with C and Windows programming in general.

Even if you are a WinSock veteran, you'll find useful information here — particularly in Part IV where the new functionality in WinSock 2 is discussed. I've also included tips and tricks that make WinSock programming easier, and documentation for some of the lesser-known, private interfaces.

What's on the CD-ROM

The CD-ROM is packed with information related to WinSock programming. All of the latest WinSock specification documents are included, as well a *complete* set of RFC documents — that means RFC 1 (dated 4/7/1969) through RFC 2097 (dated 1/30/1997).

The sample programs include POP3 and SMTP clients; a general-purpose TCP terminal, Ping and TraceRoute utilities (using both RAW sockets and Microsoft's proprietary ICMP API); a fully functioning Web server; and protocol-independent client and server applications.

The SocketAdapter library included on the CD makes it easy to discover — at run-time — what version of WinSock is installed, and to select the newest library. SocketAdapter applications can use the enhanced functionality available in WinSock 2 if it's installed, yet still run using only WinSock 1.1 functions. By using this library, a program can be not only protocol independent, but WinSock version independent as well.

In addition, the CD contains all the same summarized information about WinSock's functions and data structures that's contained in the printed Quick Reference section of this book.

Organization of This Book

Within these pages you'll find discussion of the complete WinSock API in terms of what Version 1.1 offers, and what Version 2 offers. I decided to organize the material in this way for several reasons:

- Plenty of you out there only want to use Version 1.1 of WinSock.
- If you're already familiar with Version 1.1, you don't want to have to wade through old material to learn what's new in WinSock 2.
- It just worked out that way. I discovered this organization provided a natural break in the information and avoided a lot of repetition.

The book is divided into four sections.

Part I — Introduction to Sockets

The first three chapters of the book efficiently summarize the necessary background information on networking in general and TCP/IP specifically. Part I also introduces the sockets programming model. Topics included are

- The WinSock concept: What is it?
- Fundamental concepts of networking.
- Protocol layers, specific Internet protocols, and the Internet standards process.
- WinSock programming basics: the sockets paradigm, the roles of client and server applications, WinSock version negotiation, name resolution, and sending and receiving data with sockets.
- Issues and challenges you'll encounter when using sockets with Windows. What is blocking and how do you avoid its negative effects?
- Overview of specific functionality available in WinSock Version 1.1 and in Version 2.
- Strategies that are available in each Windows platform.

Part II — The WinSock 1.1 API

Part II covers the portion of the API that is available in both Versions 1.1 and 2 of WinSock. You'll find extensive coverage of the following topics:

- *The details of using sockets efficiently in applications that use the Windows graphical user interface.* Asynchronous event notification is covered, as well as using the asynchronous database functions. You'll study a sample program that checks for the existence of waiting e-mail, using asynchronous mode, and the asynchronous database functions.
- *An examination of "optional" functionality that is available only in some implementations of WinSock.* You'll see development of a Ping utility, first using raw sockets and then using the proprietary Microsoft ICMP API. All of the socket options and ioctl commands available in WinSock 1.1 are included in this reference, whether or not they're "optional."

♦ *A look at the functionality available in the CSocket and CAsyncSocket classes,* comparing advantages and disadvantages of their use. A general-purpose TCP/IP terminal application is developed using the CAsyncSocket class, and a program that sends e-mail via SMTP is created using the CSocket class. The CSocket class is also extended to implement a time-out mechanism and allow the use of CString objects as parameters.

Part III – The WinSock 2.0 API

The third section of the book is devoted to the functions, data structures, and strategies that are available only in Version 2 of WinSock and therefore available only on Windows 95 and Windows NT 4. You'll explore the following:

♦ *The new functionality that is available in WinSock 2,* including all of the new functions and options. We look at issues surrounding the porting of WinSock 1.1 applications to WinSock 2. There's discussion of new concepts introduced in WinSock 2: service providers, name space providers, and protocol types. Most prominent among WinSock 2's new features is protocol independence, so we'll develop a protocol information utility that illustrates all of the information available from WinSock 2 about each installed transport protocol. A general-purpose function is also developed to ease selection of protocols at run time.

♦ *The new protocol-independent name registration and resolution functions that are used to advertise and locate services.* A service query utility is developed that enables the user to find hosts and services by name using one of the many predefined GUIDs.

♦ *Advanced I/O topics* such as overlapped I/O, scatter/gather, connect and disconnect data exchange, and quality of service. Several small programs are created that demonstrate the use of overlapped I/O with event objects and completion functions.

Part IV – Applications

Part IV contains several complete, working example programs. It's here that you'll see demonstrated the key ideas developed in earlier sections of the book. I offer the following applications:

♦ *Asynchronous Server:* A simple HTTP server application that can handle multiple simultaneous client connections by using asynchronous mode. The program uses only functionality that's available in both Version 1.1 and 2 of WinSock.

- *Multithreaded Server:* The same HTTP server as is covered in Chapter 11, but this time using multiple threads. The program uses WinSock 2 specific functions and shows how blocking socket routines can be used in a multithreaded application without negatively affecting user feedback. The strategies used in this program can also be applied to multithreaded client applications.
- *Protocol-Independent Client and Server:* This demonstrates how multiple protocols can be used in WinSock 2 by creating an ECHO client and an ECHO server application that are both protocol independent. The programs developed in this chapter explicitly link to WinSock. They can run on machines that have only the earlier WinSock 1.1 installed, yet they can still use the enhanced functionality of WinSock 2 if it is available.

The Quick Reference

This is a complete, concise listing of all the functions, data structures, and error codes used in both Versions 1.1 and 2 of WinSock. The function listings include descriptions of parameters and return values.

Appendixes

Appendix A is a list of what's on the CD. It provides installation instructions, an explanation of each folder's contents, and directory information to make finding files easier.

Appendix B examines some of the Win32 functions that are related to WinSock programming, but not part of the WinSock specification. The Remote Access Service that's used with dial-up networking is discussed.

Appendix C provides links to additional WinSock information that is available via the Internet.

Appendix D is the bibliography.

Feedback

I've done my best – with some excellent technical assistance – to ensure all of the information in this book is accurate and all of the sample programs work correctly on both Windows 95 and NT 4. I can't guarantee that everything here is perfect, though – WinSock 2 is too new and I'm too human. If you have problems with any of the programs in this book, or if you'd like to shower me with adoration, please feel free to contact me at the following e-mail address.

If and when problems are reported, I'll make the appropriate fixes and post new sample programs at the Web site listed below. Links to additional resources, and other sample programs will be available there as well.

Lewis Napper
`lewis@sockaddr.com`
`http://www.sockaddr.com`

Acknowledgments

Far too many people worked behind the scenes on this book to thank them all individually. I hope they all know how much I appreciate their hard work — especially the editorial and production staffs at IDG Books Worldwide. I would like to take a moment to thank a few people personally.

Thanks to John Osborn and Matt Wagner for making my outline a reality. I'll never be able to thank Carol Henry enough; her endless patience and remarkable ability to somehow know what I meant to say made this book immensely more readable. Garrett Pease found my errors and always had a good idea of what should be discussed. My wife, Kimberly, again endured my overcommitted schedule and again proved that I did indeed marry the right woman.

I would also like to say a special thanks to Hal Burford, Mike Buring, Jim Childress, Stirling Hale, Robert Leach, David Pirch, and the Internet community.

Contents at a Glance

	Preface ix
	Acknowledgments........................... xv
Part I	Introduction to Sockets
Chapter 1	Introduction to WinSock 3
Chapter 2	Programming with Sockets.................... 23
Chapter 3	Programming with Windows Sockets 57
Part II	The WinSock 1.1 API
Chapter 4	Using Asynchronous Mode.................... 83
Chapter 5	Optional Features........................... 131
Chapter 6	MFC Socket Classes 165
Part III	The WinSock 2.0 API
Chapter 7	Introduction to WinSock 2.0 209
Chapter 8	Name Registration and Resolution 247
Chapter 9	Enhanced Input/Output 279
Part IV	Applications
Chapter 10	Asynchronous Server........................ 327
Chapter 11	Multithreaded Server 365
Chapter 12	Protocol-Independent Client and Server 389
Quick Reference to WinSock Functions, Structures, and Errors.... 431	
Appendix A	What's on the CD-ROM 515

Appendix B	Related Win32 Functions 521
Appendix C	Additional Resources 525
Appendix D	Bibliography 531

Index 535

End-User License Agreement 544

CD-ROM Installation Instructions 548

Contents

Preface ix

Acknowledgments xv

Part 1 Introduction to Sockets

Chapter 1: Introduction to WinSock 3
  What Is WinSock? 4
    Acceptance of WinSock 6
  What You Need to Work with WinSock 6
    Obtaining WinSock Files 7
  The Sockets Paradigm 7
    WinSock Extensions to the Berkeley API 7
    The Client/Server Model 8
  The Structure of the Internet 8
    Catenet Model 8
    Uniform Resource Locators (URLs) 13
    The Internet Protocol Suite 13
    Protocol Layers 14
    Internet Protocol (IP) 15
    Internet Control Message Protocol (ICMP) 16
    Transmission Control Protocol (TCP) 17
    User Datagram Protocol (UDP) 18
    Common Process Protocols 18
  Summary 22

Chapter 2 Programming with Sockets 23
  Client/Server Program Flow 23
    Application Pairs 24
  WinSock Programming Fundamentals 26
  Initializing WinSock 27
    The WSAStartup() Function 28
    Version Negotiation 30
    WinSock Return Values 32
  Name Resolution 32
    The hostent Structure 32
    The gethostbyname() Function 33
    The gethostbyaddr() Function 33
    The HostInfo.c Program 35
  Network Byte Order 39

	A Word about Internet Byte Order 40
	Creating a Socket 41
	Socket Type and Protocol............................... 41
	Socket Descriptors 42
	Connecting Sockets................................. 42
	The Client's Role: Connecting to a Server 43
	The Server's Role: Listening for Client Connections........... 47
	Sending and Receiving Data......................... 49
	Connection-Oriented Sending and Receiving................. 50
	The send() Function 50
	Connectionless Sending and Receiving 52
	Closing a Socket................................... 54
	Connectionless.. 54
	Connection-Oriented 54
	Summary 56
Chapter 3	**Programming with Windows Sockets 57**
	WinSock Versions.................................. 58
	Version 1.0.. 58
	Version 1.1.. 58
	Version 2.0.. 59
	Blocking and Event-Driven Applications 61
	The Windows Message-Driven Architecture 61
	The WinSock Extensions 62
	Blocking Mode.................................... 63
	Blocking Sockets 63
	Blocking Functions 64
	Handling Reentrant Messages 65
	Blocking Hook Functions................................ 67
	Nonblocking Mode................................. 68
	ioctlsocket() 68
	Methods to Avoid: polling and select()..................... 69
	The Preferred Method: Asynchronous Mode 71
	WSAAsyncSelect() 72
	Asynchronous Database Functions......................... 74
	WSAEventSelect()...................................... 76
	Using Overlapped I/O 76
	Overlapped I/O Functions............................... 77
	Scatter and Gather..................................... 77
	General Guidelines for Your Application Strategy 78

Contents   xxi

	Which Windows Platform?............................ 78
	Which WinSock Version?............................. 79
	Which Data Transport Protocol? 79
	What Type of Application? 79
	How Much Data? 79
	What Kind of User Interface?.......................... 79
	Which Source Code Base? 79
	Summary 80

Part II The WinSock 1.1 API

Chapter 4	Using Asynchronous Mode................... 83
	Asynchronous Mode................................ 83
	The WSAAsyncSelect() Function 84
	The Database Functions 93
	Database Function Categories 94
	The Asynchronous Database Functions 95
	Host Name and Address Resolution 96
	Service Name and Port Resolution 104
	Protocol Name and Number Resolution 110
	The WSACancelAsyncRequest() Function 114
	The CheckMail Sample Application.................... 115
	Compiling the CheckMail Sample Program............... 115
	Running the CheckMail Sample 117
	The CheckMail Source Code 117
	Summary 130
Chapter 5	Optional Features.......................... 131
	Socket Options 132
	Optional Options 132
	The getsockopt() and setsockopt() Functions.............. 133
	Option Descriptions 136
	Socket Control 145
	The ioctlsocket() Function 146
	Raw Sockets 148
	SOCK_RAW 149
	Writing a Ping Utility............................... 149
	Microsoft's Proprietary ICMP API 155
	Microsoft-Specific Extensions........................ 160

	Support for Additional Transport Protocols 160
	Performance Improvement 161
	Multicast 162
	Summary 163
Chapter 6	**MFC Socket Classes** **165**
	The Microsoft Foundation Class Library 165
	MFC Versions 166
	MFC Socket Classes 167
	Adding Support for WinSock to MFC Applications. 168
	Including AFXSOCK.H 169
	Calling AfxSocketInit() 169
	Using the CAsyncSocket Class 169
	Asynchronous Callback Functions 170
	Deriving from CAsyncSocket 171
	Using a CAsyncSocket-Derived Object 172
	Object Construction 173
	Making a Connection................................. 174
	Object Destruction 177
	WSTerm: The CAsyncSocket Class at Work............. 178
	Building WSTerm.................................... 179
	The CTermSocket Class................................ 179
	The CTermView Class 181
	Connecting to a Server............................... 189
	A Conversation with a Server.......................... 190
	Closing the Connection 190
	WSTerm Limitations.................................. 191
	Using the CSocket Class 191
	A Synchronous/Asynchronous Socket 191
	Using an Archive with CSocket 192
	Deriving from CSocket 194
	The OnMessagePending() Function........................ 194
	The CSocketX Class 194
	SendMail: The CSocketX Class at Work 199
	The SendMailMessage() Function......................... 200
	Summary 204

Part III The WinSock 2.0 API

Chapter 7	**Introduction to WinSock 2.0** **209**
	What's New in WinSock 2 209
	Summary of New Functions and Options 211
	Status of the WinSock 2 Specification 216
	WINSOCK2.H 217
	Porting from WinSock 1.1 to WinSock 2 217

	Binary Compatibility with WinSock 1.1	218
	Source Compatibility with WinSock 1.1	219
	WinSock 2 Concepts	221
	Service Providers	221
	Name Space Providers	222
	Services	223
	Protocol Types	223
	Finding Protocol Information	225
	The WSAEnumProtocols() Function	225
	The WSAPROTOCOL_INFO Structure	227
	The EnumProto Application	232
	Selecting Protocols	241
	Summary	246
Chapter 8	**Name Registration and Resolution**	**247**
	Registration and Resolution	247
	Types of Name Spaces	248
	Registering a Service	249
	Service Class	249
	The WSASERVICECLASSINFO Structure	249
	The WSANSCLASSINFO Structure	250
	The WSAInstallServiceClass() Function.	251
	Advertising Availability	253
	Name Resolution.	260
	Enumerating Available Name Spaces	260
	Finding Hosts and Services.	263
	Using WSAQUERYSET During Resolution	263
	The WSALookupServiceBegin() Function	266
	The WSALookupServiceNext() Function.	268
	Name Resolution Utility Functions.	272
	The Services Utility.	277
	Summary	278
Chapter 9	**Enhanced Input/Output**	**279**
	Asynchronous Event Notification.	279
	Event Objects.	279
	Creating Event Objects	281
	Associating Network Events.	281
	Detecting Network Events	284
	Determining What Occurred.	285
	The GetHTTP2 Sample	287
	Analysis of GetHTTP2	292
	Overlapped I/O	293

Checking for Overlapped I/O Completion 294
Scatter and Gather 298
Overlapped I/O Functions 299
The WSARecvFrom() Function 302
The WSASend() Function 303
The WSASendTo() Function 305
The GetHTTP3 Sample 307
Analysis of GetHTTP3 312
Determining Quality of Service 313
QOS Data Structures 313
Quality-of-Service Templates 316
Negotiating Quality of Service 316
RSVP 317
Exchanging Data at Connect and Disconnect 317
At Connect 317
At Disconnect 319
Multipoint and Multicast 319
Handling Different Multipoint Strategies 320
Using Multipoint Protocols 320
The WSAJoinLeaf() Function 321
Getting More Information About Multipoint/Multicast 323
Summary 323

Part IV Applications

Chapter 10   **Asynchronous Server 327**
Asynchronous Mode vs. Multithreading 327
A Brief Review of the Hypertext Transfer Protocol (HTTP) . 328
The HTTPA Application 330
Running HTTPA 331
Compiling HTTPA 333
HTTPA Architecture 333
The User Interface Module: HTTPUI.C 334
Starting and Stopping HTTP Service 337
Relaying WinSock Event Notifications 340
Receiving Event and Statistics Notification Messages 341
User Interface Summary 345
The WinSock HTTP Server Module: HTTPA.C 345

	Starting HTTP Service 345
	Obtaining the Local Address............................ 348
	Waiting for Event Notifications 350
	Accepting Client Connections........................... 351
	Tracking Connections................................... 353
	Reading the Client's Request 355
	Sending the File to the Client.......................... 357
	Sending Large Amounts of Data........................ 361
	Closing the Connection 362
	Stopping HTTP Service.................................. 363
	Summary 364
Chapter 11	**Multithreaded Server 365**
	The HTTPMT Application 365
	Running HTTPMT...................................... 366
	Compiling HTTPMT 368
	HTTPMT Architecture 368
	The User Interface Module: HTTPUI.C................. 369
	The HTTPMT.C Module 370
	Starting HTTP Service 370
	Waiting for Connection Requests...................... 373
	Synchronizing Client Threads........................... 375
	Communicating with the Client 377
	Using Overlapped I/O with Event Objects 379
	Receiving the Client's Request 379
	Sending the File to the Client.......................... 382
	Extending the HTTP Example Servers.................. 386
	HTTP/1.0 386
	Common Gateway Interface............................ 386
	Allowing Clients to Complete........................... 386
	Summary 387
Chapter 12	**Protocol-Independent Client and Server 389**
	Linking to WinSock at Run-Time 390
	The Socket Adapter Library 390
	Using the Socket Adapter Library 391
	Declaring Function Pointers........................... 392
	Loading WinSock.. 394
	Unloading WinSock..................................... 397
	Socket Adapter Library Summary....................... 397
	Adding the Socket Adapter Library to Your Applications....... 400
	The Socket Adapter ECHO Client...................... 400

The Client's User Interface 401
Linking to WinSock 401
Selecting Transport Protocols........................... 402
Sending an ECHO Request 406
Finding a Server...................................... 408
Receiving an ECHO Response......................... 412
The Socket Adapter ECHO Server 413
The Server's User Interface............................ 414
The WinSock Module................................. 415
Receiving an ECHO Request........................... 427
Summary 429

Quick Reference to WinSock Functions, Structures, and Errors.... 431
Function Reference............................. 431
Data Structures................................. 488
Error Reference................................ 505

Appendix A **What's on the CD-ROM** 515
Installation Instructions 515
Changing the Windows Read-Only Attribute 516
Contents of the CD-ROM.......................... 516
About the Official WinSock Specifications.................. 517
Additional Information Sources 517
Sample Programs Used in This Book 517

Appendix B **Related Win32 Functions** 521
RAS (Remote Access Service) Functions 521
RAS Functions Available on Windows NT and 95 521
Service Control Manager Interface 523
Windows NT Service Control Interface..................... 523
Windows 95 Service Control Interface..................... 523

Appendix C **Additional Resources** 525
WinSock 2.. 525
Network Multimedia................................. 526
Web Development 526
Internet Standards 527
Security 528
WinSock Development Tools 528
WinSock Shareware................................. 528
Mailing Lists 529
USENET Newsgroups 529

Appendix D **Bibliography** 531

Index 535

End-User License Agreement 544

CD-ROM Installation Instructions 548

Part I

Introduction to Sockets

Chapter 1: Introduction to WinSock

Chapter 2: Programming with Sockets

Chapter 3: Programming with Windows Sockets

Chapter 1

Introduction to WinSock

IN THIS CHAPTER
In Chapter 1 we discuss what WinSock is, where it came from, and why you would want to use it in your applications. We also briefly cover some of the fundamental topics that underlie the sockets paradigm. Because so many WinSock applications are written for the Internet, we also discuss some of the basics of the Internet suite of protocols. Here are the topics in Chapter 1:

- What is WinSock?
- The sockets paradigm
- Structure of the Internet
- Protocol layers

Two trends in recent computer history have made all others seem small by comparison: Microsoft Windows and the Internet. Since its release in 1985, Microsoft Windows has so completely dominated the graphical user interface market that the Federal Trade Commission has been alerted. And since the advent of the World Wide Web, the already colossal Internet has grown to the point where even TV ads for laundry detergent reference the manufacturer's Web address. The Windows Sockets (WinSock) API is the point at which these two phenomenal technologies meet.

That alone is enough to make WinSock one of the most important interfaces developed this decade. But now, WinSock is more than that. With the introduction of Version 2 and the additional capabilities it provides, WinSock promises to become the de facto standard for developing Windows network applications, regardless of the underlying protocols.

This chapter provides a broad overview of the WinSock specification and lays the foundation for the rest of the book. It provides an introduction to the fundamental concepts you must understand to use WinSock. We discuss what WinSock is, how it has been used in the past, and how it can be used now and in the future. We also examine some of the fundamental networking concepts used in WinSock.

Programming with WinSock is not difficult. Once you understand these key ideas, you'll have the background information you need to start your Windows Sockets programming with confidence.

What Is WinSock?

WinSock is a network application programming interface (API) for Microsoft Windows — a well-defined set of data structures and function calls implemented as a dynamic link library (DLL).

A group of over 30 network providers have agreed upon WinSock as an open standard, which gives the application programmer a single interface to network functionality. It clearly defines which duties are assigned to the network vendor's software and which ones are left to the application.

WinSock is a translator of sorts. In your application, you make function calls requesting generic network services; WinSock translates these generic requests into protocol-specific requests and performs the necessary tasks. Residing between your application and the network implementation, WinSock shields you from the details of low-level network protocols (see Figure 1-1).

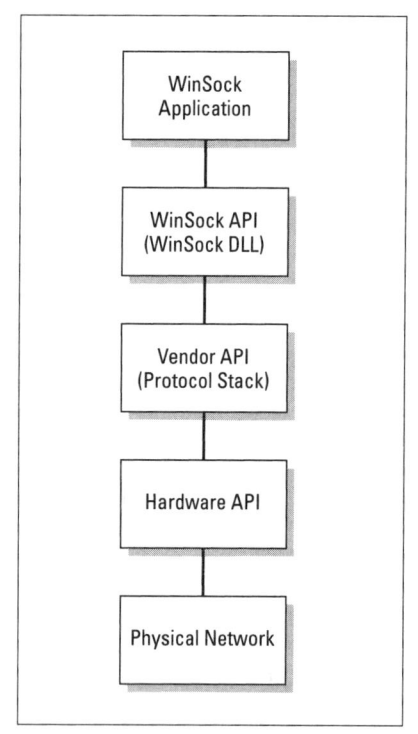

Figure 1-1: WinSock shields your application from implementation-specific details.

Before WinSock was established, each network provider developed its own interface libraries independently. The general framework and calling conventions of network applications varied greatly. Software developers were left with the daunting task of trying to code for each unique network interface. The interfaces were distinct even among equivalent network protocols and topologies. An application developed for one vendor's TCP/IP implementation wouldn't necessarily work on a TCP/IP network provided by a different vendor. The WinSock specification has changed all that.

The effort was started by Martin Hall of JSB Corp. at the fall 1991 Interop conference. Hall and others organized a "birds-of-a-feather" group, which quickly became the formal WinSock Group. This assembly of developers and network providers sought to establish a standard API for TCP/IP under Windows. They also wanted to provide for future support of additional transport protocols.

The resulting WinSock API provides not only a source code standard but also a binary standard. A WinSock-compliant application can run unchanged on any WinSock-compatible implementation without even being recompiled (see Figure 1-2).

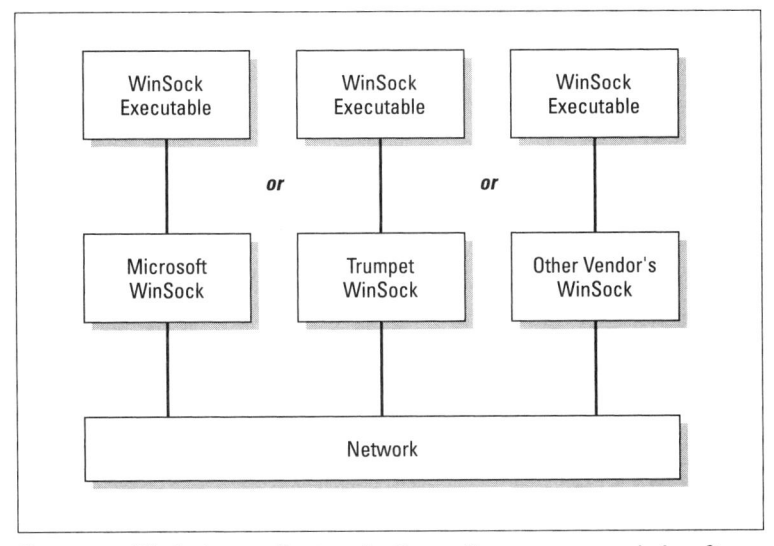

Figure 1-2: WinSock-compliant applications will run on any vendor's software.

Most of the existing WinSock software you'll come across was developed for the Internet. Even though WinSock was originally developed primarily for TCP/IP, the API is abstract enough to support other protocol families. With WinSock 2 comes substantial new functionality. It formally supports IPX/SPX, DecNet, and OSI, and expands the API to allow other protocols to be hooked in at a later date. WinSock 2 applications can even be entirely protocol independent. Using WinSock 2 services, an application that is moved from one environment to another can adapt to differences in network addressing and naming schemes.

Acceptance of WinSock

WinSock has been extremely successful since it was released in 1992. As customer demands for interconnectivity grew, providers of network hardware and software began to realize the necessity of cooperation and open standards. Closed, proprietary standards started to lose ground in the marketplace. When heavyweights such as Microsoft, Novell, IBM, Sun, 3Com, Hewlett-Packard, DEC, and others joined the WinSock group, WinSock's acceptance was virtually assured.

Microsoft was a founding member of the WinSock group and has since changed its network communications strategy from NetBIOS to WinSock. The Windows Open Services Architecture (WOSA) incorporates WinSock as a part of Microsoft's suite of open APIs.

WinSock is greatly responsible for the growth of the World Wide Web. Microsoft had already populated the world with Windows desktop PCs by the time plans for the Web started to take shape, and these PCs provided an abundant, inexpensive, natural environment for the Web's graphical hypertext model. Indeed, the Windows version of Mosaic – the first Web browser – was built with WinSock. Virtually all popular Internet applications now use WinSock, including Netscape's Web browser, Microsoft's Internet Explorer, e-mail programs, Usenet readers, and other related software.

What You Need to Work with WinSock

You probably already have everything you need to use and program for WinSock.

- ♦ Windows 95 and Windows NT Workstation both ship with WinSock included (WinSock 1.1 is on Windows 95 and earlier versions of NT; WinSock 2.0 is on NT 4).

- ♦ Several vendors make WinSock implementations available for Windows 3.1, and Microsoft offers a WinSock and TCP/IP add-on for Windows for Workgroups.

- ♦ Most commercial Windows C and C++ compilers provide the header files and import libraries needed for WinSock.

Three distributions of WinSock currently exist. Table 1.1 lists the files associated with each distribution.

TABLE 1-1 FILES AND PLATFORMS FOR THE THREE WINSOCK DISTRIBUTIONS

Dynamic Link Library	Application	Development Files	Platform
WINSOCK.DLL	16-bit WinSock 1.1	WINSOCK.H WINSOCK.LIB	16- or 32-bit Windows
WSOCK32.DLL	32-bit WinSock 1.1	WINSOCK.H WSOCK32.LIB	32-bit Windows
WS2_32.DLL	32-bit WinSock 2	WINSOCK2.H WS2_32.LIB	32-bit Windows

Obtaining WinSock Files

The official WinSock specification documents are included on the CD in the \SPECS directory. Appendix A of this book lists locations on the Internet where the latest development files can be found.

The Sockets Paradigm

The group responsible for creating WinSock made some good decisions early in the process — the most important of which was to follow the sockets model. First introduced in the Berkeley UNIX Software Distribution in the early 1980s, the concept of *sockets* was originally designed as a method of interprocess communication. Soon, however, it grew to encompass network communications as well.

The Berkeley *sockets model* conceptualizes network communications as taking place between two *endpoints,* or sockets. Analogies have been drawn between plugging an application into a network and plugging a handset into the telephone system, or an appliance into an electrical system.

A socket defines one endpoint in the communication between two processes. Before communications can start, two sockets must exist: a client socket and a server socket.

WinSock Extensions to the Berkeley API

With some exceptions, WinSock includes the complete Berkeley sockets API. A large subset of the Berkeley sockets library is available in WinSock with identical function names and parameters. WinSock also offers additional functions that are used to cope with the cooperative multitasking nature of 16-bit Windows. (All of these extension functions are prefixed with the letters *WSA*). The WinSock API is related closely enough to the Berkeley sockets library that a lot of software can be (and has been) ported from Berkeley UNIX to WinSock.

The Client/Server Model

The Berkeley sockets model (and therefore WinSock) uses a client/server approach to communications. Rather than trying to start two network applications simultaneously, one application is theoretically always available (the server) and another requests services as needed (the client).

The server creates a socket, names it so that it can be identified and found by a client, and then "listens" for service requests. A client application creates a socket, finds a server socket by name or address, and then "plugs in" to initiate a conversation. Once a conversation is initiated, data can be sent in either direction. The client can send data to and receive data from the server, and the server can send data to and receive data from the client.

The specifics of the conversation are unique to each set of client and server applications. Both applications must know what messages and data to expect from the other, and both must follow some mutual rules about when to send and when to expect to receive data. To communicate successfully, both the client and the server must speak the same language – they must both use the same protocols.

Remember, the concept of a socket is purely an abstraction used in the WinSock API. Client and server applications needn't both be written with WinSock to communicate. WinSock is a *source code interface* – a way for programmers to envision network connections. It's not a protocol or network type. A program written with WinSock can communicate with many different types of systems, as long as they use the same protocols.

The Structure of the Internet

WinSock was designed to be protocol independent, but as mentioned earlier, it was developed primarily for use with TCP/IP networks. Some WinSock 1.1 implementations do support other protocols in addition to TCP/IP, but few neglect TCP/IP altogether.

The first part of this book examines WinSock 1.1 and focuses on TCP/IP network programming. Because the Internet has been the focus of so much attention and because it is a network to which nearly everyone has access, we'll use the Internet for all of the example programs in this first section. Other protocols and protocol independence will be discussed in Part III and Part IV.

Catenet Model

The Internet is built on the catenet model of networking. The *catenet* model is a set of rules that allow data networks of widely varying types to be interconnected. A least-common-denominator approach is taken, in that as little as possible is assumed about the operation of any individual network. The functionality required to participate in a catenet can easily be developed on almost any type of computer system.

The catenet model uses the concept of packet switching for communicating between two points on the network. In *packet switching*, messages sent from one system to another are broken down into small units of data called *packets*, which are relayed from one computer to another until they reach their destination. A packet destined for some far-away machine may travel through many intermediate machines, routers, or gateways along its route. (Packet switching is used rather than *circuit switching*, in which a *direct* connection is established between just two points on a network.)

Packet switching forms the basic functionality of the catenet model and the Internet. Using the catenet model, any number of different network types can be interconnected, and any computer can send and receive packets from any other computer on any connected network. Only three basic operations are assumed to exist along this internetwork:

- ◆ A packet is carried along a path from a source machine to a destination machine.

- ◆ The format of the packet is commonly agreed upon, along with a common addressing scheme.

- ◆ Packet switching (relaying) can be performed quickly.

On the Internet, the packet is called an Internet Protocol (IP) *datagram*. We'll talk more about IP datagrams later in this chapter.

When you log on to the Internet, your machine is not automatically attached to every other computer on the network, but it does have the potential to connect with any other machine. To communicate with another computer — that is, to send IP datagrams to another machine — you must first know the other computer's address.

INTERNET ADDRESSES

Each computer connected to the Internet is assigned a unique, 32-bit integer IP address. You usually see this address written in human-readable *dotted-quad-notation* form (usually called simply *dot-notation*). In dot-notation, each of the 4 bytes of the address are written as a decimal number separated by periods. Thus 192.41.21.95 is an IP address written in dot-notation.

An address begins with a network number, followed by a local address. Some parts of the address are used to identify the network to which the computer is connected, and the remainder identify the computer itself. For instance, the first 16 bits of the address might identify the network; the next 8 bits a building, office, or floor; and the last 8 bits a particular machine.

Using a 32-bit number for the address allows for the creation of over four billion addresses (2^{32} or 4,294,967,296). Because part of the address is used to identify a particular network, however, it's not possible to use all of the addresses freely. The rapid growth of the Internet has led to the possibility of actually running out of IP addresses. Several strategies are currently being considered to overcome this limitation, one of which would make the IP address 128 bits long.

DOMAIN NAME SYSTEM (DNS)

Computers manage numbers quite well, but humans generally don't. DNS – the Domain Name System – was devised so people could connect with other computers by using a name rather than a number. These *domain names* (or *host names*) directly correspond to a specific IP address.

Like IP addresses in dot-notation, domain names are divided into two or more segments separated by periods. Let's analyze a typical domain name:

```
www.isoc.org
```

Each segment of a domain name is a *domain*. The rightmost segment of a domain name is known as a *top-level domain:* `org` in the preceding example. The top-level domain describes the type of organization or the country with which the domain name is associated. Currently about 20 top-level international domains exist for countries, from .AD (Andorra) to .ZW (Zimbabwe). Following are the identifiers for the most common top-level domains in the United States:

.COM	Commercial
.EDU	Educational
.GOV	Governmental
.INT	International
.MIL	Military
.ORG	Organization

From the top-level domain, domain names construct a sort of upside-down tree structure with second-level domains, third-level domains, and so on, as shown in Figure 1-3. Segments to the left of the rightmost domain are called *subdomains*. In our example, `isoc` is a subdomain in the domain name `isoc.org`.

Chapter 1: Introduction to WinSock 11

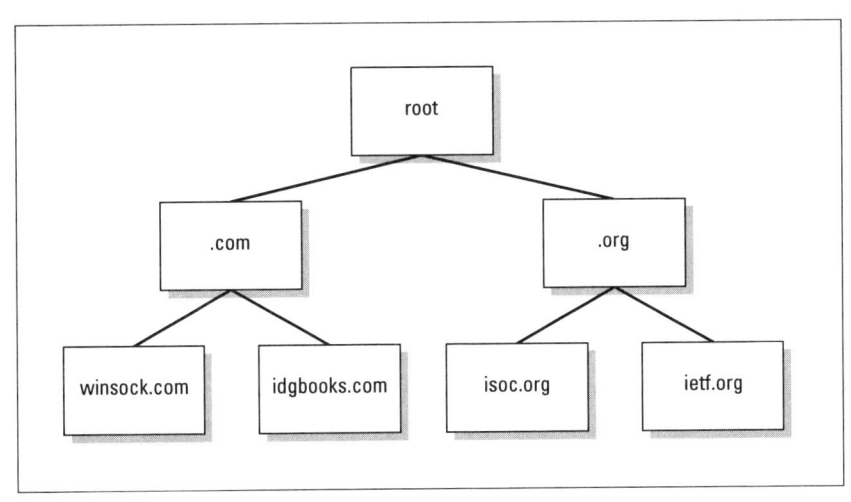

Figure 1-3: Domain-level organization

The Domain Name System uses a distributed database to relate domain names to IP addresses. Domain *resolution* (finding an IP address that relates to a given domain name) is accomplished by groups of name servers. A *name server* is a system (a program running on a computer) that will return an IP address for a given domain name.

Not all name servers know all the domain names used on the Internet. Each name server has pointers to other name servers it can use to resolve unknown domain names. In a general sense, name servers are organized like the domain levels (Figure 1-3).

For instance, take the domain name

```
sales.us.bigcompany.com
```

This domain name may be passed to several name servers before it is completely resolved. The `root` name server might pass the name to a `.com` name server. The `.com` name server might then pass the name on to a name server run by `bigcompany`, which in turn could send the name to another name server that can find IP addresses for domain names in the `us.bigcompany` domain. To start this process, every computer on the Internet must know how to connect directly to at least one name server.

Domain name assignment is completely independent from IP address assignment. A domain name can be changed to relate to a different IP address at any time by having the record changed with the registration service, Internet Network Information Center (InterNIC). Domain name registrations are handled by InterNIC in North America, Réseaux IP Européens (RIPE) in Europe, and the Asia Pacific Network Information Center (APNIC) in Asia.

The Domain Name System is documented in RFC 1034.

> ### A Word about RFCs
>
> Throughout the rest of this section, you will see references to *Request For Comments* documents (RFCs). These documents are the official publications of the Internet protocol suite. An RFC can be a proposal for a new standard, an extension of an existing standard, notes from Internet group meetings, or just someone's opinion relating to Internet communications. Examples include RFC 791, "The Internet Protocol"; RFC 959, "File Transfer Protocol"; and RFC 1118, "The Hitchhiker's Guide to the Internet." Indeed, even the specification documents for the Internet protocols are defined by the Internet Engineering Task Force (IETF) and published as a series of RFCs.
>
> An RFC editor is established by the Internet Society and the Federal Network Council. This RFC editor is the official publisher of RFC documents and is responsible for final editorial review, archival, and distribution.
>
> The RFC process begins when someone writes a proposal and mails it to the RFC editor. Newly proposed protocols then go through a series of tests, scrutiny, and debate. They pass from proposed standard to draft to official standard, with a recommendation from the Internet Engineering Steering Group at each step of the process. When a protocol completes this process, it is assigned a standard (STD) number.
>
> The RFC series was born along with the Internet in 1969 and now contains more than 2,000 documents. Most RFCs are available on line as large, precise, technical text files. A large number of the most common RFCs are included on the CD accompanying this book, in the \RFC directory. And a good source for the most up-to-date RFCs is at http://www.isi.edu/rfc-editor/.

SERVICE PORT NUMBERS

We've examined how you need the IP address of another system to communicate successfully, and how you both must "speak" using the same protocol. In addition to these requirements, you both need to understand, in a general sense, what will take place. Like WinSock, Internet applications use the client/server approach to controlling conversations. When two programs exchange data, one program assumes the role of server and the other assumes the role of client. Client applications send requests to servers, and servers respond to those requests.

Most host systems on the Internet provide a set of server applications that are collectively known as *well-known services*. These services correspond to well-defined application protocol specifications that document the rules of conversations used to perform specific tasks (file transfer or mail retrieval, for example).

Well-known services are assigned to 16-bit *service port numbers*. The service port number uniquely identifies the type of application (such as file transfer or mail) running on the host. A server application running on a host machine "listens" to one of these designated ports and waits for client applications to request services. A client application sends a formatted request to a host computer at a particular IP address on a designated service port.

A few of the well-known services are:

Port	Service
21	File transfer
25	Sending e-mail (SMTP)
80	Hypertext transfer
110	Retrieving e-mail (POP3)
119	Network news retrieval

Service names can be used rather than hard-coded port numbers. The names are usually related to port numbers in a local table.

A comprehensive list of service port numbers can be found in RFC 1010.

Uniform Resource Locators (URLs)

A Uniform Resource Locator (URL) is a string that completely specifies how to access a network resource — usually a file. Here's an example:

http://www.isoc.org/index.html

If you've spent any time on the Internet, this URL format will look familiar.

Notice all the information necessary to access the file is given in the URL. The www.isoc.org portion can be resolved to an IP address through the use of the DNS. The http portion designates the service port and protocol that will be used (HyperText Transfer Protocol/port 80 in this case). And /index.html is the name of the document to be retrieved.

The most common use of URLs is in HTML documents. When using a Web browser, every hyperlink has an associated URL. The Web browser application uses the information contained in the URL to retrieve the document when the user clicks the link.

URLs are documented in RFC 1738.

The Internet Protocol Suite

An effective technique for simplifying software design is to divide large systems into groups of common functionality. One group then calls on the services of another group to perform some task, without having to know the details of how the task was performed.

In kind, the Internet protocols are structured so they rely on one another for services. Each protocol is designed to perform a specific function (and nothing else) and is, therefore, kept as simple as possible. The protocols are then layered one on top of the other; the resulting ensemble can provide more sophisticated services. Collectively, these protocols are known as the *Internet Protocol Suite*.

Protocol Layers

The core set of Internet protocols (TCP, IP, and UDP) was developed prior to the establishment of the now widely accepted Open Systems Interconnection (OSI) model. These lower levels of the Internet were designed using the older U.S. Department of Defense (DOD) model. The DOD model is made up of the four layers shown in Figure 1-4 and described in the following paragraphs.

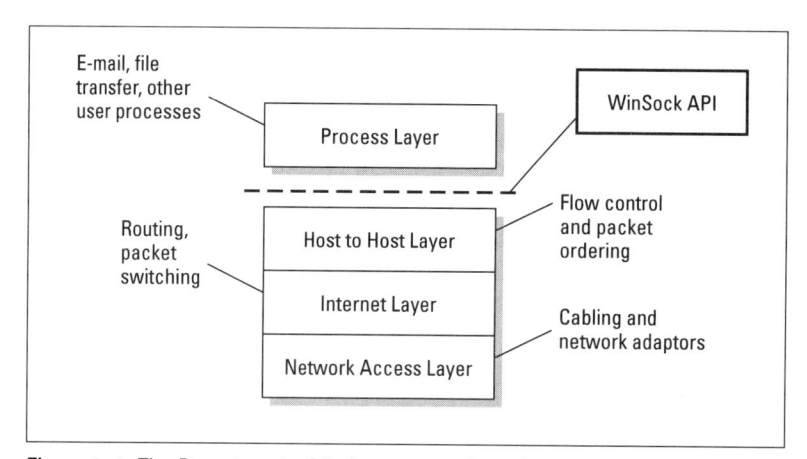

Figure 1-4: The Department of Defense network model, on which the core set of Internet protocols is based.

NETWORK ACCESS LAYER

At the bottom of the model, the *Network Access layer* is responsible for managing communications over the network's physical media — the cabling and network adapters. Today, this corresponds to the Ethernet level.

INTERNET LAYER

The *Internet layer* is responsible for routing packets across the interconnected physical networks and for reporting errors in transmission. This is the Internet Protocol (IP) layer.

HOST TO HOST LAYER

The *Host To Host layer* manages connections between computers, flow control, and the transmission and ordering of packets. This is the Transmission Control Protocol (TCP) layer.

PROCESS LAYER

At the top of the model, the *process layer* is responsible for the highest level of communication. This layer consists of end-user applications using protocols such as Post Office Protocol (POP) for mail or the File Transfer Protocol (FTP) for sending and receiving files.

Internet Protocol (IP)

The *Internet Protocol (IP)* is the Internet's most fundamental protocol. All communication on the Internet is performed either directly or indirectly through IP, which provides two essential services:

◆ Addressing

◆ Datagram fragmentation

IP is primarily responsible for routing datagrams from one computer to another. The IP datagrams contain both the source and destination addresses, data from a higher-level protocol, a checksum, and a few other network housekeeping fields. IP modules reside on each host connected to the Internet and in each gateway that interconnects networks. These modules use the address fields contained in IP datagrams to make routing decisions and send the datagrams toward their final destination. Some systems can handle larger datagrams than others. If necessary, IP can break relatively large datagrams into smaller ones so they can be transmitted though "small-packet" networks.

Note, IP treats each datagram as an independent entity completely unrelated to any other Internet datagram. Connections or logical circuits are irrelevant at this layer. IP simply finds a route and sends datagrams from a source to a destination.

Routing datagrams for delivery on the Internet is quite a job. Before a datagram reaches its destination, it may have to travel through several different machines and gateways. IP is responsible for transporting individual datagrams through a maze of various systems that use different types of transport media.

Oddly enough, much of the success of IP is due to its use of an *unreliable delivery* scheme. That is, IP datagrams are not guaranteed to be delivered to their destination. They may be lost, discarded, duplicated or delivered out of order. No error checking occurs on the data contained in the datagram, no flow control or retransmission of lost packets. This scheme is used in an effort to build a fault-tolerant network. Higher-level protocols are responsible for ensuring data sequence and delivery and must gracefully handle situations, such as temporarily overloaded or rerouted connections. IP is only responsible for routing datagrams, not for ensuring they are delivered.

> ### TCP/IP and UDP/IP
>
> Although it's common practice to say the Internet uses TCP/IP, some applications don't use TCP at all. (TCP — Transmission Control Protocol — will be discussed shortly.) It's true *most* Internet applications use TCP, but some actually use other protocols on top of IP to send and receive information. (Examples are UDP/IP and ICMP, discussed later in this chapter.) None of the example programs created in this book use IP directly. They all use either TCP or UDP, which, in turn, rely on IP to perform lower-level tasks.

Internet Control Message Protocol (ICMP)

The *Internet Control Message protocol* is a thin layer on top of IP primarily used to transmit out-of-band data. *Out-of-band data* consists of error messages and other types of urgent notifications. ICMP has two primary uses:

- Error messaging
- Troubleshooting

ICMP's responsibility is to report unreachable servers, network congestion, and other types of network transmission errors. Because all implementations of IP are required to include ICMP functionality, this protocol is sometimes considered part of IP.

ICMP messages are sent when a datagram cannot reach its destination, when the gateway does not have the buffering capacity to forward a datagram, or when the gateway can direct the host to send traffic on a shorter route. Note, the use of ICMP still does not make IP reliable. It simply provides some feedback about the problems encountered.

ICMP is also used to assist in troubleshooting. ICMP provides an *echo* function that simply sends a packet to a distant machine; when received, the packet is routed back to the sender. The network management utility, Ping, uses this echo function to measure connection speeds and to tally lost datagrams. ICMP, like IP, does not ensure delivery of datagrams. This functionality is left to applications that use ICMP.

ICMP is documented in RFC 792.

Transmission Control Protocol (TCP)

Transmission Control Protocol (TCP) is layered on top of IP. TCP uses IP to deliver datagrams (or packets) of information, adding the following important functions:

- Byte streams
- Reliable delivery
- Data integrity
- Flow control
- Logical connections

TCP provides the application programmer with the concept of a full-duplex (two-way) connection-oriented, reliable byte stream. The datagram organization of the network is hidden from the programmer. Programs read from and write to a TCP byte stream in much the same way as they would to a file.

TCP is responsible for breaking up the byte stream into IP datagrams, and then putting them back together at the other end. In addition, it ensures proper sequencing and datagram delivery. TCP uses sequence numbers to keep track of what datagrams have been sent and received and, if necessary, will retransmit lost packets.

A method of data integrity is also built into this protocol. A checksum is calculated on all data sent with TCP and transmitted along with the IP datagram. The checksum is then checked at the receiving end; data corrupted during transmission is discarded and not acknowledged as having been received. This causes the sender to retransmit the data.

Flow control is also provided by TCP. It provides a means for the receiver to govern the amount of data sent by the sender. Along with every acknowledgment of receipt, the receiver indicates the number of bytes that the sender may transmit before it will be given permission to send more.

TCP is known as a *connection-oriented* protocol. Before an application can begin to send and receive information using TCP, it must first establish a connection through an IP address and service port. Both sides of the connection then exchange packets, establishing datagram size and initial sequence numbers. The connection or circuit provided by TCP is known as a *virtual circuit*. It is actually just a logical route between two points for IP datagrams to travel along.

TCP belongs to the Host To Host layer of the DOD networking model. It is intended to provide a reliable process-to-process communications facility. It interfaces on one side to the lower-level IP and to higher-level application protocols on the other side. This reliable, convenient means of communicating across the network is why most Internet applications use TCP to send and receive messages.

TCP is documented in RFC 793.

User Datagram Protocol (UDP)

User Datagram Protocol (UDP) is also layered on top of IP, but it intentionally does not provide much in the way of extended functionality. This protocol neither conceals the datagram nature of the network as TCP does nor requires that you first establish a connection before exchanging information.

UDP is referred to as an *unreliable protocol* because UDP datagrams are delivered just like IP datagrams: They may be discarded or lost before reaching their destination. All the work that TCP does for you — acknowledging datagram delivery, resending lost packets, and so forth — is left to the applications that use UDP. The only services UDP offers over IP are service port numbers and a checksum for the data being sent. Datagrams that are corrupted during transmission fail the checksum test at the receiving end and are simply discarded.

In some instances, UDP does have advantages over TCP. UDP is much faster than TCP and has a much lower packet overhead. It is ideal for applications that exchange very small amounts of information. UDP is used when TCP would be too slow or is thought to be unnecessary.

UDP is documented in RFC 768.

Common Process Protocols

Layered on top of UDP/IP or TCP/IP are the process protocols — the top layer of the DOD model. The *process protocols* are the protocols most Internet applications use directly. To give you some idea of the services available in the Internet protocol suite, a brief overview of some of the most common process protocols follows.

DAYTIME PROTOCOL

The *Daytime protocol* provides a simple service and is, therefore, layered on top of UDP. A Daytime server application running on a host listens on port 13. When the Daytime server receives a datagram, it sends a datagram back to the sender that contains the current date and time as an ASCII character string. The data in the datagram sent to the server is ignored.

The Daytime protocol is documented in RFC 867.

FILE TRANSFER PROTOCOL (FTP)

File Transfer Protocol (FTP) is layered on top of TCP to provide the capability of transferring files from one computer to another. FTP uses two connections between the client and server applications (most protocols require only one). One connection is used to send commands and receive error messages, while the other is used for the actual transmission and receipt of file data.

FTP commands are simple ASCII character strings. FTP client applications send these commands to the FTP server and receive ASCII character string responses and error messages. FTP servers listen on port 21.

Following are some common FTP commands:

FTP Command	Function
CWD	Changes working directory
RETR	Retrieves a file
STOR	Sends a file
MKD	Makes a directory
RMD	Removes a directory
LIST	Sends directory listing

FTP is documented in RFC 959.

HYPERTEXT TRANSFER PROTOCOL (HTTP)

HyperText Transfer Protocol (HTTP) is layered on top of TCP and provides the services that make the World Wide Web possible. Once a connection is established between an HTTP client and an HTTP server, the client application issues simple ASCII commands such as `GET /index.html`. The server then responds by sending either data or an error message back over the same connection. HTTP servers listen on port 80.

HTTP 1.0 is documented in RFC 1945.

HTTP is generally used to retrieve HyperText Markup Language (HTML) documents. Currently a client can send only three HTTP commands: GET, HEAD, and POST.

GET A GET *url* command retrieves whatever information is identified by the resource identified by *url*.

The GET command can be modified to a *conditional* GET if the request message includes an `If-Modified-Since` header field. The conditional GET requests that the identified resource be transferred only if it has been modified since the date given. This method is intended to reduce network usage by allowing cached entities to be refreshed without requiring multiple requests or transferring unnecessary data.

HEAD The HEAD command is identical to GET except the server only transmits back information about the resource rather than the resource itself. This method is often used for testing hypertext links for validity, accessibility, and recent modification. There is no conditional HEAD request as there is for GET. If an `If-Modified-Since` header field is included with a HEAD request, it is ignored.

POST A POST *url* command sends information to a resource rather than receiving information from a resource. This method can be used to send data gathered in a form, post messages to bulletin board system, append records to databases, or some other function.

NETWORK NEWS TRANSPORT PROTOCOL (NNTP)

Network News Transport Protocol (NNTP) is layered on top of TCP and provides the mechanisms necessary to support reading Usenet news messages.

Once a connection is established between an NNTP client and server, the client application can issue ASCII commands to select a newsgroup, post a message, retrieve a list of posted articles, or any other Usenet-related service. The server sends the text of Usenet messages, error messages, and other responses back over the same connection. NNTP servers listen on port 119.

A list of some common NNTP commands follows:

NNTP Command	Function
LIST	Sends a list of all available newsgroups.
GROUP	Selects a newsgroup with which to work.
ARTICLE	Sends the text of an article.
HELP	Sends a list of available commands.

NNTP is documented in RFC 977.

POST OFFICE PROTOCOL (POP)

Post Office Protocol (POP) is layered on top of TCP and provides functionality for retrieving electronic mail. Simple ASCII commands are sent from the client to the host to identify the user, retrieve mail messages, and manage saved messages. The host sends responses and the text of mail messages back over the connection. POP servers listen on port 110.

Some common POP commands are listed in the following table:

POP Command	Function
USER *argument*	Identifies the mail user to the POP server.
PASS *argument*	Gives the password for the identified user.
STAT	Tells the server to respond with the number of e-mail messages waiting to be read.
RETR *argument*	Retrieves the e-mail message specified by *argument*.

POP Command	Function
DELE *argument*	Deletes the e-mail message specified by *argument*.
QUIT	Logs off from the POP server and closes the connection.

POP version 3 (POP3) is documented in RFC 1725.

SIMPLE MAIL TRANSFER PROTOCOL (SMTP)

Simple Mail Transfer Protocol (SMTP) is layered on top of TCP and provides the capability of sending electronic mail. Much like the POP protocol, the client sends simple, printable ASCII commands to the server indicating the recipient's e-mail address, the subject line, and the text body of the message. SMTP servers listen on port 25.

Some of the most used SMTP commands are listed here:

SMTP Command	Function
MAIL FROM:	Specifies the return address for the mail message about to be sent.
RCPT TO:	Specifies the recipient of the message.
DATA	Begins transmission of the text of the message body.
QUIT	Logs off from the SMTP server and closes the connection.

SMTP is documented in RFC 821.

TELNET

The *TELNET protocol* was devised to provide terminal emulation capabilities. It establishes a standard method of interfacing terminals and terminal-oriented processes. TELNET uses TCP to provide a general, bidirectional, 8-bit byte-oriented communications facility.

This protocol is generally used to create applications that enable users to log on remotely to larger host computers. Users can then access the resources on the host computer just as if they were seated at a local terminal.

TELNET is documented in RFC 854, but has numerous options and extensions. A list of option RFCs can be found in RFC 1880.

Summary

In this chapter we've covered what WinSock is and why you'd want to use it. WinSock is a widely accepted API that is fast becoming the de facto standard for all Windows network development. We've examined the sockets paradigm and the basics of the client/server model. These concepts are fundamental to the structure of all WinSock applications. We also reviewed some of the more commonly used protocols, including TCP, UDP, and IP, and the sophisticated services these simple protocols – layered together – can provide.

With this groundwork firmly laid, we're ready to move on to find out about programming with sockets.

Chapter 2

Programming with Sockets

IN THIS CHAPTER
In Chapter 2 we look at the flow of typical client and server sockets applications. We move right into programming with WinSock by looking at the steps each type of application must perform and the functions and data structures involved in the process. By the end of the chapter, we will have written fully functioning client and server WinSock applications. Here are the topics in this chapter:

- Client/server program flow
- Initializing WinSock
- Version negotiation
- Name resolution
- Creating a socket
- Connecting sockets
- Sending and receiving data
- Closing a socket

Client/Server Program Flow

As explained in Chapter 1, socket applications are designed using the client/server model. This is usually accomplished by creating two distinct applications: a client application and a server application. Each of these two types of applications assumes a predetermined role in starting a conversation.

A server application is *passive* – it simply waits for requests from clients. A client application is *active* – it seeks out a server and sends data to initiate a conversation. For example, an HTTP server application runs on a machine and waits for requests. When directed by the user, an HTTP client application (a Web browser) sends a request to the server asking for the contents of a particular file. The server responds to this request by reading the file from a local disk and sending the contents back to the client. The client receives the contents of the file and displays it for the user.

In terms of sockets, the server application creates a socket, names the socket so it can be found by a client, and then "listens" on the socket for service requests. The client application creates a socket, finds a server socket by name or address, and then "plugs in" to initiate a conversation. Once a conversation is started, data can be sent in either direction. The client can send data to the server, and the server can send data to the client.

Almost all WinSock programs follow this general client/server design. Pairs of applications are developed to provide the needed service.

Application Pairs

Two fundamental types of client/server application pairs exist: *connection-oriented* applications and *connectionless* applications. Whether an application is connection-oriented or connectionless is usually determined by the protocols used by the application to communicate and the amount of data to be exchanged.

For example, programs such as e-mail and file transfer that transmit large amounts of data are usually connection-oriented. Programs that transmit small amounts of data, such as daytime and echo applications, are generally connectionless.

CONNECTION-ORIENTED APPLICATIONS

Applications that send and receive data as a stream of bytes are *connection-oriented*. A connection is established between the two processes before any data is transmitted or received. The identity of each endpoint (socket) is established only once, at the beginning of the conversation. From that point on, the origin and destination of data sent and received are understood to come from and go to the other end of this established connection. The applications do not identify themselves again each time data is transmitted.

In the Internet Protocol suite, connection-oriented applications are usually applications that rely on the Transmission Control Protocol (TCP) for transport.

Figure 2-1 shows the steps connection-oriented clients and servers perform to establish a conversation.

Chapter 2: Programming with Sockets 25

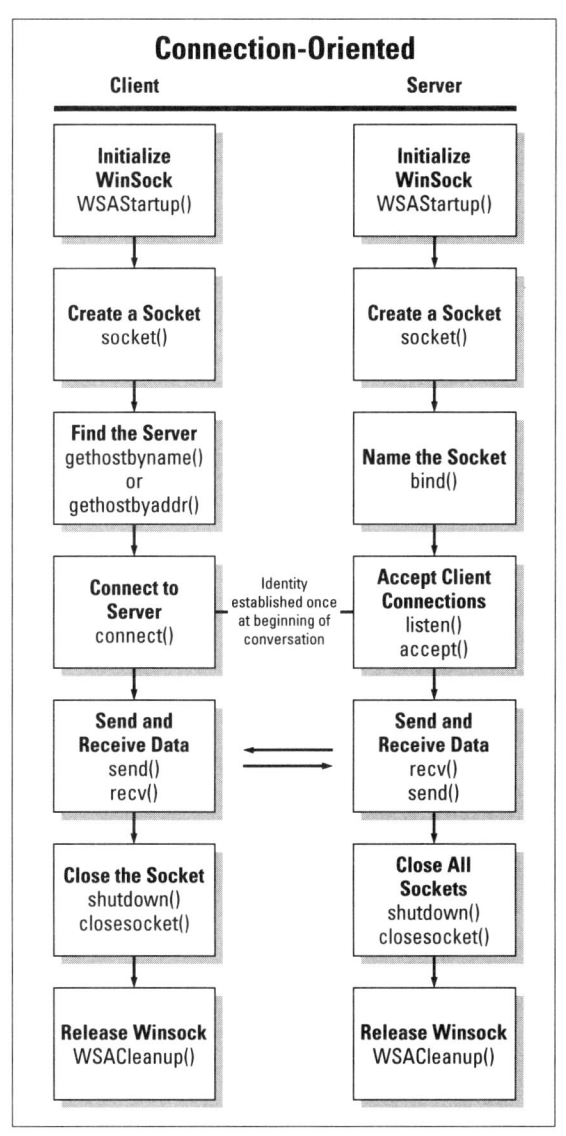

Figure 2-1: The steps performed by connection-oriented client and server applications.

The server application starts first. It creates a socket using the socket() function and then "names" the socket with bind(). Naming the socket identifies the server's address, the port it is attached to, and the protocol it uses. After the socket is named, the server waits for requests from clients, with the listen() and accept() functions.

Then the client application can execute. It uses socket() to create a socket and finds a host socket by name or address using one of the gethostbyX() functions. It then "plugs in" to the server with connect() and sends a request for services. The identity of both applications is established at this point — a *virtual circuit* is established. At least one socket in each application is dedicated to communicating to the other application. Data can now be sent and received in either direction with the send() and recv() functions. When the applications are finished communicating, they close their sockets with the closesocket() function.

CONNECTIONLESS APPLICATIONS
Applications that send and receive data in datagrams are typically connectionless. (They needn't be, but it is common practice.) The identity of each endpoint in the conversation is established each time data is sent. This scheme is only recommended for applications that transmit small amounts of information.

In the Internet Protocol suite, this usually corresponds to applications that use the User Datagram Protocol (UDP). Figure 2-2 shows the steps connectionless clients and servers perform.

The server application starts first. It creates a socket using the socket() function, names the socket with bind(), and then waits for requests from clients. Note, servers of this type don't generally use the listen() and accept() functions; they wait for client requests by calling the recvfrom() function. The recvfrom()function works exactly like the recv() function used in connection-oriented servers, but it also tells the server from where the data came. The server can then use this information to communicate back to the client, with the sendto() function.

Like the connection-oriented client, a connectionless client application uses socket() to create a socket and finds a host socket by name or address by using one of the gethostbyX() functions. But it doesn't call connect() to establish a connection; it sends data directly to the server with the sendto() function. The identity of each application is reestablished every time data is sent or received. When the applications are finished communicating, they close their sockets with the closesocket() function.

WinSock Programming Fundamentals

The rest of this chapter examines the mechanics of these two basic types of client/server application pairs. We'll look at the details of how all the steps are performed and the socket functions used to perform them. This is meant as an introduction to sockets programming, to acquaint you with the functions and data structures that make up the core of the WinSock API. Many of the details of writing real-world sockets applications are deferred to later chapters.

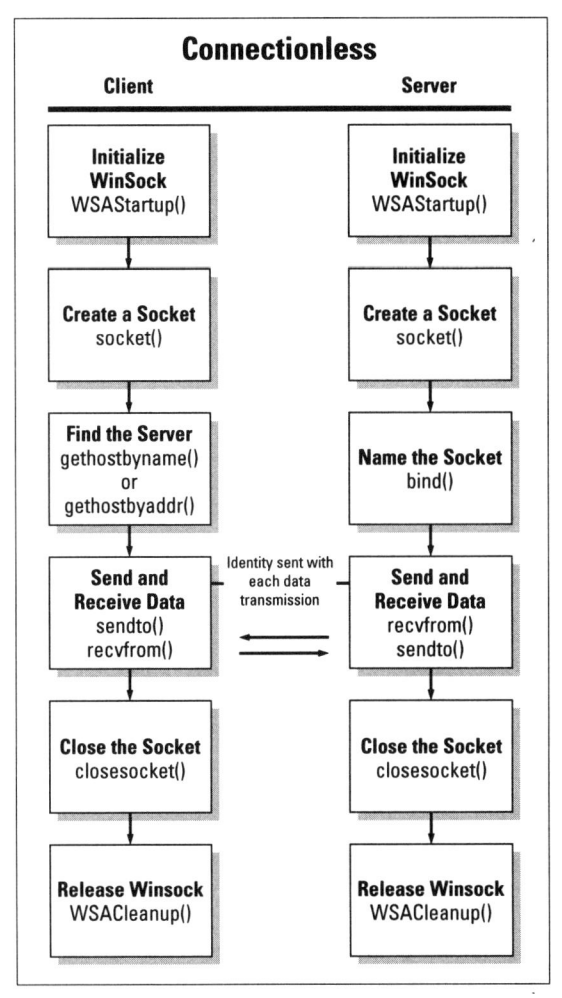

Figure 2-2: The steps performed by connectionless client and server applications.

Initializing WinSock

We will start with the three functions — WSAStartup(), WSACleanup(), and WSAGetLastError() — because they are used in all WinSock applications.

WinSock includes some functions that weren't part of the original Berkeley API. Most were added to make applications more Windows-friendly, and their use is highly recommended. All these extension functions, discussed as appropriate in subsequent chapters, are prefixed with the letters *WSA*, which stands for *Windows Sockets API*.

Part I: Introduction to Sockets

Every WinSock application *must* make a successful call to WSAStartup() before making any other WinSock calls and should call WSACleanup() before it exits. Any call made to a WinSock function before successfully executing WSAStartup() will fail, returning the WSAENOTINITIALISED error.

The WSAStartup() Function

The call to WSAStartup() gives the WinSock DLL a chance to allocate resources, register the calling process, and possibly refuse service if no system resources are available. It gives the calling application a chance to check the WinSock DLL to see if it supports the version and features the application needs to proceed.

This is the prototype for WSAStartup() from the WINSOCK.H header file:

```
int PASCAL FAR WSAStartup(
                    WORD wVersionRequired,
                    LPWSADATA lpWSAData
                    );
```

When calling WSAStartup(), the application fills in the *wVersionRequired* parameter with the major and minor WinSock version it wants to use. The least significant byte of the word must contain the major version number, and the most significant byte must contain the minor version number. As shown in the following example, the MAKEWORD macro defined in WINDOWS.H comes in handy for this.

```
// Call WSAStartup requesting WinSock 2.0 support
WSAStartup(MAKEWORD(2,0), lpWSAData);
```

Note: The 16-bit WINDOWS.H does not include the MAKEWORD macro, so I supplied one on the CD. It's in the \CH02 directory.

The second parameter in the call to WSAStartup() is a pointer to a WSADATA structure. Before the WSAStartup() function returns, it fills this structure with information about the WinSock DLL. WSADATA is defined as follows:

```
typedef struct WSAData {
        WORD                wVersion;
        WORD                wHighVersion;
        char                szDescription[WSADESCRIPTION_LEN+1];
        char                szSystemStatus[WSASYS_STATUS_LEN+1];
        unsigned short      iMaxSockets;
        unsigned short      iMaxUdpDg;
        char FAR *          lpVendorInfo;
} WSADATA;
```

WSADATA has the following members:

Field	Description
wVersion	The version of the WinSock API that the DLL expects the calling application to use. This is usually the same as the *wVersionRequired* parameter passed to WSAStartup().
wHighVersion	The highest version of WinSock this DLL can support. Normally, this is the same as the *wVersion* member, but it can be higher. For example, if you request Version 1.1 from a WinSock 2 DLL, then *wVersion* on return will be 1.1 and *wHighVersion* will be 2.0.
szDescription	A null-terminated ASCII string (up to 256 characters long) containing a text description of the WinSock DLL and vendor. Each vendor is free to use this field as they see fit — no predefined format exists.
szSystemStatus	A null-terminated ASCII string (up to 128 characters long) containing a text description of the WinSock DLL's current status or configuration information. Each vendor is free to use this field as needed; no formal format exists.
iMaxSockets [1]	The maximum number of sockets available to the calling application at the time of the call to WSAStartup().
iMaxUdpDg [1]	The size in bytes of the largest UDP datagram an application may send or receive (or can be handled by the DLL).
pVendorInfo [1]	A pointer to a buffer containing vendor-specific information. The format of the buffer pointed to by *lpVendorInfo* is completely up to the implementer. Its contents are not defined in the WinSock specification.

---

[1] The *iMaxSockets*, *iMaxUdpDg*, and *lpVendorInfo* fields should only be used with WinSock 1.1. WinSock 2 provides other means of retrieving these values. See Chapter 7 for details.

Figure 2-3 shows the contents of the WSADATA structure returned from WSAStartup() in the Version 1.1 WinSock that comes with Windows 95.

Part 1: Introduction to Sockets

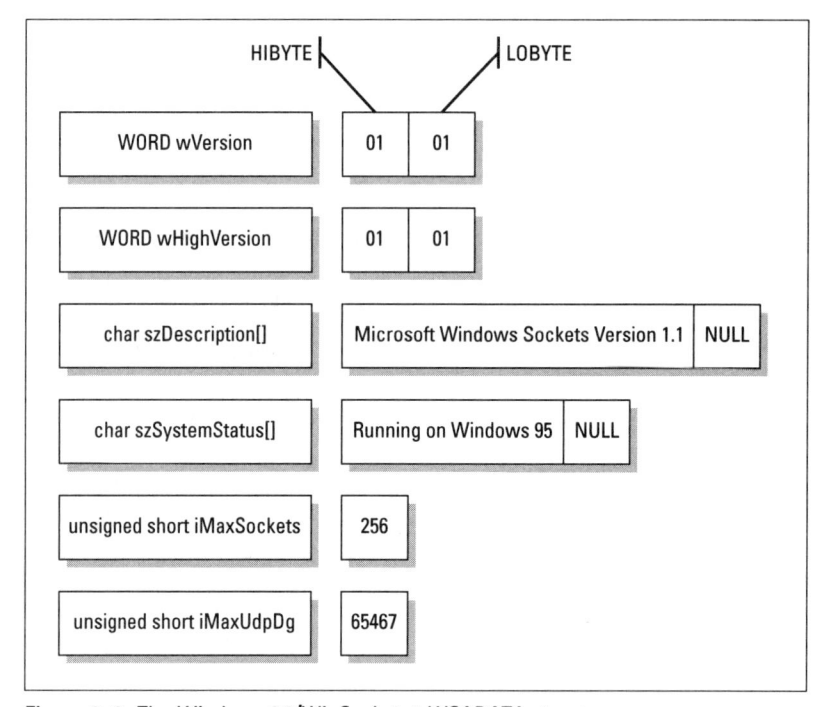

```
          HIBYTE         LOBYTE

WORD wVersion        | 01 | 01 |

WORD wHighVersion    | 01 | 01 |

char szDescription[]   | Microsoft Windows Sockets Version 1.1 | NULL |

char szSystemStatus[]  | Running on Windows 95 | NULL |

unsigned short iMaxSockets | 256 |

unsigned short iMaxUdpDg   | 65467 |
```

Figure 2-3: The Windows 95/WinSock 1.1 WSADATA structure

Version Negotiation

The most important value to check in this structure is the *wVersion* field. If WSAStartup() succeeds, this field will contain the version of the WinSock API that the DLL expects the application to use. You should always examine this value to verify the availability of the version you wish to use.

The *wVersion* member is in the same format as the *wVersionRequired* parameter. You can use the HIBYTE and LOBYTE macros defined in WINDOWS.H to test the return value, like this:

```
MajorVersion = LOBYTE(wsaData.wVersion)
MinorVersion = HIBYTE(wsaData.wVersion)
```

Or, you can simply compare WSADATA's *wVersion* member with the *wVersionRequired* parameter passed to WSAStartup(). For example, the following code requests and checks for the availability of WinSock 1.1. WSAStartup() returns 0 if it succeeds or an error value if it fails.

```
int nReturnCode;
WSADATA wsaData;
WORD wVersionRequired = MAKEWORD(1,1);
```

```
// Initialize the WinSock DLL
nReturnCode = WSAStartup(wVersionRequired, &wsaData);
if (nReturnCode != 0 )
{
    // Tell the user about the error.
    return;
}
// Confirm that the version requested is available.
if (wsaData.wVersion != wVersionRequired)
{
    // Tell the user that the needed version is not available.
    WSACleanup();
    return;
}
// WinSock initialized OK. Version is OK.
```

You should always check both the return value from WSAStartup() *and* the WSADATA *wVersion* field. WinSock exhibits some behavior here that you might not expect. For example, if you request Version 2.0 (or even higher) from a version 1.1 WinSock, WSAStartup() will not return an error. However, the *wVersion* field will indicate that only Version 1.1 is available. Table 2-1 shows the results you would receive in several different version negotiation situations.

TABLE 2-1 RESULTS FROM WINSOCK VERSION NEGOTIATION

WinSock Version	Version Requested	Results
1.1	1.0	WSAStartup() returns WSAVERNOTSUPPORTED error (version not supported)
1.1	1.1	WSAStartup() returns 0 *wVersion* = 1.1 *wHighVersion* = 1.1
1.1	2.0	WSAStartup() returns 0 *wVersion* = 1.1 *wHighVersion* = 1.1
2.0	1.1	WSAStartup() returns 0 *wVersion* = 1.1 *wHighVersion* = 2.0
2.0	2.0	WSAStartup() returns 0 *wVersion* = 2.0 *wHighVersion* = 2.0

Tip: The WSVer application included on the CD (in the \CH02 directory) enables you to try requesting different version numbers and shows you the contents of the resulting WSADATA structure.

WinSock Return Values

WSAStartup() is the only function in WinSock that returns an error code uniquely describing the error. All of the other WinSock functions return either SOCKET_ERROR or INVALID_SOCKET to indicate an error occurred. You must then call WSAGetLastError() to determine the exact cause of the error.

You'll find a complete listing of error values, their symbolic names, and their meanings in the Quick Reference at the end of this book.

Name Resolution

Before a client application can initiate communication with a server, it must first know the server's name or address. As mentioned in Chapter 1, the Domain Name System (DNS) will return an IP address when given a valid host name. The WinSock API provides several routines, collectively known as the *database functions*, that use either DNS, local tables, or some other process to provide name resolution services.

We'll look at all of these database functions in detail in Chapter 4. For now, we are only concerned with locating the address of a remote server. In this section, we will use two of the database functions to find host information:

- gethostbyname(), which returns information about a host for a given host name

- gethostbyaddr(), which returns information about a host for a given address

The hostent Structure

Both of the gethost functions return a pointer to a hostent (Host Entry) structure. The hostent structure and its members are defined as follows:

```
struct   hostent {
         char     FAR * h_name;
         char     FAR * FAR * h_aliases;
         short    h_addrtype;
         short    h_length;
         char     FAR * FAR * h_addr_list;
};
```

Field	Description
h_name	A null-terminated ASCII string containing the official name of the host.
h_aliases	A null-terminated array of null-terminated ASCII strings containing host alias names. This may not contain any entries.
h_addrtype	Specifies the type of address being returned. For a standard Version 1.1 WinSock, this value is always AF_INET (Address Family Internet). In other WinSock implementations, it could be AF_IPX, AF_OSI, AF_APPLETALK, or some other value.
h_length	The length in bytes of each address contained in the h_addr_list field. This value relates to the type of address specified in h_addrtype. If h_addrtype is AF_INET, this value will be 4 (32-bit IP address).
h_addr_list	A null-terminated array of pointers to network addresses. This list usually contains only one address. If it contains more than one, it means the host has several different network interfaces.

The gethostbyname() Function

The gethostbyname() function accepts a character string containing a host name. It returns a pointer to a hostent structure if it finds the host, or NULL if it does not. If gethostbyname() returns NULL, you should call WSAGetLastError() to check the exact reason for the error, as shown here:

```
LPHOSTENT lpHostEntry;
lpHostEntry = gethostbyname("www.idgbooks.com");
if (lpHostEntry == NULL)
    // Host name not found
    nReason = WSAGetLastError();
else
    // Host found, lpHostEntry points to a valid hostent
```

The gethostbyaddr() Function

If you know a server's address, you can retrieve hostent information for the server by using the gethostbyaddr() function. You might want to do this to find the name of a server whose address you already have. Here is the prototype for gethostbyaddr() from WINSOCK.H:

```
struct hostent FAR * PASCAL FAR gethostbyaddr(
                                        const char FAR * addr,
                                        int len,
                                        int type
                                        );
```

Parameter	Description
addr	Pointer to an address.
len	Length of the address in bytes.
type	The type of address (under Version 1.1 this is always AF_INET).

All we're doing here is passing an address, but because gethostbyaddr() was designed to accept addresses of different types, we're also passing a physical description of the address.

ADDRESS FAMILIES

Various types of network transport protocols use different addressing schemes. For example, TCP/IP uses 4-byte addresses, but IPX/SPX (Novell) addresses are 10 bytes long. WinSock uses the concept of *address families* to categorize these address types. WinSock 1.1 only officially supports the TCP/IP address family (AF_INET). At the time of this writing, WinSock 2 supports at least seven different address families; more may be added later as vendors make additional implementations available.

Because WinSock 1.1 focuses on TCP/IP, the *type* passed to gethostbyaddr() is always AF_INET (Address Family Internet) for Version 1.1; and the *len* parameter is always 4 (32-bit, 4-byte IP address).

Note, even though *addr* is defined as a character pointer, it won't accept an Internet address in dot-notation ("205.184.205.37"). For TCP/IP, gethostbyaddr() expects a pointer to a 32-bit integer (an unsigned long) that represents an IP address. You can use the inet_addr() function to convert an IP address in dot-notation to an unsigned long, as shown here:

```
unsigned long ulAddress = inet_addr("205.184.205.37");
```

If the character array passed to inet_addr() can't be converted, it returns the predefined value INADDR_NONE. We're going to use this behavior in our first WinSock program, HostInfo.c, coming up in Listing 2-1.

> **About Sample Programs in This Chapter**
>
> In this chapter, I have tried to make the sample applications as simple as possible. For clarity, all of the examples presented here are 32-bit console applications linked with WSOCK32.LIB. They will not work under MS-DOS or 16-bit Windows. They will only run on Windows 95 or Windows NT.
>
> Using console applications removes the complexity of programming for a GUI and greatly simplifies the source code. This enables us to focus on sockets fundamentals with as little involvement in nonsockets code as possible. Programs in subsequent chapters, however, will be full Windows applications capable of running on any Windows platform, and will represent the special cases of programming WinSock in conjunction with the Windows GUI.
>
> Even though WinSock 2 can be used with other networks and protocols, the samples here all assume the Internet address family and protocols. The global Internet is the only network we all have access to, so it makes sense to use it in these examples.

The HostInfo.c Program

Given a host name or address, the HostInfo program uses WinSock to get a pointer to a hostent structure and print out the information. The program uses the inet_addr() function to determine if the passed string represents a name or an address. It begins by assuming that the string is an address and passes it to inet_addr(). If inet_addr() returns INADDR_NONE, the program then assumes the string represents a host name.

Now let's take a look at HostInfo.c.

Listing 2-1: HostInfo.c

```
//
// HostInfo.c
//
// Use WinSock gethostbyX functions to lookup a host
// name or IP address and print the returned hostent
// structure;
//

//
// Pass a server name or IP address on the command line.
//
// Examples:
//      HostInfo www.idgbooks.com
//      HostInfo www.winsock.com
//      HostInfo 207.68.156.52
//
```

Part 1: Introduction to Sockets

```c
#include <stdio.h>
#include <winsock.h>

// Function to print a hostent structure
int Printhostent(LPCSTR lpServerNameOrAddress);

void main(int argc, char **argv)
{
    WORD wVersionRequested = MAKEWORD(1,1);
    WSADATA wsaData;
    int nRC;

    // Check arguments
    if (argc != 2)
    {
        fprintf(stderr,
            "\nSyntax: HostInfo ServerNameOrAddress\n");
        return;
    }

    // Initialize WinSock.dll
    nRC = WSAStartup(wVersionRequested, &wsaData);
    if (nRC)
    {
        fprintf(stderr,"\nWSAStartup() error: %d\n", nRC);
        WSACleanup();
        return;
    }

    // Check WinSock version
    if (wVersionRequested != wsaData.wVersion)
    {
        fprintf(stderr,"\nWinSock version 1.1 not supported\n");
        WSACleanup();
        return;
    }

    // Call Printhostent() to do all the work
    nRC = Printhostent(argv[1]);
    if (nRC)
        fprintf(stderr,"\nPrinthostent return code: %d\n", nRC);
    WSACleanup();
}

int Printhostent(LPCSTR lpServerNameOrAddress)
{
    LPHOSTENT lpHostEntry;      // Pointer to host entry structure
    struct in_addr iaHost;      // Internet address structure
    struct in_addr *pinAddr;    // Pointer to an internet address
    LPSTR lpAlias;              // Character pointer for alias names
    int iNdx;
```

```c
// Use inet_addr() to determine if we're dealing with a name
// or an address
iaHost.s_addr = inet_addr(lpServerNameOrAddress);
if (iaHost.s_addr == INADDR_NONE)
{
    // Wasn't an IP address string, assume it is a name
    lpHostEntry = gethostbyname(lpServerNameOrAddress);
}
else
{
    // It was a valid IP address string
    lpHostEntry = gethostbyaddr((const char *)&iaHost,
                    sizeof(struct in_addr), AF_INET);
}

// Check return value
if (lpHostEntry == NULL)
{
    fprintf(stderr,"\nError getting host: %d",
            WSAGetLastError());
    return WSAGetLastError();
}

// Print structure
printf("\n\nHOSTENT");
printf("\n-----------------");

// Host name
printf("\nHost Name.......: %s", lpHostEntry->h_name);

// List of host aliases
printf("\nHost Aliases....");
for (iNdx = 0; ; iNdx++)
{
    lpAlias = lpHostEntry->h_aliases[iNdx];
    if (lpAlias == NULL)
        break;
    printf(": %s", lpAlias);
    printf("\n                    ");
}

// Address type
printf("\nAddress type....: %d", lpHostEntry->h_addrtype);
if (lpHostEntry->h_addrtype == AF_INET)
    printf(" (AF_INET)");
else
    printf(" (UnknownType)");

// Address length
printf("\nAddress length..: %d", lpHostEntry->h_length);

// List of IP addresses
printf("\nIP Addresses....");
for (iNdx = 0; ; iNdx++)
```

```
    {
        pinAddr = ((LPIN_ADDR)lpHostEntry->h_addr_list[iNdx]);
        if (pinAddr == NULL)
            break;
        printf(": %s", inet_ntoa(*pinAddr));
        printf("\n                    ");
    }
    printf("\n");
    return 0;
}
```

OUTPUT FROM HOSTINFO.C

Compile HostInfo.c and link it with WSOCK32.LIB. Pass a host name or IP address to HostInfo on the command line to see the resulting hostent structure. Here is some sample output from the HostInfo program:

```
>HostInfo www.yahoo.com

HOSTENT
-----------------
Host Name........: www9.yahoo.com
Host Aliases.....: www.yahoo.com

Address type.....: 2(AF_INET)
Address length...: 4
IP Addresses.....: 204.71.177.74


>HostInfo www.microsoft.com

HOSTENT
-----------------
Host Name........: www.microsoft.com
Host Aliases.....:
Address type.....: 2(AF_INET)
Address length...: 4
IP Addresses.....: 207.68.156.52
                 : 207.68.137.62
                 : 207.68.156.53
```

THE in_addr STRUCTURE

The Printhostent() function in HostInfo.c uses an in_addr structure to represent an IP address rather than just using an unsigned long.

In Versions 1.1 and 2 of WinSock, in_addr is defined as a union of 4 bytes. In Berkeley sockets this structure was sometimes used to access the pieces of an IP address. The macro s_addr is a macro used to access the unsigned long portion of the union. The structure of in_addr could change at some time in the future (possibly to expand IP addresses), so you should use this structure rather than an unsigned long. Using this structure makes the source code more portable.

Network Byte Order

In addition to using inet_addr() to convert the dot-notation string to an unsigned long, we're using it to perform one more bit of work for us: It gives us an IP address in *network byte order.* Network byte order is related to the method by which processors store multibyte scalar values in memory and on disk.

Most PCs running Windows have Intel processors. Intel processors store multibyte values in *little-endian format,* in which the least significant byte is stored ahead of the most significant byte ("little end first"). *Big-endian processors* store the most significant byte ahead of the least significant byte ("big end first"). Figure 2-4 shows several values as they are stored in both little- and big-endian formats.

Data	Big-Endian (Network Byte Order)	Little-Endian (Intel Byte Order)
16-bit, 2-byte integer Short Number = 0x1234;	12 | 34	34 | 12
32-bit, 4-byte integer long Number = 0xAAABACAD;	AA | AB | AC | AD	AD | AC | AB | AA
Character array "WinSock"	W | I | N | S | O | C | K	W | I | N | S | O | C | K

Figure 2-4: Sample values in big-endian and little-endian byte order

As you can see in Figure 2-4, byte order is only important in multibyte scalar values — values that use more than one byte to represent a single quantity. Single bytes and arrays of bytes (such as character strings) are not affected. You *must* use network byte order on any multibyte value passed to WinSock. If you want to share information among systems with different processors, you should also ensure that any data transmitted across the network is in network byte order.

The WinSock API provides four functions that convert the byte order of scalar values to and from network order:

Function	Description
htons()	Host To Network Short. Converts 16-bit values from host to network order.
ntohs()	Network To Host Short. Converts 16-bit values from network to host order.
htonl()	Host To Network Long. Converts 32-bit values from host to network order.
ntohl()	Network To Host Long. Converts 32-bit values from network to host order.

Each of these functions accepts a numeric value parameter and returns a converted value of the same size. When compiled on an Intel machine and run on a TCP/IP WinSock, the comments in the following code would be True:

```
ShortIntelValue = 0x1234;         // Stored in memory as 3412
ShortNetworkValue = htons(ShortIntelValue);
// ShortNetworkValue = 0x3412; // Stored in memory as 1234
LongIntelValue = 0x12345678;
LongNetworkValue = htonl(LongIntelValue);
// LongNetworkValue = 0x78563412;
ShortIntelValue = ntohs(ShortNetworkValue);
// ShortIntel = 0x1234;
LongIntelValue = ntohl(LongNetworkValue);
// LongIntelValue = 0x12345678;
```

These conversion functions are network dependent. If the machine on which you are developing uses the same byte order as the network, then these functions do nothing. The safest and most portable way to code is to always use these functions on all multibyte scalar values. There is nothing to lose by using them, and it ensures that your source is portable not only to different machines, but different transport protocols as well.

A Word about Internet Byte Order

It was long ago agreed that network byte order on the Internet would be big-endian. Most processors at the time (PDP series, IBM 370 family, Motorola, and so forth) were all big-endian — that's the reverse of most PCs running Windows. Byte ordering is extremely important when programming for the Internet on an Intel machine.

Lively discussion on this topic occurred in the early days of the Internet. The terms *big-endian* and *little-endian* became associated with computer architecture in a now famous paper Danny Cohen wrote on the subject, "On Holy Wars and a Plea for Peace." Cohen borrowed the terms from Swift's *Gulliver's Travels*, in which citizens argued over how eggs should be broken — from the little end or the big end. Cohen's paper, IEN 137, is included on the CD in the \RFC directory.

Creating a Socket

We've done all our work so far without a socket. Before we can connect to a server or accept connections from clients, we have to create a socket — our endpoint in the communication circuit.

When you successfully create a socket, you get a *socket descriptor*. A socket descriptor is analogous to a file handle, and you use a socket descriptor in much the same way. You pass the socket descriptor to WinSock functions to designate the socket you want to connect with, send data over, and so forth.

A socket is associated with three elements: an address family, a socket type, and a protocol. You create a socket by calling the socket() function:

SOCKET PASCAL FAR socket(int *af*, int *type*, int *protocol*);

Parameter	Description
af	Address family. For a standard Version 1.1 WinSock, this value is always AF_INET (Address Family Internet). In other WinSock implementations, it could be AF_IPX, AF_OSI, AF_APPLETALK or some other value.
type	Socket type.
protocol	Transport protocol.

Socket Type and Protocol

The second parameter of the socket() function denotes a socket type. WinSock 2 defines many types of sockets and they will be discussed later in the book. Here, we'll examine the two most common types:

- SOCK_STREAM, which supports byte-stream, connection-oriented, reliable communication. Uses TCP for the Internet address family (AF_INET).

- SOCK_DGRAM, which supports datagram, connectionless, "unreliable" communication. Uses UDP for the Internet address family (AF_INET).

The third parameter to socket() specifies a protocol. The combination of socket type and address family implies a protocol. The WinSock specification only requires a single protocol for each socket type using a given address family. For this reason, the protocol parameter can be set using one of the predefined types (IPPROTO_TCP, IPPROTO_UDP, etc.) or simply set to 0 to let WinSock choose a default.

For example, if you create a socket specifying AF_INET and SOCK_DGRAM, WinSock will assume you want to use UDP. If you create a socket specifying AF_INET and SOCK_STREAM, WinSock will assume you want to use TCP.

```
MYUDPSocket = socket(AF_INET, SOCK_DGRAM, 0);
MyTCPSocket = socket(AF_INET, SOCK_STREAM, 0);
```

Socket Descriptors

The socket() function returns a socket descriptor (SOCKET) if it succeeds or INVALID_SOCKET if it fails. SOCKET is defined in WINSOCK.H as an unsigned integer, but you should never manipulate a SOCKET directly or assume any value or characteristics. A SOCKET value should only be compared to the constant INVALID_SOCKET.

For example, it was common practice in Berkeley sockets to test for errors like this:

```
SocketDescriptor = socket(af, type, protocol);
if (SocketDescriptor < 0)
    // Error
else
    // OK
```

The WinSock specification makes no restrictions on SOCKET values. Each vendor is free to use any range of values. Always use INVALID_SOCKET when checking the results of a call to socket, as shown here:

```
SocketDescriptor = socket(af, type, protocol);
if (SocketDescriptor == INVALID_SOCKET)
    // Error
else
    // OK
```

Connecting Sockets

Three pieces of information must be known before a client can communicate with a server:

- ◆ Protocol (must be the same for both the server and the client)
- ◆ Server address
- ◆ Server port number

The Client's Role: Connecting to a Server

In the HostInfo.c program, we chose a protocol (TCP) and learned how to find a server address. If we get a port number, we can then completely fill in an address structure and connect to a server.

THE connect() FUNCTION
The connect() function is used to connect a client socket to a server socket.

```
int PASCAL FAR connect(
                SOCKET s,
                const struct sockaddr FAR *name,
                int namelen
                );
```

Parameter	Description
s	Socket descriptor (obtained from the socket() function).
name	Pointer to a socket address (sockaddr) structure.
namelen	The length in bytes of the sockaddr structure.

THE sockaddr STRUCTURE
Let's take a closer look at the second parameter of connect(), which is a pointer to a sockaddr structure:

```
struct sockaddr {
        u_short sa_family;
        char    sa_data[14];
};
```

This structure has the following members:

sa_family	Address family
sa_data	Protocol-specific data

The sockaddr structure is a generic definition of a socket address. The first field, sa_family, contains a number designating the address family. This number also identifies the format of the remainder of the structure. The sa_data member is a buffer for protocol-specific socket information. Each address family has its own sockaddr_ structure. These protocol-specific socket address structures define in detail the sa_data portion.

To access a server on the Internet, we will use a sockaddr_in (socket address Internet) structure:

```
struct sockaddr_in {
        short    sin_family;
        u_short  sin_port;
        struct   in_addr sin_addr;
        char     sin_zero[8];
};
```

The sockaddr_in structure breaks the endpoint address into its two components: port number (sin_port) and IP address (sin_addr). It fills the remaining 8 bytes of the structure with an unused character string (sin_zero).

The sockaddr_in structure is the same size as the generic sockaddr, but it defines the sa_data area with transport-specific fields. Figure 2-5 shows the relationship between these two structures.

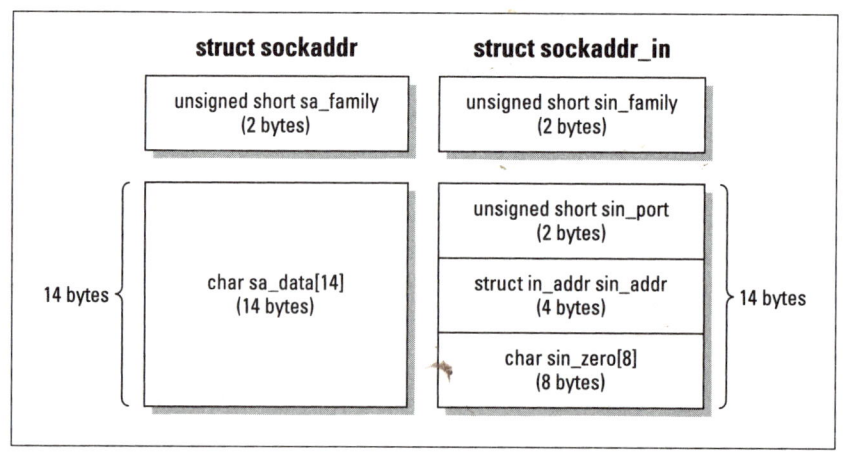

struct sockaddr	struct sockaddr_in
unsigned short sa_family (2 bytes)	unsigned short sin_family (2 bytes)
char sa_data[14] (14 bytes)	unsigned short sin_port (2 bytes)
	struct in_addr sin_addr (4 bytes)
	char sin_zero[8] (8 bytes)
14 bytes	14 bytes

Figure 2-5: A sockaddr_in structure defines the sa_data portion of a sockaddr structure with TCP/IP-specific fields.

For our needs here (TCP/IP), we'll set the sin_family member to AF_INET and fill in the in_addr member from a hostent structure. All we're missing now is the sin_port field.

FINDING THE CORRECT PORT

In the sockaddr_in structure, the sin_port field identifies the port number we want to use. The concept of ports allows more than one socket to be used at a given machine address. The *full* address of a socket — its sockaddr — is made up of an address (IP address on the Internet), a protocol (TCP, UDP, and so forth), and a port. These three pieces of information *together* uniquely identify a socket.

Only one socket can be associated with an address that uses a particular protocol and port. For instance, you can't have two sockets on the same machine attached to the same port using the same protocol. You *can* have two sockets attached to the same port if they each use a different protocol.

Note: WinSock allows multiple sockets to be assigned to the same port, as long as they each use a different protocol. This makes it possible for the same service to be provided at a given port through different protocols. For example, port 7 (the well-known *echo port*) commonly has two sockets attached to it — one providing echo services through UDP, and the other providing echo services through TCP.

The port number corresponds to the application or process we want to call on for services. As explained in Chapter 1, some services have well-known port numbers as assigned by the Internet Assigned Numbers Authority (IANA). One way to go is to fill in the port number with one of the well-known services, like this:

```
// Assign port number to "well-known" port
// for File Transfer Protocol (FTP) in network order.
SocketAddressServer.sin_port = htons(21);
```

A more portable way of assigning this value, however, is to once again call on the WinSock database services — in this case, getservbyname().

THE getservbyname() FUNCTION

The getservbyname() function can be used to find a port number corresponding to a given service name.

```
struct servent FAR * PASCAL FAR getservbyname(
                            const char FAR * name,
                            const char FAR * proto
                            );
```

Parameter	Description
name	A pointer to a null-terminated ASCII string containing a service name.
proto	A pointer to a null-terminated ASCII string containing a protocol name. If this parameter is NULL, getservbyname() returns the first service matching *name*. If it isn't NULL, getservbyname() attempts to match both the *name* and *proto*.

THE servent STRUCTURE

If getservbyname() fails, it returns NULL. If it succeeds, it returns a pointer to a servent (service entry) structure:

```
struct  servent {
        char    FAR * s_name;
        char    FAR * FAR * s_aliases;
        short   s_port;
        char    FAR * s_proto;
};
```

Parameter	Description
s_name	Official name of the service. These are always lowercase ("ftp"; "http"; and so forth).
s_aliases	A null-terminated array of null-terminated ASCII strings containing host alternate service names.
s_port	Port number in network order.
s_proto	Null-terminated ASCII string containing the name of the protocol associated with this service name and port.

The *s_port* field is the one we're after here. Note, like all return values from WinSock, the port number returned by getservbyname() is already in network byte order.

Now that we have a port number, we can completely fill in the sockaddr_in structure and call connect(). Here's the code:

```
// Find the port number for the FTP service on TCP
lpServEnt = getservbyname("ftp", "tcp");
if (lpServEnt == NULL)
{
    // Service resolution failed,
    //    use well-known number
    //    in network order
    saServer.sin_port = htons(21);
}
else
{
    // Service resolution succeeded
    //    use supplied number
    saServer.sin_port = lpServEnt->s_port;
}
```

```
// Fill in the rest of the server address structure
saServer.sin_family = AF_INET;
// Use the first address in the list
saServer.sin_addr = *((LPIN_ADDR)*lpHostEntry->h_addr_list);

// Connect the socket
rc = connect(Socket, (LPSOCKADDR)&saServer, sizeof(SOCKADDR));
if (rc == SOCKET_ERROR)
    nReason = WSAGetLastError();
```

The Server's Role: Listening for Client Connections

Because they don't initiate conversations, server applications don't call connect(). Instead, after creating a socket, the server application calls the bind() function to "name" its socket.

THE bind() FUNCTION

The bind() function allows the server to name its socket fully. Here's the prototype for bind():

```
int bind(
        SOCKET s,
        const struct sockaddr FAR* name,
        int namelen
        );
```

Parameter	Description
s	Socket descriptor.
name	Pointer to a socket address structure (sockaddr).
namelen	The length in bytes of the sockaddr structure.

Note, the parameters to bind() are identical to the ones required for connect(). The bind() function associates the server's local address and port with a socket so a client can find it. The socket already has a socket type and protocol associated with it in the call to socket().

THE listen() FUNCTION

After binding a socket to its address, connection-oriented servers then call the listen() function to wait for client requests:

```
int PASCAL FAR listen(
                  SOCKET s,
                  int backlog
                  );
```

Parameter	Description
s	A socket descriptor identifying a bound, unconnected socket.
backlog	The maximum length to which the queue of pending connections may grow.

The socket descriptor passed to listen() must not already be connected, and it must be named — that is, bound to an address with bind().

The listen() function tells WinSock that the server intends to use this socket to listen for client requests, and it specifies a backlog for incoming connections. The *backlog* parameter is the number of incoming requests the server wants to allow to stack up without being accepted before a connection is refused. Valid ranges for this number are determined by each WinSock vendor, but are typically larger than 1 and less than 5. If a legal value is not specified here, WinSock will substitute the nearest valid number.

The listen() function allows the WinSock DLL to prepare a queue for waiting connections and places the socket into passive mode. Processing does not stop and wait when listen() is called; the function is used to set up the pending connection queue. Incoming connections for the socket are then placed in the queue until they are accepted by the server. Servers that can't immediately complete requests from clients use this function to queue requests until they can be serviced. If the queue is full when a connection request arrives, the client will receive the error WSAECONNREFUSED.

THE accept() FUNCTION

After calling listen(), a connection-oriented server then calls accept() to wait for client connection requests.

```
SOCKET PASCAL FAR accept(
                  SOCKET s,
                  struct sockaddr FAR * addr,
                  int FAR * addrlen
                  );
```

Parameter	Description
s	Socket descriptor identifying a listening socket.
addr	An optional pointer to a buffer that receives the address of the client requesting the connection.
addrlen	An optional pointer to an integer that contains the length of the address *addr*.

When a server calls accept(), processing stops and waits for a connection request from a client. The optional *addr* and *addrlen* parameters are filled in by accept() with the address of the client application requesting the connection. You don't have to initialize these values before calling accept().

The accept() function returns a *new* socket that is already associated with the client. The sockaddr associated with the new socket contains the address and port number of the client and can be used to send data back to the client application.

Remember: Because accept() returns a *new* socket descriptor, connection-oriented servers may have multiple sockets to close before exiting.

Connectionless servers must call bind() to name their socket, but they don't typically call listen()or accept(). After binding their socket, this type of server simply calls the recvfrom() function (discussed in the upcoming section) to begin reading data from clients. Connectionless servers usually communicate small amounts of information and only provide services that can be completed quickly (such as returning the time of day) and, therefore, do not require a queue of pending connections.

Sending and Receiving Data

After all we've been through to create a socket, find a server, and connect to it, the sending and receiving of data is refreshingly familiar. It is similar to reading and writing files. In fact, the Berkeley API sends and receives data with the standard read() and write() functions used with normal files. Under WinSock, however, socket descriptors are not always equivalent to file handles. WinSock provides specialized send() and recv() functions to read and write data over sockets, but their usage is still much like file I/O.

The most significant difference between socket I/O and file I/O is you may not send or receive all the bytes requested with one function call. If you attempt to send more data than the protocol stack can buffer, only part of the data will be sent. If you ask to receive more data than is currently available, you will only receive what is waiting to be received. All of the WinSock I/O functions return the number of bytes transmitted. It is important to check these values and continue to send or receive until all the data has been transferred.

Connection-Oriented Sending and Receiving

As we'll see in this section, the transfer of data is handled slightly differently in connectionless applications than it is in connection-oriented programs.

The send() Function

Once a client has established a connection with a server, it can send data with the send() function.

```
int PASCAL FAR send(
                    SOCKET s,
                    const char FAR * buf,
                    int len,
                    int flags
                    );
```

Parameter	Description
s	Socket descriptor.
buf	Pointer to a buffer that contains the data to be sent.
len	Length of *buf* in bytes.
flags	Optional flags that affect the way data is sent.

Because connection-oriented applications establish a virtual circuit (connection) with the connect() function, the SOCKET supplied to send() already has an associated remote socket. The destination of the data being sent is understood to be the address and port specified in the call to connect().

The *buf* parameter is a pointer to the first byte in a buffer of data you want to send; and *len* is the total number of bytes you want to send from the buffer. The *flags* parameter affects the way in which the data is sent. This parameter is typically set to 0 (no flags). Valid options for the *flags* parameters are discussed in the Quick Reference.

If send() fails, it returns SOCKET_ERROR. If it succeeds, it returns the total number of bytes sent. The only thing tricky about sending data is that the entire buffer may not be sent in one call. It's up to the application to keep track of how much data was sent and how much is left. Sending a large amount of data may require several calls to send(). The following code sends a large buffer over a connected socket:

```
do
{
    BytesSent = send(MySocket, BufferPointer, BufferLength, 0);
    if (BytesSent == SOCKET_ERROR)
    {
        nReason = WSAGetLastError();
        // Tell the user about the error
        return;
    }
    BufferPointer += BytesSent;
    BufferLength -= BytesSent;
} while (BufferLength > 0);
```

THE recv() FUNCTION

To receive data, connection-oriented applications use the recv() function. The remote socket associated during the call to connect() is understood as the origin of the data being received. Here are recv() and its parameters:

```
int PASCAL FAR recv(
                SOCKET s,
                char FAR * buf,
                int len,
                int flags
                );
```

Parameter	Description
s	Socket descriptor.
buf	Pointer to a buffer that will receive the data.
len	Length of *buf* in bytes.
flags	Optional flags that affect the way the data is received.

As much information as is currently available, up to the size of the supplied buffer, is returned by recv(). If no data is available to be received, the recv() function will wait for data to arrive. Like send(), recv() returns either the number of bytes transferred or SOCKET_ERROR. You may have to call recv() multiple times to receive a predetermined amount of data.

The *flags* parameter affects the way in which the data is received. If this value is MSG_PEEK, the incoming data is copied into the buffer but not removed from the input queue. The same data will be read again on the next call to recv(). This parameter is typically set to 0 (no flags). Other valid options for the *flags* parameters are discussed in the Quick Reference.

RECORD BOUNDARIES ON STREAM SOCKETS

Stream sockets don't preserve record boundaries — there isn't necessarily a one-to-one relationship between send() and recv() calls. For example, if a client application sent 200 bytes to a server with two calls to send(), the server might receive all of that data in one call to recv(). The network system is free to coalesce the two calls to send() into one network packet. The system is also free to break large send() buffers into smaller packets if necessary.

Connectionless Sending and Receiving

Because no connection has been established, connectionless applications must designate the destination address when sending data.

THE sendto() FUNCTION

The sendto() function allows the destination address to be specified as follows:

```
int PASCAL FAR sendto(
                SOCKET s,
                const char FAR * buf,
                int len,
                int flags,
                const struct sockaddr FAR * to,
                int tolen
                );
```

Parameter	Description
s	A descriptor identifying a socket.
buf	A buffer containing the data to be transmitted.
len	The length of the data in *buf*.
flags	Specifies the way in which the call is made.
to	The address of the target socket.
tolen	The size of the address in *to*.

The sendto() function operates exactly as send() does, but it requires a destination address. The *to* and *tolen* parameters specify the address of the process that is to receive the data being sent.

THE recvfrom() FUNCTION

Connectionless applications receive data with the recvfrom() function, which is similar to recv():

```
int PASCAL FAR recvfrom(
                   SOCKET s,
                   char FAR * buf,
                   int len,
                   int flags,
                   struct sockaddr FAR * from,
                   int FAR * fromlen
                   );
```

Parameter	Description
s	Socket descriptor identifying a bound socket.
buf	Buffer for the incoming data.
len	Length of *buf* in bytes.
flags	Specifies the way in which the call is made.
from	Pointer to a buffer that will receive the source address.
fromlen	The length in bytes of the *from* buffer.

The recvfrom() function operates exactly as recv() does, but it requires a pointer to a destination address. The *from* and *fromlen* parameters specify a buffer that will *receive* the address of the sending process.

Note: You do not fill in the *from* and *fromlen* parameters before calling recvfrom(). The recvfrom() function fills these parameters before it returns so that the calling process can determine the source of the received data. This origin address information can then be used to return messages to the application that sent the data.

RECORD BOUNDARIES ON DATAGRAM SOCKETS

Unlike stream sockets, datagram sockets *do* preserve record boundaries. There is a one-to-one relationship between sendto() and recvfrom() calls. If a client makes two calls to sendto(), each sending 100 bytes, the server will have to perform two calls to recvfrom() (of at least 100 bytes) to receive all the data.

Closing a Socket

Closing a socket is not quite as simple as closing a file. Because two applications are involved in a connection, each must know when the conversation is ending. (It's considered rude to walk out of a room while someone is still talking.)

Connectionless

Because connectionless applications aren't dedicated to a conversation, they can simply call the closesocket() function.

```
int PASCAL FAR closesocket(SOCKET s);
```

Connection-Oriented

Connection-oriented applications, as well, can call closesocket(), but should first notify the peer application before closing a socket. A stream socket may have data waiting that it has not yet received, or the protocol stack may not have completed sending all the data in the buffer. Or the application at the other end of the conversation may still be sending data.

The shutdown() function is used for this task of more gracefully closing a socket connection.

```
int PASCAL FAR shutdown (SOCKET s, int how)
```

This function disables sending or receiving data on a socket, or both sending and receiving. The *how* parameter determines what type of shutdown is performed. This parameter takes three possible values:

Value of how Parameter	Definition
SD_RECEIVE	Receives are no longer allowed on the socket.
SD_SEND	Send operations are no longer allowed.
SD_BOTH	Both send and receive are disabled.

The recommended procedure is to first call shutdown() with

```
how = SD_SEND
```

which tells the other side that you will not send any more data. Then call recv() until there is no more data to be received. Then call shutdown() with

how = SD_BOTH

and then closesocket(). Here's how it looks:

```
// Disable sends, tell other side we want to shutdown.
nReturnCode = shutdown(MySocket, SD_SEND);
if (nReturnCode == SOCKET_ERROR)
    ReportError(WSAGetLastError());

// Receive any pending data
while(1)
{
    nReturnCode = recv(MySocket, BufferPointer, BufferLen, 0);
    if (nReturnCode == SOCKET_ERROR)
    {
        ReportError(WSAGetLastError());
        break;
    }
    if (nReturnCode == 0)    // Connection has been closed
        break;
}
// Let peer know we are finished
nReturnCode = shutdown(MySocket, SD_BOTH);
if (nReturnCode == SOCKET_ERROR)
    ReportError(WSAGetLastError());
nReturnCode = closesocket(MySocket);
if (nReturnCode == SOCKET_ERROR)
    ReportError(WSAGetLastError());
```

Summary

We've covered a lot of ground in one chapter, discussing many new functions and data structures. But what you've learned comprises the entire core of the sockets API.

Five example programs are on the CD, in the \CH02 folder, that use only the functions described here in this chapter:

- DServer.c – a datagram, connectionless server example
- DClient.c – a datagram, connectionless client example
- SServer.c – a stream, connection-oriented server example
- SClient.c – a stream, connection-oriented client example
- GetHTTP.c – a stream, connection-oriented client utility to retrieve files from the World Wide Web

All of these applications are short, extremely simple Win32 console programs that demonstrate the concepts from this chapter. The comments at the top of each source file include instructions for compiling and running the sample.

We've written real, working WinSock applications in this chapter, but none of them have a graphical user interface. In the following chapter, you'll examine the special considerations required for writing WinSock applications that use the Windows GUI.

Chapter 3

Programming with Windows Sockets

IN THIS CHAPTER
Chapter 3 will discuss how the Windows Sockets API differs from the Berkeley sockets API, and why the Berkeley standard was extended. Various techniques used to avoid the use of blocking routines are previewed, along with some general guidelines for writing WinSock applications. Here are the topics covered in Chapter 3:

- Overview of services available in each WinSock version
- The message-driven architecture and blocking of Windows
- WinSock extensions to the Berkeley API
- Blocking and nonblocking operations
- Using asynchronous mode
- The benefits of overlapped I/O and event objects
- Choosing a strategy and architecture for your application

WHEN THE WINSOCK GROUP BEGAN designing a sockets interface for Windows, the goal was to comply as closely as possible with the Berkeley API and add only those functions that were necessary to make WinSock applications fit cleanly into the Windows environment. This chapter provides a broad overview of these extensions to the standard Berkeley API. You'll learn how programming sockets for Windows is different, and why.

Several strategies are available to build WinSock programs under WinSock Version 1.1. WinSock 2 includes these methods and adds some new ones. Even though the WinSock API is the same under various Windows platforms, there are significant differences in the approaches that are appropriate for 16-bit and 32-bit Windows applications. This chapter gives you a broad understanding of the issues involved in WinSock programming and points out the alternative solutions available in each version of WinSock on each Windows platform.

WinSock Versions

Before WinSock was established, each network provider developed their own interface libraries independently. Software developers had to write code for each unique network interface they wanted to support.

The Berkeley Sockets API established a standard that would alleviate this dilemma of incompatible network interfaces, but the Berkeley solution didn't fit cleanly into the event-driven programming model of Windows. With blocking functions – functions that don't return immediately – a Windows program often appeared to stall. The WinSock group set out to emulate the Berkeley API, but they knew that they had to add extensions to this standard to make it fit the Windows programming model.

Version 1.0

Windows Sockets Version 1.0 was the initial release made by the WinSock group. At that time, there were no commercially available WinSock implementations. This version was used mainly by network software suppliers to start the process of building and testing what would become their first WinSock releases. During this period of development, several changes were made to the specification to meet the requirements of various vendors and to qualify the specification further.

Version 1.1

The first official release, WinSock 1.1, soon became the industry standard and is still widely in use today. Version 1.1 follows the guidelines laid out in Version 1.0 but incorporates several changes that resulted from the experiences of early WinSock implementers. The following key features in WinSock 1.1 made it attractive to developers:

- *Standardized API.* It supported one well-defined interface to the TCP/IP suite of protocols, rather than different interfaces for each protocol stack vendor.
- *Binary compatibility.* The dynamic link library (DLL) design provides binary compatible services from various vendors.
- *Consistent network byte-order conversion.* WinSock implementations are required to provide the standard set of byte-order conversion routines that are unique to each type of CPU.
- *WSA extensions.* New functions, data types, and structures allow network applications to fit cleanly into the Windows programming model.

The WinSock 1.1 specification focuses exclusively on the TCP/IP suite of network protocols. Some vendors (most notably Microsoft) added other protocols, but they are not part of the official WinSock specification. WinSock 1.1 vendors do not have to support these additional protocols to be WinSock compliant.

WinSock's DLL design even makes it unnecessary for applications to be recompiled when being moved from one vendor's implementation to another. Well-written WinSock applications that adhere to the standard WinSock API will run on any vendor's WinSock.

There are 16-bit and 32-bit versions of WinSock 1.1. It ships with Windows 95 and versions of Windows NT prior to Version 4.

Version 2.0

Windows Sockets Version 2 greatly expands the original standard. Most important, it officially supports protocols other than TCP/IP and provides mechanisms that allow applications to be protocol independent.

With only a few exceptions, WinSock 2 encapsulates the entire Version 1.1 API at the source level. At the binary level, WinSock 2 is 100% compatible with Version 1.1. Applications compiled and linked with Version 1.1 will run on Version 2 unchanged. In addition to this strict backward compatibility with Version 1.1, WinSock 2 provides significant new functionality. It further extends the standard Berkeley API to provide the following new services. (In this chapter, we discuss only the most notable features of WinSock 2; you'll find a more detailed examination in Chapter 7.)

- *Multiprotocol support.* WinSock 2 allows an application to use the familiar socket interface to achieve simultaneous access to any number of installed transport protocols. WinSock is no longer restricted to use on TCP/IP only.

- *Asynchronous I/O and event objects.* WinSock 2 uses the overlapped I/O model introduced in Win32 environments. *Asynchronous I/O* enables an application to continue with other processing while waiting for the I/O operation to complete. *Event objects* can be used to determine when operations conclude even if the application does not have a graphical window.

- *Quality of service.* To support emerging network technologies such as real-time multimedia communications, WinSock 2 establishes conventions for applications to negotiate required service levels of communication service for parameters such as bandwidth and latency.

WinSock 2 uses the design proposed by the Windows Open Services Architecture (WOSA) guidelines. WOSA defines a common set of interfaces for connecting front-end applications with back-end services. This format provides both an Application Program Interface (API) and a Service Provider Interface (SPI). The *API* defines the functions and data structures that give applications programmers access to services. The *SPI* defines the hooks that allow protocol stack vendors to make their network services available.

Part 1: Introduction to Sockets

The WinSock 2 DLL (WS2_32.DLL) is not supplied by each protocol stack vendor, as WINSOCK.DLL and WSOCK32.DLL were. Instead, each stack vendor supplies a *service provider library* that can be hooked into the WinSock 2 DLL. Any number of service provider libraries can be dynamically linked to WinSock at run-time, allowing a WinSock 2 application to access services from one or more transport protocols *simultaneously*. This is an improvement over the WinSock 1.1 design, which is implemented as a single DLL provided by a specific protocol stack vendor and thus prohibits simultaneous use of multiple protocol stacks.

Figure 3-1 illustrates the difference in design of WinSock Versions 1.1 and 2.

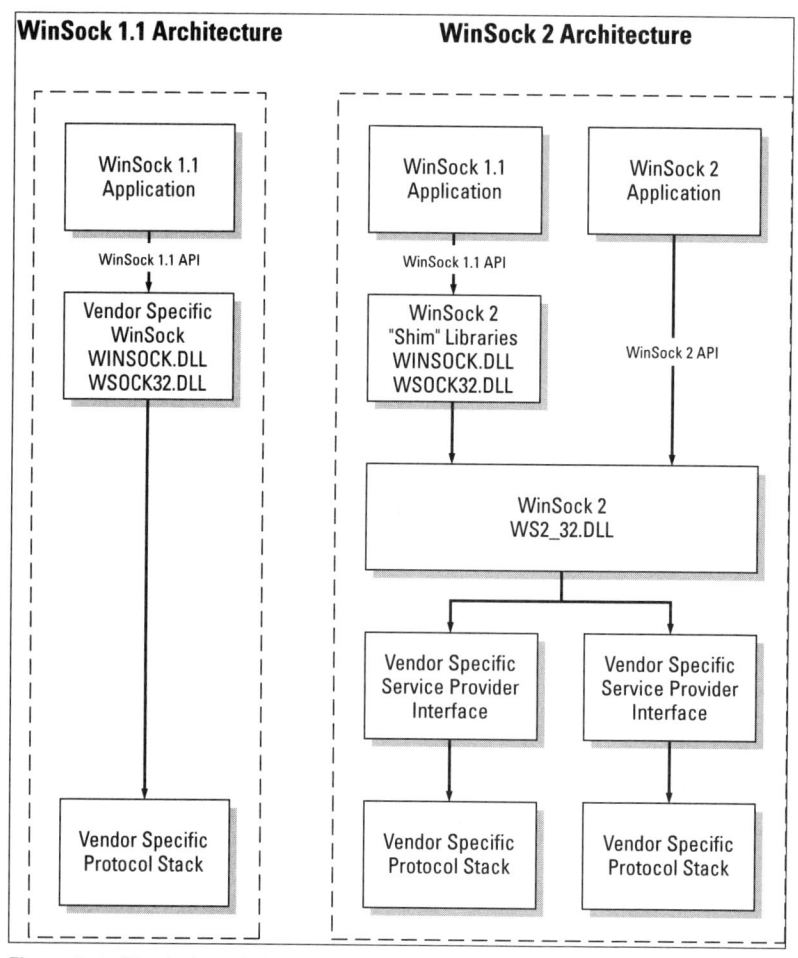

Figure 3-1: The design of the WinSock 2 architecture allows simultaneous access to one or more service providers.

WinSock 2 is only available in 32-bit Windows platforms (Windows 95 and Windows NT 4). NT 4 includes WinSock 2 as part of its normal distribution. WinSock 2 is not available for 16-bit Windows environments; no plans currently exist to develop Version 2 for any other platforms, including versions of NT prior to Version 4.

Remember, throughout the rest of this chapter, services available in WinSock 1.1 are also available in Version 2, except where noted in the text. All of the example programs developed for Version 1.1 in Chapter 4 will compile and run on WinSock 2 as well.

Blocking and Event-Driven Applications

The programs you studied in Chapter 2 work fine, but they all use *blocking* socket routines. Blocking means that when a function is called, it stops all other processing in the application and does not return until it has completed. This is all right for Win32 console applications like the ones in Chapter 2, but it can be a problem in the Windows GUI environment. Applications that use the Windows GUI are *event driven*. They receive and must quickly respond to messages from Windows each time a keystroke, mouse movement, or other event occurs.

Even in the GUI world, blocking isn't an issue for functions that complete quickly, such as socket() and bind(). It can be a *big* problem, however, on operations such as connect() and recv(), which may take a long time to finish their work. In fact, under 16-bit Windows, the use of blocking routines can completely stop the entire application from responding at all to user input. Although blocking routines in 32-bit Windows won't stop other applications from responding, the applications may seem unresponsive when blocking routines are used. The user won't be able to select menu options (or perhaps a Cancel button), and the window may not repaint for long periods of time.

In general, WinSock programs that are designed to run on 16-bit Windows should avoid blocking altogether. In 32-bit Windows programs that use the GUI, blocking in the user interface thread (the thread that contains the message pump) should be avoided. Each WinSock specification provides functions and data structures that can be used to defeat the negative effects of blocking.

The Windows Message-Driven Architecture

Traditional procedural programs execute from top to bottom, performing operations in a predetermined sequence. The program, not the operating system, decides what gets called and when. Windows programs aren't structured that way. They are event driven; they must respond to event messages sent by the operating system and must carry out the appropriate actions in a timely manner.

Under 16-bit Windows, applications cooperate by frequently yielding control of the CPU to other programs. This kind of *cooperative multitasking* means that an application has control of the CPU until it relinquishes it. Each time a 16-bit Windows program checks for incoming messages, it implicitly yields processing time to other applications. Because of this dependency on cooperation, if a 16-bit application stops checking for messages, the whole system is adversely affected.

Windows 95 and Windows NT, on the other hand, use *preemptive multitasking*. In these environments, it isn't absolutely necessary to check frequently for Windows messages. Nevertheless, even 32-bit Windows applications must respond to incoming messages quickly so the application remains responsive to the user. Because Windows applications must regularly call GetMessage() or PeekMessage(), they shouldn't block for an arbitrarily long period of time waiting for a network operation to complete. So, to support applications that fit better within this Windows programming model, WinSock provides several methods to use sockets without blocking.

The WinSock Extensions

As mentioned earlier, the WinSock specification adds many extensions to the original Berkeley API. These extension functions, provided to enable developers to create software that conforms to the Windows programming model, all begin with the letters *WSA*. The use of these extension functions in your Windows programs isn't mandatory, but it is strongly recommended. (The exceptions to this guideline are WSAStartup() and WSACleanup(), which are required.)

Table 3-1 lists all of the extension functions added in WinSock 1.1.

TABLE 3-1 WINDOWS-SPECIFIC EXTENSION FUNCTIONS ADDED IN WINSOCK 1.1

Function Name	Description
WSAStartup()	Requests use of the Windows Sockets DLL
WSACleanup()	Releases the Windows Sockets DLL
WSAAsyncGetHostByAddr()	Asynchronous version of gethostbyaddr()
WSAAsyncGetHostByName()	Asynchronous version of gethostbyname()
WSAAsyncGetProtoByName()	Asynchronous version of getprotobyname()
WSAAsyncGetProtoByNumber()	Asynchronous version of getprotobynumber()

WSAAsyncGetServByName()	Asynchronous version of getservbyname()
WSAAsyncGetServByPort()	Asynchronous version of getservbyport()
WSACancelAsyncRequest()	Cancels an outstanding call to one of the asynchronous database functions

Function Name	Description
WSAAsyncSelect()	Asynchronous version of select()
WSAIsBlocking()	Determines if WinSock is waiting for a blocking call to complete
WSACancelBlockingCall()	Cancels an outstanding blocking function call
WSASetBlockingHook()	Replaces the standard blocking hook function with an application defined routine
WSAUnhookBlockingHook()	Restores the standard blocking function
WSAGetLastError()	Obtains details of the last WinSock error
WSASetLastError()	Sets the error to be returned by subsequent calls to WSAGetLastError()

The role of some of these functions may not make sense at this point. Don't worry about that; we're going to discuss them further in this chapter. The important thing to remember is almost all of the extensions added to Version 1.1 of WinSock were necessary to deal with the issue of blocking. Before we discuss ways to avoid blocking, let's look at what functions cause WinSock to block and what happens when you use them.

Blocking Mode

Some WinSock functions never block — they always complete immediately. For functions such as socket() and bind(), no difference exists between blocking and nonblocking mode because they always complete immediately. Some WinSock functions always block; others only block when used on a blocking socket.

Blocking Sockets

Sockets used with WinSock can be placed into one of two modes: blocking or nonblocking. This mode affects the way some WinSock operations are carried out when the socket descriptor is used as a parameter. By default, a newly created socket returned

64   Part 1: Introduction to Sockets

from the socket() function is a *blocking socket*. When a blocking socket descriptor is used, WinSock functions will not return until the operation has completed.

When a nonblocking socket descriptor is used, all WinSock functions will return immediately, and some will post the WSAEWOULDBLOCK error condition. This isn't really an error in the general sense, because the function may complete successfully. By returning WSAEWOULDBLOCK, the WinSock DLL is telling the application that it has returned immediately because the function *would have* blocked. The function returned, but the operation is not yet complete. WinSock will still carry out the operation, but the application must be designed to know when the operation has actually finished the requested task. Later in the chapter, we'll discuss several methods used by applications to recognize completion of a task.

The following WinSock functions block when used with a blocking socket:

- **accept()**. The accept() function is by nature a blocking function – it is designed to wait for a connection.

- **closesocket()**. Datagram sockets don't block when calling closesocket(), but stream sockets do if a nonzero *timeout* value has been specified with setsockopt() and the SO_LINGER option. Chapter 5 covers the setsockopt() function; it is also defined in the Quick Reference.

- **connect()**. The amount of time it takes to complete the connect() function depends on network performance and whether the connection attempt succeeds.

- **recv() and recvfrom()**. The recv() and recvfrom() functions won't complete until the peer has sent something for the application to receive.

- **send() and sendto()**. The amount of time it takes for the send() and sendto() functions to complete depends on the current state of WinSock's internal buffers and network performance.

Blocking Functions

Some WinSock functions always block no matter what type of socket is used with them. In fact, almost all of the standard database functions block, and none of them requires a socket as a parameter. (The only exception is gethostname(), which is used to retrieve the name of the local machine.) The following functions always block:

- gethostbyaddr()
- gethostbyname()
- getprotobyname()
- getprotobynumber()

- getservbyname()
- getservbyport()
- select()

The first set of functions in this list (the "getXbyY" functions, as they are known) may take a long time to complete, or they may finish quickly. If one of these functions is retrieving information from tables stored on the local machine, it will likely be done quickly. On the other hand, if the function is using a network service (such as DNS), it may require some time to finish.

The select() function is used to detect the state of nonblocking sockets and is discussed later in the section "Nonblocking Mode."

Note: WinSock allows only one active blocking operation *per task or thread*. Note, this is not *per socket*. Only one blocking operation is allowed per thread, even on different sockets. This can be a significant limitation, especially for connection-oriented servers that have many sockets.

In blocking mode, whether a function succeeds or fails, you know that the action has completed when the function returns. At first look, using blocking code seems to be easy because network events take place sequentially. Under 16-bit Windows however, this apparent simplicity is deceptive. Let's see why this is so.

Handling Reentrant Messages

In an attempt to keep Windows responsive while waiting for network events, the WinSock DLL enters a PeekMessage() loop when an application makes a blocking call. The DLL starts the operation and then periodically checks for completion in this loop. While the DLL waits for the operation to complete, this PeekMessage() loop dispatches Windows messages. This yields the CPU to other processes if necessary and keeps Windows and other applications active. When the operation has completed, the DLL returns control to the calling application.

The drawback in this procedure is that the application making the blocking call may receive new messages from Windows while waiting for the blocking call to complete. The application may then attempt to make another call to a WinSock function. If it does, the called function will always fail — because WinSock only allows one blocking call per thread. Figure 3-2 illustrates one way this might happen.

Part I: Introduction to Sockets

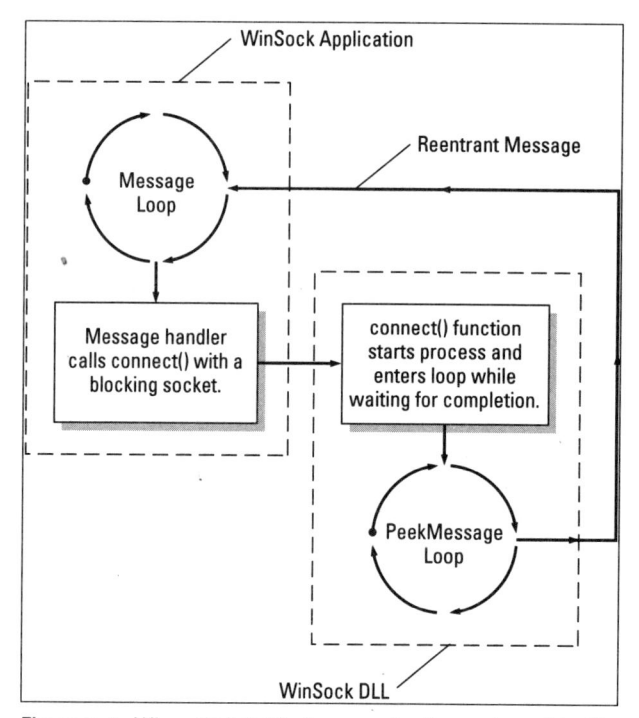

Figure 3-2: When 16-bit Windows applications rely on blocking calls, they may receive reentrant messages.

Under 16-bit Windows, a blocking call isn't really blocking the whole system. Because the DLL is executing a PeekMessage() loop, Windows messages are still being dispatched. One or more of these messages could be destined for the application that made the blocking call. The requisite handling of this reentrancy problem is just one of the reasons WinSock applications shouldn't use blocking routines.

Because 32-bit WinSock (WSOCK32.DLL) doesn't perform the PeekMessage() loop, 32-bit applications don't have to deal with this reentrancy problem. The preemptive multitasking built into Windows 95 and Windows NT ensures that other processes receive their messages. Blocking functions can be used in 32-bit Windows programs, but shouldn't be used in the user interface thread. The thread won't receive messages from Windows during the blocking call, and the application will seem unresponsive to the user.

The WinSock 1.1 API provides two functions that help when using blocking operations: WSAIsBlocking() and WSACancelBlockingCall().

Let's examine WSAIsBlocking() first:

```
BOOL PASCAL FAR WSAIsBlocking(void);
```

WSAIsBlocking() returns True if a blocking WinSock call is in progress, or False if not. Note that WSAIsBlocking() doesn't take a socket as a parameter. This is because only one blocking call is allowed per process or thread. To manage the reentrancy problem, 16-bit Windows applications can check WSAIsBlocking() before making any WinSock calls.

If WSAIsBlocking() returns True, the only WinSock function that can be legally called is WSACancelBlockingCall():

```
int PASCAL FAR WSACancelBlockingCall(void);
```

As the name suggests, WSACancelBlockingCall() will cancel any blocking operation that is currently in progress. You can't make any other WinSock function calls while a blocking function is still processing. Any WinSock function call other than WSACancelBlockingCall() made while a blocking operation is in progress will fail with a WSAEINPROGRESS error code.

The WSACancelBlockingCall() function always returns immediately. It does not wait until the blocking operation has stopped. The function call that started the blocking operation will eventually fail, returning the WSAEINTR error; however, because of this delay, it is possible for the operation to complete before it is canceled. This introduces another problem when using blocking routines: You need to code for the situation where a function is canceled, but then completes successfully.

Blocking Hook Functions

During processing of the PeekMessage() loop, the WinSock DLL checks for completion, checks for a cancel request, and also calls a *blocking hook* function. This loop may be implemented in various ways by vendors but, in general, the WinSock PeekMessage() loop looks something like this:

```
while(1)
{
    if (PeekMessage(lpMsg, hWnd, wFilterMin, wFilterMax, PM_REMOVE))
    {
        TranslateMessage(lpMsg);
        DispatchMessage(lpMsg);
    }
    // Check to see if operation is complete
    if(OperationIsComplete()) // Return operations normal error code
        break;
    // Check for WSACancelBlockingCall()
    if (BlockingWasCancelled())
    {
        nErrorCode = WSAEINTR; // "Interrupted function call"
        break;
    }
    // Call blocking hook function
    BlockingHook();
}
```

WinSock enables you to replace this blocking hook function with a function of your own; you do this with WSASetBlockingHook(). The original function can be put back into place with a call to WSAUnhookBlockingHook().

Caution: Some attempts have been made to use this replaceable blocking hook feature to solve the message reentrancy problem, by selectively dispatching Windows messages. This may work on one vendor's WinSock, but not on others. Schemes like this are *not* recommended.

It is generally accepted that sophisticated Windows applications should not use blocking sockets or blocking functions. In fact, the functions WSACancelBlockingCall(), WSAIsBlocking(), WSASetBlockingHook(), and WSAUnhookBlockingHook() have all been removed in WinSock 2. Applications using these functions that were compiled and linked with a WinSock 1.1 library will still run under Version 2, but they are no longer supported at the source code level.

Nonblocking Mode

WinSock supports the concept of *nonblocking* sockets. If an application sets a socket to nonblocking mode, then any operation that would block for an extended period of time will "fail" with the error code WSAEWOULDBLOCK. This error indicates to the application that the system started the process but was unable to complete the requested operation immediately. The operation will eventually complete.

Two ways exist to make a socket nonblocking: by calling either WSAAsyncSelect() or ioctlsocket(). We'll save WSAAsyncSelect() for the upcoming section on asynchronous mode. In this section we'll discuss the traditional use of nonblocking sockets as done on UNIX, where nonblocking sockets are used without WinSock's asynchronous extensions. If you are porting code from Berkeley sockets, you may see code similar to this.

ioctlsocket()

To make a socket nonblocking without using the WinSock asynchronous extensions, you call the ioctlsocket()function:

```
int ioctlsocket(
            SOCKET s,
            long cmd,
            u_long FAR* argp
            );
```

The first parameter, *s*, is a socket descriptor. The second, *cmd,* is one of several predefined commands. And the third, *argp,* is a pointer to an argument for the command. In some cases, the unsigned long value pointed to by *argp* is also used to return information.

Passing the predefined command FIONBIO along with any nonzero argument will make a socket nonblocking, as shown here:

```
// Create a socket and make it nonblocking
SOCKET MySocket;
u_long arg;

// Create a socket (Blocking by default)
MySocket = socket(af, type, protocol);
if (MySocket == INVALID_SOCKET)
{
    // Display error
    return;
}
// Make the socket nonblocking
arg = 1L;
nReturnCode = ioctlsocket(MySocket, FIONBIO, &arg);
```

On some WinSock implementations, the ioctlsocket() function can be used with FIONBIO and a zero argument to set a socket back to blocking mode, but this is not recommended. Once a socket is set to nonblocking mode, it should never be set back to blocking mode.

As stated earlier, once a socket is in nonblocking mode, all WinSock functions return immediately. Functions that may succeed, but that can't be completed immediately will return SOCKET_ERROR, with WSAGetLastError() equal to WSAE-WOULDBLOCK. To continue with the previous code example, here's how you would check for errors when attempting to connect a nonblocking socket:

```
// Connect a nonblocking socket
nReturnCode = connect(MySocket, lpName, NameLen);
if (nReturnCode == SOCKET_ERROR)
{
    nReason = WSAGetLastError();
    if (nReason != WSAEWOULDBLOCK)
        // We have a "real" error
    else
        // connect operation started OK
}
```

After receiving the WSAEWOULDBLOCK error on a nonblocking socket, the application must then determine when the operation is complete.

Methods to Avoid: polling and select()

One method of determining when a nonblocking operation is complete is by polling. This is *not* recommended. The following code is presented here only as background material.

```
// This is NOT recommended
// Polling on nonblocking recv()
while(1)
{
```

```
        nReturnCode = recv(NonBlockSocket, lpBuffer, BufferLen, 0);
        if (nReturnCode == 0)
        {
            // Connection was closed by peer
            // No data will ever be received
            break;
        }
        if (nReturnCode == SOCKET_ERROR)
        {
            nReason = WSAGetLastError();
            if (nReason != WSAEWOULDBLOCK)
            {
                // Handle "real" error
                break;
            }
            else
            {
                // We're still waiting
                // for the operation to complete
                continue;
            }
        }
        // recv() completed
        nBytesReceived = nReturnCode;
        break;
    }
```

In this example, the recv() function is simply called continually until data is received, or an error occurs, or the connection is closed. Using nonblocking sockets in this way on 16-bit Windows systems is actually worse than using blocking sockets. With blocking sockets, the DLL will at least occasionally call PeekMessage(), allowing Windows to continue to pump messages. But if you use polling on a blocking recv() operation like this, Windows can't dispatch any messages to any program until recv() completes. Worse yet, if the WINSOCK.DLL uses Windows messages internally, the recv() operation will *never* complete. Using this method in the GUI thread of a 32-bit application is almost as bad; unfortunately, you don't have to look hard to find examples of programs that do this.

Select()

For determining when an operation is complete, an alternative to polling that is commonly used in Berkeley sockets applications is the select() function.

Caution: This isn't recommended on WinSock either — there are better ways as we'll see later in this chapter. We mention it here only to familiarize you with the concept. Knowledge of this technique does come in handy if you are porting applications from Berkeley sockets.

The select() function can be used to check the status of any number of sockets with one function call. For each socket, you can request read, write or error status.

```
int select(
```

```
int nfds,
fd_set FAR * readfds,
fd_set FAR * writefds,
fd_set FAR * exceptfds,
const struct timeval FAR * timeout
);
```

The select() function accepts three sets (*fd_set*) of socket arrays and a *timeout* value. The *nfds* parameter (number of *fd_set*) is ignored in WinSock and only included for compatibility with Berkeley sockets.

The sockets contained in the *readfds* array are checked for readability. This means queued data is waiting to be received and, therefore, a call to recv() or recvfrom() is guaranteed not to block. In the case of a connection-oriented server, this can also mean the socket is waiting for accept() to be called.

The *writefds* array of sockets are checked for writeability. This can mean a socket waiting for a connect() to complete is ready, or it can mean that the protocol stack buffers are ready for a call to send() or sendto(). Calls to send() or sendto() can't be guaranteed not to block, because the application may try to send more data than the protocol stack can buffer.

The sockets contained in the *exceptfds* array are checked for errors and urgent data messages (out-of-band data).

Any two of the *fd_set* parameters can be NULL, if you don't want to check any sockets for that particular condition. At least one *fd_set* parameter must be non-NULL, and any non-NULL set must contain at least one socket.

The optional *timeout* parameter specifies how long the select() function will wait to complete. If *timeout* is NULL, then select() will block until at least one socket meets the specified criteria. If *timeout* isn't NULL it must point to a valid TIMEVAL structure that contains two long integers: one for the number of seconds to wait and the other for the number of microseconds to wait. If both of these values in *timeout* are set to 0, select() will return immediately. This is sometimes done to poll with select(). The same rules apply for polling with select() as applies for polling on other WinSock functions – the PeekMessage() loop will not be called and WinSock will not yield.

The Preferred Method: Asynchronous Mode

As emphasized in the foregoing sections, blocking mode and traditional nonblocking methods are unacceptable for professional Windows applications. *Asynchronous notification* is *the* preferred method for avoiding blocking in WinSock 1.1 applications.

As with traditional nonblocking operations, asynchronous operations return immediately – they do not block. Unlike traditional nonblocking, however, you don't have to resort to polling or another less-than-perfect alternative. In asynchronous mode, the WinSock DLL sends the application a message indicating an operation has completed.

Asynchronous mode is portable among Windows platforms. It is available on 16- and 32-bit Windows in both WinSock Versions 1.1 and 2. Asynchronous mode takes advantage of the Windows architecture rather than trying to work around it. As with traditional nonblocking, functions that would block are set to begin the operation and then immediately return the WSAEWOULDBLOCK error. When the processing is complete, the WINSOCK.DLL will post a message to the calling application's window indicating success or failure.

Much of Chapter 4 is devoted to the details of using the asynchronous extensions. For now, let's look at a brief synopsis of how the asynchronous mechanisms work.

WSAAsyncSelect()

To use asynchronous mode, an application should call WSAAsyncSelect() immediately after calling socket(). WSAAsyncSelect() automatically sets a socket to nonblocking mode. It also allows the application to notify WinSock that it is interested in receiving messages for certain events. For example, an application may indicate interest in the FD_READ event, so that when data arrives on a socket, WinSock will post a notification to the application's window indicating that data is waiting to be read.

The following code creates a socket, sets it to nonblocking mode, and requests notification for these events:

- When a connection has been established
- When data is ready to be read on the socket without blocking
- When data can be sent on the socket
- When the peer system has closed the socket

```
// Define the message we want WinSock to send with notifications
#define SM_EVENT WM_USER+1      // Event Socket Message

// Create a socket
MySocket = socket(af, type, protocol);
// Check MySocket for errors here!

// Make socket nonblocking and request asynchronous notifications
nRet = WSAAsyncSelect(MySocket, hWnd, SM_EVENT,
                      FD_CONNECT|FD_CLOSE|FD_READ|FD_WRITE
                      );
```

In the previous example, the window attached to *hWnd* will receive the user-defined SM_EVENT message whenever one of the specified events occurs. When an event message is received, the *wParam* parameter contains the socket descriptor on which the event took place. The *lParam* passed along with the message will contain one of the event codes signifying the specific event that occurred and the error code.

WinSock provides two macros (WSAGETSELECTEVENT and WSAGETSE-LECTERROR) for extracting these codes from the *lParam*. Listing 3-1 shows the part of an application's main window procedure that handles asynchronous messages from WinSock.

Listing 3-1 Handling asynchronous messages

```
// WndProc with socket message handlers
long WINAPI WndProc(HWND hWnd, UINT msg, UINT wParam, LONG lParam)
{
    int nEventCode;
    int nErrorCode;
    switch(msg)
    {
        case WM_. . .
            // Handle Windows messages here
            break;
        case SM_EVENT:
        {
            // Extract event and error codes from lParam
            nEventCode = WSAGETSELECTEVENT(lParam);
            nErrorCode = WSAGETSELECTERROR(lParam);
            switch(nEventCode)
            {
                case FD_CONNECT:
                    // connect() function has completed
                    // nErrorCode contains return value
                    break;
                case FD_CLOSE:
                    // Connection has been closed
                    // nErrorCode contains return value
                    break;
                case FD_READ:
                    // Data is waiting to be read
                    nRet = recv(MySocket, lpBuf, nBufLen, 0);
                    if (nRet == SOCKET_ERROR)
                    {
                        if (WSAGetLastError() != WSAEWOULDBLOCK)
                            // Handle "real" error
                    }
                    else
                        nBytesReceived += nRet;
                    break;
                case FD_WRITE:
                    // If we have data to send, we can send it now
```

```
                        nRet = send(MySocket, lpBuf, nBufLen, 0);
                        // Check for errors here!
                        break;
                    }
                }
            }
        }
```

The use of asynchronous mode can greatly improve and simplify the organization of a WinSock application. Indeed, it is the best answer for all WinSock applications that use the Windows GUI. The Windows event-driven model is consistently deployed so that the application responds to network events in the same way it handles user and system events. By frequently receiving and dispatching Windows messages, asynchronous mode WinSock applications coexist well in all Windows environments. They are highly portable across all of the Windows platforms and WinSock versions. Asynchronous mode works exactly the same way on 16-bit and 32-bit Windows, using WinSock 1.1 or 2.

Asynchronous Database Functions

With one exception, all of the database functions *always* block. The type of socket in use has no effect on this behavior. Even if you are using asynchronous mode for socket operations, functions such as gethostbyname() will still block. If these functions are configured to use DNS or some other network name-resolution service (as they usually are), they can block for quite some time.

Again, Windows-specific asynchronous functions were added to the Berkeley API to alleviate this situation:

- WSAAsyncGetHostByAddr()
- WSAAsyncGetHostByName()
- WSAAsyncGetProtoByName()
- WSAAsyncGetProtoByNumber()
- WSAAsyncGetServByName()
- WSAAsyncGetServByPort()
- WSACancelAsyncRequest()

These functions behave much like the standard synchronous versions, but they do not block. As with WSAAsyncSelect(), completion is signaled when the WINSOCK.DLL posts a message back to the calling application's window. Unlike WSAAsyncSelect(), though, the list of asynchronous database functions includes the WSACancelAsyncRequest() function. As its name suggests, this function can be used to cancel a WSAGetXbyY() function that is still pending.

NT Services

Windows NT supports an application type known as a service. A *service* is a Win32-based application that conforms to the interface rules of the Service Control Manager (SCM). Services can be started automatically at system boot, or when a connection request is made. They can be started manually by a user through the Services control panel, or by a Win32-based application that uses the service control manager functions. Services can execute even when no user is logged on to the system.

WinSock server applications designed to run exclusively on Windows NT are ideal candidates to be written as NT services.

Win32 Event Objects

Concurrently running threads often need to communicate with one another. If thread A starts thread B to perform some operation, then thread B must have a way to signal back to thread A that the operation is complete. Another example of "talking threads" is when they need to share a common resource. For example, if two threads both need to read and write from a buffer in memory, there must be some mechanism by which the threads know when it is safe to use the buffer. Otherwise, they might both try to use the buffer at the same time.

The Win32 API supports several methods for synchronizing multiple threads. One method involves the use of synchronization objects and wait functions. WinSock 2 uses a type of synchronization object known as an event object. Basically, an *event object* is a variable in memory that can be signaled (set) or nonsignaled (reset). Other types of Win32 synchronization objects include mutexes, semaphores, and timers.

An event object's state can be explicitly set to signaled by the SetEvent() or PulseEvent() functions. It can be placed into a nonsignaled state by the ResetEvent() function. Wait functions, such as WaitForSingleObject() and WaitForMultipleObjects(), can be used by a thread to block its own execution until one or more event objects are signaled.

WinSock 2 can use both event objects and wait functions to signal network events and completion of overlapped I/O. See Chapter 9 for details.

WSAEventSelect()

As you observed in Chapter 2, writing Win32 console applications is much simpler than writing programs that use the Windows GUI. Some sockets applications, including server applications and NT services, run for long periods of time unattended. They have no need for a sophisticated interface; essentially you start them up and let them run. WinSock 2 provides mechanisms that allow such applications, which have no Window handle, to use asynchronous mode.

The WSAEventSelect() function works almost exactly like WSAAsyncSelect(). The only major difference is that, rather than posting a message to a Window handle when a network event occurs, WSAEventSelect() sets an event object. Here is the WSAEventSelect() function:

```
nRet = WSAEventSelect(mySocket, hEventObject, FD_READ|FD_WRITE);
```

It accepts a socket, a handle to an event object, and an event bitmask as parameters. The event bitmask parameter uses the same event codes as WSAAsyncSelect(). WSAEventSelect() automatically sets the socket to nonblocking mode, which is also like WSAAsyncSelect().

When one of the specified events occurs, WinSock sets the event object. WinSock 2's event objects are Win32 event objects. Even though WinSock 2 provides functions like WSAWaitForMultipleEvents(), you can still use the native Win32 event object functions. This is especially useful if you want to use Win32 WaitForMultipleObjects() function to wait for both socket and nonsocket events to occur.

Once an event has been signaled, you then use WSAEnumNetworkEvents() to determine exactly which event occurred. WinSock keeps a list of all events that occur between successive calls to WSAEnumNetworkEvents() and one call to WSAEnumNetworkEvents() may indicate that more than one event has occurred since the last call.

Use of WSAEventSelect() gives console applications and NT services the advantages of asynchronous notification without the need for a graphical Window handle. Note, this is only available on 32-bit platforms and only in WinSock 2. Event notification is discussed in detail in Chapter 9.

Using Overlapped I/O

In addition to all the asynchronous functions described, WinSock 2 offers another means of performing input and output asynchronously: *overlapped I/O*. Asynchronous input and output (overlapped I/O) functions return immediately, even when an I/O request is still pending. They don't block. Through the use of overlapped I/O, an application can continue with other processing while waiting for a send or receive operation to complete.

Like the overlapped file I/O operations introduced in Win32, WinSock 2 includes functions that allow I/O requests to return immediately and then signal the application that they've concluded. These functions use the same OVERLAPPED structure for asynchronous socket I/O that Win32 uses for asynchronous file input and output.

Overlapped I/O Functions

The WinSock 2 specification includes the following functions that can perform overlapped I/O:

- WSASend()

- WSASendTo()

- WSARecv()

- WSARecvFrom()

All of these functions can indicate completion by signaling an event object or by calling an application-designated completion function.

The WinSock overlapped I/O functions accept optional parameters for either an OVERLAPPED structure (*lpOverlapped*) or a pointer to an exported CALLBACK function (*lpCompletionRoutine*). The OVERLAPPED structure contains a handle to an event object. If the *lpOverlapped* parameter isn't NULL, WinSock signals completion by setting the event object referenced in the OVERLAPPED structure. The *lpCompletionRoutine* parameter can be used to point to an exported CALLBACK function. If *lpCompletionRoutine* isn't NULL, the function pointed to is called when I/O is complete.

Overlapped send and receive calls always return immediately. A return value of zero indicates that the I/O operation completed immediately, during the function call. A return value of SOCKET_ERROR with an error code of WSA_IO_PENDING indicates the overlapped operation has begun and completion of the operation will be signaled by the chosen means (event signaling or completion routine).

One significant advantage to using overlapped I/O is increased throughput. When using overlapped I/O, send and receive buffers need not be copied multiple times. Receive buffers are posted to WinSock before any data arrives, so the WINSOCK.DLL can copy incoming data directly into the application's buffers. No need exists to queue incoming data in the protocol stack and then copy it to the application during a call to recv(). In the same way, multiple send buffers can be used to allow WinSock to transmit data directly from buffers owned by the application.

Overlapped I/O is discussed in detail in Chapter 9.

Scatter and Gather

WinSock 2 extends its OVERLAPPED I/O functionality with the concept of *scatter and gather.* Scattered/gathered I/O is much like vectored I/O that is available in UNIX.

The WSASend(), WSASendTo(), WSARecv(), and WSARecvFrom() functions all take an array of buffers as input parameters and can be used for scatter/gather I/O.

This technique can be useful when the data being transmitted is structured into two or more logical pieces. For example, if each data transmission contains a fixed header portion followed by data that changes in each transmission, the static header portion can be kept in one buffer and the data in another. Both of the buffers can then be *gathered* and transmitted in the appropriate order with one function call. When receiving data like this, the two buffers and their sizes can be specified so incoming data is *scattered* into the appropriate place. This automatically parses the data.

General Guidelines for Your Application Strategy

You've had a chance now to see several valid options in the design of a WinSock application. Choosing the right WinSock functionality when designing an application is extremely important. The strategy you select and the basic architecture used to develop it will have profound effects on an application's efficiency and user appeal. Several choices influence design. Questions and answers to help you determine which of the various strategies to use follow.

These design choices are all interrelated — there is no one best answer for all applications. Optimum choices for a server that will run only on Windows NT aren't appropriate at all for a client that must run on 16-bit Windows, for example. Strategies that make an application extremely portable may lack crucial features that would be provided by a more specialized version. Hopefully, the following considerations will point you in the right direction.

Which Windows Platform?

Will the application need to run on 16-bit Windows or can the program rely on features only available on Windows 95 or Windows NT? If the program must run on 16-bit Windows, only one choice exists. Programs designed for 16-bit Windows can only use WinSock 1.1 and should always use the asynchronous notification provided by WSAAsyncSelect().

You have more options if your application will run only on 32-bit Windows. Most notably, you then have a choice between Version 1.1 or 2 of WinSock. Also, blocking is not as much of an issue. The preemptive multitasking available in 32-bit Windows enables you to use simpler blocking socket operations without adversely affecting other processes. Multiple threads can be used to keep blocking operations outside of the user-interface thread. Multithreading can simplify connection-oriented server design by allocating threads for each socket or each operation.

Which WinSock Version?

Will WinSock 2 be available or should the application be restricted to the functionality available in WinSock 1.1? WinSock 2 ships with Windows NT 4, but it is not yet widely available. No plans exist to make it available on 16-bit Windows, not even through Win32s. You can make an application extremely portable by using only the nonoptional parts of the 1.1 API, but WinSock 2 provides many additional valuable services.

Which Data Transport Protocol?

Will the application use TCP/IP or some other protocol? WinSock 2 officially supports transports other than TCP/IP and UDP/IP, but WinSock 1.1 does not. Microsoft and other vendors make implementations of Version 1.1 that can be used with other protocols, but the application is then restricted to one vendor's implementation only. The application almost assuredly will not work on another vendor's WinSock.

What Type of Application?

Will the application be a client, server, or both? Will the application communicate connectionless or will it be connection-oriented? Connection-oriented servers should be able to handle many sockets simultaneously. Multithreading and other services available in the Win32 environment simplify the challenge of writing robust server applications. Most client applications can operate with only one socket and are reasonably easy to implement without these extended services.

How Much Data?

Will the application intermittently transmit small amounts of data or will it transfer large bulk amounts of data? If data transfer rates are paramount, then perhaps the faster overlapped I/O available in WinSock 2 should be used.

What Kind of User Interface?

Is the application interactive? Does it require a sophisticated user interface or is it started and left to run? WinSock programs designed for 16-bit Windows must use the Windows GUI, but 32-bit programs can use the Win32 console or NT service interface. This can greatly simplify program design.

Which Source Code Base?

Are you writing the application from scratch or porting it from Berkeley sockets? Porting any UNIX application to 16-bit Windows can be a daunting task. The

Win32 environment (especially with the console interface) makes moving Berkeley sockets applications to Windows much easier.

Summary

Writing WinSock programs that fit well into the graphical Windows environment requires the use of techniques that were not part of the original Berkeley API. Windows specific extension functions were added to the specification to allow WinSock programs to be Windows friendly.

Blocking is the major issue when using sockets under Windows. So that they still send and receive messages frequently, 16-bit Windows applications should use the asynchronous notification functions. This keeps the 16-bit Windows event-driven, cooperative multitasking mechanism working smoothly.

WinSock 2 provides many new features — most notably protocol independence, overlapped input/output, and event objects.

Part II
The WinSock 1.1 API

Chapter 4: Using Asynchronous Mode

Chapter 5: Optional Features

Chapter 6: MFC Socket Classes

Chapter 4

Using Asynchronous Mode

IN THIS CHAPTER
We will now take a more in-depth look at programming with asynchronous mode. All of the methods and functions used in this chapter are available in Version 1.1 of WinSock as well as in Version 2. The core of the WinSock API was covered in Part I, so here we'll focus primarily on using asynchronous, nonblocking code. Topics in this chapter include

- Using the WSAAsyncSelect() function
- Understanding the three categories of asynchronous database functions
- CheckMail: a sample Windows-friendly WinSock application

IN CHAPTER 3 WE DISCUSSED VARIOUS METHODS used to avoid blocking and the reasons why asynchronous mode is the method of choice. The bulk of this chapter deals with asynchronous mode in detail. We'll look closely at the methods and options used to detect socket state and perform name resolution asynchronously. We'll also develop a sample application that operates completely in asynchronous mode.

By the end of this chapter, you will have been introduced to almost all of the functionality available in WinSock 1.1. In addition, you'll be familiar with the preferred mechanisms for performing network communications under the Windows GUI.

Asynchronous Mode

As explained in Chapter 3, blocking mode and traditional nonblocking methods are unacceptable for professional Windows applications that make use of the Windows GUI. Asynchronous notification is the preferred method for avoiding blocking anywhere in a 16-bit Windows application or in the user-interface thread of a 32-bit Windows program.

Asynchronous mode takes advantage of the Windows architecture rather than trying to work around it. In asynchronous mode, functions that would ordinarily block begin the process that has been requested and then immediately return the WSAEWOULDBLOCK error. When the operation is complete, WinSock posts a message to the calling application's window indicating success or failure.

The WSAAsyncSelect() Function

After creating a socket, an application that wishes to use asynchronous mode calls WSAAsyncSelect().

```
int WSAAsyncSelect(
                SOCKET s,
                HWND hWnd,
                unsigned int wMsg,
                long lEvent
                );
```

Parameter	Description
s	Socket descriptor.
hWnd	Handle to window that will receive asynchronous notifications.
wMsg	Application-defined message that will be received when a network event occurs.
lEvent	A bitmask specifying the combination of network events in which the application is interested.

The first parameter, *s*, is the socket you want to use in asynchronous mode. WSAAsyncSelect() automatically makes this socket nonblocking. In asynchronous mode, there is no need to call the ioctlsocket() function to make the socket non-blocking.

The second parameter, *hWnd*, is a handle to a window that will receive asynchronous notifications. This is usually the application's main window, but it can be any window for which the application can receive messages.

The *wMsg* parameter defines the message you want WinSock to use when it notifies the application of network events. This message is usually defined using the WM_USER manifest constant, like this:

```
#define SM_EVENT WM_USER+1     // SocketMessage - Event
```

REQUESTING ASYNCHRONOUS EVENTS

You use the *lEvent* parameter in the call to WSAAsyncSelect() to tell WinSock which events you're interested in receiving. Table 4.1 lists all of the valid event codes that can be used in *lEvent*. These values can be combined with the OR operator (|) to request notifications for more than one event.

Note: Additional event codes added with WinSock 2 are covered in Chapter 7.

Chapter 4: Using Asynchronous Mode 85

TABLE 4.1 OPTIONS FOR THE WSAAsyncSelect() EVENT PARAMETER

Event Code	Event That Generates Notification
FD_ACCEPT	A connection request is received. (Stream sockets only)
FD_CLOSE	A connection is closed. (Stream sockets only)
FD_CONNECT	A connection has been established.
FD_OOB	Out-of-band data has arrived. (Stream sockets only)
FD_READ	Data is available to be read.
FD_WRITE	It is safe to send data.

For example, the following code creates a socket, sets it to nonblocking mode, and requests notification for several events:

```
// Define the message we want WinSock to send with notifications
#define SM_EVENT WM_USER+1    // SocketMessage - Event

SOCKET MySocket;
int    nRet;

// Create a socket
MySocket = socket(af, type, protocol);
// Check MySocket for errors here!

// Make socket nonblocking and request asynchronous notifications
nRet = WSAAsyncSelect(MySocket, hWnd, SM_EVENT,
                      FD_CONNECT|FD_CLOSE|FD_READ|FD_WRITE
                      );
```

In the foregoing example, the window attached to *hWnd* will receive the SM_EVENT message whenever one of the specified events occurs. The application must provide a handler for this message, as explained next.

HANDLING EVENT MESSAGES

When an application receives an event message, *wParam* contains the socket descriptor on which the event took place. The *lParam* passed along with the message contains one of the event codes signifying the event that occurred *and* the error code. WinSock provides two macros for extracting these codes from *lParam*, as shown in Listing 4-1.

Part II: The WinSock 1.1 API

Listing 4-1 Handling Event Messages

```
// WndProc with socket message handlers
int nRet;
int nEventCode;
int nErrorCode;
SOCKET socket;

socket = (SOCKET)wParam;
switch(msg)
{
    case SM_EVENT:
    {
        // Use supplied macros to extract
        // event and error codes from lParam
        nEventCode = WSAGETSELECTEVENT(lParam);
        nErrorCode = WSAGETSELECTERROR(lParam);
        switch(nEventCode)
        {
            case FD_CONNECT:
                // connect() function has completed
                // nErrorCode contains return value
                break;
            case FD_CLOSE:
                // Connection has been closed
                // nErrorCode contains return value
                break;
            case FD_READ:
                // Data is waiting to be read
                nRet = recv(socket, lpBuf, nBufLen, 0);
                if (nRet == SOCKET_ERROR)
                {
                    if (WSAGetLastError() != WSAEWOULDBLOCK)
                        // A "real" error has occurred
                }
                else
                {
                    // No error, return code represents
                    // the number of bytes received
                    nBytesReceived += nRet;
                }
                break;
            case FD_WRITE:
                // If we have data to send, we can send it now
                // This also occurs when we connect
                nRet = send(socket, lpBuf, nBufLen, 0);
                // Check for errors here!
                break;
        }
    }
}
```

Only one message — the message specified in the call to WSAAsyncSelect() — is received for all network events. The window's message procedure must determine what event happened by extracting the value from *lParam*. The same event codes that tell WSAAsyncSelect() which events you're interested in, are also used by WinSock to tell you what event has been triggered.

Important: Always use the WSAGETSELECTERROR() macro on the message's *lParam,* as shown in Listing 4-1, to determine the error status when handling an asynchronous event. *Don't* call WSAGetLastError(). The WSAGetLastError() function uses a global error code variable, and it's possible for another WinSock operation to change that value after the event message is posted. The WSAGetLastError() may only be used immediately following a call to a WinSock function.

REENABLING FUNCTIONS

Once WinSock has sent notification of a particular event, it will not send notification of that same event again until one of the event's *reenabling functions* has been called. This design prevents WinSock from flooding the application with messages.

For example, once the FD_READ notification has been sent for a socket, it won't be sent again until either recv() or recvfrom() has been called — these are the reenabling functions for the FD_READ event. Even if WinSock receives data again after posting the FD_READ event, it won't post the notification again until the application has received data. If the reenabling call to recv() or recvfrom() does not read all the data WinSock has available, the FD_READ message will be immediately posted again. So, one call to recv() or recvfrom() (even with a small buffer) is sufficient for each FD_READ notification received. If still more data is to be read after the call, WinSock will post another event notification. Figure 4-1 illustrates the logic WinSock uses with the FD_READ event.

Part II: The WinSock 1.1 API

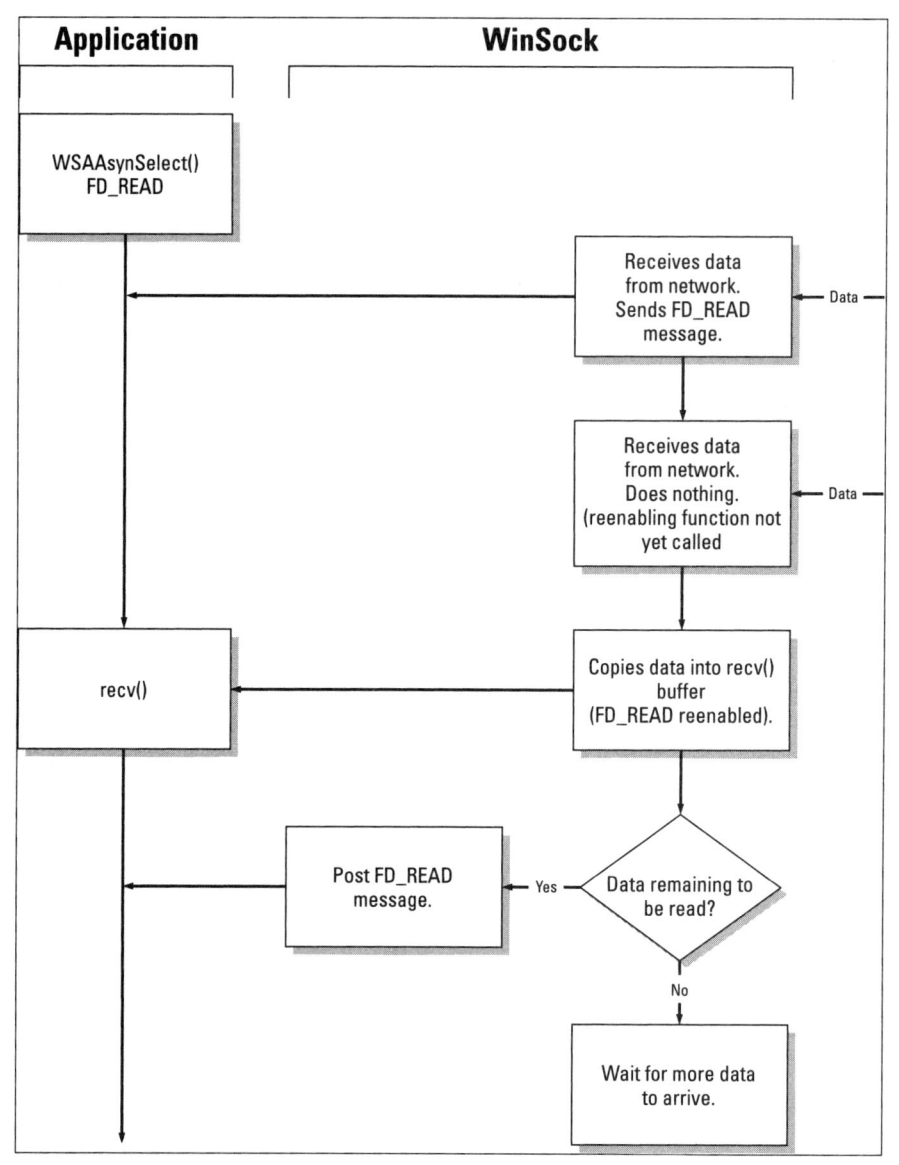

```
Application              WinSock

WSAAsynSelect()
FD_READ
                    ┌──────────────────┐
                    │ Receives data    │
                    │ from network.    │◄── Data
                    │ Sends FD_READ    │
                    │ message.         │
                    └──────────────────┘

                    ┌──────────────────┐
                    │ Receives data    │
                    │ from network.    │◄── Data
                    │ Does nothing.    │
                    │ (reenabling      │
                    │ function not     │
                    │ yet called       │
                    └──────────────────┘

                    ┌──────────────────┐
recv()   ◄───────── │ Copies data into │
                    │ recv() buffer    │
                    │ (FD_READ         │
                    │  reenabled).     │
                    └──────────────────┘

      ┌──────────┐         ◇
      │ Post     │   Yes   Data remaining
      │ FD_READ  │◄──────  to be read?
      │ message. │         
      └──────────┘         │ No
                           ▼
                    ┌──────────────────┐
                    │ Wait for more    │
                    │ data to arrive.  │
                    └──────────────────┘
```

Figure 4-1: WinSock uses reenabling functions to minimize the number of event notifications that are posted to an application.

The reenabling mechanism is used on a per-socket basis. If an application has more than one socket receiving asynchronous notifications (as would be the case with a connection-oriented server), one notification is sent for each socket. Table 4-2 lists the reenabling functions for each asynchronous event code.

TABLE 4-2 REENABLING FUNCTIONS FOR ASYNCHRONOUS EVENTS

Event	Reenabling Functions
FD_ACCEPT	accept()
FD_CLOSE	None
FD_CONNECT	None
FD_OOB	recv(), recvfrom()
FD_READ	recv(), recvfrom()
FD_WRITE	send(), sendto()

Note, FD_CLOSE and FD_CONNECT don't have reenabling functions. Because these two event codes signal completion, they don't require reenabling. They occur only once during the lifetime of a socket. Once a socket is closed, it should not be reused. Instead, a new socket descriptor should be obtained from socket().

NETWORK EVENT TRIGGERS

The FD_CLOSE and FD_CONNECT event codes signal completion. All of the other event codes indicate when it is safe to perform an operation with the reasonable assumption that it will not block. For example, FD_READ signals when data is waiting to be read. This means a call to one of the receive functions will not block. FD_WRITE signals that the protocol stack buffers are ready to accept data and it is, therefore, safe to use one of the send functions.

The following sections describe the network events that trigger each event code.

FD_ACCEPT The FD_ACCEPT event indicates a connection request has been made. It can only occur in connection-oriented servers and only on sockets in the listening state — that is, bind() and listen() have been called. When a client application calls connect(), specifying the address and service port to which a server is bound, the server receives an FD_ACCEPT message.

FD_ACCEPT will be sent in three situations:

- When a connection request arrives.
- After accept() is called, if another connection request is pending. This happens because the call to accept() reenables FD_ACCEPT messages.
- When WSAAsyncSelect() is called, if a connection request is already waiting.

When a server receives the FD_ACCEPT notification, it can reasonably assume that a call to accept() will succeed and return immediately. The socket descriptor returned from accept() will inherit all of the attributes of the listening socket. It will automatically be nonblocking, and event notifications will be received for all of the events specified for the listening socket.

FD_CLOSE   The FD_CLOSE event indicates a connection (virtual circuit) has been closed or is about to be closed. This event can only occur in connection-oriented clients and servers.

The error code sent along with the message designates whether the close was *graceful* (remote sent a close request) or *abortive* (remote reset the connection). If the error code is 0, then the close was graceful. If the error code is WSAECONNRESET, then the socket's virtual circuit was reset.

An application will also receive FD_CLOSE notification after initiating a close with shutdown() when the remote system acknowledges receipt of the close request.

WinSock posts the FD_CLOSE message in the following situations:

- The remote system initiated a graceful close.

- The local system initiated a graceful close with the shutdown() function, and the remote system acknowledged receipt of the request.

- The remote system aborted the connection.

- Immediately after a call to WSAAsyncSelect(), if the connection has already been closed.

Even though this message signals the connection has been terminated, data may still be available to read from the peer system. For this reason, you should always call recv() immediately after receiving the FD_CLOSE notification. You don't have to worry about recv() blocking in this situation. If data is available to read, recv() will return it immediately. If no data is available, recv() will immediately return 0 indicating the connection has been closed.

FD_CONNECT   The FD_CONNECT event indicates a connection request has completed. It only occurs in connection-oriented clients and denotes completion of a call to connect().

Once a connection has been established and the FD_CONNECT message has been received, an FD_WRITE message is also sent to indicate the socket is now writeable. (An explanation of FD_WRITE is coming up.) Applications that do not need to perform specific operations when initially connected may rely on the FD_WRITE message to signal connected status and not register for FD_CONNECT notification at all.

WinSock posts the FD_CONNECT message in the following situations:

- A call to connect() has completed.

- Immediately after a call to WSAAsyncSelect(), if a connection is already established.

FD_OOB   As the following explains, the implementation of OOB differs among TCP vendors and, if at all possible, you shouldn't use OOB in your applications at all.

Out-of-band data is information that a protocol marks as being special in some way. This data may consist of error messages, transmission control signals, or other information thought of as urgent and outside the normal sequence of data. For example, during a large data transfer, an application might choose to send a cancel request "out-of-band" to ask the sender to stop. You can set up your application to receive these special data blocks *out-of-band* (outside the normal sequence of data) or *in-band* (sent along in the normal data stream). By default, sockets receive this type of data out-of-band, and the FD_OOB event indicates that out-of-band (OOB) data is available to be read. To enable the receipt of urgent data in-band, use the setsockopt() function with the SO_OOBINLINE option turned on. Each special data block is then included as one more piece of data for the application to read and interpret, and its presence is signaled by an FD_READ notification rather than FD_OOB.

The FD_OOB event is only used on stream sockets and only on those configured to receive urgent data out-of-band. When an application receives the FD_OOB event message, a subsequent call to recv() or recvfrom() with the MSG_OOB flag set should successfully return urgent data.

WinSock posts FD_OOB in these situations:

- When out-of-band data arrives.

- After a call to recv() or recvfrom(), with or without the MSG_OOB flag, if OOB data is still available to be received. (These are the reenabling functions for FD_OOB.)

- Immediately after a call to WSAAsyncSelect(), if OOB data has already arrived.

The concept of out-of-band data in TCP was introduced in the Transmission Control Protocol specification, RFC 793. There are two conflicting interpretations of this RFC, and the implementation of out-of-band data in the Berkeley Software Distribution doesn't conform to the host requirements laid down in RFC 1122. All this causes a conflict in the way various TCP implementations set the TCP urgent pointer in a TCP packet. An RFC 793-compliant implementation sets the pointer to the byte that comes *after* the urgent data byte. An RFC 1122-compliant implementation points directly *to* the urgent data byte. As a result, if an application sends urgent data from a BSD-compatible implementation to an RFC 1122-compatible implementation, the receiver will read the wrong urgent data byte. (Are you still with me?)

Note: WinSock vendors are urged to document the specific out-of-band semantics — that is, either RFC 793 or RFC 1122. However, you still need to know which implementation is used by the service with which you are connecting. Some applications (such as Telnet) *require* you use OOB data. But, if this is not the case for you, then you should not use out-of-band data at all in your applications for the reasons explained in this section.

FD_READ   The FD_READ event indicates that data is available to be read. It occurs on all types of applications — connection-oriented and connectionless; clients as well as servers. When an application receives the FD_READ event message, the application can assume a call to either recv() or recvfrom() will succeed and return immediately. WinSock posts the FD_READ message in the following situations:

- When data arrives.

- After a call to recv() or recvfrom(), if more data is waiting to be read. (These are the reenabling functions for FD_READ.)

- Immediately after a call to WSAAsyncSelect(), if data is already available to be received.

- When out-of-band data arrives, if the socket option SO_OOBINLINE is enabled.

Caution: After receiving the FD_READ notification to reenable FD_READ messages, you should always call one of the receive functions. This should be done even if the message signals an error.

It's unnecessary to read all the data available when processing any one FD_READ message. A single call to a receive function for each FD_READ message will eventually read all incoming data. If data still remains to be read after a call to recv() or recvfrom(), WinSock will post another FD_READ message.

If your application receives large amounts of data, you can substantially increase data throughput by calling recv() or recvfrom() multiple times for a single FD_READ message. Calling one of the receive functions until it blocks ensures the application has read all the information the protocol stack currently has available. In fact, calling recv() or recvfrom() multiple times even after they have blocked will cause WinSock to post multiple FD_READ messages and will keep the application responding as quickly as possible. This can significantly increase data throughput.

FD_WRITE   The FD_WRITE event indicates the socket is writeable. This means the protocol stack has buffer space available for sending data. A call to send() or sendto() should complete immediately without blocking. The call might block if the application attempts to send more data than the protocol stack can buffer. If a call to send() or sendto() does result in the WSAEWOULDBLOCK error, WinSock will post another FD_WRITE message when it is again safe to send more data.

A stream socket requires a connection be established before data can be transmitted. Once this connection is established, an FD_WRITE notification is sent for the socket to signal it is now writeable. When an application requests both FD_WRITE and FD_CONNECT notification, the FD_CONNECT message will be received first.

A connectionless datagram socket does not require a connection because it uses the sendto() function. The FD_WRITE notification is, therefore, sent for a datagram socket, after a call to bind() has succeeded.

WinSock posts the FD_WRITE notification message in the following situations:

- A call to connect() establishes a connection.
- A call to accept() establishes a connection.
- The WINSOCK.DLL has cleared some of the protocol stack buffers after a call to either send() or sendto() failed with WSAEWOULDBLOCK (when it is again safe to call a send() function).
- After a call to bind() on a datagram socket.
- Immediately after a call to WSAAsyncSelect() if a send() or sendto() is possible.

CANCELING ASYNCHRONOUS MESSAGES

When a socket is closed, asynchronous notification for that socket is automatically canceled. You can also cancel asynchronous notifications for a socket by calling WSAAsyncSelect() again with the *wMsg* and *lEvent* parameters set to zero.

```
nRet = WSAAsyncSelect(MySocket, hWnd, 0, 0);
```

Each time you call WSAAsyncSelect() on a given socket, it cancels any previous WSAAsyncSelect() requests for the same socket. So, by calling the function with nothing specified in the *lEvent* parameter, asynchronous notifications are canceled.

Note: Even though WSAAsyncSelect() immediately disables event notification for the socket, it is possible unread messages may still be waiting in the application's message queue. In the same way, queued notifications may be read and dispatched after a socket has been closed. For these reasons, applications must be prepared to deal with event messages even after cancellation.

The Database Functions

Chapter 2 briefly covered some of the database functions and the data structures they use. We used gethostbyname() and gethostbyaddr() to find the address of a host so we could establish a connection, and we used getservbyname() to find a port number. In this chapter we'll look at the other database functions and corresponding data structures.

Database Function Categories

All database functions fall into these three categories:

- *Host Resolution.* Provides host name and address information by name or address.

- *Service Resolution.* Provides service port numbers information by name or number.

- *Protocol Resolution.* Provides protocol information by name or number.

Let's consider host resolution first. As mentioned in Chapter 3, almost all of the standard database functions *always* block. (The gethostname() function, which is used to retrieve the name of the local machine, is the only standard database function that does not block.) Even if you are using asynchronous mode for socket operations, functions like gethostbyname() will still block.

The amount of time any of these functions will actually take to complete is specific to the implementation. The host resolution functions — gethostbyX() — typically use DNS (or some other network resolution service) and will almost always traverse the network to complete their task. This can happen quickly (in a matter of seconds) or take some time (several minutes or more). On some implementations, these functions use local files to resolve host names and complete quickly, but this is not the norm. Host names and their corresponding addresses change so often it isn't practical to keep host tables updated on lots of different machines. For this reason, most implementations use some form of network communication to resolve host names.

Resolution of services and protocols is less likely to block than is host resolution. The getservbyX() and getprotobyX() functions typically use local files to perform their services and, therefore, complete quickly. Local files can be used for these functions because service names and associated port numbers seldom change, and protocol names and numbers almost never change.

The standard Microsoft WinSock implementations that ship with Windows 95 and Windows NT use local tables to perform service and protocol resolution. These files, listed below, are plain text files that can be viewed with Notepad or any other text editor. On Windows 95, these files are stored in the \Windows\ directory. On Windows NT, they are kept in the Systemroot\System32\Drivers\Etc\ directory.

Standard Database File	Contents
services	Well-known service names and related port numbers and transport protocols.
protocol	The Internet protocols as defined by RFC 1060.

Some typical entries from the Services file are listed in the following table. Note, as mentioned in Chapter 2, some ports are listed more than once to provide the same service through different protocols. Remember, however, this is not always the case — some services use different port numbers when they are provided through more than one protocol.

Service Name	Port Number/Protocol	Optional Alias
echo	7/tcp	
echo	7/udp	
ftp	21/tcp	
telnet	23/tcp	
smtp	25/tcp	mail
pop3	110/tcp	postoffice
nntp	119/tcp	usenet

Here are some typical entries from a protocol file:

Protocol Name	Assigned Number	Optional Alias
ip	0	IP
icmp	1	ICMP
ggp	3	GGP
tcp	6	TCP

The Asynchronous Database Functions

The asynchronous database functions are what your application uses to request name resolution services in an asynchronous manner. You use the collection of WSAAsyncGetXByY() functions to request name resolution services that would otherwise block the operation of the whole Windows environment if the standard Berkeley function were used. Here is the group of Windows-specific, asynchronous functions that were added to the Berkeley API to alleviate this situation:

- WSAAsyncGetHostByAddr()
- WSAAsyncGetHostByName()
- WSAAsyncGetProtoByName()
- WSAAsyncGetProtoByNumber()
- WSAAsyncGetServByName()
- WSAAsyncGetServByPort()
- WSACancelAsyncRequest()

These functions behave much like their synchronous versions, but they do not block. They are like WSAAsyncSelect() in that they signal completion when the WINSOCK.DLL posts a message back to the calling application's window. Unlike WSAAsyncSelect(), however, a WSACancelAsyncRequest() function is included here. As its name suggests, this function can be used to cancel a WSAGetXbyY() function that is still pending (as discussed later in the chapter).

Host Name and Address Resolution

A client application must have the network address of a host to establish a connection. The connect() and sendto() functions both require an address in network order as a parameter. To acquire the host name and address (returned in the *hostent* structure), WinSock includes two sets of functions:

gethostbyname() and WSAAsyncGetHostByName()	Return information about a host for a given host name.
gethostbyaddr() and WSAAsyncGetHostByAddr()	Return information about a host for a given address.

CONTENTS OF THE RETURNED hostent STRUCTURE

All of the host resolution functions return a *hostent* structure, which is defined as follows. (The *hostent* structure and the gethostbyname() and gethostbyaddr() functions were used in Chapter 2. They are included here also, defined in more detail, to make this chapter's reference complete.)

```
struct    hostent {
          char     FAR * h_name;
          char     FAR * FAR * h_aliases;
```

```
                short       h_addrtype;
                short       h_length;
                char        FAR * FAR * h_addr_list;
};
```

Parameter	Description
h_name	A null-terminated ASCII string containing the official name of the host.
h_aliases	A null-terminated array of null-terminated ASCII strings containing host alias names. This may not contain any entries.
h_addrtype	The type of address being returned. For a standard Version 1.1 WinSock, this value is always AF_INET (Address Family Internet). In other WinSock implementations, it could be AF_IPX, AF_OSI, AF_APPLETALK, or some other value.
h_length	The length in bytes of each address contained in the *h_addr_list* field. This value relates to the type of address specified in *h_addrtype*. If *h_addrtype* is AF_INET, this value will be 4 (32-bit IP address).
h_addr_list	A null-terminated array of pointers to network addresses. This list usually contains only one address. If it contains more than one, that means the host has several different network interfaces.

gethostbyname()

The gethostbyname() function accepts a character string containing the host name to resolve. The function prototype for gethostbyname() is as follows:

```
struct hostent FAR * PASCAL FAR gethostbyname(
                                    const char FAR * name
                                    );
```

This function returns a pointer to a hostent structure if it finds the host or NULL if it does not. If it returns NULL, you should call WSAGetLastError() to check the exact reason for the error.

Note: The gethostbyname() function always blocks and can take time to complete. The return value points to a *hostent* buffer owned and allocated by the WINSOCK.DLL. After a successful call to gethostbyname(), you should copy whatever information you need from the structure immediately. WinSock may reuse this buffer while servicing a call from another process. Also, you should never attempt to change any of the information in the structure; this can cause a general protection fault. You should only *read* information from the buffer.

The HostInfo example program in Chapter 2 demonstrates the use of the gethostbyname() function.

WSAAsyncGetHostByName()

The WSAAsyncGetHostByName() function is probably the asynchronous database function you'll use the most. Although it provides access to the same information as the standard synchronous gethostbyname() version previously described, it operates much differently.

WSAAsyncGetHostByName() returns a *hostent* structure containing host address information for a given name, just as gethostbyname() does. But it doesn't block; it operates asynchronously. Here is the function prototype for WSAAsyncGetHostByName():

```
HANDLE PASCAL FAR WSAAsyncGetHostByName(
                         HWND hWnd,
                         u_int wMsg,
                         const char FAR * name,
                         char FAR * buf,
                         int buflen
                         );
```

Parameter	Description
hWnd	The handle of the window that will receive a message when the asynchronous request has completed.
wMsg	The application-defined message that will be posted to the window.
name	A pointer to a NULL-terminated character string containing the name of the host.
buf	A pointer to the data area to receive the *hostent* data. Note, this must be larger than the size of a *hostent* structure. On successful completion, this buffer will contain not only a *hostent* structure but all of the strings referenced in the *hostent* structure as well. Ensure that this buffer is at least MAXGETHOSTSTRUCT bytes long.
buflen	The size of data area pointed to by the *buf* parameter above.

When WSAAsyncGetHostByName() has completed, WinSock copies the results into the provided buffer and notifies the application by posting the message specified in *wMsg* to the window associated with *hWnd*.

Important: The standard gethostbyname() database function uses a buffer owned by WinSock to return information. Using WSAAsyncGetHostByName(), however, the *application* must supply the buffer. The memory area pointed to by the *buf* parameter must be available from the time the request is made until the call to WSAAsyncGetHostByName() completes. This memory area should *not* be an

Chapter 4: Using Asynchronous Mode

automatic variable created on the stack. It should be a global or static buffer or an area of memory allocated from the heap.

If the name resolution operation cannot be started, WSAAsyncGetHostByName() returns zero; a specific error number can be retrieved by calling WSAGetLastError(). When the operation is successfully initiated, WSAAsyncGetHostByName() returns a nonzero asynchronous task handle that uniquely identifies a particular request. For example, if two or more asynchronous database operations are processing at the same time, this task handle can be used to identify which operation has completed. (The task handle can also be used to cancel the operation, using the WSACancelAsyncRequest() function described later in this section.)

Following is a demonstration of a call to WSAAsyncGetHostByName():

```
#define SM_GETHOST WM_USER+2      // SocketMessage - GetHost

// Note that bufHostEnt should be declared globally
// or with static storage class or allocated from
// the system
char    bufHostEnt[MAXGETHOSTSTRUCT];
HANDLE  hndlTask;
int     nReason;

hndlTask = WSAAsyncGetHostByName(
                                 hWnd,
                                 SM_GETHOST,
                                 "www.idgbooks.com",
                                 bufHostEnt,
                                 MAXGETHOSTSTRUCT
                                 );
if (hndlTask == 0)
{
    // Tell user about error
    nReason = WSAGetLastError();
}
// Task started.
// Message will be posted when complete
```

In this example, when the asynchronous operation completes, WinSock will post the specified message to the application's window.

The *wParam* value passed along with the message will contain the same task handle returned by the original function call, and the high word of *lParam* will contain the error code. WinSock supplies the WSAGETASYNCERROR macro to retrieve the error code from *lParam*. Note, this macro should always be used instead of the HIWORD macro. (Future versions of Windows or WinSock might change the exact location of this value.) An error code of zero indicates the operation completed successfully and the supplied buffer now contains the requested information.

Part II: The WinSock 1.1 API

The code in Listing 4-2 handles a message posted from a call to WSAAsyncGetHostByName().

Listing 4-2 Handling a WSAAsyncGetHostByName() notification message

```
void HandleGetHostMsg(
             HWND hWnd,
             WPARAM wParam,
             LPARAM lParam
)
{
    LPHOSTENT lpHostEnt;      // Pointer to host entry structure
    int               nRet;         // Return code
    int               nErrorCode;   // Error code

    //
    // Compare the task handle to the one
    // returned from the call to WSAAsyncGetHostByName()
    //
    if ((HANDLE)wParam != savedTaskHandle)
    {
        // Not our task handle
        return;
    }

    // Check error code
    nErrorCode = WSAGETASYNCERROR(lParam);
    if (nErrorCode != 0)
    {
        // Report the error
        return;
    }

    //
    // Server found OK, global buffer
    // contains server info
    //
    lpHostEnt = (LPHOSTENT)bufHostEnt;

    // Processing continues
    // lpHostEnt->h_addr contains
    // the primary interface address
    // for the host.
    .
    .
    .
}
```

The most common error returned by WSAAsyncGetHostByName() is WSA-HOST_NOT_FOUND, which indicates information for the host was not found.

Chapter 4: Using Asynchronous Mode 101

If the returned error code is WSAENOBUFS, then the size of the buffer passed to WSAAsyncGetHostByName() was too small. Although unlikely, this *can* happen even if the specified buffer is MAXGETHOSTSTRUCT bytes in length. This is the size recommended for use, but no guarantee exists it will always be sufficient in every case. As you saw in Chapter 2, when using the HostInfo sample program, some hosts have more than one alias or address associated with them. The size of the *hostent* structure (along with all related information) for a host with many aliases or addresses could possibly exceed MAXGETHOSTSTRUCT bytes. The buffer size is not an issue for the application when calling gethostbyname() because WinSock supplies the buffer in that case.

When the WSAENOBUFS error occurs, the low word of *lParam* will contain the size the buffer must be to hold all of the hosts information. A new, larger buffer can then be allocated and another call to WSAAsyncGetHostByName() started. WinSock supplies the WSAGETASYNCBUFLEN macro to extract the needed buffer size value from *lParam*.

We'll use WSAAsyncGetHostByName() in the CheckMail sample program in this chapter.

gethostbyaddr()

Usually, host resolution is performed by name, but occasionally you may find you only have an address. If you already have an address, you may be looking for the official host name, aliases for the host, or possibly alternate interface addresses. As shown earlier, all this information is contained in the *hostent* structure.

You can retrieve the *hostent* information for a given address by using the gethostbyaddr() function. Here is the prototype for gethostbyaddr() from WINSOCK.H:

```
struct hostent FAR * PASCAL FAR gethostbyaddr(
                                        const char FAR * addr,
                                        int len,
                                        int type
                                        );
```

Parameter	Description
addr	Pointer to an address.
len	Length of the address in bytes.
type	The type of address (under Version 1.1 this is always AF_INET).

The second and third parameters are needed so WinSock can support the address formats for various transport protocols.

Like gethostbyname(), the gethostbyaddr() function always blocks. In most WinSock implementations, it communicates across the network to resolve the host information and may take some time to complete. It returns a pointer to a *hostent* structure if it finds the host or NULL if it does not. If it returns NULL, you should call WSAGetLastError() to check the exact reason for the error.

Note: The same warnings about use of the WinSock-owned *hostent* structure described for gethostbyname() also apply to gethostbyaddr().

The HostInfo example program in Chapter 2 demonstrates use of the gethostbyaddr() function.

WSAAsyncGetHostByAddr()

The WSAAsyncGetHostByAddr() function can be used to provide the same service that gethostbyaddr() provides, but without blocking. WSAAsyncGetHostByAddr() operates almost identically to WSAAsyncGetHostByName(). It always returns immediately. The return value indicates whether the process was started successfully, and when the function completes it posts a message to the application's window. The only difference between WSAAsyncGetHostByAddr() and WSAAsyncGetHostByName() is in the calling parameters.

Here is the function prototype for WSAAsyncGetHostByName():

```
HANDLE PASCAL FAR WSAAsyncGetHostByAddr(
                          HWND hWnd,
                          u_int wMsg,
                          const char FAR * addr,
                          int len,
                          int type,
                          char FAR * buf,
                          int buflen
                          );
```

Parameter	Description
hWnd	The handle of the window that will receive a message when the asynchronous request has completed.
wMsg	The application-defined message that will be posted to the window.
addr	A pointer to an address in network byte order.
len	The length of the address in bytes. Under Version 1.1 (*type* = AF_INET), this is always 4.
type	The type of address. Under Version 1.1, this is always AF_INET.

Parameter	Description
buf	A pointer to the data area to receive the *hostent* data. Note, this must be larger than the size of a *hostent* structure. On successful completion, this buffer will contain not only a *hostent* structure but all of the strings referenced in the *hostent* structure as well. Ensure that this buffer is at least MAXGETHOSTSTRUCT bytes long.
buflen	The size of data area pointed to by the *buf* parameter above. (Must be MAXGETHOSTSTRUCT or larger.)

If the address resolution operation cannot be started, WSAAsyncGetHostByAddr() returns zero; a specific error number can be retrieved by calling WSAGetLastError(). If the operation is successfully initiated, WSAAsyncGetHostByAddr() returns a nonzero asynchronous task handle that uniquely identifies the request, just as WSAAsyncGetHostByName() does. The task handle can be used to identify which operation has completed; or it can be used to cancel the operation using the WSACancelAsyncRequest() function described later in this chapter.

Note: The same warnings about buffer availability and size relevant to WSAAsyncGetHostByName() also apply to WSAAsyncGetHostByAddr().

Listing 4-3 demonstrates a call to WSAAsyncGetHostByAddr().

Listing 4-3 Calling WSAAsyncGetHostByAddr()

```
#define SM_GETHOST WM_USER+2      // SocketMessage - GetHost

// Note that bufHostEnt should be declared globally
// or with static storage class or allocated from
// the system
char            bufHostEnt[MAXGETHOSTSTRUCT];
struct in_addr       iaHost;         // Internet address structure
HANDLE          hndlTask;            // Task Handle
int             nReason;

// Convert address from dot notation
iaHost.s_addr = inet_addr("206.61.229.23");

hndlTask = WSAAsyncGetHostByAddr(
                                hWnd,
                                SM_GETHOST,
                                &iaHost,
                                sizeof(struct in_addr),
                                AF_INET,
                                bufHostEnt,
                                MAXGETHOSTSTRUCT
                                );
```

```
if (hndlTask == 0)
{
   // Tell user about error
   nReason = WSAGetLastError();
}
// Task started.
// Message will be posted when complete
```

When the operation completes, WinSock will post the specified message to the application's window, exactly as for WSAAsyncGetHostByName(). The *wParam* value will contain the same task handle returned by the original function call, and the error code can be extracted from *lParam* with the WSAGETASYNCERROR macro. The exact message handler shown earlier for WSAAsyncGetHostByName() can be used to process messages posted from a call to WSAAsyncGetHostByAddr().

Service Name and Port Resolution

To use the connect() or sendto() functions, a client application must know the port number where it can expect to find a particular server application. In addition, server applications must know the port number clients will use to find them so they can bind() to the correct port.

The port numbers for the most common applications are well-known and can be coded directly into the program. Nevertheless, using the service resolution functions can make an application both more portable and more flexible. Some server applications are intentionally bound to ports other than the "well-known" ones, to "hide" them from intruders. For example, some private ftp sites are intentionally bound to a port other than the well-known port 21. This affords an added measure of security because hackers are less likely to find the ftp server.

As discussed earlier, service resolution is usually performed through local tables. Both client and server applications should first attempt to find the correct port by using the service resolution functions, and then use a well-known port number if the function fails.

To find the service name and port, WinSock includes two sets of functions:

getservbyname()
and
WSAAsyncGetServByName()   Return information about a service for a given
                                 service name and protocol.

getservbyport()
and
WSAAsyncGetServByPort()   Return information about a service for a given
                                 port and protocol.

CONTENTS OF THE servent STRUCTURE

All of the service resolution functions return information contained in a *servent* structure:

```
struct  servent {
                char      FAR * s_name;
                char      FAR * FAR * s_aliases;
                short     s_port;
                char      FAR * s_proto;
                };
```

Parameter	Description
s_name	Official name of the service. These are always lowercase (ftp, http, and so forth).
s_aliases	A null-terminated array of null-terminated ASCII strings containing alternate service names.
s_port	Port number in network order.
s_proto	Null-terminated ASCII string containing the name of the protocol associated with this service name and port.

getservbyname()

The getservbyname() function is used to find the port number corresponding to a service name and protocol. It returns a pointer to a *servent* structure if it succeeds, or to NULL if it fails. Here is the function's prototype:

```
struct servent FAR * PASCAL FAR getservbyname(
                                    const char FAR * name,
                                    const char FAR * proto
                                    );
```

Parameter	Description
name	A pointer to a null-terminated ASCII string containing a service name. Returned name is typically case-sensitive and almost always kept in lowercase.

(continued)

Parameter	Description
proto	An optional pointer to a null-terminated ASCII string containing a protocol name. If this parameter is NULL, getservbyname() returns the first service matching *name*. If it isn't NULL, getservbyname() attempts to match both the *name* and *proto*.

The getservbyname() function always blocks, but this is usually not a problem because service resolution typically uses local tables. The function should complete quickly.

The return value from a successful call to getservbyname() points to a buffer owned by the WINSOCK.DLL. Field values from this structure should be used or copied to local storage immediately. WinSock may write over this buffer when servicing a call from another process. Never assume you can write to this structure — use it only to read the required information.

Because some services designate different port numbers for the same service available through different protocols, a good practice is always to specify both the name and the protocol, as shown in this example:

```
LPSERVENT    lpServEnt;      // Pointer to a servent structure
SOCKADDR_IN  saServer;       // Socket address for server

// Find the port number for the FTP service on TCP
lpServEnt = getservbyname("ftp", "tcp");
if (lpServEnt == NULL)
{
    // Service resolution failed,
    //    use well-known number
    //    in network order
    saServer.sin_port = htons(21);
}
else
{
    // Service resolution succeeded
    // use supplied number
    // (already in network order)
    saServer.sin_port = lpServEnt->s_port;
}
```

The preceding example uses the scheme mentioned earlier, first to look for a port number using getservbyname() and then to assign directly the number if the function fails. Note, the port number returned in the *servent* structure is already in network order and does not need to be converted, as the hard-coded number does.

WSAAsyncGetServByName()

The WSAAsyncGetServByName() function provides the same service as getservbyname() but is guaranteed not to block. It always returns immediately. The return value indicates whether the process was started successfully, and when the function completes it posts a message to the application's window. The WSAAsyncGetServByName() isn't commonly used because getservbyname() typically doesn't take long to complete.

WSAAsyncGetServByName() operates almost identically to the other asynchronous database functions and differs significantly only in its required parameters and value returned. Here is the function prototype for WSAAsyncGetServByName():

```
HANDLE PASCAL FAR WSAAsyncGetServByName(
                                        HWND hWnd,
                                        u_int wMsg,
                                        const char FAR * name,
                                        const char FAR * proto,
                                        char FAR * buf,
                                        int buflen
                                        );
```

Parameter	Description
hWnd	The handle of the window that will receive a message when the asynchronous request has completed.
wMsg	The application-defined message that will be posted to the window.
name	A pointer to a null-terminated ASCII string containing a service name.
proto	An optional pointer to a null-terminated ASCII string containing a protocol name. If this parameter is NULL, WSAAsyncGetServByName() returns the first service matching *name*. If it isn't NULL, WSAAsyncGetServByName() attempts to match both the *name* and *proto*.
buf	A pointer to the data area to receive the *servent* data. Note, this must be larger than the size of a *servent* structure. On successful completion, this buffer will contain not only a *servent* structure but all of the strings referenced in the *servent* structure as well. Ensure that this buffer is at least MAXGETHOSTSTRUCT bytes long.
buflen	The size of data area pointed to by the *buf* parameter above.

If the address resolution operation cannot be started, then the WSAAsyncGetServByName() function returns zero; a specific error number can be retrieved by calling WSAGetLastError(). If the operation is successfully initiated, WSAAsyncGetServByName() returns a nonzero asynchronous task handle that uniquely identifies the request. This works as it does for the other asynchronous database functions. The task handle can be used to identify which operation has completed, or it can be used to cancel the operation using the WSACancelAsyncRequest() function described later in this chapter.

Note: The same warnings about buffer availability and size that were stated for WSAAsyncGetHostByName() also apply to WSAAsyncGetServByName().

The following demonstrates a call to WSAAsyncGetServByName():

```
#define SM_GETSERV WM_USER+3      // SocketMessage - Get Service

// Note that bufServEnt should be declared globally
// or with static storage class or allocated from
// the system
char    bufServEnt[MAXGETHOSTSTRUCT];
HANDLE  hndlTask;                 // Task Handle
int     nReason;

hndlTask = WSAAsyncGetServByName(
                                 hWnd,
                                 SM_GETSERV,
                                 "ftp",
                                 "tcp",
                                 bufServEnt,
                                 MAXGETHOSTSTRUCT
                                 );
if (hndlTask == 0)
{
    // Tell user about error
    nReason = WSAGetLastError();
}
// Task started.
// Message will be posted when complete
```

When the operation completes, WinSock will post the specified message to the application's window. The *wParam* value will contain the same task handle returned by the original function call, and the error code can be extracted from *lParam* with the WSAGETASYNCERROR macro.

getservbyport()

Although it's not often necessary, you can retrieve information about a service by using a port number. One case where you might want to do this is when a port is already in use and you want to display the name of the service that's assigned to the port.

Here is the function prototype for getservbyport():

```
struct servent FAR * PASCAL FAR getservbyport(
                                              int port,
                                              const char FAR * proto
                                              );
```

Parameter	Description
port	A port number in network byte order.
proto	An optional pointer to a null-terminated ASCII string containing a protocol name. If this parameter is NULL, getservbyport() returns the first service matching the name. If it isn't NULL, getservbyport() attempts to match both the *port* and *proto*.

The getservbyport() function operates much like getservbyname() and only differs in its required parameters. See that section for a description of the returned values.

As discussed in Chapter 2, the address, port number, and protocol *together* uniquely identify a socket. Only one socket is allowed to use the same values for all of these attributes. Any attempt to bind() another socket to the same address will fail with the WSAEADDRINUSE error code. When an application receives this error, it means another process is already bound to that socket address. At this point, the application can use getservbyport() to retrieve the name of the service currently using that particular port and protocol.

Because more than one socket *can* use the same port if each uses a different protocol, it's best to specify the *proto* parameter when calling getscrvbyport() rather than setting it to NULL.

WSAAsyncGetServByPort()

The WSAAsyncGetServByPort() function provides an asynchronous operation for obtaining the same information provided by getservbyport(). The asynchronous version of this function is rarely used, however, because service port resolution is typically provided by local tables and, therefore, completes quickly.

Here is the function prototype for WSAAsyncGetServByPort():

```
HANDLE PASCAL FAR WSAAsyncGetServByPort(
                        HWND hWnd,
                        u_int wMsg,
                        int port,
                        const char FAR * proto,
                        char FAR * buf,
                        int buflen
                        );
```

Parameter	Description
hWnd	The handle of the window that will receive a message when the asynchronous request has completed.
wMsg	The application-defined message that will be posted to the window.
port	A port number in network byte order.
proto	An optional pointer to a null-terminated ASCII string containing a protocol name. If this parameter is NULL, WSAAsyncGetServByName() returns the first service matching name. If it isn't NULL, WSAAsyncGetServByName() attempts to match both the *port* and *proto*.
buf	A pointer to the data area to receive the *servent* data. Note, this must be larger than the size of a *servent* structure. On successful completion, this buffer will contain not only a *servent* structure but all of the strings referenced in the *servent* structure as well. Ensure that this buffer is at least MAXGETHOSTSTRUCT bytes long.
buflen	The size of data area pointed to by the *buf* parameter above.

WSAAsyncGetServByPort() operates in the same fashion as the other asynchronous database functions and returns the same information as WSAAsyncGetServByName(). See the preceding sections on asynchronous database functions for a detailed explanation.

Protocol Name and Number Resolution

Like port numbers, protocols are assigned a number by the Internet Assigned Number Authority (IANA). These protocol numbers are the ones we saw in the protocol file earlier in this chapter. These numbers have manifest constants assigned to them in WINSOCK.H, such as IPPROTO_IP and IPPROTO_TCP.

Although they are rarely used (because protocol names and numbers hardly ever change), WinSock provides two sets of functions to perform protocol resolution services.

getprotobyname()
and
WSAAsyncGetProtoByName()   Return information about a protocol for a given protocol name.

Chapter 4: Using Asynchronous Mode   111

getprotobynumber()
and
WSAAsyncGetProtoByNumber()   Return information about a protocol for a given
                                  protocol number.

THE protoent STRUCTURE

All of the protocol resolution functions return a pointer to a *protoent* structure, which is defined as follows:

```
struct   protoent {
                char    FAR * p_name;
                char    FAR * FAR * p_aliases;
                short   p_proto;
                };
```

Parameter	Description
p_name	Official name of the protocol. These are always in lowercase (ip, icmp, tcp, and so forth).
p_aliases	A null-terminated array of null-terminated ASCII strings containing alternate protocol names.
p_proto	The protocol number in host byte order.

The p_proto Field in Host Byte Order

The WinSock specification states the *p_proto* field is in "host byte order" and, indeed, because the protocol numbers' manifest constants are compiled on the host machine (by including WINSOCK.H), they, too, are in host order. I don't know if this was done intentionally or if it was just expedient. The manifest constants are commonly used as a parameter for the socket() and getprotobynumber() functions. Manifest constants like this are the only multibyte scalar values passed to any WinSock function in host order.

Keeping the *p_proto* field in host order doesn't really matter, though, because the only time the protocol number is sent across the network is in an IP header field — which is only one byte long anyway, so byte order isn't important.

getprotobyname()

The getprotobyname() function accepts the name of a protocol (which should be specified in lowercase) and returns a pointer to a WinSock-owned *protoent* structure defined as follows:

```
struct protoent FAR * PASCAL FAR getprotobyname(
                                       const char FAR * name
                                       );
```

If getprotobyname() fails, it returns NULL. You can then call WSAGetLastError() to find the exact reason for the failure. The most common error is WSANO_DATA, which means the protocol name was not found.

WSAAsyncGetProtoByName()

The WSAAsyncGetProtoByName() function is the asynchronous version of getprotobyname(). This function is rarely used, however, because protocol numbers rarely, if ever, change. Also, protocol resolution is typically provided by local tables and therefore completes quickly.

Here is the function prototype for WSAAsyncGetProtoByName():

```
HANDLE PASCAL FAR WSAAsyncGetProtoByName(
                                       HWND hWnd,
                                       u_int wMsg,
                                       const char FAR * name,
                                       char FAR * buf,
                                       int buflen
                                       );
```

Parameter	Description
hWnd	The handle of the window that will receive a message when the asynchronous request has completed.
wMsg	The application-defined message that will be posted to the window.
name	A pointer to a null-terminated character string containing the name of the protocol to be resolved.
buf	A pointer to the data area to receive the *protoent* data. Note, this must be larger than the size of a *protoent* structure. On successful completion, this buffer will contain not only a *protoent* structure but all of the strings referenced in the *protoent* structure as well. Ensure that this buffer is at least MAXGETHOSTSTRUCT bytes long.
buflen	The size of data area pointed to by the *buf* parameter above.

WSAAsyncGetProtoByName() operates in the same fashion as the other asynchronous database functions and returns the same information as getprotobyname(). See the preceding sections on asynchronous database functions for a detailed explanation.

getprotobynumber()
The getprotobynumber() function accepts a protocol number as a parameter and returns a pointer to a *protoent* structure. It returns NULL if it fails. Here is the function prototype for getprotobynumber():

```
struct protoent FAR * PASCAL FAR getprotobynumber(int proto);
```

This function can be used to increase the portability of a conscientious program. To find a port number with the getservbyname() function, you should specify both the name of the service *and* the name of the protocol. The getprotobynumber() function provides a good means of obtaining a protocol name rather than placing it directly into the source code.

WSAGetProtoByNumber()
The WSAAsyncGetProtoByNumber() function is the asynchronous version for obtaining the same information provided by getprotobynumber(). Like its counterparts, the WSAGetProtoByNumber()function is rarely used because protocol resolution is typically provided by local tables and completes quickly. Therefore, the simpler getprotobynumber() function can be used.

Here is the function prototype for WSAAsyncGetProtoByNumber():

```
HANDLE PASCAL FAR WSAAsyncGetProtoByNumber(
                        HWND hWnd,
                        u_int wMsg,
                        int number,
                        char FAR * buf,
                        int buflen
                        );
```

Parameter	Description
hWnd	The handle of the window that will receive a message when the asynchronous request has completed.
wMsg	The application-defined message that will be posted to the window.
number	The protocol number to be resolved.

Parameter	Description
buf	A pointer to the data area to receive the *protoent* data. Note, this must be larger than the size of a *protoent* structure. On successful completion, this buffer will contain not only a *protoent* structure but all of the strings referenced in the *protoent* structure as well. Ensure that this buffer is at least MAXGETHOSTSTRUCT bytes long.
buflen	The size of data area pointed to by the *buf* parameter above.

WSAAsyncGetProtoByNumber() operates in the same fashion as the other asynchronous database functions and returns the same information as getprotobynumber(). See the preceding sections on asynchronous database functions for a detailed explanation.

The WSACancelAsyncRequest() Function

The request made to any of the asynchronous database functions can be canceled by using the WSACancelAsyncRequest() function.

Note: This function *only* works on the *asynchronous* database functions. It does not cancel outstanding asynchronous socket functions created by using WSAAsyncSelect().

The WSACancelAsyncRequest() function requires as a parameter the task handle obtained from a call to one of the WSAAsyncGetXByY() functions. It returns zero to indicate success or an explicit error code if it fails. (No need exists to call WSAGetLastError() in this case.)

Here is the function prototype for WSACancelAsyncRequest():

```
int PASCAL FAR WSACancelAsyncRequest(HANDLE hAsyncTaskHandle);
```

The two most common reasons for failure of WSACancelAsyncRequest() are WSAEINVAL (invalid handle) and WSAEALREADY (operation already completed or already canceled). According to the WinSock specification, these two errors should be treated as equivalent. This is because in both cases the error indicates no asynchronous database operation is in progress with the indicated handle.

The function can be called to enable the end-user to cancel an asynchronous database function request thought to be taking too long to complete. Full-featured WinSock applications may also set a timer when calling an asynchronous database function and cancel the request if it has not completed after a specified amount of time.

The CheckMail Sample Application

The CheckMail application presented in this section puts all of the information from this chapter to work. CheckMail is a client application that requests services from a POP3 (Post Office Protocol Version 3) server to determine if mail is waiting to be retrieved.

CheckMail uses asynchronous mode to avoid blocking. For educational purposes, its user interface does more than just give a Yes or No answer about the existence of incoming mail. As it executes, it displays messages in an edit box about each step of the process. This enables you to see the sequence and timing of events as they occur. The event code messages received as a result of using WSAAsyncSelect() are all shown, as well as all data sent to and received from the server.

Figure 4-2 shows what the CheckMail application looks like as it is processing messages.

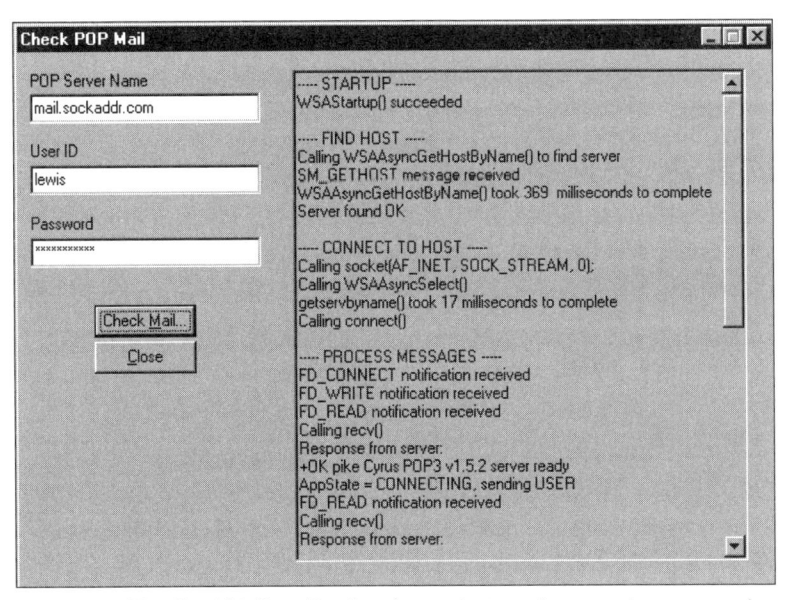

Figure 4-2: The CheckMail application demonstrates using asynchronous mode.

Compiling the CheckMail Sample Program

The CheckMail application will compile and run on both 16- and 32-bit Windows platforms using any version of WinSock. The full source code for the CheckMail application is supplied on the CD accompanying this book, located in the \CH04 directory. A project file is included for Microsoft Visual C++ Version 1.52, and the included workspace was created with Visual C++ Version 5.

A POP3 Conversation

As mentioned in Chapter 1, the Post Office Protocol is layered on top of TCP and provides services for retrieving electronic mail. Once connected, simple ASCII strings terminated by a carriage return/line feed pair are exchanged between the client and the server. These commands are used to identify the user and then to retrieve statistics and mail messages.

Here is an outline of the conversation CheckMail carries out with the POP3 server:

```
Client connects to server.
Server replies with message: "+OK POP3 Server Ready"
Client sends USER command: "USER <username>"
Server responds: "+OK User name accepted, password
please"Client sends PASS command: "PASS <password>"
Server responds: "+OK Mailbox open"
Client sends STAT command: "STAT"
Server responds: "+OK 1 4021"
Client sends QUIT command: "QUIT"
Server responds: "+OK BYE"
```

The connection is then closed. (The strings shown here are for example purposes; the exact response from the server may differ.)

The only exceptions to this sequence are the "+OK" portion, which is required by RFC1725, and the response to the "STAT" command. The "STAT" command asks the server to send the number of messages waiting to be retrieved, and the form of the response the server sends is as follows:

```
+OK <NumberOfMessages> <SizeOfMessages>
```

Thus, in the example shown above, one message containing 4,021 bytes is waiting to be retrieved.

Applications used to check intermittently for the existence of incoming mail should use the APOP command for subsequent logins instead of sending the full username and password each time mail is checked. Full documentation for the POP3 protocol, including the APOP command, can be found in RFC 1725.

Running the CheckMail Sample

The CheckMail application has a simple user interface. To use the program to check for the existence of incoming mail on a POP3 server, follow these instructions:

1. Copy the source files from the CD and compile them, or run the compiled version from the CD.

2. Enter the name of your mail server in the POP Server Name edit box. (For example, my e-mail address is lewis@sockaddr.com, so for my POP server name I enter mail.sockaddr.com.) Check with your Internet provider if you are not sure of the correct name.

3. Enter your User ID in the User ID edit box. (For example, my e-mail address is lewis@sockaddr.com, so for my User ID I enter **lewis**.)

4. Enter your password in the appropriate edit box. (I'm not telling you what my password is.)

5. Click the Check Mail button.

The application will attempt to connect with your POP server and determine if any mail is waiting to be retrieved.

The CheckMail Source Code

Listing 4-4 is the source code for CheckMail. Following the listing are sections that discuss the most important portions of the program.

You may be surprised to find little WinSock-specific code is actually in this program. Most of the source code deals with the Windows GUI and interpretation of the data received from the server. In an effort to make the source code as short and as simple as possible, CheckMail uses a dialog box for its main window.

Listing 4-4 ChekMail.c

```
//
// ChekMail.c  - Check for mail waiting on a
//                POP3 server
//

#include <windows.h>
#include <string.h>
#include <stdio.h>
#include <winsock.h>

#include "chekmail.h"
#include "resource.h"

// --- Global Variables
```

Part II: The WinSock 1.1 API

```c
// POP3 Host Name
char        gszServerName[255];
// User ID
char        gszUserId[80];
// Password
char        gszPassword[80];
// Handle for WSAAsyncGetHostByName()
HANDLE      hndlGetHost;
// HostEnt buffer for WSAAsyncGetHostByName()
char        bufHostEnt[MAXGETHOSTSTRUCT];
// The socket
SOCKET      socketPOP;
// Scratch buffer for wsprintf()
char        gszTemp[255];
// Variables used for timing
// For example only—not really needed
DWORD       gdwTicks;
DWORD       gdwElapsed;
// recv() data buffer
char        gbufRecv[256];

// --- Application State
int         gnAppState;
#define     STATE_CONNECTING    1
#define     STATE_USER          2
#define     STATE_PASS          3
#define     STATE_STAT          4
#define     STATE_QUIT          5

//
// WinMain() - Entry Point
//
int PASCAL WinMain(
            HINSTANCE       hinstCurrent,
            HINSTANCE       hinstPrevious,
            LPSTR           lpszCmdLine,
            int             nCmdShow)
{
    int nReturnCode;
    WSADATA wsaData;
    #define MAJOR_VERSION_REQUIRED 1
    #define MINOR_VERSION_REQUIRED 1

    // Prepare version for WSAStartup()
    WORD wVersionRequired = MAKEWORD(MAJOR_VERSION_REQUIRED,
                                     MINOR_VERSION_REQUIRED
                                    );

    // Initialize the WinSock DLL
    nReturnCode = WSAStartup(wVersionRequired, &wsaData);
    if (nReturnCode != 0 )
    {
        MessageBox(NULL,"Error on WSAStartup()",
```

Chapter 4: Using Asynchronous Mode   119

```
                    "CheckMail", MB_OK);
        return 1;
    }

    // Confirm that the version requested is available.
    if (wsaData.wVersion != wVersionRequired)
    {
        // Version needed is not available.
        MessageBox(NULL,"Wrong WinSock Version",
                    "CheckMail", MB_OK);
        WSACleanup();
        return 1;
    }

    // Use a dialog box for our main window
    DialogBox(
            hinstCurrent,
            MAKEINTRESOURCE(IDD_DIALOG_MAIN),
            NULL, MainDialogProc);

    // Release WinSock DLL
    WSACleanup();
    return 0;
}


//
// MainDialogProc() - Main Window Procedure
//
BOOL CALLBACK MainDialogProc(
                    HWND hwndDlg,
                    UINT msg,
                    WPARAM wParam,
                    LPARAM lParam)
{
    BOOL fRet = FALSE;

    switch(msg)
    {
        case WM_INITDIALOG:
            // Display info from WSADATA
            Display("--- STARTUP ---\r\n");
            Display("WSAStartup() succeeded\r\n\r\n");
            break;

        case WM_COMMAND:
            switch(wParam)
            {
                // User clicked button to check mail
                case ID_CHECKMAIL:
                    // Retrieve POP info
                    // Server Name, User ID and Password
                    if (!GetDlgItemText(hwndDlg,
```

```
                                IDC_SERVERNAME,
                                gszServerName,
                                sizeof(gszServerName)
                                ))
            {
                MessageBox(hwndDlg,
                    "Please enter a server name",
                    "POP Info", MB_OK);
                break;
            }
            if (!GetDlgItemText(hwndDlg, IDC_USERID,
                gszUserId, sizeof(gszUserId)))
            {
                MessageBox(hwndDlg,
                    "Please enter a user ID",
                    "POP Info", MB_OK);
                break;
            }
            if (!GetDlgItemText(hwndDlg,
                                IDC_PASSWORD,
                                gszPassword,
                                sizeof(gszPassword)
                                ))
            {
                MessageBox(hwndDlg,
                    "Please enter a password",
                    "POP Info", MB_OK);
                break;
            }

            // Request a lookup of the host name
            // using the asynchronous version
            // of gethostbyname()
            // SM_GETHOST message will be posted
            // to this  window when it completes.
            Display("--- FIND HOST ---\r\n");
            Display("Calling WSAAsyncGetHostByName()"
                " to find server\r\n");
            // Time WSAAsyncGetHostByName() function for
            // example purposes.
            gdwTicks = GetTickCount();
            hndlGetHost = WSAAsyncGetHostByName(
                            hwndDlg, SM_GETHOST,
                            gszServerName,
                            bufHostEnt,
                            MAXGETHOSTSTRUCT);
            if (hndlGetHost == 0)
            {
                MessageBox(hwndDlg,
                    "Error initiating "
                    "WSAAsyncGetHostByName()",
                    "CheckMail", MB_OK);
            }
```

Chapter 4: Using Asynchronous Mode 121

```
                    else
                    {
                        EnableButtons(FALSE);
                        gnAppState = 0;
                    }
                    fRet = TRUE;
                    break;

                // User pressed cancel button on main window
                case IDCANCEL:
                    if (gnAppState)
                        CloseSocket(socketPOP);
                    PostQuitMessage(0);
                    fRet = TRUE;
                    break;
            }
            break;

        // Handle asynchronous gethostbyname() return
        case SM_GETHOST:
            HandleGetHostMsg(hwndDlg, wParam, lParam);
            fRet = TRUE;
            break;

        // Hanlde asynchronous messages
        case SM_ASYNC:
            HandleAsyncMsg(hwndDlg, wParam, lParam);
            fRet = TRUE;
            break;
    }
    return fRet;
}

//
// HandleGetHostMsg()
// Called when WSAAsyncGetHostByName() completes
void HandleGetHostMsg(
          HWND hwndDlg,
          WPARAM wParam,
          LPARAM lParam)
{
    SOCKADDR_IN saServ;       // Socket address for Internet
    LPHOSTENT   lpHostEnt;    // Pointer to host entry
    LPSERVENT   lpServEnt;    // Pointer to server entry
    int nRet;                 // Return code

    Display("SM_GETHOST message received\r\n");
    if ((HANDLE)wParam != hndlGetHost)
        return;

    // For example purposes, display elapsed time
    // for WSAGetHostByName() function
    gdwElapsed = (GetTickCount() - gdwTicks);
```

Part II: The WinSock 1.1 API

```c
    wsprintf((LPSTR)gszTemp,
        (LPSTR)"WSAAsyncGetHostByName() took %ld "
        " milliseconds to complete\r\n",
        gdwElapsed);
    Display(gszTemp);

    // Check error code
    nRet = WSAGETASYNCERROR(lParam);
    if (nRet)
    {
        wsprintf((LPSTR)gszTemp,
            (LPSTR)"WSAAsyncGetHostByName() error: %d\r\n",
            nRet);
        Display(gszTemp);
        EnableButtons(TRUE);
        return;
    }

    // Server found OK, bufHostEnt
    // contains server info
    Display("Server found OK\r\n\r\n");

    Display("--- CONNECT TO HOST ---\r\n");
    // Create a socket
    Display("Calling socket(AF_INET, SOCK_STREAM, 0);\r\n");
    socketPOP = socket(AF_INET, SOCK_STREAM, 0);
    if (socketPOP == INVALID_SOCKET)
    {
        Display("Could not create a socket\r\n");
        EnableButtons(TRUE);
        return;
    }

    // Make socket nonblocking and register
    // for asynchronous notification
    Display("Calling WSAAsyncSelect()\r\n");
    if (WSAAsyncSelect(socketPOP, hwndDlg, SM_ASYNC,
            FD_CONNECT|FD_READ|FD_WRITE|FD_CLOSE))
    {
        Display("WSAAsyncSelect() failed\r\n");
        EnableButtons(TRUE);
        return;
    }

    // Try to resolve the port number
    // with getservbyname()
    // Simpler synchronous version used since
    // it almost always completes quickly.
    // Time getservbyname() function for
    // example purposes.
    gdwTicks = GetTickCount();
    lpServEnt = getservbyname("pop3", "tcp");
    gdwElapsed = (GetTickCount() - gdwTicks);
```

```c
        wsprintf((LPSTR)gszTemp,
                (LPSTR)"getservbyname() took %ld milliseconds"
                " to complete\r\n",
                gdwElapsed);
        Display(gszTemp);

        // If servent not found
        if (lpServEnt == NULL)
        {
           // Fill in with well-known port
            saServ.sin_port = htons(110);
            Display("getservbyent() failed. Using port 110\r\n");
        }
        else
        {
            // Use port returned in servent
            saServ.sin_port = lpServEnt->s_port;
        }
        // Fill in the server address structure
        saServ.sin_family = AF_INET;
        lpHostEnt = (LPHOSTENT)bufHostEnt;
        saServ.sin_addr = *((LPIN_ADDR)*lpHostEnt->h_addr_list);
        // Connect the socket
        Display("Calling connect()\r\n");
        nRet = connect(socketPOP,
                   (LPSOCKADDR)&saServ,
                   sizeof(SOCKADDR_IN));
        if (nRet == SOCKET_ERROR)
        {
            if (WSAGetLastError() != WSAEWOULDBLOCK)
            {
                Display("Error connecting\r\n");
                EnableButtons(TRUE);
                return;
            }
        }
        gnAppState = STATE_CONNECTING;
        Display("\r\n--- PROCESS MESSAGES ---\r\n");
}


//
// HandleAsyncMsg()
// Called when a WSA WSAAsyncSelct() event is triggered.
void HandleAsyncMsg(
                   HWND hwndDlg,
                   WPARAM wParam,
                   LPARAM lParam)
{
    int nBytesRead;

    switch(WSAGETSELECTEVENT(lParam))
    {
```

```
            case FD_CONNECT:
                Display("FD_CONNECT notification received\r\n");
                break;

            case FD_WRITE:
                Display("FD_WRITE notification received\r\n");
                break;

            case FD_READ:
                Display("FD_READ notification received\r\n");
                Display("Calling recv()\r\n");
                // Receive waiting data
                nBytesRead = recv(
                    socketPOP,              // socket
                    gbufRecv,               // buffer
                    sizeof(gbufRecv),       // max len to read
                    0);                     // recv flags
                // Check recv() return code
                if (nBytesRead == 0)
                {
                    // Connection has been closed.
                    MessageBox(hwndDlg,
                        "Connection closed unexpectedly",
                        "recv() error", MB_OK);
                    break;
                }
                if (nBytesRead == SOCKET_ERROR)
                {
                    wsprintf((LPSTR)gszTemp,
                        (LPSTR)"recv() error: %d", nBytesRead);
                    MessageBox(
                        hwndDlg,
                        gszTemp,
                        "recv() error",
                        MB_OK);
                    break;
                }
                // NULL terminate the buffer
                gbufRecv[nBytesRead] = '\0';
                // And pass it to be interpreted
                ProcessData(hwndDlg, gbufRecv, nBytesRead);
                break;
            case FD_CLOSE:
                Display("FD_CLOSE notification received\r\n");
                EnableButtons(TRUE);
                break;
        }
    }


//
// ProcessData()
// Read incoming data and break it
```

```
// into lines
//
void ProcessData(HWND hwndDlg, LPSTR lpBuf, int nBytesRead)
{
    static char szResponse[512];
    static int nLen = 0;
    char *cp;

    // Is there enough room in our buffer for the new data?
    if ((nLen + nBytesRead) > sizeof(szResponse))
    {
        Display("!!!!! Buffer overrun, data truncated\r\n");
        nLen = 0;
        szResponse[0] = '\0';
        return;
    }
    // Append the new data to our buffer
    strcat(szResponse, lpBuf);
    nLen = strlen(szResponse);

    // Process all full lines
    while(1)
    {
        // Does the buffer contain a full line?
        cp = strchr(szResponse, '\n');
        if (cp == NULL)
            break;
        // We have a CR/LF pair
        // Replace the LF with a NULL
        *cp = '\0';
        // And pass it to the ProcesLine() function
        ProcessLine(hwndDlg, szResponse);
        // Move the remaining data to the front
        // of the buffer
        cp++;
        if (strlen(cp))
            memmove(szResponse, cp, strlen(cp)+1);
        else
            szResponse[0] = '\0';
    }
}

//
// ProcessLine()
// Handle response lines from server
// and decide what to do next.
//
void ProcessLine(HWND hwndDlg, LPSTR lpStr)
{
    int nRet;
    long lCount;
    long lSize;
```

```
Display("Response from server:\r\n");
Display(lpStr);
Display("\r\n");

// Check response for error
if (lpStr[0] == '-')
{
    Display("Negative response: ");
    switch(gnAppState)
    {
        case STATE_CONNECTING:
            Display("Connection denied\r\n");
            break;
        case STATE_USER:
            Display("Unknown UserID\r\n");
            break;
        case STATE_PASS:
            Display("Wrong Password\r\n");
            break;
        case STATE_STAT:
            Display("STAT command not supported\r\n");
            break;
        case STATE_QUIT:
            Display("QUIT command not supported\r\n");
            break;
    }
    Display("Sending QUIT\r\n");
    wsprintf(gszTemp, "QUIT\r\n");
    Display(gszTemp);
    nRet = send(
            socketPOP,         // socket
            gszTemp,           // data buffer
            strlen(gszTemp),   // length of data
            0);                // send flags
    gnAppState = STATE_QUIT;
    return;
}

// We have a positive response
switch(gnAppState)
{
    case STATE_CONNECTING:
        // Send the USER portion of the login
        // request and set the app state
        Display("AppState = CONNECTING, "
                "sending USER\r\n");
        wsprintf(gszTemp, "USER %s\r\n", gszUserId);
        nRet = send(
                socketPOP,         // socket
                gszTemp,           // data buffer
                strlen(gszTemp),// length of data
                0);                // send flags
        gnAppState = STATE_USER;
```

```
        break;

case STATE_USER:
    // Send the PASSword portion of the login
    // request and set the app state
    Display("AppState = USER, sending PASS\r\n");
    wsprintf(gszTemp, "PASS %s\r\n", gszPassword);
    nRet = send(
            socketPOP,      // socket
            gszTemp,        // data buffer
            strlen(gszTemp),// length of data
            0);             // send flags
    gnAppState = STATE_PASS;
    break;

case STATE_PASS:
    // Send the STAT command
    // request and set the app state
    Display("AppState = PASS, sending STAT\r\n");
    wsprintf(gszTemp, "STAT\r\n");
    nRet = send(
            socketPOP,      // socket
            gszTemp,        // data buffer
            strlen(gszTemp),// length of data
            0);             // send flags
    gnAppState = STATE_STAT;
    break;

case STATE_STAT:
    // Read the STAT response
    // and print the results
    Display("AppState = STAT, reading response\r\n");
    sscanf(lpStr, "%s %ld %ld",
            gszTemp, &lCount, &lSize);
    Display("--- RESULT ---\r\n");
    wsprintf(gszTemp, "%ld messages %ld bytes\r\n",
            lCount, lSize);
    Display(gszTemp);
    // Send the QUIT command
    // and set the app state
    Display("Sending QUIT\r\n");
    wsprintf(gszTemp, "QUIT\r\n");
    nRet = send(
            socketPOP,          // socket
            gszTemp,            // data buffer
            strlen(gszTemp),    // length of data
            0);                 // send flags
    gnAppState = STATE_QUIT;
    break;

case STATE_QUIT:
    Display("Host QUIT OK\r\n");
    Display("Closing socket\r\n");
```

```
            CloseSocket(socketPOP);
    }
}


//
// CloseSocket()
// Closes a socket after an attempt to clear the
// protocol stack buffers
//
void CloseSocket(SOCKET sock)
{
    int nRet;
    char szBuf[255];

    // Tell the remote that we're not going
    // to send any more data
    shutdown(sock, 1);
    while(1)
    {
        // Try to receive data.
        // This clears any data that
        // may still be buffered in
        // the protocol stack
        nRet = recv(
                sock,            // socket
                szBuf,           // data buffer
                sizeof(szBuf),   // length of buffer
                0);              // recv flags
        // Stop receiving data if connection
        // closed or on any other error.
        if (nRet == 0 || nRet == SOCKET_ERROR)
            break;
    }
    // Tell the peer that we're not
    // going to receive any more either.
    shutdown(sock, 2);
    // Close the socket
    closesocket(sock);
}
```

USING DATABASE FUNCTIONS

Once you've filled in all of the edit boxes with the appropriate information and clicked the Check Mail button, the ID_CHECKMAIL message handler in MainDialogProc requests asynchronous host resolution by using the WSAAsyncGetHostByName() function. The message returned for this request is handled by the HandleGetHostMsg() procedure. To give you an idea of how long a host-resolution request can actually take to complete, the elapsed time for completion of WSAAsyncGetHostByName() is calculated here in HandleGetHostMsg().

In my testing, it never took more than half a second, even on a machine attached to the Internet with a 28.8 modem. Watch out, however – if you intentionally (or even unintentionally) type in a nonexistent host name, the SM_GETHOST message may not return for several seconds. Remember, receiving a response from WSAAsyncGetHostByName() takes approximately the same amount of time a blocking call to gethostbyname() would take. Several seconds is plenty of time to annoy or confuse any end-user if the blocking version had been called and caused Windows to be unresponsive for that long.

Note, I didn't use the asynchronous version of getservbyname() to find the POP3 port. The amount of time elapsed for the call to this standard synchronous, blocking version is also timed in the application. It never took more than 15 milliseconds to complete on my machine.

These two demonstrations point out that host resolution should always be performed with the asynchronous functions, whereas service and protocol resolution can almost always be performed using the simpler synchronous versions.

RESPONDING TO ASYNCHRONOUS EVENTS

The HandleAsyncMsg() function is called to deal with all asynchronous event codes when they are received. No processing occurs upon receipt of the FD_CONNECT, FD_WRITE, and FD_CLOSE messages – only a message is displayed to show when they occur. A more robust application might use these notifications to keep track of connection status and socket state.

Most of the processing occurs in response to the FD_READ notification. Each time an FD_READ event is received, the program simply calls recv() requesting as much data as will fit in the read buffer. No attempt is made to ensure that all of the available data is read at one time. If more data is waiting to be read, WinSock will post another FD_READ message after the call to recv() reenables that message. Data read into the buffer is passed to the ProcessData() function to be interpreted.

PARSING THE DATA

Much of the processing in this program deals with examining data coming in from the server to find the end of lines and with interpreting the line's meaning. Remember, stream sockets don't preserve record boundaries. Each time we call recv() and send the data to the ProcessData() function, we may have only received part of a line. Or, we may have received several lines. The application's responsibility is to inspect the incoming data and make sense of it – WinSock only delivers it in sequence.

The ProcessData() function keeps its own copy of all incoming data until it has been used. Each time it is called, it first appends the new data to its internal buffer and searches for end-of-line characters. Then, it passes each full line to the ProcessLine() function.

MAINTAINING APPLICATION STATE

At several key points in the program, the variable *gnAppState* is set to a new value to keep track of where we are in the conversation with the server. These roughly correspond to the states laid out in RFC 1725 (POP3).

Each time a new line is passed to ProcessLine(), it is first examined to see if there is a positive or negative response from the server. POP3 servers literally place a plus (+) character in the first position of a response line to indicate success or a minus (-) character to indicate failure.

If ProcessLine() receives a negative response from the server, it uses a *switch* statement with the *gnAppState* variable to attempt to give the end-user a descriptive reason for the failure. If a positive response is received from the server, the *gnAppState* variable is used to decide what step to take next.

CLOSING THE CONNECTION
CheckMail uses the technique described in Chapter 2 to attempt to ensure the protocol stack buffers are cleared before closing the socket. The CloseSocket() function first uses the shutdown() function to let the server know it does not intend to send any more data. Then it calls recv() to empty any data that might possibly still be buffered for the socket. It stops calling recv() when *any* error message is received. It then calls shutdown() again to tell the server the socket will no longer receive any data, and then calls closesocket().

Summary

With a good understanding of this chapter and Chapter 2, you have mastered the most-often used portions of the Version 1.1 set of the WinSock API. As you'll see in Chapter 7, the new portions of the WinSock 2 API do offer some performance enhancements. But by using the methods outlined in this chapter, you can write TCP/IP applications that will compile and run with WinSock 1.1 or 2 and work in a Windows-friendly manner, on any platform from Windows 3.0 forward.

In Chapter 5 you'll get a chance to examine some of the less often used WinSock 1.1 functions and portions of the API that are not mandatory for a vendor to implement. That some of these functions are rarely used definitely does not mean they are unuseful, however. For example, in the next chapter we will develop our own version of the familiar Ping network utility.

Chapter 5

Optional Features

IN THIS CHAPTER
Portions of the official WinSock specification were designated as optional — vendors were not required to support these features to be WinSock compliant. Some WinSock vendors include support for these optional features and others don't. In this chapter we discuss what these optional features offer, who supports them, and who doesn't. We also explore additional functionality that wasn't mentioned in the WinSock specification at all, but is provided by some of the more prominent WinSock vendors. We'll cover these topics:

- Using setsockopt() and getsockopt()
- Writing utilities with raw sockets
- Using protocols other than TCP/IP in WinSock 1.1
- Using Microsoft-specific extensions

MOST OF THE WINSOCK API IS SUPPORTED by all WinSock vendors, but some features described in the WinSock specification were designated as optional. Vendors were urged to support these optional features, but it wasn't mandatory for WinSock compliance.

Because some features of the API weren't precisely documented in the WinSock specification, their exact behavior was left open to interpretation. Each vendor decided on its own implementation of these features; and, of course, they didn't all do it the same way. The folks at Stardust Technologies (www.winsock.com), who specialize in testing WinSock applications, report that there are over 70 different WinSock 1.1 TCP/IP stacks now in circulation. That leaves a lot of room for differences in these arbitrary areas.

Over time, other functionality that was not intended to be part of the specification has been added into various WinSock implementations. The WinSock specification includes a section detailing how vendors may implement their own private interfaces inside the WINSOCK.DLL by using ordinal values outside the range employed by the standard functions. Some vendors (most notably Microsoft and Novell) have added extensions to their WinSock implementations that weren't mentioned in the WinSock specification at all.

I've collected all of this optional behavior into one chapter to emphasize that it may not be available on all WinSock implementations, and that you may not want to use it. Some of the functions described in this chapter aren't optional at all – they are required as part of every WinSock implementation. On the other hand, several of the options and command codes used with these function are optional, and that's why they're discussed in this chapter. For example, the getsockopt(), setsockopt(), and ioctlsocket() functions aren't optional, but the behavior they exhibit and some of the options used with them are.

Socket Options

WinSock supports several options (or attributes) for sockets. Options affect a wide variety of socket operations and behavior. Table 5-1 lists the options that are available and briefly describes their meaning.

Note: Only the options that are available in both WinSock 1.1 and 2 are listed in Table 5-1. Several new options that are only available in WinSock 2 are discussed in Part III and in the Quick Reference.

Optional Options

No, that's not a typo. WinSock has "optional" options. The WinSock 1.1 specification states that all WinSock implementations must *recognize* all of the socket options, but it also says that some of the options may be "silently ignored." So, a valid WinSock implementation could accept a new value for one of these optional options without indicating an error, and yet not use the new value in any way!

The various options available for a socket can be enabled, disabled, or specified with the setsockopt() function. Their current value can be found by using the getsockopt() function. You can usually tell if an option is supported, by first setting a new value with setsockopt() and then checking to see if getsockopt() returns the new value. However, under strict adherence to the guidelines of the WinSock specification, a valid WinSock implementation could conceivably return the new value from getsockopt() and still not actually use the value.

The options that are...well...*optional* are indicated as such in Table 5-1 and in the detailed discussion of each option later in this chapter.

TABLE 5-1 SOCKET OPTIONS AND THEIR MEANING

Option	Meaning
SO_ACCEPTCONN	Will socket accept() a connection? (Has listen() been called?)
SO_BROADCAST	Should the socket be allowed to send broadcast messages?
SO_DEBUG (optional)	Is debug output enabled?

Option	Meaning
SO_DONTLINGER	Should the socket block while waiting for closesocket() to complete?
SO_DONTROUTE (optional)	Should WinSock bypass the protocol routing mechanisms?
SO_ERROR	Retrieve and then clear the error status for the socket.
SO_KEEPALIVE (optional)	Should WinSock send keep-alive requests for the socket?
SO_LINGER	Should the socket block while waiting for closesocket() to complete? And if so, for how long?
SO_OOBINLINE	Receive out-of-band data for the socket in the normal data stream?
SO_RCVBUF (optional)	Set the size of the buffer used for receiving data.
SO_REUSEADDR	Should other sockets be allowed to use this socket's address?
SO_SNDBUF (optional)	Set the size of buffer used for sending data.
SO_TYPE	Retrieve the socket type (SOCK_STREAM, SOCK_DGRAM, etc.).
TCP_NODELAY	Use the Nagle algorithm for send coalescing? (The Nagle algorithm is explained in the section on TCP_NODELAY.)

The getsockopt() and setsockopt() Functions

Most of the socket options are simple Boolean flags that are turned on or off (enabled or disabled). A few of the options use an integer value rather than a flag, and one uses a *linger* structure that is described later in this section.

As mentioned earlier, you use the setsockopt() function to enable, disable, or specify the various options available for a socket. You use the getsockopt() function to find the options' current values. All of the options can be used with getsockopt(), but (as you'll see in the upcoming discussions) some of the options can't be set with setsockopt(). Both getsockopt() and setsockopt() return 0 when they succeed or SOCKET_ERROR when they fail.

Here is the function prototype for getsockopt():

```
int PASCAL FAR getsockopt(
                SOCKET s,
                int level,
                int optname,
```

```
                         char FAR * optval,
                         int FAR *optlen
                         );
```

Parameter	Description
s	The socket descriptor for which you want to retrieve an option value.
level	The protocol level to which the option belongs.
optname	The option to retrieve (acceptable values are listed in Table 5.1).
optval	A pointer to a buffer where the value for the requested *optname* will be copied. The appropriate size for this buffer depends on the option being retrieved. It is always either *sizeof(int)* or *sizeof(struct linger)* in WinSock 1.1.
optlen	The length of the buffer referenced by *optval*.

This is the function prototype for setsockopt():

```
int PASCAL FAR setsockopt(
                         SOCKET s,
                         int level,
                         int optname,
                         const char FAR * optval,
                         int optlen
                         );
```

Parameter	Description
s	The socket descriptor for which you want to change an option value.
level	The protocol level to which the option belongs.
optname	The option to set (acceptable values are listed in Table 5.1).
optval	A pointer to a buffer containing the new value for the option. The appropriate size for this buffer depends on the option being retrieved. In WinSock 1.1, it is always either *sizeof(int)* or *sizeof(struct linger)*.
optlen	The length of the buffer referenced by *optval*.

The parameters for getsockopt() and setsockopt() are *almost* identical. There are only two differences:

Chapter 5: Optional Features 135

- The area pointed to by the *optval* parameter (option value) includes the *const* modifier in the call to setsockopt(). This means WinSock won't *write* to this area during the call to setsockopt(); it will only *read* from that area. WinSock *will* write to the area pointed to by *optval* during the call to getsockopt().

- The *optlen* parameter is an integer in the call to setsockopt(), but it is a *pointer* to an integer in getsockopt(). When calling setsockopt(), the application is telling WinSock how large the area pointed to by *optval* is; but in the call to getsockopt(), WinSock is telling the application the size of this area.

The second parameter indicates an *option level*. The option level refers to the protocol layer that the option affects. There are two distinct option levels: The SOL_SOCKET level affects the application protocol layer, and the IPPROTO_TCP level affects the transport protocol layer. In the WinSock 1.1 specification, only one option (TCP_NODELAY) affects the IPPROTO_TCP level; all of the others affect the SOL_SOCKET protocol layer. WinSock 2 introduces several new values for the *level* parameter. These are discussed in Part III and in the Quick Reference.

The *optname* parameter in both getsockopt() and setsockopt() is actually an integer value. All of the values accepted in this parameter have constants defined in WINSOCK.H and will be discussed shortly.

The *optval* parameter points to an area of memory to hold the option value. This area is filled with a value by the application in a call to setsockopt() and is used by WinSock to return a value in a call to getsockopt(). The size and contents of this buffer depend on the option being used. With one exception, *optval* always points to an integer, either as a value or a Boolean flag. The one exception is when the *linger* structure is used in the SO_LINGER and SO_DONTLINGER options (explanation coming up).

SETTING SOCKET OPTIONS

To enable a Boolean option with a call to setsockopt(), *optval* must point to a nonzero integer. To disable the option, *optval* must point to an integer equal to zero. Other options require a value. In these cases, *optval* is used to point to the first byte of the value, and *optlen* specifies the size of the value.

In all cases, the *sizeof* operator should be used to set *optlen* to the appropriate size, as shown in the following code sample:

```
// Enable the SO_OOBINLINE option
int nLevel          = SOL_SOCKET;
int nOption         = SO_OOBINLINE;    // Data type for SO_OOBINLINE
BOOL nOptionValue   = TRUE;             // is defined as BOOL
int nOptionValLen   = sizeof(BOOL);

nRet = setsockopt(MySocket,
                  nLevel,
```

```
                        nOption,
                        (char *)&nOption,
                        nOptionValLen
                        );
if (nRet == SOCKET_ERROR)
{
    // Handle error here
}
```

Note: An example of using setsockopt() with the *linger* structure is given in the section that describes the SO_LINGER option.

GETTING SOCKET OPTIONS

Retrieving an option value with getsockopt() is very similar to using setsockopt(). The only significant difference is that the *optlen* parameter is now a pointer to an integer rather than an integer value. Note that even though WinSock is returning a value in the *optlen* parameter, you still must set *optlen* to the appropriate size before making the call to getsockopt(). Here's an example:

```
// Get the current value for the SO_OOBINLINE option
int nLevel        = SOL_SOCKET;
int nOption       = SO_OOBINLINE;    // Data type for SO_OOBINLINE
int nOptionValLen = sizeof(BOOL);    // is defined as BOOL
BOOL nOptionValue;

nRet = getsockopt(MySocket,
                  nLevel,
                  nOption,
                  (char *)&nOption,
                  &nOptionValLen
                  );
if (nRet == SOCKET_ERROR)
{
    // Handle error here
}
```

Option Descriptions

Many of the options are only valid for stream sockets, some are valid for any type of socket, and one is valid only for datagram sockets. Some of these options can greatly improve an application's efficiency, some don't seem to be very useful at all, and others should be avoided altogether. The following sections describe each option in detail.

SO_ACCEPTCONN

The SO_ACCEPTCONN option isn't really an option at all — it is a means of discovering whether a particular socket is in the *listening* (passive) state. You can use SO_ACCEPTCONN with getsockopt() but not with setsockopt(). The return value (*optval*) will be True if listen() has been called for the socket and False if it hasn't. The SO_ACCEPTCONN option isn't supported on datagram sockets (SOCK_DGRAM).

SO_BROADCAST

The SO_BROADCAST option is used to indicate whether or not the socket should be allowed to send or receive broadcast messages. Before you can send a datagram to a broadcast address, you must call setsockopt() and enable SO_BROADCAST. Only datagram sockets (SOCK_DGRAM) are used with a broadcast address, so this option isn't supported for stream sockets (SOCK_STREAM).

About Broadcast Addresses

Broadcast addresses are used to send datagrams to more than one host with a single call to sendto(). They are typically used with peer-to-peer applications to establish communication patterns with one-to-many or many-to-many relationships. Some typical applications for broadcast addresses are conferencing systems such as IRC, and multiplayer games that connect players across a network. More recently, they have been used to simultaneously distribute multimedia content to multiple destinations (LAN TV is one example of this).

Broadcast addresses can be used to find host systems bound to a particular port number by sending datagrams to every machine attached to a network or subnetwork.

On a large network, a single broadcast can result in a lot of traffic being sent over the network, so broadcast addresses should be used with caution. Multicast addresses are a special type of broadcast address that were created in an attempt to alleviate this problem. Multicasting allows hosts to register as members of a group interested in receiving a particular type of multicast traffic. This allows an application to simultaneously communicate with any number of hosts without adversely affecting hosts that don't wish to receive the information.

The Internet community is currently focusing significant effort on new techniques for this kind of multipoint routing, and the WinSock 2 specification officially includes support for it. The IP Multicast Initiative supports precise routing of multicast traffic and allows systems to dynamically register and unregister for receipt of different types of multicast messages. Unfortunately, most of the routers employed on the Internet today don't support multicasting. The IETF has established a multicast backbone (MBONE) that allows multicast datagrams to be sent across routers that don't support multicast.

(continued)

> **About Broadcast Addresses** *(continued)*
>
> Multicasting is probably *the* biggest thing to happen on the Internet since the World Wide Web. It may even replace TV someday, though it may still have to rely heavily on reruns of *Gilligan's Island*. For more information, check in at these sites:
>
> http://www.ipmulticast.com
> http://www.best.com/~prince/techinfo/mbone.html

STANDARD BROADCAST ADDRESSES

To send broadcast datagrams, an application must use special broadcast addresses. There are three categories of broadcast addresses:

- *Local Broadcast.* The address "255.255.255.255" (defined in WINSOCK.H as INADDR_BROADCAST) designates a broadcast across a local network or subnetwork. Routers never forward packets with this address beyond the local network. If you are multihomed (attached to more than one network), these are typically only sent across the primary interface.

- *Net-Directed Broadcast.* An IP address made up of a standard network address, coupled with all bits set in the host portion, designates that the datagram should be sent to all systems attached to that particular network. The exact address depends on the network address class being used. Examples are "Net.255.255.255," "Net.B.255.255," and "Net.B.C.255." Routers usually forward this type of address, although they may be configured otherwise.

- *IP Multicast.* This is a special IP address in the Class D range. An address of this type will only work with network routers that support the Internet Group Management Protocol (IGMP). SO_BROADCAST does not have to be enabled to use multicast addresses.

SO_DEBUG (OPTIONAL)

The SO_DEBUG option is used to enable or disable debug output from the WinSock implementation itself. Even though support of this option is encouraged by the WinSock specification, it is not required. Neither the exact mechanism for generating the debug information nor the form it takes is defined in the specification. A WinSock vendor may implement this any way it wants.

None of the standard Microsoft WinSock implementations returns an error when enabling SO_DEBUG, but none of them actually supports it, either – it is simply ignored. This unique neutrality exists in the Winsock 1.1 implementations for

- Windows for Workgroups 3.11 (MS TCP/IP-32)
- Windows NT 3.1, 3.5, and 3.51
- Windows 95

WinSock 2 provides new debug and trace facilities. You can find documentation for this in the \SPECS\2\DBGSPEC.DOC file on the CD. There are also several affordable WinSock trace utilities available that are much more powerful and effective than using the SO_DEBUG option. You can find links to these utilities in the "Additional Resources" Appendix C of this book, as well as in the \LINKS\INDEX.HTM file on the CD.

SO_DONTLINGER

The SO_DONTLINGER option affects the behavior of the closesocket() function. When this option is enabled (which it is by default), closesocket() returns immediately — regardless of whether the socket is in blocking or nonblocking mode. When SO_DONTLINGER is disabled on a blocking socket (creating a double-negative: Don't linger = no), closesocket() will block until it completes negotiation with the peer system. When SO_DONTLINGER is disabled on a nonblocking socket, closesocket() will fail and WSAGetLastError() will return WSAEWOULDBLOCK.

Note: The best method for closing a socket is the one detailed in Chapter 2. You use shutdown() together with closesocket() to terminate the connection gracefully.

The SO_LINGER option (explained later in this section), which allows you to specify a value, effectively disables SO_DONTLINGER.

The SO_DONTLINGER option is only relevant to connection-oriented applications and isn't supported on datagram sockets.

SO_DONTROUTE (OPTIONAL)

When enabled, the SO_DONTROUTE option indicates that outgoing messages should bypass the standard *internal* routing tables. This option is only significant if the local machine is multihomed. For example, the PC I'm using to write this book is attached through a network card to a local intranet, and to the global Internet through a dial-up. SO_DONTROUTE is used to reroute messages before they leave the local machine, so that they use the interface with the shortest (or possibly only) route to the destination.

Normally, IP selects a network interface based on an entry in a routing table. When SO_DONTROUTE is enabled, packets are sent along the interface whose network number or full IP address matches the destination address.

The MSG_DONTROUTE flag, which can be used with send() and sendto(), has the same effect. Both the MSG_DONTROUTE flag and SO_DONTROUTE are optional in the WinSock specification. Therefore, WinSock vendors may choose to ignore either or both.

SO_ERROR

The SO_ERROR option retrieves and then clears the error status for the socket. SO_ERROR can only be used with getsockopt().

WinSock implementations *should* maintain error codes on both a per socket and per thread basis. Indeed, SO_ERROR was designed to return the per-socket error code rather than the thread-global error code returned by WSAGetLastError(). Unfortunately, the WinSock 1.1 specification didn't specify this precisely, and some WinSock 1.1 implementations return the thread-global error for this option. This can cause a problem if you rely on SO_ERROR to return an error code for a particular socket. Since the thread-global error changes each time a WinSock function is called, you may not get the error code for the socket specified in the call to getsockopt(). The WinSock 2 specification does specify the socket-based error code for this option, so all WinSock 2 service providers should return the correct error code.

SO_KEEPALIVE (OPTIONAL)

On WinSock implementations that support it, the SO_KEEPALIVE option enables the periodic transmission of messages on a connected socket.

The only way to determine if a connection to a peer is still valid at any point in time is to attempt to communicate with it. The periodic transmission of "keep-alive" messages was introduced as a method of determining whether a connection has been lost during long idle periods when no application data is being transmitted.

When using asynchronous mode with FD_CLOSE notification requested, WinSock will notify the application if a connection is dropped as the result of lost keep-alive messages. No matter what the mode, any WinSock calls made after the keep-alive mechanism has failed will return SOCKET_ERROR, with WSAGetLastError() set to either the WSAENETRESET or WSAENOTCONN error codes.

SO_KEEPALIVE is not supported on datagram sockets.

About the TCP Keep-Alive Mechanism

The WinSock specification states that implementations choosing to support the SO_KEEPALIVE option should conform to section 4.2.3.6 of RFC 1122, "Requirements for Internet Hosts – Communication Layers." However, saying that this RFC is not enthusiastic about the use of keep-alives is like saying some Native Americans weren't fond of Custer. It states that TCP implementations *may* provide support for keep-alives, but that the practice is "not universally accepted." It suggests that keep-alive packets only be used in server applications that might hang indefinitely as a result of a client's abruptly aborting a connection. Further, it suggests that keep-alives be sent at an interval of *two hours*! In other words, the keep-alive mechanism isn't recommended at all.

(continued)

> If you feel that your application needs some type of keep-alive mechanism, the best alternative is to implement it yourself in the application. Of course, this is only possible if you have access to the source code for both the server and the client applications.

SO_LINGER

The SO_LINGER option affects the behavior of the closesocket() function. This option is disabled by default. If you enable it, closesocket() will block until it completes negotiation with the peer system or until the specified period expires.

The SO_LINGER option is the only one listed in the WinSock 1.1 specification that does *not* use an integer as the buffer for the *optval* parameter. In a call to either getsockopt() or setsockopt() with SO_LINGER, the *optval* parameter must point to a *linger* structure:

```
struct linger {
        u_short l_onoff;
        u_short l_linger;
};
```

If the *l_onoff* field in the *linger* structure is zero (False), SO_LINGER is disabled; and if *l_onoff* is nonzero (True), SO_LINGER is enabled. The *l_linger* member specifies a value in seconds.

The following code enables SO_LINGER with a of 30 seconds:

```
struct linger Linger;
int nLevel = SOL_SOCKET;
int nOption = SO_LINGER;
int nOptionValLen = sizeof(struct linger);
int nRet;

Linger.l_onoff = TRUE;      // Enable SO_LINGER
Linger.l_linger = 30;       // Timeout in 30 seconds
nRet = getsockopt(theSocket,
                  nLevel,
                  nOption,
                  (char *)&Linger,
                  &nOptionValLen
                  );
```

- If SO_LINGER is enabled with *l_linger* set to zero, closesocket() will close the connection even if queued data is still buffered in the protocol stack waiting to be sent. This is called a "hard" or "abortive" close, because the virtual circuit between the two sockets is reset immediately and any buffered data is discarded. Any recv() call on the remote end of the circuit will fail with WSAECONNRESET.

- If SO_LINGER is enabled with a nonzero interval set in *l_linger*, closesocket() will attempt to gracefully close the connection with the peer system until the expires. On a blocking socket, the call to closesocket() will block during this time. If the circuit has not been closed by the time *l_linger* seconds have elapsed, then closesocket() will perform a hard close.

- If SO_LINGER is disabled (the default), closesocket() won't block, but WinSock will continue to try to gracefully close the connection in the background. Any data still buffered in the protocol stack awaiting transmission will be sent before the connection is closed if possible.

Again, the best method for closing a socket is the one detailed in Chapter 2: Use shutdown() together with closesocket() to terminate the connection gracefully.

The SO_LINGER option implicitly affects the SO_DONTLINGER option — if SO_LINGER is enabled then SO_DONTLINGER is disabled and vice versa.

SO_LINGER is only relevant to connection-oriented applications and isn't supported on datagram sockets.

SO_OOBINLINE

The SO_OOBINLINE option affects the way urgent data is received on a given socket. You can choose to receive urgent data out-of-band (outside the normal sequence of data) or in-band (sent along in the normal data stream).

When SO_OOBINLINE is disabled (the default), applications receive urgent data outside the normal data stream.

When SO_OOBINLINE is enabled, you must use the SIOCATMARK command with ioctlsocket(), as discussed in the next section, to determine if out-of-band data is available to be read in the normal data stream. If out-of-band data is waiting to be read and SO_OOBINLINE is enabled, a call to recv() or recvfrom() will only return the out-of-band data. Any normal data waiting to be received won't be read until all out-of-band data has been retrieved.

As mentioned in Chapter 4, you should avoid using out-of-band data in your applications if at all possible. But if you must, the preferred method is to receive out-of-band data with SO_OOBINLINE disabled (the default). In asynchronous mode, with SO_OOBINLINE disabled, you can receive notification of the arrival of out-of-band data by registering to receive the FD_OOB event. When an application receives the FD_OOB event message, a subsequent call to *recv()* or *recvfrom()* with the MSG_OOB flag set will return out-of-band data only.

If you enable SO_OOBINLINE, on the other hand, you *can't* use WSAAsyncSelect() to detect the arrival of out-of-band data — it will just arrive in the normal data stream. Note that in either case — with SO_OOBINLINE either enabled or disabled — recv() and recvfrom() will never return out-of-band and normal data in the same call.

SO_OOBINLINE is not supported on datagram sockets.

SO_RCVBUF (OPTIONAL)

The SO_RCVBUF option allows you to adjust the size of the receive buffer that is used for the socket by the protocol stack. An application may request a larger buffer size for high-volume connections, or a smaller size to limit the possible backlog of incoming data.

Some implementations may statically allocate the receive buffer and not support this option. Because this is an optional option, a call to setsockopt() may fail with WSAENOPROTOOPT or WSAEINVAL. Also, the call to setsockopt() may indicate success even though the implementation does not support SO_RCVBUF, or even if a buffer of the requested size could not be allocated. The protocol stack may also limit the maximum size through negotiation with the peer. Generally, you can deduce whether or not an implementation supports this option by first calling setsockopt() with a new value and then checking to see if getsockopt() returns the new buffer size.

This option and the SO_SNDBUF options (described later) can dramatically improve throughput on implementations that support them, but because they are optional your application should not rely on them.

SO_REUSEADDR

As explained in Chapter 2, the full address of a socket (its *sockaddr*) is made up of an IP address, a protocol such as TCP or UDP, and a port number. These three pieces of information *together* uniquely identify a socket. By default, a socket may not be bound to a local address which is already in use; bind() will fail with the WSAEADDRINUSE error. The SO_REUSEADDR option can be used to inform WinSock that a call to bind() on a socket should not be disallowed because the desired address is already in use by another socket.

The WinSock specification points out that since every connection is uniquely identified by the combination of local and remote addresses, it is possible to have two sockets bound to the same local address as long as their remote addresses are different. Even though this is true, use of this option still causes problems. Since bind() is the only WinSock function this option affects, we can assume that SO_REUSEADDR would probably be used in a server application. If two servers were each to bind() their sockets to the same address, the protocol stack would have no way of knowing which one should be allowed to accept() an incoming connection request.

> **Reusing Socket Addresses**
>
> The Berkeley sockets documentation states that the SO_REUSEADDR option allows multiple applications bound to the same port to receive the same *broadcast* datagrams. However, the WinSock specification does not explicitly say that this behavior must be supported by WinSock vendors.
>
> I ran some tests on the standard WinSock implementations that ship with Windows 95 and Windows NT and got the same results on both. By using the SO_REUSEADDR option, I successfully bound two servers to the same address and port, both using the same protocol (UDP). Then I sent a datagram from a client to that address and port to see what would happen.
>
> When I used the server's specific IP address from the client, only one server received the datagram. The server that first called bind() received the datagram — the other server received nothing. However, when I used the local broadcast address (INADDR_BROADCAST), *both* servers received the datagram.
>
> Since the WinSock specification doesn't specifically require support of this feature, you can't rely on it to work this way on all implementations. However, the standard WinSock implementations shipped with Windows do, in fact, support this behavior.

SO_SNDBUF (OPTIONAL)
The SO_SNDBUF option allows you to adjust the size of the send buffer that is used for the socket by the protocol stack. An application may request a larger buffer size for high-volume connections.

Some implementations may statically allocate the send buffer for each socket and not support this option. Because this is an optional option, a call to setsockopt() may fail with WSAENOPROTOOPT or WSAEINVAL. In addition, the call to setsockopt() may indicate success even though the implementation does not support the option, or even if a buffer of the requested size could not be allocated. Generally, you can deduce whether or not an implementation supports this option by first calling setsockopt() with a new value and then checking to see if getsockopt() returns the new buffer size.

This option and the SO_RCVBUF options can dramatically improve throughput on implementations that support them, but because they are optional your application should not rely on them.

SO_TYPE
The SO_TYPE option can be used with getsockopt() to determine a socket's type. It *cannot* be used with setsockopt() to change the socket's type. The option value returned from getsockopt() corresponds to the *type* value used in a call to the socket() function. This is either SOCK_STREAM, SOCK_DGRAM or SOCK_RAW on TCP/IP implementations.

TCP_NODELAY

Of all the socket options available in both WinSock 1.1 and 2, TCP_NODELAY is the only one that affects the transport protocol layer. It uses IPPROTO_TCP as the value of the *level* parameter where all of the other options use the SOL_SOCKET level.

The TCP_NODELAY option *enables or disables* the Nagle algorithm. Enabling TCP_NODELAY *disables* the Nagle algorithm.

Note: The *Nagle algorithm* was introduced by John Nagle in RFC 896 as a means of controlling network congestion. It reduces the number of packets sent by some applications, by buffering small packets and joining them together into a larger packet before transmitting them from the local protocol stack.

A large amount of overhead can be incurred when very small amounts of data are sent over a TCP/IP network. For example, one byte of data sent through a TCP connection is sent inside a 14-byte TCP header and a 20-byte IP header. That's 35 bytes of data sent across the network to transmit just one byte of application data! And this doesn't include the transport media header – that's another 14 bytes on Ethernet.

The Nagle algorithm delays sending packets if any previously transmitted data on the connection remains unacknowledged. The only way data will be sent before any outstanding data is acknowledged is if the maximum segment size (MSS) is reached. Applications that transmit very small packets and expect the data to be sent immediately can be adversely affected by the Nagle algorithm. The classic case is Telnet applications that routinely transmit a single keyboard character typed by the end-user. Some specialized applications may choose to enable TCP_NODELAY.

It should be noted that disabling the Nagle algorithm and sending many small packets on a busy network can have a profoundly negative effect on both network congestion and network performance and should be avoided if at all possible. For the vast majority of applications, the Nagle algorithm actually *increases* application performance by lessening the data-to-header overhead ratio.

The WinSock specification "highly recommends" that WinSock vendors enable the Nagle algorithm by default (TCP_NODELAY *disabled*), and the official default value for this option is False. However, some WinSock implementations may enable TCP_NODELAY by default. TCP applications should check this value and, if possible, disable the TCP_NODELAY option.

Socket Control

In the Berkeley API, a socket descriptor is always the same thing as a file handle, and the standard C run-time function ioctl() is used to control various aspects of a socket's operation. Socket descriptors aren't necessarily the same thing as file handles under WinSock – each vendor is free to use any design they wish in implementing socket descriptors. Since socket descriptors aren't necessarily the same thing as file handles, WinSock includes a function not found in the Berkeley API called ioctlsocket().

The ioctlsocket() Function

The ioctlsocket() function controls the I/O mode of a socket. Through the use of predefined commands, it is used to set or retrieve operating parameters associated with a socket's input and output. Here is the function prototype for ioctlsocket():

```
int PASCAL FAR ioctlsocket(SOCKET s, long cmd, u_long FAR
    *argp);
```

The first parameter is the socket to be controlled, the second is one of three predefined commands, and the third parameter is a pointer to a command specific value.

The following sections describe commands supported by the ioctlsocket() function.

FIONBIO

By default, when a socket is created with the socket() function, it operates in blocking mode. As mentioned in Chapter 3, the FIONBIO command can be used with ioctlsocket() to place a socket in nonblocking mode. The *argp* parameter points to an unsigned long, which is nonzero to make the socket nonblocking or zero to make the socket blocking again.

Note: Some WinSock implementations don't allow a nonblocking socket to be set back to blocking mode. Once a socket is set to nonblocking mode, it should never be set back to blocking mode.

The following example demonstrates how to explicitly make a socket nonblocking:

```
// Create a socket and make it nonblocking
SOCKET MySocket;
u_long arg;          // Argument for ioctlsocket()
int nRet;            // Return code

// Create a socket (Blocking by default)
MySocket = socket(af, type, protocol);
if (MySocket == INVALID_SOCKET)
{
    // Handle error here
    return;
}
// Make the socket nonblocking
arg = 1L;
nRet = ioctlsocket(MySocket, FIONBIO, &arg);
if (nRet == SOCKET_ERROR)
{
    // Handle error here
    return;
}
// Socket is now nonblocking
```

WSAAsyncSelect() automatically sets a socket to nonblocking mode. So, in asynchronous mode there is no need to use ioctlsocket() and FIONBIO to make the socket nonblocking. If WSAAsyncSelect() has been issued on a socket, then any attempt to use ioctlsocket() to set the socket back to blocking mode will fail and WSAGetLastError() will return WSAEINVAL.

You *may* be able to set a socket that has been used in asynchronous mode back to blocking mode by first canceling asynchronous notifications (by calling WSAAsyncSelect() with the *lEvent* parameter set to zero) and then calling ioctlsocket() with FIONBIO and *arg* set to zero.

FIONREAD

The FIONREAD command can be used to determine the amount of data that the socket currently has waiting to be read: the number of bytes still buffered in the protocol stack. On return from ioctlsocket(), the long pointed to by *argp* will contain the result as shown here:

```
u_long arg;          // Argument for ioctlsocket()
int nRet;            // Return code

nRet = ioctlsocket(theSocket, FIONREAD, &arg);
if (nRet == SOCKET_ERROR)
{
   // Handle error here
   return;
}
// arg now equals the number of bytes waiting to be read
```

The number returned by using FIONREAD depends on the socket type. For stream sockets (SOCK_STREAM), FIONREAD returns the total number of bytes waiting to be read for the socket. For datagram sockets (SOCK_DGRAM), the number returned indicates the size of the first datagram queued on the socket even if more than one datagram is waiting to be retrieved.

Because stream sockets don't preserve record boundaries, some application designers attempt to use this command to delay a call to recv() until a predetermined number of bytes are available to be read. They poll with FIONREAD until an entire record has arrived and then call recv() to read the data. This scheme is not recommended. A deadlock situation can arise from using this method. If the protocol stack buffers become filled, WinSock will wait for the application to recv() some of the data before accepting anything else from the peer system. If, at the same time, the application is waiting for more data to arrive, WinSock and the application are then both locked, waiting for the other to take some action.

The best method to use is to not use FIONREAD at all. Simply read data from WinSock as it becomes available and buffer it internally in the application. Then a parsing routine (like the one illustrated in the CheckMail application in Chapter 4) can be used to break the data into records.

SIOCATMARK

The SIOCATMARK command can be used to determine if out-of-band data is waiting to be read. This command only applies to stream sockets that have been configured to receive urgent or expedited data in the normal data stream (with the SO_OOBINLINE socket option described previously in this chapter).

For some protocols, the position of the OOB data in the normal data stream is meaningful. Such applications may therefore choose to receive OOB data in-line, and rely on the WinSock implementation to maintain a logical "mark" indicating where in the stream OOB data is present. The SIOCATMARK indicates whether or not there is any unread data preceding this mark. For example, this might be used to discard all information received prior to the OOB data.

The return value from using the SIOCATMARK command is probably not what you would expect. It returns True if there is *no* out-of-band data waiting to be read and False if there *is*. If OOB data is waiting to be read, the application should then call recv() with the MSG_OOB flag to receive it, as shown here:

```
u_long arg;          // Argument for ioctlsocket()
int nRet;            // Return code
int nBytesRead;

// Check for OOB data
nRet = ioctlsocket(theSocket, SIOCATMARK, &arg);
// Check return code
if (nRet == SOCKET_ERROR)
{
   // Handle error here
   return;
}
// Check return value
if (arg == FALSE)
{
   // There is OOB data waiting to be read
   nBytesRead = recv(theSocket, BufferPointer, BufferLen, MSG_OOB);
   if (nBytesRead == SOCKET_ERROR)
   {
      // Handle error
      return;
   }
   // Buffer contains OOB data
}
```

Note that recv() and recvfrom() will never mix out-of-band with normal data in the same function call.

Raw Sockets

In the Berkeley API, a *raw* socket is a socket that allows the lowest level of access to the underlying transport protocols. Just as datagram sockets allow access to UDP, and stream sockets allow access to TCP, raw sockets can be used to directly access IP and ICMP. By far the most common use of raw sockets is in the creation of Ping and TraceRoute utilities. We'll talk more about those later in this section.

The WinSock 1.1 specification leaves raw-socket support optional – it may or may not be implemented by the vendor. Some vendors do provide raw socket support in their WinSock 1.1 implementations. Raw sockets are supported by WinSock 2.

The most notable exception among vendors supporting raw sockets is Microsoft. Microsoft's WinSock 2 implementations for NT4 and Windows 95 do support raw sockets, but none of their WinSock version 1.1 implementations do. Still, there is a way to create low-level utilities like Ping with the Microsoft 1.1 implementations, as you'll see later in this chapter.

SOCK_RAW

To create a raw socket, you specify SOCK_RAW for the *type* parameter in a call to socket() just as you normally use SOCK_STREAM or SOCK_DGRAM. The Berkeley API allowed raw sockets to directly access IP by creating a socket and specifying IPPROTO_IP in the call to socket(). This isn't supported on any of the most popular WinSock implementations. Some WinSocks do allow access to ICMP, though, by creating a socket and specifying IPPROTO_ICMP, like this:

```
// Create a RAW ICMP socket
SOCKET rawSocket;

rawSocket = socket(AF_INET, SOCK_RAW, IPPROTO_ICMP);
if (rawSocket == INVALID_SOCKET)
{
   if (WSAGetLastError() == WSAESOCKTNOSUPPORT)
   {
       // Raw sockets is not supported.
   }
   // Handle other errors here
  return;
}
// Raw socket opened successfully
```

This code example also demonstrates the best way to determine if a WINSOCK.DLL supports raw sockets. If an attempt to create a raw socket fails and WSAGetLastError() returns the WSAESOCKTNOSUPPORT error, then the WinSock in use doesn't support raw sockets.

Access to a raw socket using ICMP gives an application all it needs to create a Ping utility.

Writing a Ping Utility

I've never seen a TCP/IP protocol stack distribution that didn't include a Ping utility. So why create another one? I have no idea, but from the number of messages on Usenet concerning Ping source code, it seems everyone needs to write a Ping program. Actually, adding Ping capability to a network program might be useful to the end-user. If the WinSock in use supports raw sockets, a failing application might be able to provide useful diagnostic information about the cause of the error.

Ping is an invaluable tool for every network administrator's toolbox. It enables easy determination of whether a connection to some distant machine is possible and how long the round-trip takes.

> ### Ping's History
>
> Mike Muuss is the original author of Ping. He says he wrote it one evening in 1983 using Berkeley sockets on BSD UNIX to diagnose odd behavior on the network he was trying to use. Inspired by the principle of echo location, he says he named the now famous utility after the sound that a sonar makes.

Ping works by sending an ICMP echo request packet to a distant IP address. The TCP/IP stack on the other end will automatically send back an echo reply containing the same data that was in the request. Typical Ping applications repeat this process several times to ensure a connection and calculate the time elapsed form sending the echo request to receiving the echo reply. An application can send multiple echo requests and then use the ICMP header's sequence field to match requests to replies.

Listing 5-1 is the source code for a very simple Ping application. This program will work on any WinSock 2 implementation and several vendors' WinSock 1.1 offerings. It will *not* work on any of the standard Microsoft version 1.1 WINSOCK.DLLs shipped with Windows. A Ping application that will work with Microsoft's 1.1 WinSock implementations is listed in the upcoming section.

Listing 5-1 PING.C

```
//
// PING.C - Ping program using ICMP and RAW Sockets
//

#include <stdio.h>
#include <stdlib.h>
#include <winsock.h>

#include "ping.h"

// Internal Functions
void Ping(LPCSTR pstrHost);
void ReportError(LPCSTR pstrFrom);
int  WaitForEchoReply(SOCKET s);
USHORT InternetChecksum(PUSHORT pBuf, int nLen);
```

```
// ICMP Echo Request/Reply functions
int     SendEchoRequest(SOCKET, LPSOCKADDR_IN);
DWORD   RecvEchoReply(SOCKET, LPSOCKADDR_IN, u_char *);


// main()
void main(int argc, char **argv)
{
    WSADATA wsaData;
    WORD wVersionRequested = MAKEWORD(1,1);
    int nRet;

    // Check arguments
    if (argc != 2)
    {
        fprintf(stderr,"\nUsage: ping hostname\n");
        return;
    }

    // Init WinSock
    nRet = WSAStartup(wVersionRequested, &wsaData);
    if (nRet)
    {
        fprintf(stderr,"\nError initializing WinSock\n");
        return;
    }

    // Check version
    if (wsaData.wVersion != wVersionRequested)
    {
        fprintf(stderr,"\nWinSock version not supported\n");
        return;
    }

    // Go do the ping
    Ping(argv[1]);

    // Free WinSock
    WSACleanup();
}


// Ping()
// Calls SendEchoRequest() and
// RecvEchoReply() and prints results
void Ping(LPCSTR pstrHost)
{
    SOCKET      rawSocket;
    LPHOSTENT   lpHost;
    struct      sockaddr_in saDest;
    struct      sockaddr_in saSrc;
    DWORD       dwTimeSent;
    DWORD       dwElapsed;
```

```c
    u_char      cTTL;
    int         nLoop;
    int         nRet;

    // Create a Raw socket
    rawSocket = socket(AF_INET, SOCK_RAW, IPPROTO_ICMP);
    if (rawSocket == SOCKET_ERROR)
    {
        ReportError("socket()");
        return;
    }

    // Lookup host
    lpHost = gethostbyname(pstrHost);
    if (lpHost == NULL)
    {
        fprintf(stderr,"\nHost not found: %s\n", pstrHost);
        return;
    }

    // Setup destination socket address
    saDest.sin_addr.s_addr = *((u_long FAR *) (lpHost->h_addr));
    saDest.sin_family = AF_INET;
    saDest.sin_port = 0;

    // Tell the user what we're doing
    printf("\nPinging %s [%s] with %d bytes of data:\n",
            pstrHost,
            inet_ntoa(saDest.sin_addr),
            REQ_DATASIZE);

    // Ping multiple times
    for (nLoop = 0; nLoop < 4; nLoop++)
    {
        // Send ICMP echo request
        SendEchoRequest(rawSocket, &saDest);

        // Use select() to wait for data to be received
        nRet = WaitForEchoReply(rawSocket);
        if (nRet == SOCKET_ERROR)
        {
            ReportError("select()");
            break;
        }
        if (!nRet)
        {
            printf("\nTimeOut");
            break;
        }

        // Receive reply
        dwTimeSent = RecvEchoReply(rawSocket, &saSrc, &cTTL);
```

Chapter 5: Optional Features   153

```c
        // Calculate elapsed time
        dwElapsed = GetTickCount() - dwTimeSent;
        printf("\nReply from: %s: bytes=%d time=%ldms TTL=%d",
               inet_ntoa(saSrc.sin_addr),
               REQ_DATASIZE,
               dwElapsed,
               cTTL);
    }
    printf("\n");
    nRet = closesocket(rawSocket);
    if (nRet == SOCKET_ERROR)
        ReportError("closesocket()");
}


// SendEchoRequest()
// Fill in echo request header
// and send to destination
int SendEchoRequest(SOCKET s,LPSOCKADDR_IN lpstToAddr)
{
    static ECHOREQUEST echoReq;
    static nId = 1;
    static nSeq = 1;
    int nRet;

    // Fill in echo request
    echoReq.icmpHdr.Type       = ICMP_ECHOREQ;
    echoReq.icmpHdr.Code       = 0;
    echoReq.icmpHdr.Checksum   = 0;
    echoReq.icmpHdr.ID         = nId++;
    echoReq.icmpHdr.Seq        = nSeq++;

    // Fill in some data to send
    for (nRet = 0; nRet < REQ_DATASIZE; nRet++)
        echoReq.cData[nRet] = ' '+nRet;

    // Save tick count when sent
    echoReq.dwTime             = GetTickCount();

    // Put data in packet and compute checksum
    echoReq.icmpHdr.Checksum = InternetChecksum(
                                     (u_short *)&echoReq,
                                     sizeof(ECHOREQUEST));

    // Send the echo request
    nRet = sendto(s,                        // socket
                  (LPSTR)&echoReq,          // buffer
                  sizeof(ECHOREQUEST),
                  0,                        // flags
                  (LPSOCKADDR)lpstToAddr,   // destination
                  sizeof(SOCKADDR_IN));     // address length

    if (nRet == SOCKET_ERROR)
```

```
            ReportError("sendto()");
        return (nRet);
}


// RecvEchoReply()
// Receive incoming data
// and parse out fields
DWORD RecvEchoReply(SOCKET s, LPSOCKADDR_IN lpsaFrom, u_char *pTTL)
{
    ECHOREPLY echoReply;
    int nRet;
    int nAddrLen = sizeof(struct sockaddr_in);

    // Receive the echo reply
    nRet = recvfrom(s,                         // socket
                    (LPSTR)&echoReply,         // buffer
                    sizeof(ECHOREPLY),         // size of buffer
                    0,                         // flags
                    (LPSOCKADDR)lpsaFrom,      // From address
                    &nAddrLen);                // pointer to address len

    // Check return value
    if (nRet == SOCKET_ERROR)
        ReportError("recvfrom()");

    // return time sent and IP TTL
    *pTTL = echoReply.ipHdr.TTL;
    return(echoReply.echoRequest.dwTime);
}

// What happened?
void ReportError(LPCSTR pWhere)
{
    fprintf(stderr,"\n%s error: %d\n",
        WSAGetLastError());
}


// WaitForEchoReply()
// Use select() to determine when
// data is waiting to be read
int WaitForEchoReply(SOCKET s)
{
    struct timeval Timeout;
    fd_set readfds;

    readfds.fd_count = 1;
    readfds.fd_array[0] = s;
    Timeout.tv_sec = 5;
    Timeout.tv_usec = 0;

    return(select(1, &readfds, NULL, NULL, &Timeout));
}
```

```
//
// InternetChecksum() As per RFC 791, "Internet Protocol"
//
// The one's complement of the one's complement sum of
// all 16 bit words.
//
USHORT InternetChecksum(PUSHORT pBuf, int nLen)
{
    int nSum = 0;

    while(nLen > 0)
    {
        nSum += (*pBuf++);
        nLen -= 2;
    }

    nSum = (nSum > 16) + (nSum & 0xffff);
    nSum += (nSum > 16);
    return(~nSum);
}
```

Microsoft's Proprietary ICMP API

None of the standard Microsoft WinSock 1.1 implementations that shipped with Windows NT 3.*x* and Windows 95 support raw sockets. Instead, Microsoft uses a private, proprietary interface for ICMP services through ICMP.DLL.

The Microsoft Knowledge Base article Q139459, "Programatically Using ICMP Echo Request and Reply (Ping)" says that it is possible to use their ICMP services, and that documentation is available in the \ICMP directory of the Win32 SDK CD. The Knowledge Base article as well as the README.TXT file contained on the SDK CD both warn against using this API, however, and point out that it is a temporary solution to be used only until WinSock 2 is available. Nonetheless, Microsoft currently still supports the proprietary ICMP API in the WinSock 2 that shipped with NT 4.

Still, Microsoft doesn't consider the functions exported from ICMP.DLL to be part of the Win32 API, and it's a good bet that this it will eventually be dropped at some point in the future.

With all those warnings stated, let's look at the functions contained in ICMP.DLL and how they can be used.

WRITING A PING UTILITY USING ICMP.DLL

There are three functions in ICMP.DLL that can be used to provide low-level ICMP services. All of the functions work in blocking mode, so if you are going to create a GUI application using these functions, you should create a worker thread and do all the work there. (We'll look at multithreading in Part IV of this book.)

To begin, you first create a context handle with the IcmpCreateFile() function:

```
HANDLE WINAPI IcmpCreateFile(VOID);
```

IcmpCreateFile() takes no parameters and returns a HANDLE. It returns INVALID_HANDLE if it fails; any other value indicates success. The HANDLE returned from this function must be closed before the application exits using the IcmpCloseHandle() function:

```
BOOL WINAPI IcmpCloseHandle(HANDLE IcmpHandle);
```

IcmpCloseHandle accepts one parameter — the handle returned from IcmpCreateFile() — and returns True if it succeeds or False if it fails.

Once a context handle has been obtained from IcmpCreateFile(), echo requests can be sent with the IcmpSendEcho() function: The IcmpSendEcho() function sends an ICMP echo request to the specified destination IP address and returns any replies received within the *Timeout* value specified.

```
DWORD WINAPI IcmpSendEcho(
                          HANDLE IcmpHandle,
                          DWORD DestAddress,
                          LPVOID RequestData,
                          WORD RequestSize,
                          LPIPINFO RequestOptns,
                          LPVOID ReplyBuffer,
                          DWORD ReplySize,
                          DWORD Timeout
                         );
```

Parameter	Description
IcmpHandle	The handle returned from the call to IcmpCreateFile().
DestAddress	The destination IP address in network order.
RequestData	A pointer to an echo request buffer to send.
RequestSize	Length of the echo request buffer in bytes.
RequestOptions	A pointer to a buffer specifying echo request options.
ReplyBuffer	A pointer to an echo reply buffer.
ReplySize	Length of the reply buffer in bytes.
Timeout	Time in milliseconds to wait before canceling reply.

The source for a very simple Ping application using ICMP.DLL is in Listing 5-2. This program will work on the standard Microsoft version 1.1 WINSOCK.DLLs shipped with Windows 95 and Windows NT 3.x. Rather than using a .LIB file to

Chapter 5: Optional Features   157

import the functions from ICMP.DLL, the program dynamically loads the library at run-time and finds pointers to the required functions with GetProcAddress().

Listing 5-2 PINGI.C

```c
//
// PingI.c—Simple ping program using the proprietary
//          Microsoft ICMP API
//

#include <windows.h>
#include <winsock.h>
#include <stdio.h>
#include <string.h>

// Echo request options
typedef struct tagIPINFO
{
    u_char Ttl;                // Time To Live
    u_char Tos;                // Type Of Service
    u_char IPFlags;            // IP flags
    u_char OptSize;            // Size of options data
    u_char FAR *Options;       // Options data buffer
}IPINFO, *PIPINFO;

// Echo reply structure
typedef struct tagICMPECHO
{
    u_long Source;             // Source address
    u_long Status;             // IP status
    u_long RTTime;             // Round trip time in milliseconds
    u_short DataSize;          // Reply data size
    u_short Reserved;          // Unknown
    void FAR *pData;           // Reply data buffer
    IPINFO  ipInfo;            // Reply options
}ICMPECHO, *PICMPECHO;

// ICMP.DLL Export Function Pointers
HANDLE (WINAPI *pIcmpCreateFile)(VOID);
BOOL (WINAPI *pIcmpCloseHandle)(HANDLE);
DWORD (WINAPI *pIcmpSendEcho)
    (HANDLE,DWORD,LPVOID,WORD,PIPINFO,LPVOID,DWORD,DWORD);

// main()
void main(int argc, char **argv)
{
    WSADATA wsaData;           // WSADATA
    ICMPECHO icmpEcho;         // ICMP Echo reply buffer
    HANDLE hndlIcmp;           // LoadLibrary() handle to ICMP.DLL
    HANDLE hndlFile;           // Handle for IcmpCreateFile()
    LPHOSTENT pHost;           // Pointer to host entry structure
```

Part II: The WinSock 1.1 API

```c
    struct in_addr iaDest;       // Internet address structure
    DWORD *dwAddress;            // IP Address
    IPINFO ipInfo;               // IP Options structure
    int nRet;                    // General use return code
    DWORD dwRet;                 // DWORD return code
    int x;

    // Check arguments
    if (argc != 2)
    {
        fprintf(stderr,"\nSyntax: pingi HostNameOrIPAddress\n");
        return;
    }

    // Dynamically load the ICMP.DLL
    hndlIcmp = LoadLibrary("ICMP.DLL");
    if (hndlIcmp == NULL)
    {
        fprintf(stderr,"\nCould not load ICMP.DLL\n");
        return;
    }
    // Retrieve ICMP function pointers
    pIcmpCreateFile = (HANDLE (WINAPI *)(void))
        GetProcAddress(hndlIcmp,"IcmpCreateFile");
    pIcmpCloseHandle = (BOOL (WINAPI *)(HANDLE))
        GetProcAddress(hndlIcmp,"IcmpCloseHandle");
    pIcmpSendEcho = (DWORD (WINAPI *)
        (HANDLE,DWORD,LPVOID,WORD,PIPINFO,LPVOID,DWORD,DWORD))
        GetProcAddress(hndlIcmp,"IcmpSendEcho");
    // Check all the function pointers
    if (pIcmpCreateFile == NULL    ||
        pIcmpCloseHandle == NULL   ||
        pIcmpSendEcho == NULL)
    {
        fprintf(stderr,"\nError getting ICMP proc address\n");
        FreeLibrary(hndlIcmp);
        return;
    }

    // Init WinSock
    nRet = WSAStartup(0x0101, &wsaData );
    if (nRet)
    {
        fprintf(stderr,"\nWSAStartup() error: %d\n", nRet);
        WSACleanup();
        FreeLibrary(hndlIcmp);
        return;
    }
    // Check WinSock version
    if (0x0101 != wsaData.wVersion)
    {
        fprintf(stderr,"\nWinSock version 1.1 not supported\n");
        WSACleanup();
```

```
        FreeLibrary(hndlIcmp);
        return;
}

// Lookup destination
// Use inet_addr() to determine if we're dealing with a name
// or an address
iaDest.s_addr = inet_addr(argv[1]);
if (iaDest.s_addr == INADDR_NONE)
    pHost = gethostbyname(argv[1]);
else
    pHost = gethostbyaddr((const char *)&iaDest,
                  sizeof(struct in_addr), AF_INET);
if (pHost == NULL)
{
    fprintf(stderr, "\n%s not found\n", argv[1]);
    WSACleanup();
    FreeLibrary(hndlIcmp);
    return;
}

// Tell the user what we're doing
printf("\nPinging %s [%s]", pHost->h_name,
        inet_ntoa((*(LPIN_ADDR)pHost->h_addr_list[0])));

// Copy the IP address
dwAddress = (DWORD *)(*pHost->h_addr_list);

// Get an ICMP echo request handle
hndlFile = pIcmpCreateFile();

// Ping 4 times
for (x = 0; x < 4; x++)
{
    // Set some reasonable default values
    ipInfo.Ttl = 255;
    ipInfo.Tos = 0;
    ipInfo.IPFlags = 0;
    ipInfo.OptSize = 0;
    ipInfo.Options = NULL;
    //icmpEcho.ipInfo.Ttl = 256;
    // Reqest an ICMP echo
    dwRet = pIcmpSendEcho(
        hndlFile,       // Handle from IcmpCreateFile()
        *dwAddress,     // Destination IP address
        NULL,           // Pointer to buffer to send
        0,              // Size of buffer in bytes
        &ipInfo,        // Request options
        &icmpEcho,      // Reply buffer
        sizeof(struct tagICMPECHO),
        5000);          // Time to wait in milliseconds
    // Print the results
    iaDest.s_addr = icmpEcho.Source;
```

```
            printf("\nReply from %s  Time=%ldms   TTL=%d",
                    inet_ntoa(iaDest),
                    icmpEcho.RTTime,
                    icmpEcho.ipInfo.Ttl);
            if (icmpEcho.Status)
            {
                printf("\nError: icmpEcho.Status=%ld",
                    icmpEcho.Status);
                break;
            }
        }
        printf("\n");
        // Close the echo request file handle
        pIcmpCloseHandle(hndlFile);
        FreeLibrary(hndlIcmp);
        WSACleanup();
}
```

Microsoft-Specific Extensions

As mentioned earlier in this chapter, the WinSock specification suggests that vendors may add functionality to a WINSOCK.DLL by adding their own private API in a range of ordinal values set aside for this. WSOCK32.DLL, which ships with Windows NT 3.*x* and Windows 95, contains just such a private API. Unlike the ICMP API discussed earlier, documentation for the functions in the Microsoft version of WSOCK32.DLL is included along with the rest of the Win32 API.

Even though these functions are more formally supported by Microsoft, an application that uses the Microsoft-specific extension will almost certainly not work correctly on another vendor's TCP/IP stack. There is a way to determine if these extension functions are available at run-time and only rely on their use if they are available.

To do this, rather than linking with an import library at build time, an application can use the GetProcAddress() function to retrieve pointers to these nonstandard functions and determine if they are available. The PINGI.C listing from the previous section demonstrates how to do this.

Complete coverage of all of the functionality available in this private API could fill another book this size, so I'm just going to point out the names of the functions and briefly describe the services they provide. See the Win32 API documentation for full details. Also, you can find several sample programs that use this API by searching the Knowledge Base at www.microsoft.com.

Support for Additional Transport Protocols

As stated earlier, the WinSock 1.1 specification focused only on the TCP/IP protocol suite. However, the sockets paradigm is abstract enough to support almost any network protocol. Microsoft added support for AppleTalk, IPX/SPX, ISO TP4, and NetBEUI to its WSOCK32.DLL.

To support these protocols, Microsoft added new address-family constants, socket type definitions, and other related structures in the following header files:

Protocol	Header File
AppleTalk	ATALKWSH.H
ISO TP4	WSHISOTP.H
Novell IPX/SPX	WSIPX.H and WSNWLINK.H
NetBEUI	WSNETBS.H

Microsoft also developed an API for registering services and resolving names for these other protocols, called "Registration and Resolution" (RNR). It is very similar to the WinSock 2 architecture. The following Microsoft-specific functions were added to provide service registration and name-resolution capabilities:

EnumProtocols()	Obtains information about a specified set of network protocols that are active on a local host.
GetAddressByName()	Queries a name space, or a set of default name spaces, to obtain network address information for a specified network service.
GetNameByType()	Obtains the name of a network service specified by its service type.
GetService()	Obtains information about a network service in the context of a set of default name spaces or a specified name space.
GetTypeByName()	Obtains a service-type, globally unique identifier (GUID) for a network service specified by name.
SetService()	Registers or unregisters a network service within one or more name spaces.

Performance Improvement

In the Win32 environment (Windows 95 and Windows NT), the standard I/O functions can be used with sockets. If used properly, they can dramatically improve throughput. The socket descriptor must be opened in the normal way with one of the WinSock functions – socket() or accept() – but it can then be used with I/O functions in place of the file handle parameter. The ReadFile(), ReadFileEx(), WriteFile(), and WriteFileEx() functions will all accept a socket descriptor for the file handle parameter, and they all support asynchronous (overlapped) operation. Note however, that there is no way to transfer out-of-band data using these functions.

The following Microsoft-specific functions were added to provide improved application performance:

AcceptEx()	Accepts a new connection, returns the local and remote address, and receives the first block of data sent by the client application.
GetAcceptExSockaddrs()	Parses the data obtained from a call to the AcceptEx() function and passes the local and remote addresses to a SOCKADDR structure.
TransmitFile()	Transmits file data over a connected socket handle. This function uses the operating system's cache manager to retrieve the file data, and provides high-performance file transfer over sockets.
WSARecvEx()	Performs the same functionality as the recv() function, but allows receipt of the MSG_PARTIAL flag. For protocols that support it, the indication of this flag means that the supplied buffer is not large enough to hold the entire record and that a partial record is being returned (message-boundaries are not being preserved). The entire record can be retrieved by calling WSARecvEx() again with a larger buffer.

Multicast

Microsoft's WSOCK32.DLL also recognizes the following socket options that are used for IP multicast:

IP_ADD_MEMBERSHIP	IP_DEFAULT_MULTICAST_LOOP
IP_DEFAULT_MULTICAST_TTL	IP_DONTFRAGMENT
IP_DROP_MEMBERSHIP	IP_MAX_MEMBERSHIPS
IP_MULTICAST_IF	IP_MULTICAST_LOOP
IP_MULTICAST_TTL	

Summary

There is a substantial amount of functionality to be found in the optional features and vendor-specific extensions of the standard WinSock API. However, relying on the existence of these optional features comes at the expense of portability. It's up to you to decide whether the additional functionality is worth restricting your applications to specific WinSock providers.

Many of the features discussed in this chapter are now an official part of the WinSock 2 specification – most notably, transports other than TCP/IP, raw sockets, and multicast. If WinSock 2 is available, the methods outlined in Part III of this book should be used rather than the extensions discussed here.

Chapter 6

MFC Socket Classes

IN THIS CHAPTER
The Microsoft Foundation Classes include support for WinSock. In this chapter we look at the functionality available in the CSocket and CAsyncSocket classes and discuss the advantages and disadvantages of their use. We cover the following topics:

- Versions of the Microsoft Foundation Classes (MFC)
- Deriving from the CAsyncSocket class
- Using the CSocket class
- Using archives with sockets
- Extending the CSocket class

UP TO THIS POINT, we've covered all of the functionality that is available in WinSock 1.1. We're going to switch gears a little here and discuss the sockets support provided by the Microsoft Foundation Class (MFC) Library.

I routinely read the articles posted in the various Usenet newsgroups. (By the way, a list of these newsgroups is provided in Appendix C, "Additional Resources.") As part of my research for this book, I tracked the number of questions asked about various WinSock subjects. There were so many questions regarding the MFC socket classes that I decided to devote a chapter to them here.

The Microsoft Foundation Class Library

The MFC Library is a large set of C++ classes that encapsulates most of the Windows API. Currently about 150 classes provide access in C++ form to windows, dialog boxes, GDI objects and other standard Windows elements. The library also includes application framework classes that provide the basic requirements of a Windows application. Using these classes you can write very little code and yet create complete, fully functioning Windows programs.

MFC is fast becoming *the* standard set of C++ classes used for writing Windows applications. This has been fueled by Microsoft's decision to license MFC to other compiler vendors. MFC currently comes with the following compilers:

- Microsoft Visual C++
- Borland C++
- Watcom C++
- Symantec C++

MFC is also striving to become a real multiplatform development environment. Microsoft distributes highly compatible versions of MFC for Intel, Macintosh, Alpha, and MIPS platforms. Several vendors make MFC-compliant X-Windows libraries and Motif/MFC cross-platform products available.

> ### About Windows C++ Class Libraries
>
> Borland was the first to release a commercial set of C++ classes for Windows programming: the Object Windows Library (OWL). Microsoft soon followed with the first release of MFC. The debate raged for years as loyal devotees of each class library espoused the merits of their brand. These were dark days for me indeed, because on many occasions the program code I wanted to steal from a magazine or off the Internet was written with OWL rather than MFC.
>
> The top contenders for Windows class library dominance were always limited to just Microsoft and Borland. Borland's OWL was (and is) an excellent class library with many advantages over MFC. However, when I saw that Borland had licensed MFC for release with its C++ compiler, I assumed the war was over.

MFC Versions

Since its initial release, MFC has been regularly upgraded through the addition of new classes, methods, and bug fixes for previous versions. There are two distinctly different releases of MFC: 16-bit and 32-bit. The 16-bit implementation makes calls to the standard 16-bit Windows API and runs on Windows 3.1 and Windows for Workgroups. The 32-bit release uses the Win32 API and only runs on Windows NT and Windows 95. (Programs written with a subset of Win32 can run on Windows 3.1 with Win32s.)

Each release of MFC on either platform is assigned a version number. The _MFC_VER constant is defined near the top of AFXVER_.H and looks something like this:

```
#define _MFC_VER 0x0253 // Microsoft Foundation Classes 2.53
```

Note that the MFC version is not necessarily the same as the Visual C++ version number. The latest versions currently available (at the time of this writing) are as follows:

Platform	MFC Version	Visual C++ Version
Win16	2.53	1.52
Win32	4.21	5.0

WinSock support was added to Win16 MFC in version 2.52 and to Win32 MFC in version 3.1. The classes discussed in this chapter are only available in these (or newer) MFC releases.

MFC Socket Classes

MFC now supports several classes related to WinSock and Internet programming, and the number is growing all the time. Some are more related to specific application protocols than to WinSock itself. Others – the ones we'll discuss here – are directly related to the WinSock API.

WinSock support from MFC comes in two flavors:

- ◆ **CAsyncSocket:** This class encapsulates asynchronous mode WinSock programming and provides callback functions for event notifications. This is a virtual base class and you must derive a new socket class to use it.

- ◆ **CSocket:** This class is derived from CAsyncSocket to provide a higher-level abstraction for working with WinSock. It manages blocking and background processing of Windows messages, to provide the application with a synchronous interface to the underlying asynchronous CAsyncSocket class.

Note: The Microsoft documentation does a thorough job of covering the CSocket class and provides good examples of its use. The CAsyncSocket class, however, gets brushed over. This class seems to cause quite a bit of confusion, so the bulk of this chapter deals with the CAsyncSocket class exclusively.

Both of these classes only use WinSock 1.1; at the time of this writing, MFC does not provide any MFC classes for WinSock 2. Under Windows NT and Windows 95, MFC applications that use these classes are linked with WSOCK32.LIB. Win16 MFC applications must be linked to WINSOCK.LIB.

This chapter's discussion of the CAsyncSocket and CSocket classes assumes that you are familiar with C++, Windows programming with MFC, and the portion of WinSock that has been covered in Chapters 1 through 5 of this book.

A NOTE ABOUT WinInet
The WinInet classes provide high-level support for creating HTTP, FTP, and Gopher client applications through MFC. All of these classes allow you to create Internet

client applications without knowing much about WinSock or TCP/IP. However, since the purpose of this book is to make sure you *do* get to know a *lot* about WinSock, I've omitted the WinInet classes from the discussion here. In this chapter, we're only going to explore the classes that provide direct access to the WinSock API and help you to write server applications as well as clients.

Adding Support for WinSock to MFC Applications

Any application that uses either CAsyncSocket or CSocket must add global support for WinSock. Specifically, the application must include AFXSOCK.H and call the AfxSocketInit() function.

In the latest versions of Visual C++, AppWizard includes an option to provide this global WinSock support (see Figure 6-1). None of the earlier versions of Visual C++ — including those that support WinSock classes — provides an option for the global support. It's easy enough, however, to make the necessary changes to your application.

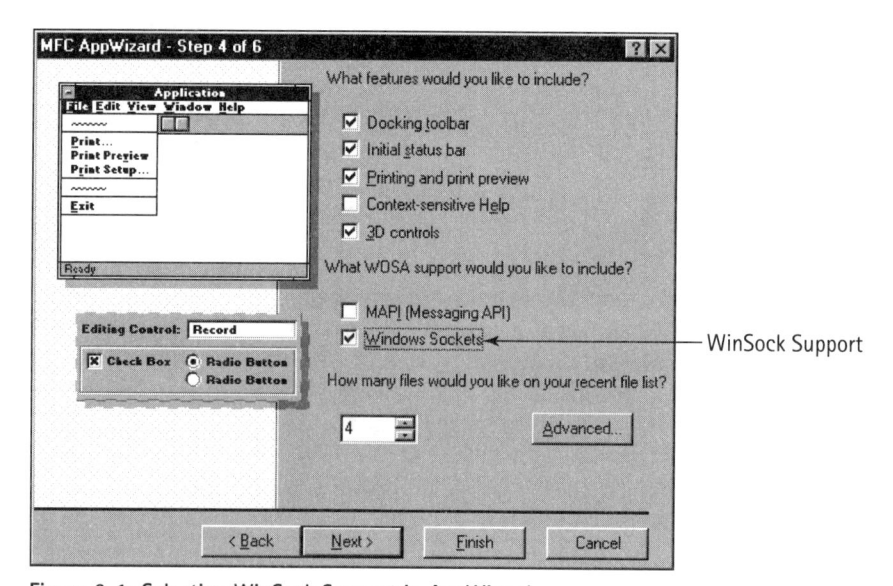

Figure 6-1: Selecting WinSock Support in AppWizard

Including AFXSOCK.H

Of course, you can just include AFXSOCK.H in the source files that actually use the socket classes, but generally this file is included in STDAFX.H. Selecting the Windows Sockets Support option in AppWizard adds the following line to STDAFX.H:

```
#include <afxsock.h>        // MFC socket extensions
```

Including AFXSOCK.H defines the CSocket and CAsyncSocket classes and also includes WINSOCK.H, so that everything you need is available everywhere in your application.

Calling AfxSocketInit()

Before using either of the socket classes, a call must first be made to AfxSocketInit(). This function calls WSAStartup() and checks to ensure that version 1.1 of WinSock is available. The CWinApp::InitInstance() class member is a convenient place to call this function, and when you select WinSock support in AppWizard, the following code is added to your application's InitInstance():

```
if (!AfxSocketInit())
{
    AfxMessageBox(IDP_SOCKETS_INIT_FAILED);
    return False;
}
```

AfxSocketInit() returns True if it succeeds and False if it fails. AfxSocketInit() will fail if the call to WSAStartup() returns an error or if version 1.1 of WinSock isn't available. In the code above, if AfxSocketInit() returns False, a message box is displayed telling the user that WinSock isn't available. Then False is returned from InitInstance(), which tells the framework that the application should not continue.

There is also an AfxSocketTerm() function that calls WSACleanup(), but you should never have to call this function directly. AfxSocketInit() sets a flag so that the application framework automatically calls AfxSocketTerm() before exiting. By using this one call to AfxSocketInit(), you avoid having to call WSAStartup() or WSACleanup().

Using the CAsyncSocket Class

The CAsyncSocket class is a thin C++ layer that encapsulates a socket using asynchronous mode. It essentially just provides an object-oriented interface to a socket and the methodologies used in asynchronous mode. Little is done to abstract the WinSock API, and you must have a good understanding of WinSock and asynchronous mode in order to use CAsyncSocket. You're still responsible for handling blocking, accommodating byte-order differences, ensuring the correct sequence of function calls, and dealing with all errors.

This isn't to say that the class isn't useful. It provides a familiar, logical interface to WinSock from C++. The CAsyncSocket class provides the following advantages:

- *Simplified socket creation.* The Create() function establishes the most used parameters as defaults, automatically makes the socket nonblocking, and also registers the socket for receipt of asynchronous network events.

- *Combination of host resolution with the connect() function.* The Connect() function will accept a fully qualified socket address just as the WinSock connect() function does; in addition, it is overloaded to accept a character string and port number. The string and port number are then resolved into a socket address before WinSock's connect() function is called.

- *Network byte order conversion for parameters.* The Bind(), Connect(), and SendTo() member functions all convert their port number parameters to network order before calling any WinSock function. Note that network byte order conversion does *not* automatically happen for application data; that is still left to the programmer.

- *Callback functions for asynchronous event notification.* The CAsyncSocket class manages its own window for receiving event notification messages and can dispatch them to callback functions the programmer defines. The error code associated with the notification is extracted from LPARAM and passed to the callback function.

- *Automatic conversion of IP addresses.* Several functions accept or return IP addresses in their dot-quad notation form ("206.80.51.140").

- *Destructor automatically calls the Close() function.* When a CAsyncSocket object is destroyed (either explicitly by being deleted, or implicitly by losing scope), the associated socket is first automatically closed.

Asynchronous Callback Functions

Let's take a look at the callback functions included in the CAsyncSocket class that handle asynchronous network events. These callback functions directly relate to the asynchronous notification events discussed in Chapter 4. The following callback functions are available to notify the application of events:

Callback Function	Notification
OnAccept	A connection is pending, ready to be accepted with the Accept() function.
OnClose	The connection is now closed.

Callback Function	Notification
OnConnect	A connection request has completed.
OnOutOfBandData	Out-of-band data is waiting to be received.
OnReceive	Data is waiting to be received by calling Receive().
OnSend	WinSock has buffer space available so that data can be sent with either the Send() or SendTo() function.

The default implementations of these functions in CAsyncSocket do nothing — they are merely placeholders. CAsyncSocket takes event notifications received from WinSock in the form of Windows messages and converts them into calls to these notification functions, but you must implement how the functions actually respond. You have to derive a new class from CAsyncSocket and override these callback functions to implement the desired behavior.

Deriving from CAsyncSocket

To use the CAsyncSocket class effectively, you must first derive a new class that inherits from CAsyncSocket. Then define overrides for the callback notification functions that you want to process. To begin this process, define a class based on CAsyncSocket, like this:

```
class CMyNewSocketClass : public CAsyncSocket
{
    DECLARE_DYNAMIC(CMyNewSocketClass);

// Attributes
public:
    BOOL m_fConnected; // Flag to track connection state

protected:
    virtual void OnConnect(int nErrorCode);
    virtual void OnSend(int nErrorCode);
    virtual void OnReceive(int nErrorCode);
    virtual void OnClose(int nErrorCode);
};
```

Then, in the implementation of the new class, define the behavior of each of the overridden notification functions, like this:

```
void CMyNewSocketClass::OnConnect(int nErrorCode)
{
    // Connection request has completed.
    // Examine nErrorCode to see if we're
```

```
        // connected and set flag.
        if (!nErrorCode)
            m_fConnected = True;
        else
        {
            // Tell user about error
            m_fConnected = False;
        }
    }

    void CMyNewSocketClass::OnSend(int nErrorCode)
    {
        // If we have data to send, we can send it now.
        int nRet = Send(lpBuf, nBufLen, 0);
        // Check for errors here!
    }

    void CMyNewSocketClass::OnReceive(int nErrorCode)
    {
        // Data is waiting to be received,
        // call Receive() member function.
        char szBuf[256];
        int nBytes = Receive(szBuf, sizeof(szBuf), 0);
        // Check for errors here!
    }

    void CMyNewSocketClass::OnClose(int nErrorCode)
    {
        m_fConnected = False;
    }
```

The preceding code is just one example of the steps the callback functions might actually perform. It is intentionally brief and leaves out some of the details you would want to handle in an actual implementation. You'll study a real-world example of overriding the CAsyncSocket later in this chapter, in the section "WSTerm: The CAsyncSocket Class at Work." The important thing to learn at this point is that you have to override CAsyncSocket and provide the functionality for the notification functions.

Using a CAsyncSocket-Derived Object

Now let's look at how the class we defined above might be used in an application. Creation of a CAsyncSocket-based object follows the MFC pattern of two-stage construction.

Object Construction

To create an instance of the CMyNewSocketClass object defined above, you would normally create a copy of the object on the heap — with the C++ *new* operator — and then call the Create() function, like this:

```
CMyNewSocketClass *pSock = new CMyNewSocketClass;
pSock.Create();
```

The constructor for CAsyncSocket (which will be used by CMyNewSocketClass) contains only one line of code:

```
    m_hSocket = INVALID_SOCKET;
```

The constructor does nothing else.

The Create() function actually creates a socket descriptor. It calls socket() to create a socket descriptor and then WSAAsyncSelect() to make the socket nonblocking and register it for receipt of asynchronous event notifications. Here is the function prototype for CAsyncSocket::Create():

```
BOOL Create(
        UINT nSocketPort = 0,
        int nSocketType = SOCK_STREAM,
        long lEvent = FD_READ | FD_WRITE | FD_OOB | FD_ACCEPT |
                      FD_CONNECT | FD_CLOSE,
        LPCTSTR lpszSocketAddress = NULL
        );
```

Parameter	Description
nSocketPort	A port number to be used with the socket, or 0 if you want WinSock to select a port. When creating a client socket, you should always leave this set to 0. For a server socket, you will always specify this number.
nSocketType	SOCK_STREAM or SOCK_DGRAM.
lEvent	A bitmask specifying the combination of asynchronous events in which the application is interested.
lpszSocketAddress	A pointer to a null-terminated ASCII string containing the socket address or name ("www.idgbooks.com," or an IP address in dot-quad notation, "206.61.229.23").

Create() returns True if it succeeds or False if it fails. If it fails, a specific error code can be obtained by calling the GetLastError() member function.

If you simply call Create() with no parameters, you get a nonblocking stream socket that's registered to receive all event notifications. This is normally what you want when creating a TCP client application. To create a simple TCP server socket, you call Create() and specify the *nSocketPort* parameter with a well-known port number. It's important to note that Create() expects the *nSocketPort* parameter to be in *host* order — not in network order as in WinSock.

Making a Connection

If the socket is to be used as a connection-oriented client, you connect to a server using the Connect() function. A connectionless client simply begins by calling SendTo(). If the socket is to be used as a server, you will either call Listen() and Accept() for a connection-oriented server, or call ReceiveFrom() for a connectionless server.

CONNECTING A CLIENT SOCKET TO A SERVER

To establish a connection with a server from a client application, you call the Connect() member function. Connect() is overloaded with two interfaces. Both of these overloads return True if they are successful; if they fail, they return False, with a specific reason for the error available through GetLastError().

Here are the function prototypes for Connect():

```
BOOL Connect(const SOCKADDR* lpSockAddr, int nSockAddrLen);
BOOL Connect(LPCTSTR lpszHostAddress, UINT nHostPort);
```

The first version of Connect() is almost identical to the WinSock connect() function. It accepts a fully qualified socket address and address length. The *lpSockAddr* parameter points to a SOCKADDR structure, which has been filled in with a host address (in *network* order) and host service port number. The only difference between this overload of Connect() and the WinSock connect() function is the return value: Connect() returns True when it succeeds, whereas connect() returns 0.

The second overload of Connect() is much handier than the WinSock connect() function. It accepts a string containing the host's name or IP address in dot-quad notation and a port number. When this overload of Connect() is called, it first attempts to convert the *lpszHostAddress* parameter into an address by using the inet_addr() function. If this fails, it then calls gethostbyname() to resolve the host name.

Note: This is a blocking WinSock function call. The CAsyncSocket class does not use WSAAsyncGetHostByName() to resolve host names. If you need to operate in purely asynchronous mode, you must call WSAAsyncGetHostByName() yourself and pass the resulting SOCKADDR to the first overload of Connect().

Like the Create() member function and all of the other member functions that accept a port number, Connect() expects the port number parameter to be in *host* order.

Both of the Connect() functions call the WinSock connect() function. Since the underlying socket has been placed into nonblocking mode during the call to Create(), then Connect() will nearly always "fail," with WSAEWOULDBLOCK returned from GetLastError(). As discussed in Chapters 3 and 4, this is not really a failure in the general sense. This error indicates to the application that WinSock has begun the connect process but was unable to complete the requested operation immediately. The operation will eventually complete. You should always examine the specific reason for the error from Connect() with GetLastError(), but be aware that most of the time it will return WSAEWOULDBLOCK.

CONNECT() RETURN VALUE

Some peculiar behavior is introduced into the Connect() function due to the fact that the Connect() overload accepting *lpszHostAddress* as a parameter may call gethostbyname() and block. If an invalid host name is passed to Connect(), as in the following example, the gethostbyname() function called by Connect() will fail. If this happens, Connect() sets WSAEINVAL with the WSASetLastError() function. Connect() then blocks and eventually returns False. But you don't get the WSAHOST_NOT_FOUND error from GetLastError() as you might expect; you get WSAEINVAL.

```
// Connect to the host
// Program execution will block here!
if (!pSocket->Connect("www.notasite.com", nHostPort))
{
    if (pSocket->GetLastError() != WSAEWOULDBLOCK)
    {
        // Tell the user about the error
        // If error == WSAEINVAL
        // it could mean that the host
        // was not found
        delete pSocket;
        return;
    }
}
// OnConnect member function will be called
// when the WinSock connect() operation
// completes.
```

Once the Connect() operation has completed, the framework will call the OnConnect() callback notification function discussed earlier. The error code passed to OnConnect() was extracted from the *lParam* passed with the FD_CONNECT event message sent from WinSock.

LISTENING FOR CLIENTS WITH A SERVER SOCKET

You use a CAsyncSocket-derived object as a server socket in much the same way you would a normal socket descriptor. If you specified the port you want to use in the call to Create() — as you should for a server socket — then there is no need to call Bind(). The call to Create() binds the socket to an address.

Connectionless servers simply call ReceiveFrom() to begin communicating with clients. ReceiveFrom() will return immediately and, unless there is already data waiting to be read, will return the WSAEWOULDBLOCK error. The application should then respond to the OnReceive() callback notification with another call to ReceiveFrom() to read data when it is available.

Connection-oriented servers first call the Listen() member function and specify the number of incoming connections to queue. This simply calls the WinSock bind() function. Listen() returns True if it is successful and False if it fails. After a successful call to Listen(), connection-oriented servers then call Accept() to wait for connection requests.

Here is the function prototype for Accept():

```
virtual BOOL Accept(CAsyncSocket& rConnectedSocket,
                    SOCKADDR* lpSockAddr = NULL,
                    int* lpSockAddrLen = NULL
                    );
```

Parameter	Description
rConnectedSocket	A reference to a new client socket that is available for connection.
lpSockAddr	An optional pointer to a SOCKADDR structure, which receives the address of the client requesting the connection.
lpSockAddrLen	If *lpSockAddr* is specified, this points to an integer containing the length of the *lpSockAddr* in bytes.

Important: As a parameter, Accept() takes a reference to a *new, empty* CSocket object. You must construct this object before you call Accept(), but you shouldn't call Create(). The following sample code demonstrates the correct way to call Accept():

```
// Create a new client socket on the heap
CClientSocket* pSocket = new CClientSocket();
// Call Accept()
if (pServerListeningSocket->Accept(*pSocket))
{
    // Accept() succeeded
    // Send and receive through pSocket
}
else
{
    // Accept() failed
    // Call pServerListeningSocket->GetLastError()
}
```

Code similar to this would be placed in the server socket's OnAccept() callback notification function. This example assumes that *pServerListeningSocket* points to a server socket object that has been prepared with the Create(), Listen(), and Accept() functions.

Object Destruction

CAsyncSocket-derived objects are often created on the heap with the C++ *new* operator. In this case, you are responsible for destroying the object when it is no longer needed, with the *delete* operator. The destructor for CAsyncSocket will automatically call the object's Close() member function before destroying the object.

To initiate a graceful close, connection-oriented applications should use Shutdown() and Receive() to clear the protocol stack's buffers before destroying the object, like this:

```
// Tell the peer that we're
// not going to send anymore
pSocket->ShutDown(CAsyncSocket::sends);

// Receive any pending data
int nRet;
char szBuf[256];
while(1)
{
    nRet = pSocket->Receive(szBuf, sizeof(szBuf));
    if (nRet == 0 || nRet == SOCKET_ERROR)
        break;
}

// Tell the peer that we're not going
// to send or receive anymore
pSocket->ShutDown(CAsyncSocket::both);

// Close the socket
pSocket->Close();
// And delete it
delete pSocket;
```

The foregoing sample assumes that *pSocket* points to a previously created socket. This code follows the recommendations discussed in Chapter 2 for closing a connection.

WSTerm: The CAsyncSocket Class at Work

The WSTerm (WinSock Terminal) application presented in this section illustrates the use of the CAsyncSocket class and the methods we've discussed so far in this chapter. WSTerm is a general-purpose, TCP client utility. It allows you to connect to various types of TCP servers and interactively hold a conversation with them. For example, you can use WSTerm to connect to

- An SMTP server to interactively send e-mail
- A POP3 server to receive e-mail
- An HTTP server to request a Web page and watch as it is received
- An NNTP server and retrieve Usenet Network News articles

With WSTerm you can connect and "talk" to any type of server that communicates using plain text commands — which, in the Internet suite of protocols, includes most of them. Figure 6-2 shows a sample WSTerm session with an NNTP server.

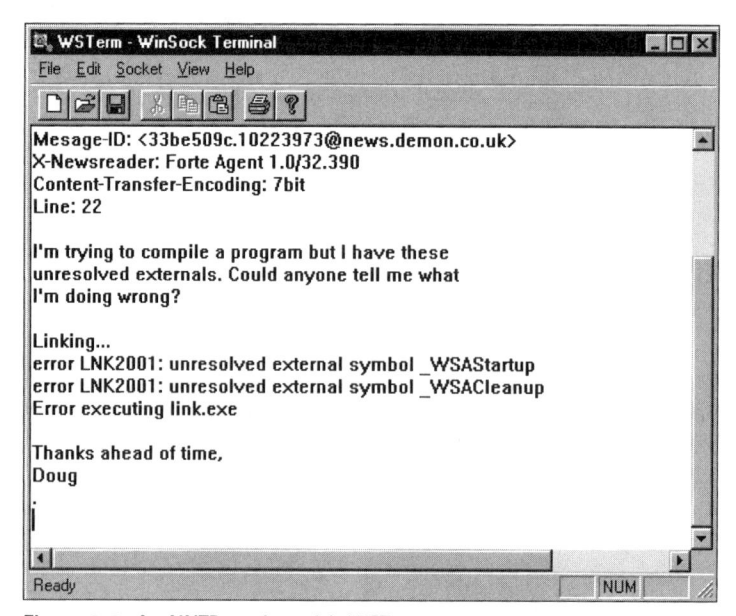

Figure 6-2: An NNTP session with WSTerm

WSTerm will compile with the current versions of either the 16-bit or 32-bit MFC libraries. It uses the standard Document/View architecture, and CEditView class as its primary user interface.

Note: A complete source listing for WSTerm is stored on the CD in the \CH06\WSTERM folder. Only the source files of particular interest to the subject at hand are listed here in Chapter 6, and we'll discuss each one in the following sections.

Building WSTerm

So that WSTerm will compile in both 16-bit and 32-bit environments, I generated the program skeleton for WSTerm with the AppWizard in Visual C++ 1.52. I then added code to the document class member functions OnNewDocument() and Serialize(), to load and restore plain text files. This allows you to save conversation sessions to file.

I then added a dialog box in which you can specify a host name or address and a port number. This dialog is displayed when you select the Socket / Connect menu option. When you click the Connect button in this dialog, WSTerm attempts to connect to the server on the specified port number and displays the result in the edit view.

From that point, the View class does almost all of the work. When you type a line into the edit control, WSTerm sends the line to the server. When the server sends data back to WSTerm, the data is displayed on the next line. Not exactly Telnet, but a perfectly acceptable quick-and-dirty terminal emulation for WinSock.

The CTermSocket Class

The view class in WSTerm (CTermView) owns a member variable (m_pSocket) that points to a CTermSocket object. CTermSocket is defined in TERMSOCK.H (Listing 6-1) and TERMSOCK.CPP (Listing 6-2).

Listing 6-1 TERMSOCK.H

```
// TERMSOCK.H - Socket derived from CAsyncSocket
//

#ifndef __TERMSOCK_H__
#define __TERMSOCK_H__

class CTermSocket : public CAsyncSocket
{
    DECLARE_DYNAMIC(CTermSocket);

// Operations
public:

// Implementation
```

```
protected:
    virtual void OnConnect(int nErrorCode);
    virtual void OnSend(int nErrorCode);
    virtual void OnReceive(int nErrorCode);
    virtual void OnClose(int nErrorCode);
};
#endif // __TERMSOCK_H__
```

Listing 6-2 TERMSOCK.CPP

```
// TERMSOCK.CPP - Socket derived from CAsynCAsyncSocket
//

#include "stdafx.h"
#include "wsterm.h"
#include "doc.h"
#include "termsock.h"
#include "view.h"

#ifdef _DEBUG
#undef THIS_FILE
static char BASED_CODE THIS_FILE[] = __FILE__;
#endif

IMPLEMENT_DYNAMIC(CTermSocket, CAsyncSocket)

void CTermSocket::OnConnect(int nErrorCode)
{
    CTermView *pView = CTermView::GetView();
    pView->OnConnect(nErrorCode);
}

void CTermSocket::OnSend(int nErrorCode)
{
    CTermView *pView = CTermView::GetView();
    pView->OnSend(nErrorCode);
}

void CTermSocket::OnReceive(int nErrorCode)
{
    CTermView *pView = CTermView::GetView();
    pView->OnReceive(nErrorCode);
}

void CTermSocket::OnClose(int nErrorCode)
{
    CTermView *pView = CTermView::GetView();
    pView->OnClose(nErrorCode);
}
```

As you can see, this is a very simple class. TERMSOCK.H simply defines the CTermSocket class as inheriting from CAsyncSocket, and provides function prototypes for the network-event callback functions we're interested in processing.

Chapter 6: MFC Socket Classes

The definitions of the callback functions in TERMSOCK.CPP all just acquire a pointer to the view class through its GetView() method, and then notify the view class that the event occurred and pass along the error code. As stated earlier, it's the view class that does most of the work in WSTerm.

The CTermView Class

Listings 6-3 and 6-4 contain the source for the CTermView class. A large portion of the code in these listings is standard CEditView handlers generated by AppWizard.

The constructor for CTermView initializes the CTermSocket pointer to NULL and sets a connected-state flag to False. The destructor checks to see if the CTermSocket object needs to be deleted; if the socket is still connected, the destructor performs a hard close.

The CTermView::Display() function defines a convenient method of printing messages and received data in the view's edit control. The CTermView::OnChar() function watches for keystrokes from the user. If the user types in a line and then presses the Enter key, the OnChar() function parses out the current line and sends it out the socket to the server.

Listing 6-3 VIEW.H

```
// view.h : interface of the CTermView class
//
/////////////////////////////////////////////////////////////////////

class CTermView : public CEditView
{
protected: // create from serialization only
    CTermView();
    DECLARE_DYNCREATE(CTermView)

// Attributes
public:
    CTermDoc* GetDocument();
    static CTermView *GetView();
    CTermSocket*    m_pSocket;
    BOOL            m_fConnected;
    BOOL            m_fShowNotifications;

// Operations
public:
    void Display(LPCSTR lpFormat, ...);
    void OnConnect(int nErrorCode);
    void OnSend(int nErrorCode);
    void OnReceive(int nErrorCode);
    void OnClose(int nErrorCode);

// Implementation
```

Part II: The WinSock 1.1 API

```cpp
public:
    virtual ~CTermView();
    virtual void OnDraw(CDC* pDC);  // overridden to draw this view
#ifdef _DEBUG
    virtual void AssertValid() const;
    virtual void Dump(CDumpContext& dc) const;
#endif

protected:

    // Printing support
    virtual BOOL OnPreparePrinting(CPrintInfo* pInfo);
    virtual void OnBeginPrinting(CDC* pDC, CPrintInfo* pInfo);
    virtual void OnEndPrinting(CDC* pDC, CPrintInfo* pInfo);

// Generated message map functions
protected:
    //{{AFX_MSG(CTermView)
    afx_msg void OnSocketConnect();
    afx_msg void OnUpdateSocketConnect(CCmdUI* pCmdUI);
    afx_msg void OnSocketClose();
    afx_msg void OnUpdateSocketClose(CCmdUI* pCmdUI);
    afx_msg void OnChar(UINT nChar, UINT nRepCnt, UINT nFlags);
    afx_msg void OnViewSocketNotifications();
    afx_msg void OnUpdateViewSocketNotifications(CCmdUI* pCmdUI);
    afx_msg void OnEditClearBuffer();
    //}}AFX_MSG
    DECLARE_MESSAGE_MAP()
};

#ifndef _DEBUG  // debug version in view.cpp
inline CTermDoc* CTermView::GetDocument()
    { return (CTermDoc*)m_pDocument; }
#endif
```

Listing 6-4 VIEW.CPP

```cpp
// view.cpp : implementation of the CTermView class
//

#include "stdafx.h"
#include "wsterm.h"

#include "doc.h"
#include "termsock.h"
#include "view.h"
#include "connectd.h"
```

```
#ifdef _DEBUG
#undef THIS_FILE
static char BASED_CODE THIS_FILE[] = __FILE__;
#endif


/////////////////////////////////////////////////////////////////////
// CTermView

IMPLEMENT_DYNCREATE(CTermView, CEditView)

BEGIN_MESSAGE_MAP(CTermView, CEditView)
    //{{AFX_MSG_MAP(CTermView)
    ON_COMMAND(ID_SOCKET_CONNECT, OnSocketConnect)
    ON_UPDATE_COMMAND_UI(ID_SOCKET_CONNECT, OnUpdateSocketConnect)
    ON_COMMAND(ID_SOCKET_CLOSE, OnSocketClose)
    ON_UPDATE_COMMAND_UI(ID_SOCKET_CLOSE, OnUpdateSocketClose)
    ON_WM_CHAR()
    ON_COMMAND(ID_VIEW_SOCKETNOTIFICATIONS,
 OnViewSocketNotifications)
    ON_UPDATE_COMMAND_UI(ID_VIEW_SOCKETNOTIFICATIONS,
 OnUpdateViewSocketNotifications)
    ON_COMMAND(ID_EDIT_CLEARBUFFER, OnEditClearBuffer)
    //}}AFX_MSG_MAP
    // Standard printing commands
    ON_COMMAND(ID_FILE_PRINT, CEditView::OnFilePrint)
    ON_COMMAND(ID_FILE_PRINT_PREVIEW, CEditView::OnFilePrintPreview)
END_MESSAGE_MAP()

/////////////////////////////////////////////////////////////////////
/////////
// CTermView construction/destruction

CTermView::CTermView()
{
    m_pSocket = NULL;
    m_fConnected = False;
    m_fShowNotifications = False;
}

CTermView::~CTermView()
{
    // If we allocated a socket
    if (m_pSocket != NULL)
    {
        // If it's still connected
        if (m_fConnected)
            m_pSocket->Close();
        delete m_pSocket;
    }
}

/////////////////////////////////////////////////////////////////////
```

Part II: The WinSock 1.1 API

```cpp
// CTermView drawing

void CTermView::OnDraw(CDC* pDC)
{
    CTermDoc* pDoc = GetDocument();
    ASSERT_VALID(pDoc);

    // TODO: add draw code for native data here
}

/////////////////////////////////////////////////////////////////////
// CTermView printing

BOOL CTermView::OnPreparePrinting(CPrintInfo* pInfo)
{
    // default CEditView preparation
    return CEditView::OnPreparePrinting(pInfo);
}

void CTermView::OnBeginPrinting(CDC* pDC, CPrintInfo* pInfo)
{
    // Default CEditView begin printing.
    CEditView::OnBeginPrinting(pDC, pInfo);
}

void CTermView::OnEndPrinting(CDC* pDC, CPrintInfo* pInfo)
{
    // Default CEditView end printing
    CEditView::OnEndPrinting(pDC, pInfo);
}

/////////////////////////////////////////////////////////////////////
// CTermView diagnostics

#ifdef _DEBUG
void CTermView::AssertValid() const
{
    CEditView::AssertValid();
}

void CTermView::Dump(CDumpContext& dc) const
{
    CEditView::Dump(dc);
}

CTermDoc* CTermView::GetDocument() // non-debug version is inline
{
    ASSERT(m_pDocument->IsKindOf(RUNTIME_CLASS(CTermDoc)));
    return (CTermDoc*)m_pDocument;
}
#endif //_DEBUG

CTermView *CTermView::GetView()
```

```
{
    CFrameWnd *pFrame = (CFrameWnd *)(AfxGetApp()->m_pMainWnd);
    CView *pView = pFrame->GetActiveView();
    if (!pView)
        return NULL;
    if (!pView->IsKindOf(RUNTIME_CLASS(CTermView)))
        return NULL;
    return (CTermView *)pView;
}

void CTermView::OnEditClearBuffer()
{
    SetWindowText(NULL);
}


// Helper function to display
// lines in the edit control
void CTermView::Display(LPCSTR lpFormat, ...)
{
    // Is the edit control almost full?
    CEdit& ed = GetEditCtrl();
    if (ed.GetLineCount() > 1000)
    {
        // Empty the whole thing
        SetWindowText(NULL);
    }

    va_list Marker;
    static char szBuf[256];

    // Write text to string
    // and append to edit control
    va_start(Marker, lpFormat);
    vsprintf(szBuf, lpFormat, Marker);
    va_end(Marker);
    ed.SetSel(-1,-1);
    ed.ReplaceSel(szBuf);
}

////////////////////////////////////////////////////////////////////
// CTermView message handlers

// When user presses <ENTER>
// we send the current line
void CTermView::OnChar(UINT nChar, UINT nRepCnt, UINT nFlags)
{
    // If we're not connected...
    if (!m_fConnected)
    {
        // Ask the user to connect our socket
        AfxMessageBox("Choose Socket/Connect to start\r\n");
        return;
```

```cpp
    }
    // If the user hit <ENTER>
    if (nChar == 13)
    {
        // Figure out what line we're on
        CEdit& ed = GetEditCtrl();
        int iStart, iEnd;
        ed.GetSel(iStart, iEnd);
        int iLine = ed.LineFromChar(iStart);
        if (iLine > -1)
        {
            static char szLine[256];
            memset(szLine, 0, sizeof(szLine));
            // Get the whole line
            int iNdx = ed.GetLine(iLine, szLine, sizeof(szLine)-1);
            if (iNdx > 0)
            {
                // and Send() it out our socket
                strcat(szLine, "\r\n");
                m_pSocket->Send(szLine, strlen(szLine));
            }
        }
    }
    CEditView::OnChar(nChar, nRepCnt, nFlags);
}

void CTermView::OnViewSocketNotifications()
{
    if (m_fShowNotifications)
        m_fShowNotifications = False;
    else
        m_fShowNotifications = True;
}

void CTermView::OnUpdateViewSocketNotifications(CCmdUI* pCmdUI)
{
    pCmdUI->SetCheck(m_fShowNotifications);
}

// Socket/Connect Menu handler
void CTermView::OnSocketConnect()
{
    // Display the Connect Dialog
    CConnectDialog dlg;
    if (dlg.DoModal() != IDOK)
        return;
    Display("Connect to port %d on %s...\r\n",
            dlg.m_nPort,
            dlg.m_strHostName);

    // Make sure we don't have a socket left
    // from our last connection
    if (m_pSocket != NULL)
```

```cpp
    {
        delete m_pSocket;
        m_pSocket = NULL;
    }

    // Create a new CTermSocket object on the heap.
    m_pSocket = new CTermSocket();

    // And then call the Create() member
    // accepting all defaults
    if (!m_pSocket->Create())
    {
        AfxMessageBox("Socket creation failed");
        return;
    }

    // Connect to the host
    if (!m_pSocket->Connect(dlg.m_strHostName, dlg.m_nPort))
    {
        if (m_pSocket->GetLastError() != WSAEWOULDBLOCK)
        {
            CString strError;
            strError.LoadString(m_pSocket->GetLastError());
            Display("Connect() failed: %s\r\n",
                strError);
            m_fConnected = False;
            delete m_pSocket;
            m_pSocket = NULL;
        }
    }
    // Assume we're connected until OnConnect
    // tells us otherwise. This is done to
    // make menu pCmdUI's work
    m_fConnected = True;
}

void CTermView::OnUpdateSocketConnect(CCmdUI* pCmdUI)
{
    pCmdUI->Enable(!m_fConnected);
}

void CTermView::OnSocketClose()
{
    // Initiate a graceful close
    // Tell the peer that we're
    // not going to send anymore
    m_pSocket->ShutDown(CAsyncSocket::sends);

    // Receive any pending data
    int nRet;
    char szBuf[256];
    while(1)
    {
```

```cpp
            nRet = m_pSocket->Receive(szBuf, sizeof(szBuf));
            if (nRet == 0 || nRet == SOCKET_ERROR)
                break;
        }
        // Tell the peer that we're not going
        // to send or receive anymore
        m_pSocket->ShutDown(CAsyncSocket::both);

        // Close the socket
        m_pSocket->Close();
        // And delete it
        delete m_pSocket;
        m_pSocket = NULL;
        m_fConnected = False;
    }

    void CTermView::OnUpdateSocketClose(CCmdUI* pCmdUI)
    {
        pCmdUI->Enable(m_fConnected);
    }

    void CTermView::OnConnect(int nErrorCode)
    {
        if (m_fShowNotifications)
            Display("\tOnConnect(%d)\r\n", nErrorCode);

        if (nErrorCode)
        {
            m_fConnected = False;
            Display("\tError OnConnect(): %d\r\n",
                    nErrorCode);
        }
        else
        {
            m_fConnected = True;
            Display("\tSocket connected\r\n");
        }
    }

    void CTermView::OnSend(int nErrorCode)
    {
        if (m_fShowNotifications)
            Display("\tOnSend(%d)\r\n", nErrorCode);
    }

    void CTermView::OnReceive(int nErrorCode)
    {
        if (m_fShowNotifications)
            Display("\tOnReceive(%d)\r\n", nErrorCode);

        static char szBuf[256];
        // Set buffer to all zeros
        // So that it is already
```

```
    // NULL terminated
    memset(szBuf, 0, sizeof(szBuf));
    // Receive maximum of one less byte
    // than buffer size, so NULL
    // is always last character.
    int nBytes = m_pSocket->Receive(szBuf, 255, 0);
    if (nBytes == 0)
    {
        Display("Receive() indicates that socket is closed\r\n");
        return;
    }
    if (nBytes == SOCKET_ERROR)
    {
        CString strError;
        strError.LoadString(m_pSocket->GetLastError());
        Display("Receive error %s\r\n", strError);
        return;
    }
    Display(szBuf);
}

void CTermView::OnClose(int nErrorCode)
{
    if (m_fShowNotifications)
        Display("\tOnClose(%d)\r\n", nErrorCode);

    AfxMessageBox("Socket closed");
    m_fConnected = False;
}
```

Connecting to a Server

CTermView::OnSocketConnect() responds to a menu command and handles the initiation of a connection with a server. This function displays the dialog box shown in Figure 6-3, in which the user enters a host name or address and port number.

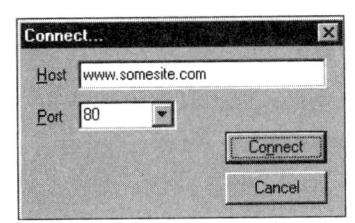

Figure 6-3: WSTerm's Connect dialog box

OnSocketConnect() then creates a new CTermSocket on the heap and calls Create(), accepting all defaults. This creates a stream, TCP, nonblocking socket registered to receive all network events. The host name and port number entered into the dialog box are then passed to Connect() to request a connection to the server.

When the connection request completes, the CTermSocket::OnConnect() function gets called by the framework. CTermSocket::OnConnect() in turn calls the CTermView::OnConnect() function. CTermView::OnConnect() simply displays the connection result in the edit control and, if the connection was successful, it sets the connection-state flag *m_fConnected* to True.

A Conversation with a Server

Once connected, WSTerm allows the user to enter command lines in the edit control. When the user presses the Enter key, the OnChar() function mentioned earlier sends the line to the server. When the server responds, the CTermSocket::OnReceive() function is called by the framework. It then notifies the view of the event by calling CTermView::OnReceive(). The CTermView::OnReceive() function simply calls the Receive() function and displays the incoming data in the edit control.

A two-way conversation is established, allowing you to interactively send and receive data from many different types of servers. With WSTerm you can visually check the response from servers by issuing commands and watching responses. Here is a typical conversation with an HTTP server:

User: I start by selecting Socket | Connect from the menu. In the WSTerm Connect dialog box, I enter www.sockaddr.com for the host name and 80 as the port number, and then click Connect.

WSTerm: Displays the message "Socket connected."

User: I enter **GET /index.html** and press Enter, making sure to type **GET** in all caps. The server then sends the contents of my Web page.

WSTerm: Displays file contents in the view.

You can test many different types of servers with WSTerm. The RFC documents included in the \RFC folder on the CD detail the commands available on different types of servers.

Closing the Connection

The CTermView::OnSocketClose() function responds to a menu command and initiates a graceful close of the connection. It uses the methods described earlier by calling the ShutDown() function and attempting to receive any data that might be buffered for the socket by WinSock.

WSTerm Limitations

The use of the standard Windows edit control in the WSTerm program introduces some limitations. For example, connecting to a typical Network News server and entering the list command will cause the server to transfer *much* more information than the edit control can hold. WSTerm uses an inelegant, brute-force workaround for this problem by simply emptying the contents of the edit control after the contents become too large.

A much more serious limitation of the edit control is line length. Attempting to place a line into the edit control that contains more than 251 characters can have disastrous effects. WSTerm does nothing to ensure that this doesn't happen.

Despite these limitations, the program is very useful – especially for educational purposes. It gives a real-world example of using the CAsyncSocket class and at the same time allows you to watch a conversation with a server.

Using the CSocket Class

The CSocket class is derived from CAsyncSocket and provides a higher-level abstraction of working with WinSock. CSocket is much easier to use than CAsyncSocket, but this added convenience comes at a cost of some flexibility and control. Depending on the application, the gained ease of use may far outweigh the loss of absolute control.

In addition to the advantages listed earlier for the CAsyncSocket class, the CSocket class provides the following services:

- *Simpler code by virtue of synchronous interface.* Because socket operations performed through the CSocket class don't return to the calling application until they complete, code can be written in a purely sequential manner. There is no need to handle a single socket operation with multiple functions.

- *A familiar, file-like operation for socket functions provided by CArchive interface.* By attaching a CSocketFile to a CSocket object, data can be transmitted in much the same manner as reading from and writing to a file. (This only works if *both* the client and the server transmit and receive MFC objects.)

A Synchronous/Asynchronous Socket

The CSocket class gives the application a synchronous interface to socket functions by handling asynchronous socket calls in the background. Since CSocket is derived from CAsyncSocket, all WinSock operations are actually handled in asynchronous mode. However, CSocket functions don't return to the calling application until the operation has completed. Functions such as Receive() and Send() don't return WSAEWOULDBLOCK when used with CSocket, as they do when used with CAsyncSocket. The CSocket class versions of these functions all wait until the operation has actually completed before returning to the calling application.

The CSocket class processes Windows messages in the background while waiting for asynchronous functions to complete, and provides a mechanism to catch particular messages so that they can be acted on immediately. The OnMessagePending() function can be overridden to watch for messages of interest (such as a Cancel request from the user).

CSocket also includes the IsBlocking() function to determine if a blocking call is in progress, and the CancelBlockingCall() function to stop a lengthy operation. Once the CancelBlockingCall() function has been used, however, the socket is left in an indeterminate state. Close() is the only socket function that can be reliably performed after the CancelBlockingCall() function has been used.

Using an Archive with CSocket

The programmer is shielded from a lot of work by the synchronous nature of CSocket Send() and Receive() calls. Data can be transferred using an even higher-level interface than this by associating a CSocketFile and one or more CArchive objects with a CSocket object.

Data can be sent and received using C++ stream I/O-like operators, as shown here:

```
// Construct a new CSocket object on the stack
CSocket theSocket;

// Create the default TCP socket descriptor
if (!theSocket.Create())
{
    // Handle error;
    return;
}

// Connect to a server
if (!theSocket.Connect(strHostName, nPort))
{
    // Handle error
    return;
}

// Create a new file object
CSocketFile socketFile(&theSocket);

// Create one archive for each
// transfer direction (sending and receiving)
CArchive arIn(&socketFile, CArchive::load);
CArchive arOut(&socketFile, CArchive::store);
```

Chapter 6: MFC Socket Classes 193

```
// Use one archive to send data
arOut << "UserID\r\n";

// and the other to receive data
arIn > strHostResponse;
```

Notice here that CArchive objects move data in only one direction. In order to both send and receive data, you must create two CArchive objects.

The archive serialization and deserialization process even takes care of network byte order — you just send and receive objects with no regard as to whether the objects are stored in big-endian or little-endian format.

CArchive LIMITATIONS

As handy as this CArchive mechanism is, it has one serious limitation: You can only communicate with other MFC applications. The MFC serialization process used with CArchive reads and writes more than just the data stored in the object; it also sends information about the type of object. So if you want to talk to a non-MFC server (say, on the Internet), you can't use an archive to transmit strings to and from the server. For example, the following code will not work when communicating with a typical TCP/IP server. The data will be transmitted to the server; the server just won't understand how to interpret it.

```
// This WILL NOT work unless the server
// is also an MFC application expecting
// a CString object

// Create CSocket, CSocketFile, and CArchives
CSocket theSocket;
theSocket.Create();
theSocket.Connect(strHostName, nPort);
CSocketFile socketFile(&theSocket);
CArchive arIn(&socketFile, CArchive::load);
CArchive arOut(&socketFile, CArchive::store);

// CString objects
// Won't work because object information is sent along
// with character string.
CString str = "UserID\r\n";
arOut << str;
// This won't work either
arOut << (LPCTSTR)str;
// And this won't either
arOut << "UserID\r\n";
```

The CArchive mechanism has one other limitation, though it's not as serious. CArchive serialization can't be used with datagram sockets. In version 1.1 of WinSock (which is used by the CSocket class), all datagram sockets are assumed to use an unreliable protocol (UDP). Because UDP datagrams aren't guaranteed to arrive and may be repeated or transmitted out of sequence, they aren't compatible with serialization. The serialization process expects data to flow reliably and in sequence. If you try to use a datagram CSocket object with an archive, an MFC assertion fails.

The CArchive mechanism is extremely convenient if you are writing a specialized application that is only going to communicate with other MFC applications. Just keep in mind that both the client and the server must understand and use the same process.

Deriving from CSocket

Unlike CAsyncSocket, you don't have to create a new class for CSocket. You can use a CSocket directly. However, you can derive a new class from CSocket to extend its behavior, just as we did for CAsyncSocket earlier in this chapter.

The OnMessagePending() Function

One reason for deriving a new class from CSocket is to override the default OnMessagePending() function. The framework calls this function while waiting for a lengthy CSocket operation to complete. The default version of OnMessagePending() calls PeekMessage() to process WM_PAINT messages. This lets the application redraw itself in the event that it is covered and then uncovered by another window while a blocking call is in progress.

The OnMessagePending() function can be overridden to watch for messages of special interest. For example, you might watch for a Cancel request from the user. Another example is to implement a timeout mechanism for CSocket calls. The CSocketX class, discussed next, does just that.

The CSocketX Class

Listings 6-5 and 6-6 present the source code for the CSocket-derived CSocketX class. CSocketX overrides OnMessagePending() to implement a timeout mechanism. It also includes overloaded versions of Send() and Receive() that accept CString objects as parameters; in addition, it accepts timeout values.

Listing 6-5 SOCKETX.H

```
// SOCKETX.H - Extension of the CSocket class
//

#ifndef __SOCKETX_H__
#define __SOCKETX_H__

class CSocketX : public CSocket
{
```

```cpp
    DECLARE_DYNAMIC(CSocketX);

// Implementation
public:
    int Send(LPCTSTR lpszStr, UINT uTimeOut = 0, int nFlags = 0);
    int Receive(CString& str, UINT uTimeOut = 0, int nFlags = 0);
    BOOL SetTimeOut(UINT uTimeOut);
    BOOL KillTimeOut();

protected:
    virtual BOOL OnMessagePending();

private:
    int m_nTimerID;
};
#endif // __SOCKETX_H__
```

Listing 6-6 SOCKETX.CPP

```cpp
// SOCKETX.CPP - Extension of the CSocket class
//

#include "stdafx.h"
#include "socketx.h"


#ifdef _DEBUG
#undef THIS_FILE
static char BASED_CODE THIS_FILE[] = __FILE__;
#endif

IMPLEMENT_DYNAMIC(CSocketX, CSocket)

int CSocketX::Send(LPCTSTR lpszStr, UINT uTimeOut, int nFlags)
{
    // If a timeout value was specified, set it
    if (uTimeOut > 0)
        SetTimeOut(uTimeOut);

    // Call base class function
    int nRet = CSocket::Send(lpszStr, strlen(lpszStr), nFlags);

    // If we previously set a timeout
    if (uTimeOut > 0)
    {
        KillTimeOut();
        // If the operation timedout, set a more
        // natural error message
        if (nRet == SOCKET_ERROR)
        {
            if (GetLastError() == WSAEINTR)
                SetLastError(WSAETIMEDOUT);
        }
```

```
    }
    return nRet;
}


int CSocketX::Receive(CString& str, UINT uTimeOut, int nFlags)
{
    static char szBuf[256];
    memset(szBuf, 0, sizeof(szBuf));

    // If a timeout value was specified, set it
    if (uTimeOut > 0)
        SetTimeOut(uTimeOut);

    // Call base class function
    int nRet = CSocket::Receive(szBuf, sizeof(szBuf), nFlags);

    // If we previously set a timeout
    if (uTimeOut > 0)
    {
        KillTimeOut();
        // If the operation timedout, set a more
        // natural error message
        if (nRet == SOCKET_ERROR)
        {
            if (GetLastError() == WSAEINTR)
                SetLastError(WSAETIMEDOUT);
        }
    }

    // Fill in the CString reference
    str = szBuf;
    return nRet;
}

BOOL CSocketX::OnMessagePending()
{
    MSG msg;

    // Watch for our timer message
    if(::PeekMessage(&msg, NULL, WM_TIMER, WM_TIMER, PM_NOREMOVE))
    {
        // If our timer expired...
        if (msg.wParam == (UINT) m_nTimerID)
        {
            // Remove the message
            ::PeekMessage(&msg,
                          NULL,
                          WM_TIMER,
                          WM_TIMER,
                          PM_REMOVE);
            // And cancel the call
            CancelBlockingCall();
```

```
            return False;
        }
    }
    // Call base class function
    return CSocket::OnMessagePending();
}


BOOL CSocketX::SetTimeOut(UINT uTimeOut)
{
    m_nTimerID = SetTimer(NULL,0,uTimeOut,NULL);
    return m_nTimerID;
}


BOOL CSocketX::KillTimeOut()
{
    return KillTimer(NULL,m_nTimerID);
}
```

USING TIMEOUTS ON SEND() AND RECEIVE()

When you call a CSocket function that could block, it might complete quickly or it might take a long time; and then again it might never return at all. The Send() and Receive() functions in CSocketX allow you to specify a timeout value to ensure that you always get a response... eventually.

Both of the overload functions use the same strategy. If the *uTimeOut* parameter is specified (if it's not 0) the functions set a Windows timer with the new CSocketX::SetTimeOut() function. The *uTimeOut* value specifies the number of milliseconds to wait for the function to complete. The override of OnMessagePending() watches for the timer to elapse. If the timer expires before the Send() or Receive() function has completed, OnMessagePending() cancels the call with the CSocket::CancelBlockingCall() function.

On return from the base class function Send() or Receive(), the overload CSocketX functions call GetLastError() to look for the WSAEINTR (call interrupted) error. This is the error posted by CancelBlockingCall(). If GetLastError() returns this error, the CSocketX functions assume that the base class function timed out and use SetLastError() to set the WSAETIMEDOUT error.

So, you can specify a timeout value (in milliseconds) in the CSocketX versions of Send() and Receive(). You can also expect to find the WSAETIMEDOUT error set if the allotted time expires before the call completes. The following sample code shows how this is implemented:

```
// Set timeout to 10 seconds
UINT uTimeOut = 10000;

// Read a response from the peer
if (theSocket.Receive(strResponse, uTimeOut) == SOCKET_ERROR)
```

```
{
    if (theSocket.GetLastError() == WSAETIMEDOUT)
    {
        AfxMessageBox("Operation timed-out");
        return;
    }
    // Handle other errors here
}
```

> ### PumpMessages() Bug in Earlier Versions of MFC
>
> There is a bug in some versions of MFC that will cause problems if you attempt to use a timer and override OnMessagePending() as shown in the timeout example in this section. The problem is documented in the following Microsoft Knowledge Base article:
>
> Article ID: Q137632
> Title: BUG: OnMessagePending Not Called When a Timer Is Active
>
> The bug applies to versions 1.52, 1.52b, 2.1, and 2.2 of Visual C++. If you are using one of these versions, the CSocketX class will not work.

Note that I only provide overloads for the Send() and Receive() functions. You might want to override other CSocket functions in the same way. Another alternative is to use the SetTimeOut() and KillTimer() functions on a per-call basis. To do this, you would surround a call to a CSocket function like this:

```
// Wait 10 seconds for a datagram
theSocket.SetTimeOut(10000);
int nRet = theSocket.ReceiveFrom(lpBuf,
                                 nBufLen,
                                 rSocketAddress,
                                 rSocketPort);
theSocket.KillTimer();
if (nRet == SOCKET_ERROR)
{
    if (theSocket.GetLastError() == WSAEINTR)
    {
        AfxMessageBox("Operation timed-out");
        return;
    }
    // Handle other errors here
}
```

USING CSTRING OBJECTS WITH SEND() AND RECEIVE()

As you'll see in the next example program, CString objects are very handy indeed when you're communicating using text. The standard CSocket implementations of Send() and Receive() don't accept CString arguments – they both require buffer pointer and buffer length parameters.

The overloaded Send() function in the CSocketX class accepts an LPCTSTR (*const TCHAR **) as a parameter and uses the strlen() function to call the base class version of Send(). A conversion operator makes it possible to substitute CString objects for the *const char** and LPCTSTR function arguments. So, by using LPCTSTR as an argument, the Send() function in CSocketX can accept either a LPCTSTR or a CString object, like this:

```
// Send() will accept a CString object
CString str = "UserID\r\n";
Send(str)
// Or a character string
Send("UserID\r\n");
```

The overloaded Receive() function in CSocketX accepts a reference to a CString object as one parameter. It uses a private character buffer to make a call to CSocket::Receive() and then places the result in the CString parameter. This allows you to call CSocketX::Receive() like this:

```
// Read the response from the peer
CString strResponse;
theSocket.Receive(strResponse);
```

The overloaded Send() and Receive() functions both return the same values as the CSocket() versions. Send() returns the total number of characters sent or SOCKET_ERROR. Receive() returns the number of bytes received; or SOCKET_ERROR if an error occurs; or 0 if the connection has been closed.

SendMail: The CSocketX Class at Work

The SendMail application uses the CSocketX class to implement a simple SMTP client. This program can be used to send e-mail (hence, its imaginative and original name). SendMail was created as a dialog-based MFC application with the AppWizard in version 5 of Visual C++. Figure 6-4 shows SendMail's main window.

Part II: The WinSock 1.1 API

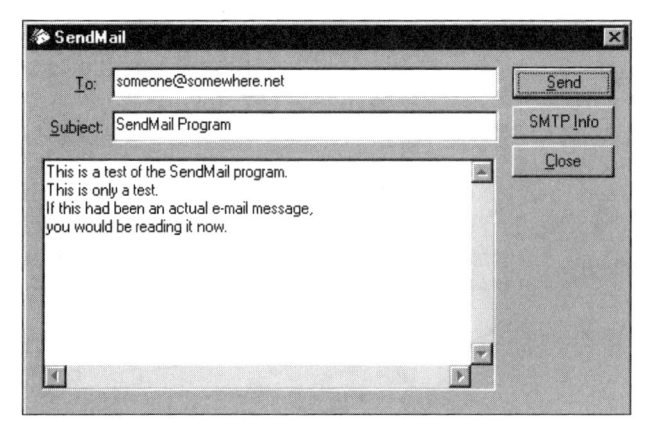

Figure 6-4: The SendMail application's main window

The SendMailMessage() Function

SendMail serves as a good example of how much the CSocket class can simplify an application. Almost all of the source code for SendMail is devoted to the user interface. Other than the CSocketX code described earlier, SendMail uses only one function to transmit an e-mail message to a server. Listing 6-7 presents the source code for the SendMailMessage() function that does all of the WinSock work in SendMail.

Listing 6-7 SendMailMessage()

```
BOOL CMailDlg::SendMailMessage(LPCTSTR szServer,
                               LPCTSTR szFrom,
                               LPCTSTR szTo,
                               LPCTSTR szSubject,
                               LPCTSTR szMessage)
{
    // Construct a socket from the derived class
    CSocketX theSocket;

    // And create the socket descriptor
    if (!theSocket.Create())
    {
        AfxMessageBox("Socket creation failed");
        return False;
    }

    // Connect to the server
    if (!theSocket.Connect(szServer, 25))
    {
        AfxMessageBox("Could not connect to server");
        return False;
```

```
    }

    // General purpose strings
    CString strCommand;
    CString strResponse;

    // Set timeout to 10 seconds
    UINT uTimeOut = 10000;

    // Read the "HELO" response from the server
    if (theSocket.Receive(strResponse, uTimeOut) == SOCKET_ERROR)
    {
        ReportSocketError(theSocket.GetLastError());
        return False;
    }

    // and check to see if we're talking to an
    // SMTP server
    if (strResponse.Left(3) != _T("220"))
    {
        CString strError = "ERROR: Not a valid SMTP "
                           "server response\r\n";
        strError += strResponse;
        AfxMessageBox(strError);
        theSocket.Send("QUIT\r\n");
        return False;
    }

    // Send the "FROM" line
    strCommand = "MAIL FROM:<";
    strCommand += szFrom;
    strCommand += ">\r\n";
    theSocket.Send(strCommand);

    // and check the response
    if (theSocket.Receive(strResponse, uTimeOut) == SOCKET_ERROR)
    {
        ReportSocketError(theSocket.GetLastError());
        return False;
    }
    if (strResponse.Left(3) != _T("250"))
    {
        CString strError = "ERROR: Sender rejected\r\n";
        strError += strResponse;
        AfxMessageBox(strError);
        theSocket.Send("QUIT\r\n");
        return False;
    }

    // Send the "RCPT" line
    strCommand = "RCPT TO:<";
    strCommand += szTo;
    strCommand += ">\r\n";
```

```cpp
    theSocket.Send(strCommand);

    // and check the response
    if (theSocket.Receive(strResponse, uTimeOut) == SOCKET_ERROR)
    {
        ReportSocketError(theSocket.GetLastError());
        return False;
    }
    if (strResponse.Left(3) != _T("250"))
    {
        CString strError = "ERROR: Recipient rejected\r\n";
        strError += strResponse;
        AfxMessageBox(strError);
        theSocket.Send("QUIT\r\n");
        return False;
    }

    // Send the "DATA" line
    theSocket.Send("DATA\r\n");

    // and check the response
    if (theSocket.Receive(strResponse, uTimeOut) == SOCKET_ERROR)
    {
        ReportSocketError(theSocket.GetLastError());
        return False;
    }
    if (strResponse.Left(3) != _T("354"))
    {
        CString strError = "ERROR: DATA command rejected\r\n";
        strError += strResponse;
        AfxMessageBox(strError);
        theSocket.Send("QUIT\r\n");
        return False;
    }

    // Send the "Subject" line
    strCommand = "Subject: ";
    strCommand += szSubject;
    strCommand += "\r\n";
    theSocket.Send(strCommand);

    // No response from server expectd

    // Send the message data
    // This code assumes the message
    // data contains CRLF pairs
    // where appropriate.
    if (theSocket.Send(szMessage) == SOCKET_ERROR)
    {
        ReportSocketError(theSocket.GetLastError());
        return False;
    }
```

```
    // No response from server expectd

    // Send the termination line
    theSocket.Send("\r\n.\r\n");

    // and check the response
    if (theSocket.Receive(strResponse, uTimeOut) == SOCKET_ERROR)
    {
        ReportSocketError(theSocket.GetLastError());
        return False;
    }
    if (strResponse.Left(3) != _T("250"))
    {
        CString strError = "ERROR: Message body rejected\r\n";
        strError += strResponse;
        AfxMessageBox(strError);
        theSocket.Send("QUIT\r\n");
        return False;
    }

    // Send the "QUIT" line
    theSocket.Send("QUIT\r\n");

    return True;
}
```

The SendMailMessage() function accepts parameters for all of the information it needs to send a small e-mail message. This makes it easier to move SendMailMessage() from one application to another.

The function begins by constructing a CSocketX object, creating a socket descriptor, and then attempting to connect to the server specified in the *szServer* parameter. If all of this succeeds, SendMailMessage() then begins a conversation with the server. Let's take a closer look.

TALKING SMTP
The Simple Mail Transfer Protocol (documented in RFC 821) specifies the characteristics of a conversation between an SMTP client and server. Once a connection request has been accepted, the SMTP server will send a line like this:

```
220 SMI-8.6/SMI-SVR4 ready at Sun, 6 Jul 1997 09:56:41 -0500
```

The 220 portion of the response is mandated by the SMTP protocol and indicates that the SMTP server is ready to communicate. The rest of the line can be anything the server would like to send.

SendMailMessage() expects to receive this greeting line immediately after making a connection and examines the line in this section of code:

```
    // Read the "HELO" response from the server
    if (theSocket.Receive(strResponse, uTimeOut) == SOCKET_ERROR)
    {
        ReportSocketError(theSocket.GetLastError());
```

```
            return False;
    }

    // and check to see if we're talking to an
    // SMTP server
    if (strResponse.Left(3) != _T("220"))
    {
        // Error
    }
```

The rest of the conversation with the server follows this same pattern. SendMailMessage() sends a command to the server and then checks the response.

A typical conversation would look like this. Server responses are prefixed with [S]; client commands are prefixed with [C].

```
[S] 220 SMI-8.6/SMI-SVR4 ready\r\n
[C] MAIL FROM:<lewis@sockaddr.com>\r\n
[S] 250 <lewis@sockaddr.com>... Sender ok\r\n
[C] RCPT TO:<someone@somewhere.net>\r\n
[S] 250 <someone@somewhere.net>... Recipient ok\r\n
[C] DATA\r\n
[S] 354 Enter mail, end with "." on a line by itself\r\n
[C] Test message\r\n
[C] sent with the SendMail program\r\n
[C] .\r\n
[S] 250 JAA22577 Message accepted for delivery
[C] quit
[S] 221 closing connection
```

As you can see, each response from the server begins with a 3-digit number. These numbers are documented in RFC 821. By examining this number at each step of the process, the SendMailMessage() function knows if the conversation is succeeding.

Fascinating as this probably is to you, "talking" SMTP is not really the point here. The important thing to note in the SendMailMessage() function is how much the process has been simplified. There are no asynchronous event messages to process, and no callback functions – just a straight sequence of code that sends a small e-mail message.

Summary

This chapter has explained the two models supplied by the Microsoft Foundation Classes for writing WinSock programs with a C++ interface: CAsyncSocket and CSocket. Both classes use asynchronous sockets mode to perform operations.

Several other functions are available in these classes that weren't discussed in this chapter, including SetSockOpt(), GetSockOpt(), and others. They are all well documented in the MFC documentation; if you understand the information on WinSock presented thus far, you'll have no trouble using them.

The CAsyncSocket class is a thin C++ layer over the WinSock C API. The CSocket class gives an application a synchronous interface to asynchronous mode. In addition, this class can help with network byte-order issues through CArchive serialization.

Part III
The WinSock 2.0 API

Chapter 7: Introduction to WinSock 2.0

Chapter 8: Name Registration and Resolution

Chapter 9: Advanced Input/Output

Chapter 7

Introduction to WinSock 2.0

IN THIS CHAPTER
Here in Chapter 7 we look at the new functionality available in WinSock 2 and the advantages it provides. Topics covered in this chapter include

- An overview of what's new
- WinSock 2 concepts
- Porting from WinSock 1.1
- Finding protocol information

IN THE PRECEDING CHAPTERS, we covered all of the functionality available in both Version 1.1 and Version 2 of WinSock. Now, in Part III, we'll focus exclusively on the new functions and data structures only available in WinSock 2. Chapters 7, 8, and 9 all assume you are familiar with WinSock 1.1 and the material presented in Parts I and II.

What's New in WinSock 2.0

Version 2 of the Windows Sockets API greatly expands the original standard. Most important, it officially supports protocols other than TCP/IP and provides mechanisms that allow applications to be protocol independent. WinSock 2 includes enhancements to the WinSock input/output mechanisms and provides new methods of network event notification. Also, WinSock 2 attempts to clarify parts of the WinSock 1.1 specification considered vague or open to interpretation.

In addition to retaining almost all of the functionality available in Version 1.1, WinSock 2 provides the following new features:

- **Multiple Protocol Support**
  Version 2 provides simultaneous access to any number of installed transport protocols. Applications can operate in a protocol-independent manner.

- Protocol-Independent Name Resolution
  A new set of functions and data structures enable applications to locate hosts and services without specific knowledge of the underlying name resolution service. One set of functions allows access to various name resolution strategies such as Domain Name Service (DNS) and Novell's Service Advertising Protocol (SAP).

- Overlapped I/O
  WinSock 2 uses the asynchronous (or overlapped) input/output model established in Win32, which allows applications to continue with other processing while waiting for an I/O operation to complete. By giving WinSock exclusive access to buffers during I/O operations, the number of times a buffer is copied can be reduced, thereby increasing transmission speed.

- Scatter/Gather
  The new I/O functions available in WinSock 2 allow multiple buffers to be used for sending and receiving data. This aids data parsing by "scattering" incoming data into multiple data structures, or "gathering" various pieces of outgoing data together from different sources.

- Event Objects
  In WinSock 2, applications can choose to be notified of asynchronous network events using Win32 event objects rather than Windows messages. This aids in the design of multithreaded applications and allows console applications a clean method for using asynchronous notification.

- Connection Setup and Teardown
  New mechanisms are provided to exchange user data when connections are established and terminated and to accept conditionally new connections based on application-supplied criteria.

- Quality of Service
  The speed of data transmission is especially critical to some applications. To support multimedia communications and other emerging network technologies, WinSock 2 establishes conventions for applications to negotiate required service levels for parameters such as bandwidth and latency.

- Multicast and Multipoint
  WinSock 2 allows applications to discover transport protocols that support multipoint or multicast. Protocol-independent multicast and multipoint functions are provided, as well.

- Other Frequently Requested Extensions
  WinSock 2 supports shared sockets and includes a standardized, protocol-specific extension mechanism.

Summary of New Functions and Options

We'll begin with a summary of the new functions, socket options, and ioctl opcodes. Tables 7-1 through 7-10 give you a big-picture view of exactly what has been added in WinSock 2. We'll discuss almost all of these new functions in detail as we work through Part III. Note, WSASocket() and WSAConnect() are listed in more than one area, to show how they are used in different situations.

TABLE 7-1 MULTIPLE PROTOCOL SUPPORT

Function	Description
WSASocket()	Extended version of socket(). Creates a socket that is bound to a specific transport service provider.
WSAEnumProtocols()	Retrieves information about all of the available transport protocols.
WSAHtonl() WSAHtons() WSANtohl() WSANtohs()	These functions convert byte order of scalar values as appropriate for a specified protocol.

TABLE 7-2 PROTOCOL-INDEPENDENT NAME RESOLUTION

Function	Description
WSAEnumNameSpaceProviders()	Retrieves information about all of the available Name Registration and Resolution service providers.
WSAGetServiceClassInfo	Retrieves information about a particular class of service applications.
WSAGetServiceClassNameByClassId()	Returns the name of the service class name associated with the given class type.
WSAInstallServiceClass()	Registers a new class of services within a name space.

(continued)

Table 7-2 (CONTINUED)

Function	Description
WSARemoveServiceClass()	Removes a service class type.
WSALookupServiceBegin()	Begins a client query to enumerate and find information for available services.
WSALookupServiceNext()	Continues enumeration of available services initiated with WSALookupServiceBegin().
WSALookupServiceEnd()	Stops enumeration of available services initiated with WSALookupServiceBegin().
WSASetService()	Registers or unregisters a particular service instance within one or more name spaces.
WSAAddressToString()	Converts an address structure into a human-readable address string as appropriate for the protocol.
WSAStringToAddress()	Converts a human-readable address string to a socket address structure suitable for passing to Windows Sockets routines.

Table 7-3 ENHANCED INPUT/OUTPUT

Function	Description
WSASocket()	An extended version of socket(); creates socket descriptors that can be used with overlapped I/O.
WSAGetOverlappedResult()	Returns the completion status of a pending overlapped I/O routine.
WSARecv()	Extended version of recv() that supports overlapped I/O and scatter/gather.
WSARecvFrom()	Extended version of recvfrom() that supports overlapped I/O, scatter/gather, and allows both input and output of the *flags* parameter.

Function	Description
WSASend()	Extended version of send() that supports overlapped I/O and scatter/gather.
WSASendTo()	Extended version of sendto() that supports overlapped I/O and scatter/gather.

TABLE 7-4 CONNECTION SETUP AND TEARDOWN

Function	Description
WSAAccept()	An extended version of accept() that allows an application-defined procedure to determine if a new connection request will be accepted or denied based on the caller information passed in as parameters.
WSAConnect()	An extended version of connect() that allows for the exchange of connect data.
WSARecvDisconnect()	Disables receiving on a socket and retrieves any available disconnect data. Similar to shutdown (SD_RECV).
WSASendDisconnect()	Disables sending on a socket and can optionally send disconnect data to the peer. Similar to shutdown (SD_SEND).

TABLE 7-5 EVENT NOTIFICATION

Function	Description
WSACreateEvent()	Creates a new event object that can be used for asynchronous notification.
WSAEventSelect()	Associates an event object with network events using the FD_EVENT codes. Similar to WSAAsyncSelect().
WSAEnumNetworkEvents()	Determines what network events have occurred for a particular socket.

(continued)

TABLE 7-5 (CONTINUED)

Function	Description
WSAResetEvent()	Resets the state of an event object to nonsignaled.
WSASetEvent()	Sets the state of an event object to signaled.
WSAWaitForMultipleEvents()	Blocks until any one or all of the specified event objects are in the signaled state, or when the timeout interval expires.
WSACloseEvent()	Destroys an event object.

TABLE 7-6 QUALITY OF SERVICE

Function	Description
WSAConnect()	Extended version of connect() that allows the needed quality of service to be exchanged.
WSAGetQOSByName()	Initializes a quality-of-service structure based on a named template, or retrieves an enumeration of the available template names.

TABLE 7-7 MULTICAST AND MULTIPOINT

Function	Description
WSASocket()	Extended version of socket(). Creates socket descriptors that can be used in multipoint sessions.
WSAJoinLeaf()	Joins a leaf node into a multipoint session.

Chapter 7: Introduction to WinSock 2.0 215

TABLE 7-8 OTHER FREQUENTLY REQUESTED EXTENSIONS

Function	Description
WSAIoctl()	Extended version of ioctlsocket() that supports new socket options and a formal, vendor-specific mechanism for function extension.
WSADuplicateSocket()	Enables socket sharing between processes and retrieves the information necessary to create a new socket to be shared.

TABLE 7-9 NEW SOCKET OPTIONS

Socket Option	Description
SO_MAX_MSG_SIZE	Returns the maximum outbound size of a message for use with message-oriented protocols. (There is no way to discover the maximum inbound size.) This option has no meaning for stream-oriented sockets.
SO_PROTOCOL_INFO	Retrieves information about the protocol that is bound to a socket.
PVD_CONFIG	Retrieves configuration information related to a service provider. The exact format of the data returned is specific to the service provider.

TABLE 7-10 NEW I/O CONTROL CODES

Control Code	Description
SIO_ASSOCIATE_HANDLE	Associates a socket with the handle of a companion interface.
SIO_ENABLE_CIRCULAR_QUEUEING	Indicates to the underlying message-oriented service provider that a newly arrived message should never be dropped because of a buffer queue overflow.

(continued)

Table 7-10 (Continued)

Control Code	Description
SIO_FIND_ROUTE	Requests the route to the remote address be discovered.
SIO_FLUSH	Discards current contents of the sending queue associated with a socket.
SIO_GET_BROADCAST_ADDRESS	Fills a buffer with a SOCKADDR struct containing a suitable broadcast address for use with sendto() or WSASendTo().
SIO_GET_EXTENSION_FUNCTION_POINTER	Retrieves a pointer to a vendor-specific extension function.
SIO_GET_QOS	Retrieves current flow specifications for the socket.
SIO_MULTIPOINT_LOOKBACK	Controls whether data sent in a multipoint session will also be received by the same socket on the local host.
SIO_MULTICAST_SCOPE	Specifies the scope over which multicast transmissions will occur.
SIO_SET_QOS	Establishes new flow specifications for the socket.
SIO_TRANSLATE_HANDLE	Obtains a corresponding handle for a socket that is valid in the context of a companion interface. (This is protocol specific.)

Status of the WinSock 2 Specification

WinSock 2 shipped with Version 4 of Windows NT even before the API's specification was officially complete; it was finalized with the release of the WinSock 2 SDK for Windows 95. Version 2.2.1 of the formal specification was released at the same time (June 10, 1997) and is considered final. Future revisions are expected only for the purpose of correcting errors or removing ambiguity. It is assumed they will not include any new functionality.

The WinSock 2 SDK for Windows 95 contains the newest run-time components for Windows 95. It also contains new development files (header and lib) that should be used on both platforms (even NT 4). If you are developing WinSock 2 applications for Windows 95, you can install the WinSock2 DLL and related files, as well as the Microsoft TCP/IP and IPX services. If you are using Version 4 of Windows NT, you will still need the latest header and library files from this distribution.

The SDK is available on Microsoft's Web site:

```
http://www.microsoft.com/win32dev/netwrk/winsock2/ws295sdk.html
```

WINSOCK2.H

The architecture of WinSock 2 enables vendors of transport protocols and name space to install their services dynamically (we'll talk about name spaces later in this chapter). WinSock 2 will continue to be updated with new functionality as more vendors make products available. The WINSOCK2.H header file now contains numerous identifiers that enable an application developer to specify programmatically such things as address families, socket types, and protocols. As more products become available for WinSock 2, new identifiers will be assigned to support them.

The WinSock Identifier Clearinghouse is responsible for assigning new identifiers and will periodically make new versions of WINSOCK2.H available, containing all the latest constants and identifiers. Developers are urged to stay current with successive revisions of WINSOCK2.H. The Clearinghouse can be reached at

```
www.stardust.com/wsrcsource/winsock2/ws2ident.html
```

UNICODE SUPPORT

If you browse through WINSOCK2.H to see what it contains, you may notice structure declarations and function prototypes that have the letters *W* and *A* appended to their names. These declarations are used to define both ANSI (A) and Unicode (W) versions of WinSock 2 functions and data structures. *Unicode* is a 16-bit character set capable of encoding all known characters and is used as a worldwide character-encoding standard. *Unicode characters* are also known as *wide characters* (thus the *W*) because they are 2 bytes wide. Windows uses Unicode exclusively at the system level.

Porting from WinSock 1.1 to WinSock 2

Even with all its new functionality, WinSock 2 is remarkably compatible with Version 1.1. In fact, all of the Version 1.1 applications developed earlier in this book and all the samples on the CD will compile and run on WinSock 2. All that is required is to change the include file from WINSOCK.H to WINSOCK2.H, to recompile the program and to link it with WS2_32.LIB rather than WINSOCK.LIB or WSOCK32.LIB. (The only exceptions to this are the programs from Chapter 6 that use MFC. Currently, MFC uses WinSock 1.1 only.)

Caution: There is one caveat to including WINSOCK2.H. If your application includes both WINDOWS.H and WINSOCK2.H directly, you may receive multiple errors and warnings resulting from type redefinitions. For example, this will cause errors:

```
#include <windows.h>
#include <winsock2.h>
```

This happens because WINDOWS.H includes the Version 1.1 WINSOCK.H. If you then include WINSOCK2.H, many of the same names are redefined. To prevent the errors, you can do one of two things: Either define WIN32_WINNT as 0x0400 before including WINDOWS.H, or delete the WINDOWS.H include and rely on WINSOCK2.H to pull in WINDOWS.H.

Defining WIN32_WINNT as greater than or equal to 0x0400 causes WINDOWS.H to include WINSOCK2.H rather than WINSOCK.H. This is from WINDOWS.H:

```
#if(_WIN32_WINNT >= 0x0400)
#include <winsock2.h>
#include <mswsock.h>
#else
#include <winsock.h>
#endif /* _WIN32_WINNT >= 0x0400 */
```

Note: The file MSWSOCK.H included along with WINSOCK2.H defines the Microsoft-specific extensions to WinSock.

If you don't include WINDOWS.H at all, WINSOCK2.H will include WINDOWS.H and force it to *not* include WINSOCK.H. This is from WINSOCK2.H:

```
#ifndef _WINSOCK2API_
#define _WINSOCK2API_
#define _WINSOCKAPI_   /* Prevent inclusion of winsock.h in
 windows.h */
[Other definitions...]
/*
 * Pull in WINDOWS.H if necessary
 */
#ifndef _INC_WINDOWS
#include <windows.h>
#endif /* _INC_WINDOWS */
```

Binary Compatibility with WinSock 1.1

WinSock 2 fully supports WinSock 1.1 executables. When compiled, WinSock 1.1-compliant applications are guaranteed to run over a WinSock 2 implementation

Chapter 7: Introduction to WinSock 2.0

without modification of any kind, as long as at least one TCP/IP service provider is properly installed.

To support WinSock 1.1 applications, WinSock 2 includes two "shim" dynamic link libraries that provide a WinSock 1.1 interface. Figure 7-1 illustrates the three distinct interfaces supplied with WinSock 2. Applications that use the WinSock 2 API make calls directly into WS2_32.DLL. The 16-bit and 32-bit applications that use the WinSock 1.1 API still use either WINSOCK.DLL or WSOCK32.DLL, respectively.

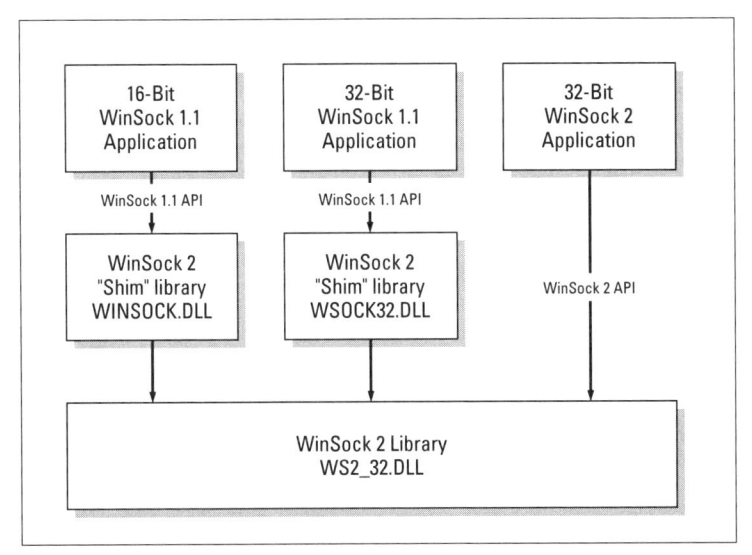

Figure 7-1: The design of the WinSock 2 architecture maintains binary compatibility with WinSock 1.1.

Source Compatibility with WinSock 1.1

With just a few exceptions, source code written for Version 1.1 is completely compatible with WinSock 2. The following sections explain the few areas where porting a program from WinSock 1.1 to WinSock 2 requires source code changes.

PSEUDOBLOCKING IS OUT

Because WinSock 2 is only available in 32-bit environments that implement preemptive multitasking, the WS2_32.DLL does not perform the pseudoblocking that was performed by WINSOCK.DLL.

WinSock 2 doesn't dispatch Windows messages in the background during blocking calls and, for this reason, blocking hooks are no longer supported in the new API. The WSAEINPROGRESS error code will never be returned, and the following functions are not available to WinSock 2 applications:

- WSACancelBlockingCall()
- WSAIsBlocking()
- WSASetBlockingHook()
- WSAUnhookBlockingHook()

Any WinSock 1.1 applications that make use of blocking hooks must be modified to use any of the new WinSock 2 functionality. If the program is compiled using WINSOCK.H and linked to either WINSOCK.LIB or WSOCK32.LIB (even if it uses blocking hooks), it will still run on WinSock 2. You only have to modify the source if you want to use any of the new WinSock 2 features.

> **About Windows Platforms and Blocking**
>
> In 16-bit Windows environments such as Windows 3.1 and Windows for Workgroups, Windows uses *cooperative multitasking*. All running programs share the same message queue. If any one program stops dispatching Windows messages, all programs stop processing and responding to user input. In an attempt to keep Windows responsive during blocking sockets calls, WinSock 1.1 implementations enter a PeekMessage() loop when waiting for an operation to complete. While the DLL waits for the operation to complete, this PeekMessage() loop dispatches Windows messages. This yields the CPU to other processes if necessary and keeps Windows and other applications active.
>
> Win32 environments such as Windows 95 and Windows NT use preemptive multitasking, and each process has its own input queue. Using a blocking call in the user interface thread of a 32-bit Windows GUI application will stop all user input to that particular program until the operation completes, but it won't stop *other* applications from receiving Windows messages.

USING VALUES FROM WSADATA

In Version 1.1 of WinSock, each transport-protocol vendor supplied the WINSOCK.DLL. Therefore, an application had access to only one vendor's protocol stack at one time. For this reason, data values for the maximum number of sockets (*iMaxSockets*), the maximum datagram size (*iMaxUdpDg*), and other vendor-specific information could be passed along in the WSADATA structure during a call to WSAStartup().

In WinSock 2, however, multiple protocols from multiple vendors can be made accessible at the same time. For this reason, information about the protocol in use should be obtained from one of the new protocol-information functions supplied in WinSock 2, rather than relying on the values from WSADATA. To support current WinSock 1.1 applications that rely on these fields, "safe" values are still supplied in the WSADATA structure. WinSock 2 applications, however, shouldn't use them.

The data value that was previously obtained from *wsadata.iMaxUdpDg* should now be retrieved by using getsockopt() with the new SO_MAX_MSG_SIZE option. The new PVD_CONFIG socket option can be used to retrieve vendor-specific information much like *wsadata.lpVendorInfo*.

WinSock 2 Concepts

WinSock 2 introduces some new concepts and some new terms. Before we actually begin using any of the new functions in WinSock 2, we need to review some of these terms.

Service Providers

As briefly mentioned in Chapter 3, WinSock 2's architecture is completely different from WinSock 1.1. The WinSock 2 DLL (WS2_32.DLL) is not supplied by each protocol stack vendor as WINSOCK.DLL and WSOCK32.DLL were. Instead, each transport protocol vendor supplies a library that can be hooked into the WinSock 2 DLL. Any number of these libraries can be dynamically linked to WinSock 2 at run-time. This architecture allows a WinSock 2 application to access services from one or more transport protocols simultaneously.

WinSock 2 defines a standard set of functions that are used to register new transport protocols. When a new transport protocol is installed, a complete set of information describing the protocol is registered along with it in the *protocol catalog*. A protocol stack that has been registered in this manner is said to be a WinSock *service provider*. Figure 7-2 illustrates the service provider's relationship with WS2_32.DLL and WinSock 2 applications.

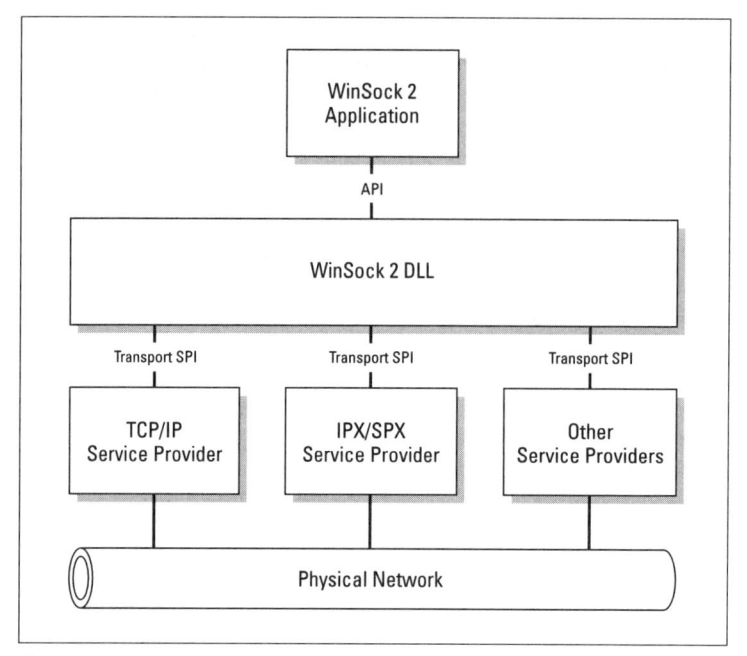

Figure 7-2: The service provider architecture allows multiple protocols to be accessed simultaneously.

THE SERVICE PROVIDER ORDER UTILITY

The program SPORDER.EXE, included with the WinSock 2 SDK, can be used to view and modify the order in which service providers are enumerated. This might be important if you have more than one service provider supporting the same protocol. By manipulating the order in which service providers are enumerated, you can indicate which of the redundant service providers should be used as the default.

The functions that SPORDER.EXE uses to manage the order of service providers are documented in the Service Provider Interface Specification (in the \SPECS\2\WSSPI22.DOC folder on this book's CD-ROM). Note, some installation programs may use these functions to change the service provider order. You may want to review the service provider order after any installation of a new service provider.

Name Space Providers

In WinSock 2, a *name space* refers to service names, host names, protocol names, *and* the resolution services available to convert names to values and values to names. A *name space provider* is a special type of service provider that performs name resolution services. Several types of name resolution services are available on various network systems; these services all provide services similar to the

Internet's Domain Name System (DNS). They all accept some sort of name and return an address, port number, or other useful network information.

WinSock 2 includes functions that standardize the way applications access and use these network naming services. Applications can use these functions to perform name resolution without having to know the details of how a particular name service works. As with service providers, there can be multiple name-space providers in use at any one time.

Figure 7-3 illustrates that name space providers are installed in much the same way as protocol service providers.

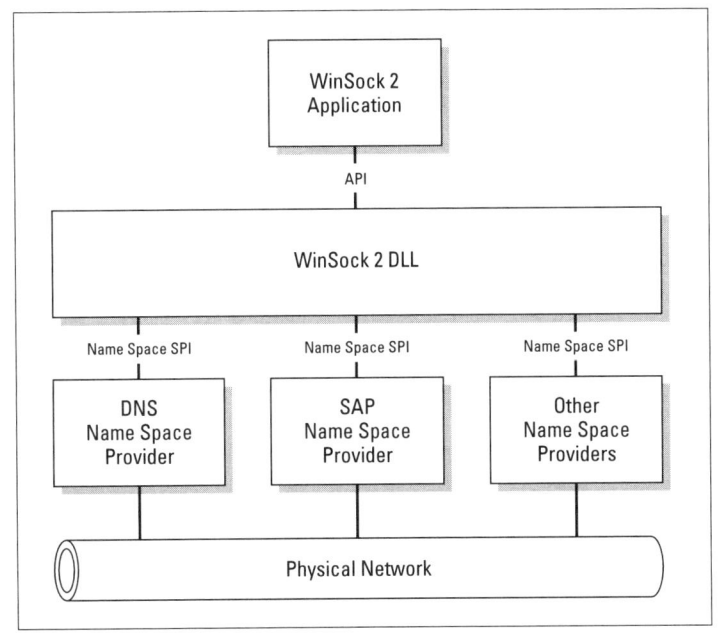

Figure 7-3: Name space providers give applications a standard interface to various name resolution services.

Services

The WinSock 2 documentation refers to a server application as a service. Don't confuse a *service* (which is a server application) with a *service provider* (which is an installed protocol stack).

Protocol Types

The term *base protocol* refers to a protocol that is capable of performing data communications with a remote endpoint. TCP, UDP, and SPX are base protocols.

A *layered protocol* is a protocol that cannot stand alone — it relies on a base protocol for services. Layered protocols perform higher-level communication functions through the use of a base protocol. The *Secure Sockets Layer (SSL)* is one example of a layered protocol. The SSL provides public-key encryption and relies on an underlying reliable, connection-oriented transport protocol to transfer data.

A *protocol chain* is a combination of one or more layered protocols attached to a suitable base protocol. In other words, a protocol chain consists of one or more layered protocols plus the base protocol needed to perform data transmission. Layered protocols that support the service provider interface for both input and output can be stacked on top of a base protocol to provide additional services.

Figure 7-4 illustrates each type of protocol discussed in this section. Only base protocols and protocol chains are capable of performing data communications. Because of this, only base protocols and protocol chains are exposed to the WinSock 2 API. Layered protocols are only used through the Service Provider Interface (SPI).

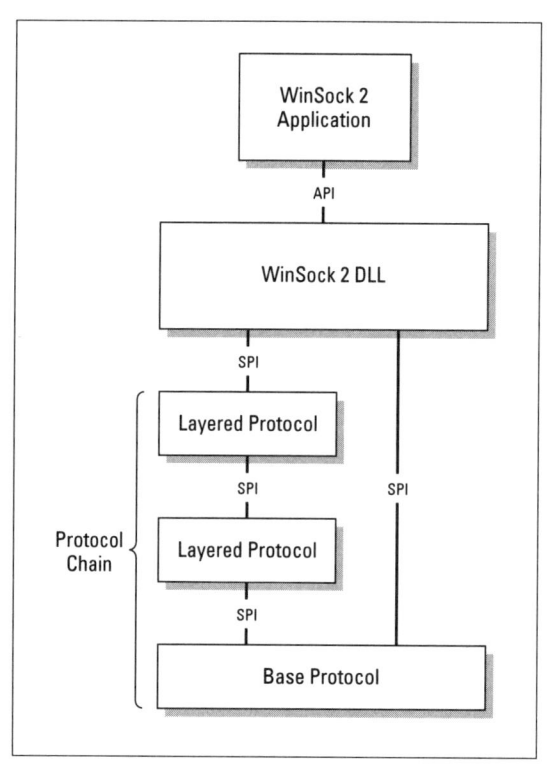

Figure 7-4: One or more layered protocols combined with a base protocol form a protocol chain.

Finding Protocol Information

With all the preliminaries now out of the way, we're ready to begin using some of the new WinSock 2 features. Foremost among WinSock 2's added capabilities is the support for protocols other than TCP/IP. As stated earlier, the new architecture of WinSock 2 makes it possible to have any number of transport protocols and protocol chains available at the same time.

If a TCP/IP service provider is installed, a WinSock 2 application can still use the familiar parameters to the socket() function to obtain TCP stream sockets and UDP datagram sockets:

```
tcpSocket = socket(AF_INET, SOCK_STREAM, IPPROTO_TCP);
udpSocket = socket(AF_INET, SOCK_DGRAM,  IPPROTO_UDP);
```

But now many more address families and socket types are available. For example, if a service provider is installed that supports Novell's IPX/SPX suite of protocols, socket descriptors can also be created like this:

```
spxSocket = socket(AF_IPX, SOCK_STREAM, NSPROTO_SPX);
ipxSocket = socket(AF_IPX, SOCK_DGRAM,  NSPROTO_IPX);
```

Although these socket descriptors work perfectly well, WinSock 2 provides a mechanism for selecting protocols that is much more powerful. Rather than explicitly specifying a particular protocol, applications can select from a list of installed protocols based on their suitability for the program's purpose. For example, an application may search for protocols that are connection oriented and reliable; or protocols that are message oriented and preserve record boundaries; or perhaps protocols that support multicast. A function for selecting protocols is developed at the end of this chapter.

A server application can obtain a list of all of the protocols that meet its needs and then create a number of listening sockets — one for each protocol. Client applications can obtain a list of protocols with the desired characteristics, locate a suitable server, and connect with any suitable protocol. Client and server applications that use strategies such as this are truly protocol independent. Because they are not limited to specific protocol names and socket types, protocol-independent applications can take advantage of the different protocols that are available in various operating environments. They can also use new protocols as they become available.

The WSAEnumProtocols() Function

The WSAEnumProtocols() function is used to retrieve information about all the available transport protocols and protocol chains installed on the local machine. Here is the function prototype for WSAEnumProtocols() from WINSOCK2.H:

```
int WSAEnumProtocols(
                    LPINT lpiProtocols,
                    LPWSAPROTOCOL_INFO lpProtocolBuffer,
                    ILPDWORD lpdwBufferLength
                    );
```

Parameter	Description
lpiProtocols	An optional pointer to a null-terminated array of integers specifying protocol types. If this parameter is NULL, information for all available protocols is returned. If the parameter is specified, only information for the listed protocols is returned.
lpProtocolBuffer	A pointer to a buffer that will be filled with WSAPROTOCOL_INFO structures.
lpdwBufferLength	A pointer to a DWORD variable. On input, it is set to the size, in bytes, of the buffer pointed to by *lpProtocolBuffer*. On output, it contains the minimum buffer size required to retrieve all the requested information.

Note, WSAEnumProtocols() returns all of the information requested in just one call. The buffer pointed to by *lpProtocolBuffer* must be large enough to hold all the requested protocol information. If the buffer is too small, then WSAEnumProtocols() will return SOCKET_ERROR, and WSAGetLastError() will be set to WSAENOBUFS. In this case, the DWORD variable pointed to by the *lpdwBufferLength* will be set to the needed size, and WSAEnumProtocols() must be called again with a larger buffer. The WSAPROTOCOL_INFO structure that is returned for each protocol is currently only 372 bytes long. Most machines only have a few protocols installed on them, so providing a buffer large enough to hold all the protocol information isn't usually a problem.

The optional *lpiProtocols* parameter can be used to restrict the call by requesting that only information about specific protocols be returned. Normally, this parameter is set to NULL to request information about all installed protocols and protocol chains, like this:

```
// Find all installed protocols
// and protocol chains
BYTE buffer[1024];
DWORD dwLen;
int nRet;

nRet = WSAEnumProtocols(NULL,
                       (LPWSAPROTOCOL_INFO)pBuf,
                       &dwLen);
if (nRet == SOCKET_ERROR)
```

```
{
    // handle errors here
    return;
}
// nRet contains the number of
// WSAPROTOCOL_INFO structures
// copied to the buffer
```

When you want to restrict the call to only a few protocols, you can point to a null-terminated array of protocol integers as shown here:

```
// Find only IP protocol(s)
char szBuf[1024];
DWORD dwLen;
int nRet;
int iProtocols[] = {IPPROTO_TCP, IPPROTO_UDP, 0};

// Call WSAEnumProtoocls and point
// the the iProtocols array
nRet = WSAEnumProtocols(iProtocols,
                        (LPWSAPROTOCOL_INFO)pBuf,
                        &dwLen);
```

If WSAEnumProtocols() fails, it returns SOCKET_ERROR, and the reason can be determined by calling WSAGetLastError(). On success, WSAEnumProtocols() fills the supplied buffer with an array of WSAPROTOCOL_INFO structures — one for each protocol or protocol chain installed on the machine. The return value from WSAEnumProtocols() represents the number of WSAPROTOCOL_INFO structures copied to the buffer. Information about layered protocols isn't included in this buffer because they aren't directly usable by an application.

The WSAPROTOCOL_INFO structures appear in the buffer in the same order as they are registered with the system — either from installation or from reordering with SPORDER.EXE.

The WSAPROTOCOL_INFO Structure

The WSAPROTOCOL_INFO structure contains a wealth of information about a protocol. By examining this structure, an application can determine if a particular protocol is suitable for its purposes. Following is the WSAPROTOCOL_INFO structure definition, and you'll find its fields defined in Table 7-11.

```
typedef struct _WSAPROTOCOL_INFO {
    DWORD dwServiceFlags1;
    DWORD dwServiceFlags2;
    DWORD dwServiceFlags3;
    DWORD dwServiceFlags4;
    DWORD dwProviderFlags;
    GUID ProviderId;
```

```
    DWORD dwCatalogEntryId;
    WSAPROTOCOLCHAIN ProtocolChain;
    int iVersion;
    int iAddressFamily;
    int iMaxSockAddr;
    int iMinSockAddr;
    int iSocketType;
    int iProtocol;
    int iProtocolMaxOffset;
    int iNetworkByteOrder;
    int iSecurityScheme;
    DWORD dwMessageSize;
    DWORD dwProviderReserved;
    WCHAR szProtocol[WSAPROTOCOL_LEN+1];
} WSAPROTOCOL_INFO, FAR * LPWSAPROTOCOL_INFO
```

TABLE 7-11 FIELDS OF WSAPROTOCOL_INFO STRUCTURE

Field	Description
dwServiceFlags1	A bitmask describing the services provided by the protocol. This is an important field; see "Service Flags Values" section in this chapter.
dwServiceFlags2 dwServiceFlags3 dwServiceFlags4	Reserved for future use.
dwProviderFlags	A bitmask describing supplementary information about the protocol and its corresponding catalog entry. See "Provider Flags Values" section in this chapter.
ProviderId	A globally unique identifier assigned to the provider. This value is useful for distinguishing between multiple service providers who provide the same protocol.
dwCatalogEntryId	A unique identifier assigned by the WS2_32.DLL for each WSAPROTOCOL_INFO structure.

Field	Description
ProtocolChain	A structure that indicates whether this entry represents a base protocol, a layered protocol, or a protocol chain. In the case of a chain, the structure holds information about the chain's protocol layers: *ProtocolChain.ChainLen* = 0: Layered protocol. Because layered protocols aren't directly usable by an application, this value should never be returned. *ProtocolChain.ChainLen* = 1: Base protocol. *ProtocolChain.ChainLen* > 1: Protocol chain. In this case, the *ProtocolChain.ChainEntries[]* array contains information about each layered protocol and the base protocol in the chain.
iVersion	Protocol version identifier.
iAddressFamily	The address family this protocol uses. This value can be used as the address family parameter in a call to socket() or WSASocket(). This value can also be used to determine the exact structure of a SOCKADDR to be used with the protocol.
iMaxSockAddr	The maximum size in bytes of an address used with this protocol.
iMinSockAddr	The minimum size in bytes of an address used with this protocol.
iSocketType	The value to use as the socket *type* parameter in a call to socket() or WSASocket() to open a socket for this protocol.
iProtocol	The value to use as the *protocol* parameter in a call to socket() or WSASocket() to open a socket for this protocol.
iProtocolMaxOffset	The maximum value that may be added to *iProtocol* when supplying a value for the *protocol* parameter to socket() and WSASocket(). Not all protocols allow a range of values, and in this case *iProtocolMaxOffset* will be zero.
iNetworkByteOrder	The network byte order used by the protocol. WINSOCK2.H defines two constants to be used with this field: BIGENDIAN and LITTLEENDIAN.

(continued)

TABLE 7-11 (CONTINUED)

Field	Description
iSecurityScheme	The type of security scheme employed (if any). WINSOCK2.H currently only defines SECURITY_PROTOCOL_NONE to indicate that the protocol does not provide any type of security. Other values would be provided by the service provider vendor. For example, SSL-enabled transports would have the value SECURITY_PROTOCOL_SSL here.
dwMessageSize	The maximum message size supported by the protocol, or one of the following special values: 0 = The protocol is stream oriented and the concept of message size is not relevant. 0x1 = The maximum message size depends on the underlying network MTU (Maximum Transmission Unit) and cannot be determined until the socket is bound. Bind the socket and then use SO_MAX_MSG_SIZ with getsockopt() to retrieve the value. 0xFFFFFFFF = The protocol is message oriented, but there is no maximum limit to the size of messages that may be transmitted.
dwProviderReserved	Reserved for use by service providers.
szProtocol	An array of up to 255 characters containing the name of the protocol. For example, Microsoft's Windows 95 TCP service provider is MS.w95.spi.tcp.

Note: The WSAPROTOCOL_INFO structure provides all the fields necessary to create a socket descriptor that uses the protocol. The *iAddressFamily*, *iSocketType*, and *iProtocol* fields can be used directly as parameters in a call to socket() or WSASocket().

The *ProviderId* field contains a *globally unique identifier* (GUID) for the service provider responsible for this protocol. GUIDs are Microsoft's implementation of the Open Software Foundation's idea of a Universal Unique Identifier (UUID). A GUID is a 128-bit value that uniquely identifies a provider or service. Like UUIDs, GUIDs can be generated that are statistically certain to be unique. Dynamically generating identifiers in this way negates the need to rely on registration with some central authority to ensure that identifiers are unique. Currently, two utility programs can be used to generate GUIDs: UUIDGEN.EXE and GUIDGEN.EXE.

Chapter 7: Introduction to WinSock 2.0

SERVICE FLAGS VALUES

The values in the *dwServiceFlags1* field in a WSAPROTOCOL_INFO structure reveal more about a protocol; they describe the type of service provided by the protocol or protocol chain. Table 7-12 presents a list of possible values and their meanings.

Note: With some values, the *absence* of the value helps describe the protocol.

TABLE 7-12 SERVICE FLAGS IN dwServiceFlags1 FIELD

Flag	Information Provided If Flag Is Set
XP1_CONNECTIONLESS	If set, this indicates the protocol is connectionless. If not set, the protocol is connection-oriented.
XP1_GUARANTEED_DELIVERY	The protocol guarantees delivery of all data sent (it is a "reliable" protocol).
XP1_GUARANTEED_ORDER	The protocol guarantees *if data is delivered*, it will arrive in the order in which it was sent, and it will not be duplicated.
XP1_MESSAGE_ORIENTED	The protocol preserves message boundaries.
XP1_PSEUDO_STREAM	A special type of message-oriented protocol has been used that does not preserve message boundaries on data being received.
XP1_GRACEFUL_CLOSE	If set, the protocol supports graceful close. If not set, only abortive closes are performed.
XP1_EXPEDITED_DATA	The protocol supports expedited (out-of-band) data.
XP1_CONNECT_DATA	The protocol supports connect data.
XP1_DISCONNECT_DATA	The protocol supports disconnect data.
XP1_SUPPORT_BROADCAST	The protocol supports a broadcast mechanism.
XP1_SUPPORT_MULTIPOINT	The protocol supports a multipoint or multicast mechanism.
XP1_QOS_SUPPORTED	The protocol supports quality-of-service requests.
XP1_UNI_SEND	The protocol is unidirectional in the send() direction.
XP1_UNI_RECV	The protocol is unidirectional in the recv() direction.
XP1_IFS_HANDLES	The socket descriptors returned by the provider are operating-system Installable File System (IFS) handles.
XP1_PARTIAL_MESSAGE	The MSG_PARTIAL flag is supported in WSASend() and WSASendTo().

PROVIDER FLAGS VALUES

The *dwProviderFlags* field holds information from the service provider about the protocol's entry in the protocol catalog. Table 7-13 lists the possible values and their meanings.

TABLE 7-13 PROVIDER FLAGS IN dwProviderFlags FIELD

Flag	Information Provided If Flag Is Set
PFL_MULTIPLE_PROTOCOL_ENTRIES	This is just one of two or more entries for this protocol from this provider. Protocols that can be configured to exhibit different behaviors will have this value set. (For example, SPX can be used as either a message-oriented protocol or a pseudostream. A *pseudostream* operates message-oriented on sends, and stream-oriented on receives.)
PFL_RECOMMENDED_PROTO_ENTRY	This is the recommended catalog entry to use for this protocol. This flag is only applicable if the protocol is capable of implementing multiple behaviors (see preceding flag).
PFL_HIDDEN	Set by a service provider to indicate this protocol should not be returned in the result buffer generated by WSAEnumProtocols(). Obviously, a WinSock 2 application should never see an entry with this bit set.
PFL_MATCHES_PROTOCOL_ZERO	This is the default protocol for this address family and socket type. (A value of zero in the *protocol* parameter of socket() or WSASocket() will create a descriptor using this protocol.)

The EnumProto Application

The EnumProto application presented in this section uses the WSAEnumProtocols() function to obtain a list of all protocols and protocol chains installed on the local machine. It parses the returned WSAPROTOCOL_INFO structures and builds a description of each available protocol, using a tree-view control. Figure 7-5 shows

Chapter 7: Introduction to WinSock 2.0   233

EnumProto running on a Windows 95 machine that has TCP, UDP, SPX, and IPX installed. This view of the IPX entry is expanded to show the information obtained from the *dwServiceFlags1* field.

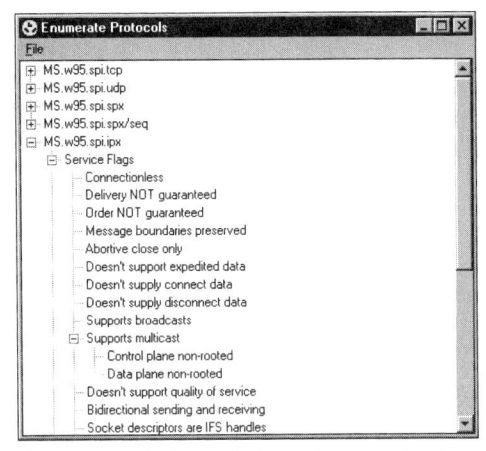

Figure 7-5: The EnumProto application displays detailed information about all installed protocols and protocol chains.

Listing 7-1 contains the source code for the AddAllProtocols() function from the EnumProto program. This function does almost all the WinSock work in the program. It calls WSAEnumProtocols(), parses the WSAPROTOCOL_INFO structures, and fills the application's tree-view control.

Note: You'll find the complete source code for EnumProto on the CD, in the \CH07\ENUMPROT folder.

Tip: Rather than guessing at the size of the buffer needed to hold all protocol information, the AddAllProtocols() function uses a little trick picked up from one of the WinSock 2 SDK samples. It intentionally passes a NULL buffer to WSAEnumProtocols(), which generates a WSAENOBUFS error. When this error occurs, WSAEnumProtocols() sets the DWORD parameter pointed to by *lpdwBufferLength*, to the needed buffer size. AddAllProtocols() then allocates a buffer of the specified size and calls WSAEnumProtocols() a second time to actually retrieve all of the protocol information.

Listing 7-1 The AddAllProtocols() function from ENUMPROT.C

```c
//
// AddAllProtocols()
// Call WSAEnumProtocols()
// and add info to TreeControl
//
void AddAllProtocols(HWND hWndTree)
{
LPBYTE pBuf;
    DWORD dwLen;
    int nRet;
    int nCount;
    LPWSAPROTOCOL_INFO pInfo;
    HTREEITEM hParent;
    HTREEITEM hParent2;
    HTREEITEM hParent3;

    //
    // Determine needed buffer size by
    // intentionally generating an error.
    //
    dwLen = 0;
    nRet = WSAEnumProtocols(NULL,
                            NULL,
                            &dwLen);
    if (nRet == SOCKET_ERROR)
    {
        // Look for the expected error
        if (WSAGetLastError() != WSAENOBUFS)
        {
            ShowWinsockError(WSAGetLastError());
            return;
        }
    }

    //
    // dwLen should now contain the needed buffer size
    // Check to see that it's at least the
    // size of 1 WSAPROTOCOL_INFO structure
    //
    if (dwLen < sizeof(WSAPROTOCOL_INFO))
    {
        MessageBox(NULL, "Internal error",
                        gszAppName,
                        MB_OK|MB_ICONERROR);
        return;
    }

    // Add 1 byte just to be paranoid
    dwLen++;
    pBuf = malloc(dwLen+1);
```

```c
    if (pBuf == NULL)
    {
        MessageBox(NULL,
                    "Couldn't allocate protocol buffer",
                    gszAppName,
                    MB_OK|MB_ICONERROR);
        return;
    }

    //
    // Make the "real" call
    //
    nRet = WSAEnumProtocols(NULL,
                            (LPWSAPROTOCOL_INFO)pBuf,
                            &dwLen);
    if (nRet == SOCKET_ERROR)
    {
        free(pBuf);
        ShowWinsockError(WSAGetLastError());
        return;
    }

    //
    // Loop through the protocols
    // nRet contains the number of
    // protocols returned
    //
    pInfo = (LPWSAPROTOCOL_INFO)pBuf;
    for(nCount = 0; nCount < nRet; nCount++)
    {
        // Each protocol begins at the root
        // of the tree view control
        hParent = AddTreeItem(hWndTree,
                                TVI_ROOT,
                                pInfo->szProtocol);

        // Service flags are added one step down
        hParent2 = AddTreeItem(hWndTree,
                                hParent,
                                "Service Flags");

        //
        // Helper macro for adding service flags
        //
        #define ADDSF(f, s1, s2)                    \
            AddTreeItem(hWndTree,                   \
                hParent2,                           \
                (pInfo->dwServiceFlags1 & f) ?      \
                s1 : s2)

        ADDSF(XP1_CONNECTIONLESS,
            "Connectionless",
            "Connection-oriented");
```

```
            ADDSF(XP1_GUARANTEED_DELIVERY,
                "Delivery guaranteed",
                "Delivery NOT guaranteed");

            ADDSF(XP1_GUARANTEED_ORDER,
                "Order guaranteed",
                "Order NOT guaranteed");

            ADDSF(XP1_MESSAGE_ORIENTED,
                "Message boundaries preserved",
                "Message boundaries NOT preserved");

            if (pInfo->dwServiceFlags1 & XP1_PSEUDO_STREAM)
                AddTreeItem(hWndTree, hParent2,
                    "Message oriented with boundaries ignored");

            ADDSF(XP1_GRACEFUL_CLOSE,
                "Can perform graceful close",
                "Abortive close only");

            ADDSF(XP1_EXPEDITED_DATA,
                "Supports expedited data",
                "Doesn't support expedited data");

            ADDSF(XP1_CONNECT_DATA,
                "Supplies connect data",
                "Doesn't supply connect data");

            ADDSF(XP1_DISCONNECT_DATA,
                "Supplies disconnect data",
                "Doesn't supply disconnect data");

            ADDSF(XP1_SUPPORT_BROADCAST,
                "Supports broadcasts",
                "Doesn't support broadcasts");

            // Multipoint/multicast
            if (pInfo->dwServiceFlags1 & XP1_SUPPORT_MULTIPOINT)
            {
                hParent3 = AddTreeItem(hWndTree,
                                hParent2,
                                "Supports multicast");
                AddTreeItem(hWndTree,
                            hParent3,
                            (pInfo->dwServiceFlags1 &
                            XP1_MULTIPOINT_CONTROL_PLANE) ?
                            "Control plane rooted" :
                            "Control plane non-rooted");

                AddTreeItem(hWndTree,
                            hParent3,
                            (pInfo->dwServiceFlags1 &
```

Chapter 7: Introduction to WinSock 2.0

```
                    XP1_MULTIPOINT_DATA_PLANE) ?
                    "Data plane rooted" :
                    "Data plane non-rooted");
}
else
    AddTreeItem(hWndTree,
                hParent2,
                "Doesn't support multicast");

ADDSF(XP1_QOS_SUPPORTED,
    "Supports quality of service",
    "Doesn't support quality of service");

if (pInfo->dwServiceFlags1 & XP1_UNI_SEND)
    AddTreeItem(hWndTree,
            hParent2,
            "Unidirectional in the send direction");

if (pInfo->dwServiceFlags1 & XP1_UNI_RECV)
    AddTreeItem(hWndTree,
            hParent2,
            "Unidirectional in the recv direction");

if (!(pInfo->dwServiceFlags1 & XP1_UNI_SEND) &&
    !(pInfo->dwServiceFlags1 & XP1_UNI_RECV))
        AddTreeItem(hWndTree,
            hParent2,
            "Bidirectional sending and receiving");

if (pInfo->dwServiceFlags1 & XP1_IFS_HANDLES)
    AddTreeItem(hWndTree,
            hParent2,
            "Socket descriptors are IFS handles");

ADDSF(XP1_PARTIAL_MESSAGE,
    "Supports MSG_PARTIAL",
    "Doesn't support MSG_PARTIAL");

// Provider flags
hParent2 = AddTreeItem(hWndTree,
                    hParent,
                    "Provider Flags");

if (pInfo->dwProviderFlags &
        PFL_MULTIPLE_PROTO_ENTRIES)
    AddTreeItem(hWndTree,
                hParent2,
                "This is one behavior of two or"
                " more for this protocol");

if (pInfo->dwProviderFlags &
        PFL_RECOMMENDED_PROTO_ENTRY)
    AddTreeItem(hWndTree,
```

```c
                            hParent2,
                            "This is the recommended entry"
                            " for this protocol.");

        if (pInfo->dwProviderFlags & PFL_HIDDEN)
            AddTreeItem(hWndTree,
                        hParent2,
                        "WS2 SPI ERROR."
                        " Hidden catalog entry shown");

        if (pInfo->dwProviderFlags &
                PFL_MATCHES_PROTOCOL_ZERO)
            AddTreeItem(hWndTree,
                        hParent2,
                        "Use zero as protocol parameter");

        // Provider ID
        AddTreeItem(hWndTree,
                    hParent,
                    "GUID: %s",
                    GUIDtoString((GUID *)&pInfo->ProviderId));

        // Catalog entry
        AddTreeItem(hWndTree,
                    hParent,
                    "Catalog entry: %ld",
                    pInfo->dwCatalogEntryId);

        // Protocol chain
        switch(pInfo->ProtocolChain.ChainLen)
        {
            case 0:
                AddTreeItem(hWndTree,
                            hParent,
                            "Layered protocol");
                break;
            case 1:
                AddTreeItem(hWndTree,
                            hParent,
                            "Base protocol");
                break;
            default:
                if (pInfo->ProtocolChain.ChainLen > 1)
                    AddTreeItem(hWndTree,
                                hParent,
                                "Protocol chain");
                else
                    AddTreeItem(hWndTree,
                                hParent,
                                "SPI ERROR:"
                                " Invalid ChainLen");
        }
```

```
// Version
AddTreeItem(hWndTree,
            hParent,
            "Version: %d",
            pInfo->iVersion);

// Address family
AddTreeItem(hWndTree,
            hParent,
            "Address family: %s",
            AFtoSTR(pInfo->iAddressFamily));

// Min/Max SOCKADDR size
AddTreeItem(hWndTree,
            hParent,
            "Min/Max Address length: %d/%d",
            pInfo->iMinSockAddr,
            pInfo->iMaxSockAddr);

// Socket type
switch(pInfo->iSocketType)
{
    case SOCK_STREAM:
        AddTreeItem(hWndTree,
                    hParent,
                    "SOCK_STREAM");
        break;
    case SOCK_DGRAM:
        AddTreeItem(hWndTree,
                    hParent,
                    "SOCK_DGRAM");
        break;
    case SOCK_RAW:
        AddTreeItem(hWndTree,
                    hParent,
                    "SOCK_RAW");
        break;
    case SOCK_RDM:
        AddTreeItem(hWndTree,
                    hParent,
                    "SOCK_RDM");
        break;
    case SOCK_SEQPACKET:
        AddTreeItem(hWndTree,
                    hParent,
                    "SOCK_SEQPACKET");
        break;
    default:
        AddTreeItem(hWndTree,
                    hParent,
                    "Unknown");
}
```

```c
            // Protocol
            AddTreeItem(hWndTree,
                        hParent,
                        "Protocol: %s",
                        PROTOtoSTR(pInfo->iProtocol));

            // Protocol max offset
            AddTreeItem(hWndTree,
                        hParent,
                        "Protocol Max Offset: %d",
                        pInfo->iProtocolMaxOffset);

            // Network byte order
            switch(pInfo->iNetworkByteOrder)
            {
                case BIGENDIAN:
                    AddTreeItem(hWndTree,
                                hParent,
                                "Big Endian");
                    break;
                case LITTLEENDIAN:
                    AddTreeItem(hWndTree,
                                hParent,
                                "Little Endian");
                    break;
                default:
                    AddTreeItem(hWndTree,
                                hParent,
                                "Unknown");
            }

            // Security
            AddTreeItem(hWndTree,
                        hParent,
                        "Security scheme: %d",
                        pInfo->iSecurityScheme);

            // Message size
            switch(pInfo->dwMessageSize)
            {
                case 0:
                    AddTreeItem(hWndTree,
                                hParent,
                                "Max message size"
                                " not applicable");
                    break;
                case 1:
                    AddTreeItem(hWndTree,
                                hParent,
                                "Max message size based on MTU");
                    break;
                case 0xFFFFFFFF:
                    AddTreeItem(hWndTree,
```

```
                            hParent,
                            "No limit on max message size");
                break;
            default:
                AddTreeItem(hWndTree,
                            hParent,
                            "Unknown max message size: %ld",
                            pInfo->dwMessageSize);
        }
        // Move pointer to next protocol
        pInfo++;
    }

    free(pBuf);
    return;
}
```

Selecting Protocols

One task that protocol-independent client and server applications must perform over and over again is selecting protocols based on their suitability for some purpose. As mentioned in the earlier section on finding protocol information, an application might search for protocols that are connection oriented and reliable, preserve record boundaries, or support multicast.

The SelectProtocols() function is included on the companion CD-ROM to help with this process. It works almost exactly like WSAEnumProtocols(), but enables you to specify only those protocols that meet some predetermined behavior.

Note: You'll find the Select Protocols() function in the \CH07\SELPROTO folder on the CD.

Here is the function prototype for the SelectProtocols() function:

```
int SelectProtocols(
                    DWORD dwSetFlags,
                    DWORD dwNotSetFlags,
                    LPWSAPROTOCOL_INFO lpProtocolBuffer,
                    LPDWORD lpdwBufferLength
                    );
```

Parameter	Description
dwSetFlags	A bitmask of values to ensure are set in the protocol's WSAPROTOCOL_INFO.*dwServiceFlags1* field.

Parameter	Description
dwNotSetFlags	A bitmask of values to ensure are NOT set in the protocol's WSAPROTOCOL_INFO.*dwServiceFlags1* field.
lpProtocolBuffer	The buffer to be filled with WSAPROTOCOL_INFO structures.
lpdwBufferLength	On input, the size in bytes of the buffer pointed to by the *lpProtocolBuffer* parameter. On output, the minimum size the buffer must be to retrieve all of the requested information.

The SelectProtocols() function compares the values specified in the *dwSetFlags* parameter with the values in WSAPROTOCOL_INFO.*dwServiceFlags1* field of each protocol. For each value specified in the *dwSetFlags* parameter (such as XP1_CONNECTIONLESS), SelectProtocols() ensures that any protocol returned has the same value set in its *dwServiceFlags1* field.

As noted earlier in the "Service Flags Values" section, the *absence* of some flag values in *dwServiceFlags1* is significant. For example, no flag specifically indicates a protocol is connection oriented. Thus the absence of the XP1_CONNECTIONLESS flag indicates a protocol is connection oriented. Therefore, SelectProtocols() also accepts a bitmask of values that are *not* set in each returned protocol's dwServiceFlags1 field. The following code calls SelectProtocols() and requests information for all protocols that guarantee delivery and are connection oriented:

```
// Request all protocols that guarantee delivery and order
#define SETFLAGS XP1_GUARANTEED_DELIVERY|XP1_GUARANTEED_ORDER
// and are connection-oriented
#define NOTSETFLAGS XP1_CONNECTIONLESS

BYTE  protocolBuf[1024];
DWORD dwLen = sizeof(protocolBuf);
int   nRet;

nRet = SelectProtocols(SETFLAGS,
                       NOTSETFLAGS,
                       (LPWSAPROTOCOL_INFO)protocolBuf,
                       &dwLen);
if (nRet == SOCKET_ERROR)
{
    if (WSAGetLastError() == WSAENOBUFS)
    {
        // protocolBuf is too small
        // dwLen is set to needed size
    }
    // Handle other error
}
```

On success, SelectProtocols() returns the number of WSAPROTOCOL_INFO structures copied to the input buffer. On failure, it returns SOCKET_ERROR, and a specific error code can be found with WSAGetLastError(). As with WSAEnumProtocols(), if the specific error is WSAENOBUFS, then the buffer pointed to by the *lpProtocolBuffer* is too small and the DWORD pointed to by *lpdwBufferLength* contains the needed buffer size.

Listing 7-2 is the source code for the SelectProtocols() function.

Listing 7-2 SELPROTO.C

```c
//
// SELPROTO.C -SelectProtocols() function
//

#include <winsock2.h>

//////////////////////////////////////////////////////////////

int SelectProtocols(
                    DWORD dwSetFlags,
                    DWORD dwNotSetFlags,
                    LPWSAPROTOCOL_INFO lpProtocolBuffer,
                    LPDWORD lpdwBufferLength
                    )
{
    LPBYTE              pBuf;
    LPWSAPROTOCOL_INFO  pInfo;
    DWORD               dwNeededLen;
    LPWSAPROTOCOL_INFO  pRetInfo;
    DWORD               dwRetLen;
    int                 nCount;
    int                 nMatchCount;
    int                 nRet;

    //
    // Determine needed buffer size
    //
    dwNeededLen = 0;
    nRet = WSAEnumProtocols(NULL, NULL, &dwNeededLen);
    if (nRet == SOCKET_ERROR)
    {
        if (WSAGetLastError() != WSAENOBUFS)
            return SOCKET_ERROR;
    }

    //
    // Allocate the buffer
    //
    pBuf = malloc(dwNeededLen);
    if (pBuf == NULL)
    {
        WSASetLastError(WSAENOBUFS);
```

```
            return SOCKET_ERROR;
    }

    //
    // Make the "real" call
    //
    nRet = WSAEnumProtocols(NULL,
                            (LPWSAPROTOCOL_INFO)pBuf,
                            &dwNeededLen);
    if (nRet == SOCKET_ERROR)
    {
        free(pBuf);
        return SOCKET_ERROR;
    }

    //
    // Helper macros for selecting protocols
    //
    #define REJECTSET(f) \
      ((dwSetFlags & f) && !(pInfo->dwServiceFlags1 & f))
    #define REJECTNOTSET(f) \
      ((dwNotSetFlags &f) && (pInfo->dwServiceFlags1 & f))
    #define REJECTEDBY(f) (REJECTSET(f) || REJECTNOTSET(f))

    //
    // Loop through the protocols making selections
    //
    pInfo = (LPWSAPROTOCOL_INFO)pBuf;
    pRetInfo = lpProtocolBuffer;
    dwRetLen = 0;
    nMatchCount = 0;
    for(nCount = 0; nCount < nRet; nCount++)
    {
        //
        // Check all of the requested flags
        //
        while(1)
        {
            if (REJECTEDBY(XP1_CONNECTIONLESS))
                break;
            if (REJECTEDBY(XP1_GUARANTEED_DELIVERY))
                break;
            if (REJECTEDBY(XP1_GUARANTEED_ORDER))
                break;
            if (REJECTEDBY(XP1_MESSAGE_ORIENTED))
                break;
            if (REJECTEDBY(XP1_PSEUDO_STREAM))
                break;
            if (REJECTEDBY(XP1_GRACEFUL_CLOSE))
                break;
            if (REJECTEDBY(XP1_EXPEDITED_DATA))
                break;
            if (REJECTEDBY(XP1_CONNECT_DATA))
```

```
                    break;
                if (REJECTEDBY(XP1_DISCONNECT_DATA))
                    break;
                if (REJECTEDBY(XP1_SUPPORT_BROADCAST))
                    break;
                if (REJECTEDBY(XP1_SUPPORT_MULTIPOINT))
                    break;
                if (REJECTEDBY(XP1_MULTIPOINT_DATA_PLANE))
                    break;
                if (REJECTEDBY(XP1_QOS_SUPPORTED))
                    break;
                if (REJECTEDBY(XP1_UNI_SEND))
                    break;
                if (REJECTEDBY(XP1_UNI_RECV))
                    break;
                if (REJECTEDBY(XP1_IFS_HANDLES))
                    break;
                if (REJECTEDBY(XP1_PARTIAL_MESSAGE))
                    break;
                //
                // If we made it here,
                //the protocol meets all requirements
                //
                dwRetLen += sizeof(WSAPROTOCOL_INFO);
                if (dwRetLen > *lpdwBufferLength)
                {
                    // The supplied buffer is too small
                    WSASetLastError(WSAENOBUFS);
                    *lpdwBufferLength = dwNeededLen;
                    free(pBuf);
                    return SOCKET_ERROR;
                }
                nMatchCount++;
                // Copy this protocol to the caller's buffer
                memcpy(pRetInfo, pInfo, sizeof(WSAPROTOCOL_INFO));
                pRetInfo++;
                break;
            }
        pInfo++;
    }
    free(pBuf);
    *lpdwBufferLength = dwRetLen;
    return(nMatchCount);
}
```

Summary

Version 2 of WinSock is an ambitious extension of the now well-established WinSock 1.1 standard. A generous assortment of new features exist in many new areas, but most important by far is that WinSock 2 now officially supports transport protocols other than TCP/IP.

Even with all its new functionality, WinSock 2 remains remarkably compatible with WinSock 1.1. All that is required to port most Version 1.1 applications to Version 2 is to include WINSOCK2.H rather than WINSOCK.H, then compile and link.

In this chapter we examined the processes for obtaining information for all of the protocols and protocol chains installed on a machine. In the next chapter, we'll look at how client and server applications can operate in a truly protocol independent fashion, through the use of the new WinSock 2 name registration and resolution functions.

Chapter 8

Name Registration and Resolution

IN THIS CHAPTER
In Chapter 8 we look at the new protocol-independent name registration and resolution functions available in WinSock 2. Topics covered are as follows:

- Understanding name space behavior
- Registering a new service class
- Advertising a service
- Enumerating available name spaces
- Finding a host or service

WINSOCK 2 STILL INCLUDES the standard database functions – gethostbyname(), getservbyport(), and so on – that were available in WinSock 1.1. These "getXbyY" functions are still limited in Version 2 to name resolution on TCP/IP only. They either use local tables or the DNS name space to perform their services.

To provide true protocol independence, WinSock 2 also includes a new set of functions that can be used to locate host machines and services using a wide variety of underlying network naming schemes and transport protocols. A single standard API allows simultaneous access to various name-resolution strategies, including the Internet's Domain Name Service (DNS) and Novell's Service Advertising Protocol (SAP) and others.

Registration and Resolution

The WinSock 2 functions for name resolution and registration provide two basic services:

- Name Registration: A standardized way for server applications to announce their availability.
- Name Resolution: A standardized way for client applications to locate server applications.

A server application (service) registers a service name to *advertise* its availability through one or more name spaces. A client application then uses the resolution functions to translate this service name into the address, protocol, and socket type information needed to connect to the service.

Types of Name Spaces

As mentioned in Chapter 7, a *name space* refers to service names, host names, protocol names, *and* the resolution services available to convert names to values and values to names. The same functions are used to find hosts and services no matter what underlying name service is in use. The exact nature of the service provided, however, is dependent on the *type* of name space in use. Three fundamental types of name spaces exist.

Dynamic name spaces allow services to register programmatically their availability at run-time. Name spaces of this type broadcast services' availability, so client applications can locate a service and determine if it is *currently* available. Novell's Service Advertising Protocols (SAP) is an example of a dynamic name space.

Persistent name spaces, like dynamic name spaces, allow services to register programmatically their availability at run-time. Persistent name spaces, however, do not continually broadcast service availability. Name spaces of this type usually maintain registration information in disk files. The Netware Directory Service (NDS) is an example of a persistent name space.

Static name spaces don't provide a mechanism for services to register programmatically their availability at run-time. Service names and their related information must be registered manually in advance of a client query. The Internet's Domain Name Service (DNS) is an example of a static name space.

Even though the specifics of how a service registers with WinSock 2 remain the same across different name spaces, exactly what happens to that information varies dramatically depending on the type of name space being used. When a service successfully calls the registration functions on a local machine using a dynamic name space, client applications on remote machines can immediately locate the service. When the same registration process takes place using a static name space, clients running on remote machines will still have no knowledge of the service's presence.

Important: I want to stress the Internet's Domain Name System does *not* support a mechanism that would allow a server application to register service information dynamically. As you'll see later in this chapter, DNS name spaces have well-known TCP/IP and UDP/IP services preregistered. Registering in a SAP or NDS name space provides many benefits; however, registering a new, unique (not well-known) service accomplishes little or nothing in a DNS name space.

Registering a Service

One of the most substantial benefits derived from protocol independence is that a service can make itself available across multiple transport protocols simultaneously. At startup, a service can search for appropriate transport protocols based on their suitability for the application's task and open one or more listening sockets, each bound to a specific address and protocol. By registering and listening on all appropriate protocols, a service makes itself available to as many different types of client applications as possible.

Certain parameters needed by a client to communicate with the service are unique to a transport. For example, the client will need to know the correct port number for a service using TCP or UDP. The next few sections explain how services register specific parameters within appropriate name spaces to make this type of information available to clients.

Service Class

Each instance of a service has a service name and is also related to a service class. A *service class* holds information that many instances of a particular service application may have in common. This set of attributes is provided at the time the service class is defined to WinSock, and is referred to as the *service class schema* information. Examples of service class names may be well-known services such as "HTTP Server"; or they may be completely unique, like "Fred's Widget Server."

Each service class has one related service-class info structure (WSASERVICECLASSINFO) that references one or more name-space-specific class information structures (WSANSCLASSINFO). A service class refers to a WSANSCLASSINFO structure for *each* name space through which the service is available.

The WSASERVICECLASSINFO Structure

The WSASERVICECLASSINFO structure simply identifies the service class by name and GUID, and points to an array of related name-space-specific structures. The class name doesn't necessarily have to be unique, but the GUID must be.

```
typedef struct _WSASERVICECLASSINFO
{
    LPGUID              lpServiceClassId;
    LPSTR               lpszServiceClassName;
    DWORD               dwCount;
    LPWSANSCLASSINFOA   lpClassInfos;
}WSASERVICECLASSINFO;
```

Developers creating new or unique services (services that are not well-known) simply choose a class name and generate a new GUID with UUIDGEN.EXE, GUIDGEN.EXE, or some other utility.

250 Part III: The WinSock 2.0 API

GUIDs for well-known services have been preassigned and can be found in SVCGUID.H. Preassigned GUIDs exist for all of the well-known TCP/IP services as defined in RFC 1060, "Assigned Numbers," as well as for many Netware services. Macros are named in SVCGUID.H that expand into the appropriate preassigned GUID. In addition, some macros accept a TCP port number or Netware SAP ID (in host order) and return a GUID. Table 8-1 lists some of the GUID macros available in SVCGUID.H.

The *lpClassInfos* field of the WSASERVICECLASSINFO structure points to an array of WSANSCLASSINFO structures, and the *dwCount* field references the number of members contained in the array.

TABLE 8-1 PREASSIGNED GUIDS FOR WELL-KNOWN SERVICES

Macro	Expanded Preassigned GUID
SVCID_TCP(Port)	GUID for the given port number when using TCP as a transport.
SVCID_UDP(Port)	GUID for the given port number when using UDP.
SVCID_ECHO_TCP	GUID for ECHO service on TCP (port 7).
SVCID_ECHO_UDP	GUID for ECHO service on UDP (port 7).
SVCID_FTP_TCP	GUID for FTP connection service on TCP (port 21).
SVCID_NETWARE(Type)	GUID for the given Netware object type.
SVCID_PRINT_QUEUE	GUID for Netware print queue service.

The WSANSCLASSINFO Structure

The name space service-class information (WSANSCLASSINFO) structures provide a series of parameters unique to each type of name space. Each structure holds a parameter name; a name space identifier to which the parameter relates; a description of the parameter's value including type and size; and the value itself. For example, an FTP service in a DNS name space would register the parameter name "TcpPort" with a value of 21. Here is the definition of the WSANSCLASSINFO structure from WINSOCK2.H:

```
typedef struct _WSANSCLASSINFO
{
    LPSTR    lpszName;
    DWORD    dwNameSpace;
```

```
    DWORD     dwValueType;
    DWORD     dwValueSize;
    LPVOID    lpValue;
}WSANSCLASSINFO;
```

Commonly used values for the *lpszName* field are contained in the name space provider API header (NSPAPI.H). These include manifest constants for parameter names, such as the following:

Constant for lpszName Field	Description
SERVICE_TYPE_VALUE_CONN	"ConnectionOriented"
SERVICE_TYPE_VALUE_TCPPORT	"TcpPort"
SERVICE_TYPE_VALUE_UDPPORT	"UdpPort"
SERVICE_TYPE_VALUE_SAPID	"SapId"

The *dwNameSpace* field of the service-class information structure specifies the type of name space as defined in WINSOCK2.H (NS_ALL, NS_DNS, and so forth). The *dwValueType* field contains a reference to a data type as defined for the registry in WINNT.H (REG_DWORD, REG_SZ, and so forth). And the *dwValueSize* field contains the size in bytes of the value; for example, `sizeof(DWORD)`.

The WSAInstallServiceClass() Function

Once a WSASERVICECLASSINFO structure and a set of related WSANSCLASS-INFO structures have been prepared, a new service class can be registered with the WSAInstallServiceClass() function. WSAInstallClass() accepts a pointer to a WSACLASSINFO structure and returns zero on success, or SOCKET_ERROR on failure.

The example in Listing 8-1 registers a new service class by preparing the needed structures and then calling WSAInstallServiceClass().

Listing 8-1 Registering a Service Class

```
//
// Install new service class for connection-oriented server
// on DNS and SAP name spaces.
//
// GUID: {2406E160-043A-11d1-85E2-444553540000}
// generated with GUIDGEN.EXE
static const GUID guid = {
```

```
                            0x2406e160, 0x43a, 0x11d1,
                            { 0x85, 0xe2, 0x44, 0x45,
                              0x53, 0x54, 0x0,  0x0
                            }
                          };
WSASERVICECLASSINFO sci;
WSANSCLASSINFO      nsciArray[4];
DWORD               dwOne   = 1;
DWORD               dwPort  = 2000;
DWORD               dwSapId = 2000;
int                 nRet;

// Service class info
sci.lpServiceClassId = (LPGUID)&guid;
sci.lpszServiceClassName = "My Widget Server";
sci.dwCount = 4;
sci.lpClassInfos = nsciArray;

//
// DNS setup
//

// Set connection-oriented to TRUE (1)
nsciArray[0].lpszName = SERVICE_TYPE_VALUE_CONN;
nsciArray[0].dwNameSpace = NS_DNS;
nsciArray[0].dwValueType = REG_DWORD;
nsciArray[0].dwValueSize = sizeof(DWORD);
nsciArray[0].lpValue    = &dwOne;
// Indicate port number
nsciArray[1].lpszName = SERVICE_TYPE_VALUE_TCPPORT;
nsciArray[1].dwNameSpace = NS_DNS;
nsciArray[1].dwValueType = REG_DWORD;
nsciArray[1].dwValueSize = sizeof(DWORD);
nsciArray[1].lpValue    = &dwPort;

//
// Novell SAP setup
//

// Set connection-oriented to TRUE (1)
nsciArray[2].lpszName = SERVICE_TYPE_VALUE_CONN;
nsciArray[2].dwNameSpace = NS_SAP;
nsciArray[2].dwValueType = REG_DWORD;
nsciArray[2].dwValueSize = sizeof(DWORD);
nsciArray[2].lpValue    = &dwOne;
// Indicate SAP Object ID
nsciArray[3].lpszName = SERVICE_TYPE_VALUE_SAPID;
nsciArray[3].dwNameSpace = NS_SAP;
nsciArray[3].dwValueType = REG_DWORD;
nsciArray[3].dwValueSize = sizeof(DWORD);
nsciArray[3].lpValue    = &dwSapId;

// Install the new class
```

```
nRet = WSAInstallServiceClass(&sci);
if (nRet == SOCKET_ERROR)
{
    // Handle the error
}
```

A service class such as this need only be installed on the machine that will host the service — it needn't be installed on each client machine. Once the service class has been established, services that use this class do not have to reinstall the class each time they run. They only need to form a relationship with a class that has already been installed.

A service class can be removed with the WSARemoveServiceClass() function. The function takes only one parameter: a pointer to the GUID identifying the service class to be removed.

Advertising Availability

Once a service class has been installed, a specific instance of a service can be *advertised* (registered for availability). During startup, the service can search for appropriate transport protocols and choose to listen with one or more sockets, each bound to a specific socket address and protocol. Then, when the service registers its availability to clients, it supplies information about the various addresses and protocols on which it is currently listening. In this way, a client application is able to find the service, choose from any one of the listening sockets, and attempt to connect.

THE CSADDR_INFO STRUCTURE

All the address and protocol information for a service's listening sockets is collected into a series of CSADDR_INFO structures. Here is the definition of the CSADDR_INFO structure:

```
typedef struct _CSADDR_INFO {
    SOCKET_ADDRESS LocalAddr ;
    SOCKET_ADDRESS RemoteAddr ;
    INT iSocketType ;
    INT iProtocol ;
} CSADDR_INFO;
```

Field	Description
LocalAddr	A SOCKET_ADDRESS structure that contains a pointer to a SOCKADDR structure (*lpSockAddr*) and the length of the SOCKADDR (*iSockaddrLength*).

(continued)

254   Part III: The WinSock 2.0 API

Field	Description
RemoteAddr	A SOCKET_ADDRESS structure that contains a pointer to a SOCKADDR structure (*lpSockAddr*) and the length of the SOCKADDR (*iSockaddrLength*).
iSocketType	An integer that can be used for the socket type parameter in a call to socket() or WSASocket().
iProtocol	An integer that can be used for the protocol parameter in a call to socket() or WSASocket()

Note, this structure contains all the information a client needs to create an appropriate socket descriptor and then communicate with the service. All of the parameters required for a call to socket() are included: socket type and protocol from the structure itself (*iSocketType* and *iProtocol)* and the address family parameter from *RemoteAddr.lpSockaddr->sa_family*.

USING WSAQUERYSET DURING REGISTRATION

As soon as one CSADDR_INFO structure has been created for each listening socket, the socket can then register for availability by putting all of this information together into one WSAQUERYSET structure. Here is the definition of the WSAQUERYSET structure from WINSOCK2.H:

```
typedef struct _WSAQuerySet
{
        DWORD              dwSize;
        LPWSTR             lpszServiceInstanceName;
        LPGUID             lpServiceClassId;
        LPWSAVERSION       lpVersion;
        LPWSTR             lpszComment;
        DWORD              dwNameSpace;
        LPGUID             lpNSProviderId;
        LPWSTR             lpszContext;
        DWORD              dwNumberOfProtocols;
        LPAFPROTOCOLS      lpafpProtocols;
        LPWSTR             lpszQueryString;
        DWORD              dwNumberOfCsAddrs;
        LPCSADDR_INFO      lpcsaBuffer;
        DWORD              dwOutputFlags;
        LPBLOB             lpBlob;
} WSAQUERYSET;
```

Note: The WSAQUERYSET structure is used by services when they are registering their availability, and also by clients when searching for available services. Many of the fields aren't relevant to registering a service, so rather than looking at

Chapter 8: Name Registration and Resolution 255

the entire structure here, we'll discuss only the fields used when registering a service. Later in this chapter, we'll look at the WSAQUERYSET structure again and examine the fields used for locating services.

Table 8-2 describes the WSAQUERYSET fields used when registering a service.

TABLE 8-2 WSAQUERYSET FIELDS WHEN REGISTERING A SERVICE

Field	Description
dwSize	Must be set to `sizeof(WSAQUERYSET)`. This is a versioning mechanism.
dwOutputflags	Not applicable to registration.
lpszServiceInstanceName	Pointer to a character array containing the service name. Holds the name of this instance of the service — *not* the service class name.
lpServiceClassId	Pointer to the GUID for the previously installed service class. Must reference a service class that was previously installed with WSAInstallServiceClass() or one of the special, preassigned service classes (see Table 8-1).
lpVersion	Optional pointer to a WSAVERSION structure containing a DWORD version number. Clients can select among instances of a service by comparing this version number (if supplied).
lpszComment	Optional pointer to a character array containing a comment; this can be anything the service would like to use.
dwNameSpace1	Identifier of a single name-space in which to register, or NS_ALL to register in all available name spaces. The combination of this field and the *lpNSProviderId* field (described next) determines which name space providers will be used by the service. If the *lpNSProviderId* field isn't NULL, then this field is ignored.
lpNSProviderId	Optional pointer to a GUID for specific name-space provider. If this field isn't NULL, then the *dwNameSpace1* field is ignored.
lpszContext	Not applicable to registration.
dwNumberOfProtocols	Not applicable to registration.

(continued)

TABLE 8-2 (CONTINUED)

Field	Description
lpafpProtocols	Not applicable to registration.
lpszQueryString	Not applicable to registration.
dwNumberOfCsAddrs	The number of elements in the array of CSADDRO_INFO structures referenced by *lpcsaBuffer*.
lpcsaBuffer	Pointer to an array of CSADDR_INFO structures that contain the protocol and address information for the socket on which the service is listening. See Figure 8-1.
lpBlob	Optional pointer to a provider-specific structure.

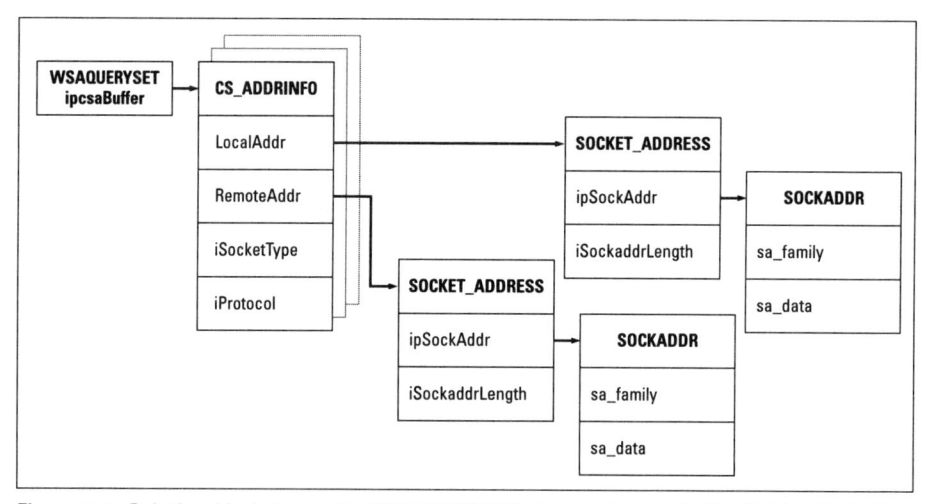

Figure 8-1: Relationship between the WSAQUERYSET structure's lpcsaBuffer field and all of the related structures

THE WSASetService() FUNCTION

Once all of this information has finally been collected, a service can use the WSASetService() function to register for availability. This function is used when the service begins to register for availability and again before it exits, to indicate that it will no longer be available. Here is the function prototype for WSASetService():

```
INT WSASetService(
                LPWSAQUERYSETA lpqsRegInfo,
                WSAESETSERVICEOP essoperation,
                DWORD dwControlFlags
                );
```

Parameter	Description
lpqsRegInfo	A pointer to the previously prepared WSAQUERYSET structure, as described in the preceding section.
essOperation	One of the operation codes: RNRSERVICE_REGISTER, RNRSERVICE_DEREGISTER, or RNRSERVICE_DELETE, as described in the paragraphs that follow.
dwControlFlags	The meaning of *dwControlFlags* is dependent on the value of the *essOperation* field. Details are discussed in the following section.

The WSASetService() function is affected by the following values used in the *essOperation* parameter:

RNRSERVICE_REGISTER A service uses this operation code when starting up and registering for availability. On dynamic name spaces such as SAP, broadcasting or some other mechanism will be initiated to inform clients of the service's availability. On persistent name spaces such as NDS, this value causes the registration information to be written to the data store. On static name spaces such as DNS, unfortunately, this value does nothing.

The SERVICE_MULTIPLE flag is used in the *dwControlFlags* parameter to signal that the registering service is represented by more than one CSADDR_INFO structure. Table 8-3 explains the behavior of RNRSERVICE_REGISTER with and without the SERVICE_MULTIPLE flag.

Part III: The WinSock 2.0 API

TABLE 8-3 EFFECTS OF THE SERVICE_MULTIPLE FLAG ON RNRSERVICE_REGISTER

Flags	Service Already Exists	Service Does Not Exist
None	Completely overwrites the object and only uses the the accompanying CSADDR_INFO structures.	Creates a new object using the addresses listed in the addresses in CSADDR_INFO structures.
SERVICE_MULTIPLE	Updates the object, adding the addresses CSADDR_INFO structures to the already installed list.	Creates a new object using the addresses listed in the listed in the CSADDR_INFO structures.

RNRSERVICE_DEREGISTER A service uses this operation code prior to shutting down, to indicate that it will no longer be available. On dynamic name spaces, this will stop the periodic broadcast. On persistent name spaces, the registration information will be removed from the data store. On static names spaces, this does nothing. Table 8-4 explains the behavior of RNRSERVICE_DEREGISTER with and without the SERVICE_MULTIPLE flag.

TABLE 8-4 EFFECTS OF THE SERVICE_MULTIPLE FLAG WHEN USED WITH RNRSERVICE_DEREGISTER

Flags	Service Already Exists	Service Does Not Exist
None	Removes all addresses, but doesn't remove the object from the name space.	SOCKET_ERROR. WSAGetLastError() equals WSASERVICE_NOT_FOUND.
SERVICE_MULTIPLE	Removes the specified addresses and only deregisters the service if no addresses remain.	SOCKET_ERROR. WSAGetLastError() equals WSASERVICE_NOT_FOUND.

RNRSERVICE_DELETE A service that is represented by multiple CSADDR_INFO structures (SERVICE_MULTIPLE) uses this operation code when it wants to no longer listen on one of the previously registered addresses. Only the supplied

Chapter 8: Name Registration and Resolution 259

address will be deleted, and this must exactly match the CSADD_INFO entry that was supplied when the service was registered. Table 8-5 explains the behavior of RNRSERVICE_DELETE with and without the SERVICE_MULTIPLE flag.

TABLE 8-5 EFFECTS OF THE SERVICE_MULTIPLE FLAG WHEN USED WITH RNRSERVICE_DELETE

Flags	Service Already Exists	Service Does Not Exists
None	Removes the object from the name space.	SOCKET_ERROR. WSAGetLastError() equals WSASERVICE_NOT_FOUND.
SERVICE_MULTIPLE	Removes the specified addresses and only removes the object if no addresses remain.	SOCKET_ERROR. WSAGetLastError() equals WSASERVICE_NOT_FOUND.

REGISTERING A SERVICE

The following example shows one way a service might collect all its address information and register for availability with WSASetService() using the RNRSERVICE_REGISTER operation code. The example assumes that the service has already selected a set of suitable protocols and successfully prepared a set of CSADDR_INFO structures.

```
//
// Register service for availability
//
WSAQUERYSET qs
WSAVERSION  Version;
GUID guid = MYGUID;
int nRet;

memset(&qs, 0, sizeof(WSAQUERYSET));
qs.dwSize = sizeof(WSAQUERYSET);
qs.lpszServiceInstanceName = "MyWidgets Version 2";
qs.lpServiceClassId = &guid;
qs.lpVersion = &Version;
    Version.dwVersion = 2;
    Version.ecHow = COMP_NOTLESS;
qs.dwNameSpace = NS_ALL;
qs.dwNumberOfCsAddrs = dwNumberOfAddressesInArray;
qs.lpcsaBuffer = lpCSAddrInfo;

nRet = WSASetService(&qs,
```

```
                         RNRSERVICE_REGISTER,
                         SERVICE_MULTIPLE);
```

Name Resolution

WinSock 2 includes a small set of functions that enable a client to locate a host or service. Equipped with a service or host name and a service class GUID, a client application can discover not only the address of the host or service, but protocol and socket information as well.

As the following table shows, only four functions are related to protocol-independent name resolution. The three WSALookupService() functions are used together and are extremely powerful – capable of returning a wide variety of information. We'll look at each of these functions in detail in the rest of this chapter.

WSAEnumNameSpaceProviders()	Retrieves information about all available name-space providers.
WSALookupServiceBegin()	Begins a client query to enumerate and find information for available hosts or services.
WSALookupServiceNext()	Continues enumeration of services initiated with WSALookupServiceBegin().
WSALookupServiceEnd()	Stops enumeration of services initiated with WSALookupServiceBegin().

Enumerating Available Name Spaces

The WSAEnumNameSpaceProviders() function is used to gather information about all of the available name spaces that are installed on the local machine. Here is the function prototype:

```
INT WSAEnumNameSpaceProviders(
                         LPDWORD lpdwBufferLength,
                         LPWSANAMESPACE_INFO lpnspBuffer
                         );
```

The *lpnspBuffer* parameter points to a buffer that will receive an array of WSANAMESPACE_INFO structures, and the *lpdwBufferLength* points to a DWORD value indicating the size of the buffer. WSAEnumNameSpaceProviders() returns information about all name spaces in just one call, so the supplied buffer must be large enough to hold all of the returned information. If it's not, the function call will return SOCKET_ERROR, and WSAGetLastError() will be set to WSAEFAULT. In this case, the DWORD pointed to by *lpdwBufferLength* will reference the needed buffer size. The application can then allocate a larger buffer and call WSAEnumNameSpaceProviders() again.

On success, the buffer pointed to by the *lpnspBuffer* parameter will be filled with an array of WSANAMESPACE_INFO structures, and the return value will indicate the number of elements in the array. Here is the definition of the WSANAMESPACE_INFO structure:

```
typedef struct _WSANAMESPACE_INFO {
    GUID    NSProviderId;
    DWORD   dwNameSpace;
    BOOL    fActive;
    DWORD   dwVersion;
    LPSTR   lpszIdentifier;
} WSANAMESPACE_INFOA;
```

Parameter	Description
NSProviderId	The GUID that has been assigned to the vendor who supplied this particular name space.
dwNameSpace	Identifies the type of name space. Acceptable values are found in WINSOCK2.H (NS_DNS, NS_SAP, NS_X500, and so forth).
fActive	If True, indicates that this provider is active. If False, the provider is inactive and is not accessible.
dwVersion	Version number.
lpszIdentifier	Pointer to a character array containing a description or name of the name space.

Note, it is possible for a given name space to have more than one name space provider installed on a given machine. Whereas the *dwNameSpace* field identifies the type of name space, the *NSProviderId* field identifies the exact vendor who supplied the implementation. As you'll see in "Finding Hosts and Services" later in this chapter, the *NSProviderId* field can be used to restrict a query operation to a specified name space provider.

Part III: The WinSock 2.0 API

The same trick that was used in calling the WSAEnumProtocols() function in Chapter 7 (see "The EnumProto Application") can be used in a call to WSAEnumNameSpaceProviders(). Rather than guessing at the buffer size needed to hold all of the name space information, a NULL pointer and 0 length can be passed in a preliminary call to the function to obtain the correct buffer size. The example code in Listing 8-2 calls WSAEnumNameSpaceProviders() in just this way, to walk through the list of name space providers and print the *lpszIdentifer* field for each one.

Listing 8-2 Enumerating Name Space Providers

```
//
// Print name of each available name space provider
//
LPWSANAMESPACE_INFO pInfo;
DWORD dwBufLen;
PBYTE pBuf;
int    nCount;
int    nRet;

//
// Intentionally generate an error
// to get the required buffer size
//
dwBufLen = 0;
nRet = WSAEnumNameSpaceProviders(&dwBufLen, NULL);
if (nRet == SOCKET_ERROR)
{
    // Look for unexpected errors
    if (WSAGetLastError() != WSAEFAULT)
    {
        printf("Error %d\n",
                    WSAGetLastError());
        return;
    }
}

//
// dwBufLen now equals needed buffer size
//
pBuf = malloc(dwBufLen);
if (pBuf == NULL)
{
    printf("\nCould not allocate buffer\n");
    return;
}

//
// Now, make the "real" call
//
nRet = WSAEnumNameSpaceProviders(&dwBufLen,
```

```
                                     (LPWSANAMESPACE_INFO)pBuf);
if (nRet == SOCKET_ERROR)
{
    printf("Error: %d\n", WSAGetLastError());
    free(pBuf);
    return;
}

//
// Loop through the returned info
//
pInfo = (LPWSANAMESPACE_INFO)pBuf;
for (nCount = 0; nCount < nRet; nCount++)
{
    printf("\n%s", pInfo->lpszIdentifier);
    printf("\nName Space: %ld", pInfo->dwNameSpace);
    pInfo++;
}
free(pBuf);
return;
```

Finding Hosts and Services

Host machines and the services running on those hosts can be found with a series of calls to the WSALookupService() functions. To find a suitable host or service, a client application enumerates the available address and protocol information with one call (query) to WSALookupServiceBegin(), followed by one or more calls to WSALookupServiceNext() and ending with a call to WSALookupServiceEnd().

Using WSAQUERYSET During Resolution

The WSALookupServiceBegin() and WSALookupServiceNext() functions both accept a WSAQUERYSET structure as a parameter. One WSAQUERYSET is initialized by the application with information about the desired query and passed to WSALookupServiceBegin(). Another WSAQUERYSET is filled in by the name space provider and returned to the application in a call to WSALookupServiceNext().

In both cases, this is the same structure that was discussed in the WSASetService() section earlier, but different fields are used this time and others are interpreted in a different way. Let's take another look at WSAQUERYSET, to examine the way fields are used both to initiate a query and to read the results of the query.

```
typedef struct _WSAQuerySet
{
    DWORD           dwSize;
    LPWSTR          lpszServiceInstanceName;
    LPGUID          lpServiceClassId;
```

Part III: The WinSock 2.0 API

```
    LPWSAVERSION        lpVersion;
    LPWSTR              lpszComment;
    DWORD               dwNameSpace;
    LPGUID              lpNSProviderId;
    LPWSTR              lpszContext;
    DWORD               dwNumberOfProtocols;
    LPAFPROTOCOLS       lpafpProtocols;
    LPWSTR              lpszQueryString;
    DWORD               dwNumberOfCsAddrs;
    LPCSADDR_INFO       lpcsaBuffer;
    DWORD               dwOutputFlags;
    LPBLOB              lpBlob;
} WSAQUERYSET;
```

Table 8-6 describes the WSAQUERYSET fields as they are used to construct a query for use with WSALookupServiceBegin().

TABLE 8-6 FIELDS OF WSAQUERYSET WHEN QUERYING A SERVICE

Field	Description
dwSize	Must be set to sizeof(WSAQUERYSET). This is a versioning mechanism.
dwOutputflags	Not applicable to queries.
lpszServiceInstanceName	Optional pointer to a character array containing the service name. Some name spaces support wildcarding to find all instances of a given service class, but the mechanisms for doing this are not well documented. For Novell's SAP and NDS name spaces, NULL matches all names.
lpServiceClassId	Pointer to a GUID indicating a service class that was either previously installed with WSAInstallServiceClass() or preassigned by the name space for a well-known service. This field (and any other field not marked as optional) is required.
lpVersion	Optional pointer to a WSAVERSION structure containing a DWORD version number (lpVersion->dwVersion) and a comparison operation code (lpVersion->ecHow). If ecHow is set to COMP_EQUALS, only services that exactly match the given version number are returned. If ecHow is set to COMP_NOTLESS, only services with a version number equal to or greater than the given version number are returned.
lpszComment	Not applicable to queries.

Chapter 8: Name Registration and Resolution

Field	Description
dwNameSpace1	Identifier of a single name-space in which to search, or NS_ALL to search in all available name spaces. The combination of this field and the next field (*lpNSProviderId*) determines which name space providers are searched. If the *lpNSProviderId* field isn't NULL, then this field is ignored. This field corresponds to the WSANAMESPACE_INFO.*dwNameSpace* field returned from WSAEnumNameSpaceProviders().
lpNSProviderId	An optional pointer to the GUID of specific name space provider. If this field isn't NULL, then the *dwNameSpace1* field is ignored. This value is the same as the WSANAMESPACE_INFO.*NSProviderId* returned from WSAEnumNameSpaceProviders().
lpszContext	An optional pointer to a character string that indicates the starting point of the query in a hierarchical name space. This field is used with name spaces organized like a directory tree, such as NDS and X.500. The following values may be used: NULL or blank (" ") starts at the default context. Backslash (\ ) starts the search at the top of the name space. Any other value starts the search at the designated point.
dwNumberOfProtocols	Number of elements contained in the optional *lpafpProtocols* constraint array. This number may be 0.
lpafpProtocols	An optional pointer to an array of AFPROTOCOLS structures that constrain the search to services using one of the designated protocols. An example using this technique is shown later in "Using the Service Lookup Functions."
lpszQueryString	An optional pointer to a character array that specifies additional query information. This pointer is only used with name spaces (such as whois++) that support simple text queries.
dwNumberOfCsAddrs	Not applicable to queries.
lpcsaBuffer	Not applicable to queries.
lpBlob	An optional pointer to a provider-specific structure.

The WSALookupServiceBegin() Function

To initiate a query, a client application first calls the WSALookupServiceBegin() function. That function returns a handle that will be used in subsequent calls to WSALookupServiceNext() to get the actual results. Here is the function prototype for WSALookupServiceBegin():

```
INT WSALookupServiceBegin(
                    LPWSAQUERYSET   lpqsRestrictions,
                    DWORD           dwControlFlags,
                    LPHANDLE        lphLookup
                    );
```

WSALookupServiceBegin() accepts

- A pointer to a WSAQUERYSET structure, which has been initialized as outlined in the preceding section
- A pointer to HANDLE that will be used with WSALookupServiceNext()
- A bitmask that controls the depth of the query and the amount of information returned

Table 8-7 defines the flags supported in the *dwControlFlags* parameter. WSALookupServiceBegin() returns zero if it succeeds, or SOCKET_ERROR if it fails.

TABLE 8-7 CONTROL FLAGS IN DWCONTROLFLAGS

Flag	Information Provided If Flag Is Set
LUP_DEEP	Query deep, as opposed to just querying the first level. This flag and the two container flags described in this table are used with hierarchical name spaces such as NDS and X.500.
LUP_CONTAINERS	Return containers only.
LUP_NOCONTAINERS	Do not return any containers.
LUP_FLUSHCACHE	Some name space providers cache previously returned information. This flag causes the provider to ignore the cache and to perform the full query again.
LUP_NEAREST	If possible, return results in the order of distance.
LUP_RES_SERVICE	This indicates whether the prime response is in the *RemoteAddr* or *LocalAddr* portion of the returned CSADDR_INFO structure. The other part should be usable in either case.

Chapter 8: Name Registration and Resolution

Flag	Information Provided If Flag Is Set
LUP_RETURN_ALIAS	Return all available alias information as well as the primary information.
LUP_RETURN_NAME	Include the service or host name in the *lpszServiceInstanceName* field of the resulting WSAQUERYSET.
LUP_RETURN_TYPE	Include the service class type in the *lpServiceClassId* field of the resulting WSAQUERYSET.
LUP_RETURN_VERSION	Include the service's version in the *lpVersion* field of the resulting WSAQUERYSET.
LUP_RETURN_COMMENT	Include the service's comment in the *lpszComment* field of resulting WSAQUERYSET.
LUP_RETURN_QUERY_STRING	Return the unparsed remainder of the service instance name in the resulting WSAQUERYSET *lpszQueryString* field.
LUP_RETURN_ADDR	Include the service's addresses and protocol information in the *lpcsaBuffer* field of the resulting WSAQUERYSET.
LUP_RETURN_BLOB	Include the service's name space specific data in the *lpBlob* field of the resulting WSAQUERYSET. On TCP/IP requests, an example of this would be a *hostent* or *servent* structure.
LUP_RETURN_ALL	Retrieve all of the information.

SPECIAL QUERY-RELATED GUIDS

As discussed earlier, GUIDs have been preassigned for well-known services (see Table 8-1). Special GUIDs have also been preassigned to perform queries. The GUID of a previously installed service, the preassigned GUID of a well-known service, or one of the following special query-related GUIDs may be used in the WSAQUERYSET passed to WSALookupServiceBegin().

SVCID_HOSTNAME This GUID refers to the name of a host rather than any particular service running on the host. This GUID can be used with any name space or address family.

SVCID_INET_HOSTADDRBYINETSTRING This GUID is used only with the AF_INET address family to find host information for a given Internet address in dot-quad notation. When used with WSALookupServiceBegin(), this GUID retrieves the same information that was available through a call to gethostbyname() with an Internet address that was converted with inet_addr(). The resulting *lpBlob* field will reference a *hostent* structure.

SVCID_INET_HOSTADDRBYNAME   This GUID is used only with the AF_INET address family to find host information for a given name – this is exactly the same as a call to gethostbyname(). The resulting *lpBlob* field will reference a *hostent* structure.

SVCID_INET_SERVICEBYNAME   This GUID is used only with the AF_INET address family to find service information for a given name. It returns exactly the same information as a call to getservbyname(). The resulting *lpBlob* field will reference a *servent* structure.

The WSALookupServiceNext() Function

The WSALookupServiceNext() function is used to retrieve the information requested in a call to WSALookupServiceBegin(). During a call to WSALookupServiceNext(), the name space provider will fill a WSAQUERYSET structure with the protocol and address information for the host or service. This function can be called repeatedly to enumerate all of the available information until it returns SOCKET_ERROR to indicate either that no more information is available or an error has occurred.

Here is the function prototype for WSALookupServiceNext():

```
INT WSALookupServiceNext(
                        HANDLE          hLookup,
                        DWORD           dwControlFlags,
                        LPDWORD         lpdwBufferLength,
                        LPWSAQUERYSETA  lpqsResults
                        );
```

Parameter	Description
hLookup	The handle returned from the previous call to WSALookupServiceBegin().
dwControlFlags	A bitmask that controls provider behavior. The value LUP_FLUSHPREVIOUS or any of the *dwControlFlags* values discussed in the WSALookupServiceBegin() section may be used here. This is discussed in the following paragraphs.

Parameter	Description
lpdwBufferLength	A pointer to a DWORD value indicating the size in bytes of the *lpqsResults* buffer. If this buffer is too small to hold all of the requested information, the function will return SOCKET_ERROR, and WSAGetLastError() will return WSAEFAULT. In this case, the DWORD pointed to by *lpdwBufferLength* will be set to the minimum buffer size needed to hold all of the information. The *dwControlFlags* parameter also affects behavior in this situation.
lpqsResults	A pointer to a buffer that will receive the resulting WSAQUERYSET structure and related information.

The *dwControlFlags* parameter is a bitmask that controls the operation. It accepts the same values as the *dwControlFlags* listed for WSALookupServiceBegin(), and/or the value LUP_FLUSHPREVIOUS. If WSALookupServiceNext() signals that the supplied buffer is not large enough to hold all of the returned information, the LUP_FLUSHPREVIOUS flag instructs the service provider to discard the result set that is too large and return the next available result set in the next call to WSALookupServiceNext(). If LUP_FLUSHPREVIOUS isn't indicated, the name space provider will continue to return the same result set in each successive call to WSALookupServiceNext() that uses the same handle.

The *dwControlFlags* passed to WSALookupServiceNext() are combined with the flags specified in the call to WSALookupServiceBegin() to further restrict the results. So, an application that can't (or won't) supply a buffer large enough for all of the results might choose to restrict the amount of information returned so that a smaller result buffer will work. For example, suppose LUP_RETURN_ALL was specified in the call to WSALookupServiceBegin(), and the resulting buffer was too large to be returned to the application. The program could call WSALookupServiceNext() again, specifying only LUP_RETURN_ADDR. This would cause only the address information to be returned, rather than *lpBlob* and all of the other information.

Note: The flags specified during a call to WSALookupServiceNext() can't *increase* the amount of information returned over what was specified in the call to WSALookupServiceBegin(). The amount of information can only be *decreased*. For example, if only the LUP_RETURN_NAME flag was specified in the call to WSALookupServiceBegin(), then adding the LUP_RETURN_ADDR flag to WSALookupServiceNext() will *not* cause the address information to be retrieved.

The LUP_FLUSHPREVIOUS and LUP_RES_SERVICE are exceptions to the combined restrictions rule because they control behavior rather than the amount of information returned. Both of these flags will work as expected when specified in the call to WSALookupServiceNext(), even if they weren't specified in the call to WSALookupServiceBegin().

USING WSALookupServiceNext() The example in Listing 8-3 uses the special query GUID SVCID_HOSTNAME to retrieve address and protocol information about a host. This example restricts the call by protocol: It supplies an array in the *lpafpProtocols* field. This is only done for purposes of illustration — the code would still work without this restriction.

Caution: Listing 8-3 also watches for the WSALookupServiceNext() function to set WSAENOMORE (10102) *or* WSA_E_NO_MORE (10110), signaling that no more information is available. Both of these error codes were defined in the WinSock 2 specification documents. WSAENOMORE will be removed in a future version, and only WSA_E_NO_MORE will remain. To be safe, however, applications should still check for either of these return codes just in case an older name space provider still uses the now-obsolete error code.

Listing 8-3 Using the Service Lookup Functions

```
//
// Find information for an Internet host
// and print out the results
void HostExample(void)
{
    WSAQUERYSET qs;
    LPWSAQUERYSET pqs;
    LPCSADDR_INFO pcsa;
    DWORD dwFlags;
    DWORD dwLen;
    HANDLE hLookup;
    DWORD dwX;
    AFPROTOCOLS afProtocols[2];
    BYTE bufResult[2048];
    char szBuf[256];
    int nRet;
    GUID guidServiceClass = SVCID_HOSTNAME;

    //
    // Initialize WSAQUERTYSET values
    // for query
    //
    memset(&qs, 0, sizeof(WSAQUERYSET));
    qs.dwSize                   = sizeof(WSAQUERYSET);
    qs.lpszServiceInstanceName  = "www.idgbooks.com";
    qs.lpServiceClassId         = &guidServiceClass;
    qs.dwNameSpace              = NS_ALL;
    qs.dwNumberOfProtocols      = 2;
    qs.lpafpProtocols           = afProtocols;
        afProtocols[0].iAddressFamily   = AF_INET;
        afProtocols[0].iProtocol        = IPPROTO_TCP;
        afProtocols[1].iAddressFamily   = AF_INET;
        afProtocols[1].iProtocol        = IPPROTO_UDP;
```

Chapter 8: Name Registration and Resolution

```
//
// Begin lookup
//
dwFlags = LUP_RETURN_ALL;
nRet = WSALookupServiceBegin(&qs,
                             dwFlags,
                             &hLookup);
if (nRet == SOCKET_ERROR)
{
    fprintf(stderr,"\nLookupBegin: %d\n",
        WSAGetLastError());
    return;
}

//
// Loop until WSALookupServiceNext() return SOCKET_ERROR
//
while(1)
{
    dwFlags = LUP_FLUSHPREVIOUS;
    dwLen = sizeof(bufResult);
    nRet = WSALookupServiceNext(hLookup,
                                dwFlags,
                                &dwLen,
                                (LPWSAQUERYSET)bufResult);
    if (nRet == SOCKET_ERROR)
    {
        nRet = WSAGetLastError();
        if (nRet != WSAENOMORE && nRet != WSA_E_NO_MORE)
            fprintf(stderr,"\nLookupNext: %d\n",
                WSAGetLastError());
        // break out of the loop
        break;
    }

    //
    // Cast the result to a WSAQUERYSET pointer
    //
    pqs = (LPWSAQUERYSET)bufResult;

    //
    // Cast the lpcsaBuffer to a CSADDR_INFO pointer
    pcsa = pqs->lpcsaBuffer;
    for (dwX = 0; dwX < pqs->dwNumberOfCsAddrs; dwX++)
    {
        //
        // Convert the returned address into
        // a display string
        //
        dwLen = sizeof(szBuf);
        nRet = WSAAddressToString(
                    pcsa->RemoteAddr.lpSockaddr,
                    pcsa->RemoteAddr.iSockaddrLength,
```

```
                            NULL,
                            szBuf,
                            &dwLen);
            if (nRet == SOCKET_ERROR)
            {
                fprintf(stderr,"\nWSAAddressToString(): %d\n",
                    WSAGetLastError());
                break;
            }
            //
            // Print out the info
            //
            printf("\n"
                    "Name      : %s\n"
                    "Address   : %s\n",
                    pqs->lpszServiceInstanceName,
                    szBuf
                    );
            pcsa++;
        }
    }
    WSALookupServiceEnd(hLookup);
}
```

This example is intentionally oversimplified and shows just one use for the new lookup service functions. It also uses a function we haven't discussed yet: WSAAddressToString(). This function and the other name-resolution utility functions and macros are discussed in the next section.

Also appearing in Listing 8-3 is a call to the WSALookupServiceEnd() function, which must be called to terminate a service-lookup session begun with WSALookupServiceBegin(). The termination function accepts the handle returned from WSALookupServiceBegin() and returns 0 on success.

Name Resolution Utility Functions

Winsock 2 provides four utility functions and a set of macros that aid in name resolution.

THE WSAAddressToString() FUNCTION

The WSAAddressToString() function converts a generic SOCKADDR into a human-readable display string. It will work on *any* SOCKADDR, no matter what the underlying transport protocol, because the address conversion actually takes place inside the name space.

```
INT WSAAddressToString(
                LPSOCKADDR          lpsaAddress,
                DWORD               dwAddressLength,
                LPWSAPROTOCOL_INFO  lpProtocolInfo,
                LPSTR               lpszAddressString,
```

Chapter 8: Name Registration and Resolution 273

```
                    LPDWORD              lpdwAddressStringLength
                    );
```

Parameter	Description
lpsaAddress	A pointer to a SOCKADDR.
dwAddressLength	The length in bytes of the SOCKADDR pointed to by *lpsaAddress*. This may vary with different protocols.
lpProtocolInfo	An optional pointer to a WSAPROTOCOL_INFO structure associated with a specific provider to be used. If this is NULL, the address conversion is performed by the first provider found that supports the address family indicated in *lpsaAddress*.
lpszAddressString	A pointer to a buffer that receives the address string.
lpdwAddressStringLength	The length in bytes of the buffer pointed to by *lpszAddressString*.

WSAAddressToString() returns zero if it succeeds or SOCKET_ERROR if it fails. If the supplied address buffer is not large enough, WSAGetLastError() will be set to WSAEFAULT, and the DWORD value pointed to by *lpdwAddressStringLength* will contain the needed size.

THE WSAStringToAddress() FUNCTION

The WSAStringToAddress() function accepts an address represented as a character string and builds a valid SOCKADDR for the indicated address family.

```
INT WSAStringToAddress(
                    LPSTR                AddressString,
                    INT                  AddressFamily,
                    LPWSAPROTOCOL_INFO   lpProtocolInfo,
                    LPSOCKADDR           lpAddress,
                    LPINT                lpAddressLength
                    );
```

Parameter	Description
AddressString	A pointer to a null-terminated character array containing a string representation of an address.

(continued)

274 Part III: The WinSock 2.0 API

Parameter	Description
AddressFamily	One of the address family designations (AF_INET, AF_IPX, and so forth).
lpProtocolInfo	An optional pointer to a WSAPROTOCOL_INFO structure associated with a specific provider to be used. If this is NULL, the conversion is performed by the first provider found that supports the address family indicated in *AddressFamily*.
lpAddress	A pointer to a SOCKADDR.
pAddressLength	The length in bytes of the SOCKADDR.

Because the actual conversion is performed by a name space provider, you must have at least one provider that supports the indicated address family.

In the case of Internet addresses, this function is capable of creating a full service address including port number. The port number can be appended to the end of the address, separated by a colon, like this:

```
208.137.132.90:80
```

If possible, any portion of the address that is missing will be filled in with default values. For example, a missing port number will default to zero. The following example converts a full Internet service address in dot-notation to a SOCKADDR:

```
SOCKADDR sockaddr;
int nLen;
int nRet;

nLen = sizeof(SOCKADDR);
nRet = WSAStringToAddress("208.137.132.90:80",
                          AF_INET,
                          NULL,
                          &sockaddr,
                          &nLen);
if (nRet == SOCKET_ERROR)
{
    // Handle error
}
```

THE WSAGetServiceClassNameByClassId() FUNCTION

Not only does the WSAGetServiceClassNameByClassId() function return the class name for a GUID, but it's also the winner of the WinSock 2 Longest Function Name Contest! In fact, at one point the function was actually named

Chapter 8: Name Registration and Resolution 275

WSAGetServiceClassNameByServiceClassId(), and it still shows up with that name in the Win32 documentation accompanying Version 5 of Visual C++. WS2_32.DLL, however, only exports WSAGetServiceClassNameByClassId().

```
INT WSAGetServiceClassNameByClassId(
                            LPGUID  lpServiceClassId,
                            LPSTR lpszServiceClassName,
                            LPDWORD lpdwBufferLength
                            );
```

Parameter	Description
lpServiceClassId	A pointer to the service class GUID.
lpszServiceClassName	A pointer to a buffer that will receive the class name.
lpdwBufferLength	A pointer to a DWORD value that indicates the length of the buffer on input and represents the number of characters copied to the buffer on output.

The name returned from WSAGetServiceClassNameByClassId() is the generic class name for the service — not the name of a specific instance of the service. An example would be `FTP Server`.

THE WSAGetServiceClassInfo() FUNCTION

The WSAGetServiceClassInfo() function retrieves all of the class schema information for a specified service class from a specified name space provider.

```
INT WSAGetServiceClassInfo(
                            LPGUID  lpProviderId,
                            LPGUID  lpServiceClassId,
                            LPDWORD  lpdwBufSize,
                            LPWSASERVICECLASSINFO lpServiceClassInfo
                            );
```

Parameter	Description
lpProviderId	A pointer to a GUID that identifies a specific name space provider.
lpServiceClassId	A pointer to a GUID identifying the service class.

(continued)

Parameter	Description
lpdwBufSize	A pointer to a DWORD value indicating the size in bytes of the buffer pointed to by *lpServiceClassInfo*.
lpServiceClassInfo	A pointer to a buffer that will receive a WSASERVICECLASSINFO structure.

WSAGetServiceClassInfo() returns zero if it succeeds or SOCKET_ERROR if it fails. If the supplied service-class information buffer is not large enough, WSAGetLastError() will be set to WSAEFAULT, and the DWORD value pointed to by *lpdwBufSize* will contain the needed size.

Note: This function only returns the information for a service as it relates to the indicated name space provider. Individual providers are only required to retain service class information that is applicable to the name spaces supported by the provider. If the service is registered in more than one name space, additional service class information may be available from other name space providers. The only way to ensure that all of the available information for a service class has been retrieved is to use WSAEnumSpaceProviders() and retrieve the information for each installed name space.

OTHER GUID MACROS

Throughout this chapter, we've discussed several preassigned or special GUIDs that are used with name registration and resolution. There are still a few more that haven't yet been mentioned, listed in Table 8-8.

TABLE 8-8 GUID MACROS

Macro	Description
IS_SVCID_TCP(GUID)	Returns True if the GUID is within the allowable range for TCP GUIDs.
IS_SVCID_UDP(GUID)	Returns True if the GUID is within the allowable range for UDP GUIDs.
IS_SVCID_NETWARE(GUID)	Returns True if the GUID is within the allowable range for Netware GUIDs.
SET_TCP_SVCID(GUID, port)	Initializes a GUID structure with the GUID equivalent for a TCP port number.
SET_UDP_SVCID(GUID, port)	Initializes a GUID structure with the GUID equivalent for a UDP port number.

Macro	Description
PORT_FROM_SVCID_TCP(GUID)	Returns the port number associated with the TCP GUID.
PORT_FROM_SVCID_UDP(GUID)	Returns the port number associated with the UDP GUID.
SAPID_FROM_SVCID_NETWARE(GUID)	Returns the SAP identifier associated with the Netware GUID.

The Services Utility

The Services utility is on the CD-ROM, in the \CH08\SERVICES directory. This application demonstrates almost all of the host and service name-resolution functions discussed in this chapter. The Services program is meant to be used as a test environment for the functions WSALookupServiceBegin(), WSALookupServiceNext(), and WSALookupServiceEnd(). Figure 8-2 shows the Lookup Services dialog after the program has found host address information.

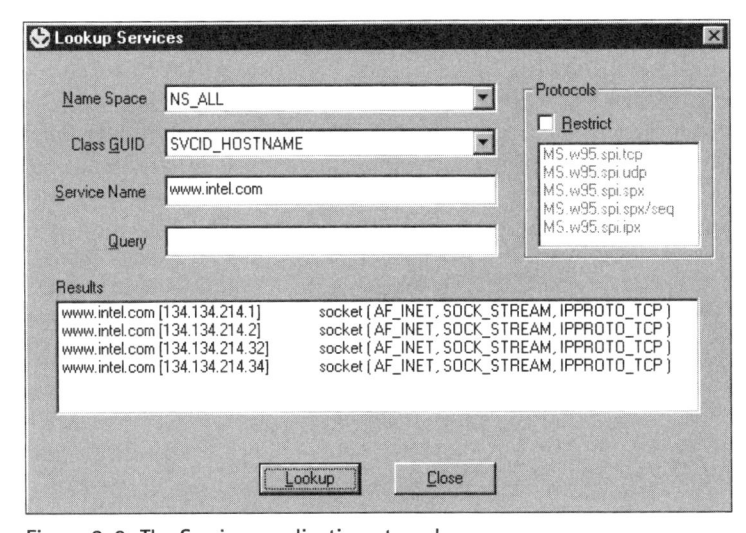

Figure 8-2: The Services application at work

The Services program provides a combo box filled with all available name space providers and an NS_ALL selection, as well as a combo box with the most commonly used service class GUIDs. To look up a service or host, you select a name space and GUID and fill in the Service Name text box with the name. When you then click the Lookup button, the program performs the lookup service request and fills the Results list box with the information provided.

This utility was written with MFC. It's not listed here in the chapter because 99% of it is user interface code. You may want to look at the file DLG.CPP on the CD; it demonstrates enumerating protocols, name spaces, and use of the lookup service functions. It also contains a static array of GUIDs that are included in the Class GUID combo box. You can add other GUIDs to this array for testing if you want, or just look at the source code.

Using this utility will give you a good sense of the new name-resolution functions and the type of information that is returned from them.

Summary

The new protocol-independent name registration and resolution functions included in WinSock 2 provide a whole new area of functionality that wasn't available before. The services are especially powerful when used with dynamic name spaces.

The functions use an intricate set of data structures to provide one standard API that allows simultaneous access to various name registration and resolution strategies, such as the Internet's Domain Name Service (DNS) and Novell's Service Advertising Protocol (SAP).

This has been a long and challenging chapter with a lot of heavily interrelated information. The name registration and resolution functions are powerful but somewhat complex. The next chapter gives us a lift — it deals with enhanced I/O, which isn't difficult to use and it can really boost the performance of your applications.

Chapter 9
Enhanced Input/Output

IN THIS CHAPTER
Here, in Chapter 9 we discuss a number of new capabilities found in WinSock 2 that are all associated in one way or another with input and output. Event objects are closely related to the subject of overlapped I/O, so they are included in this chapter as well. Here are this chapter's topics:

- Asynchronous event notification
- Overlapped I/O
- Scatter and gather
- Connect and disconnect data exchange
- Quality of service
- Protocol-independent multipoint and multicast

Asynchronous Event Notification

Some WinSock applications have no need for a sophisticated GUI. Applications such as servers and batch-oriented clients can run for long periods of time unattended. These applications — console applications and NT applications that use the Service Control Manager interface — have no window handle to use with the WSAAsyncSelect() asynchronous notification mechanism. WinSock 2's WSAEventSelect() function behaves in much the same way as WSAAsyncSelect(), but rather than sending a message to a window handle to notify an application of a network event, WSAEventSelect() sets an *event object*. Thus applications that have no window handle can still use asynchronous mode.

Event Objects

One fundamental difference between 16-bit and 32-bit Windows is that 32-bit Windows applications can have multiple threads. Concurrently running threads often need to communicate with one another, so that one thread can tell another that some operation is complete or that some common resource is in use.

Event objects were introduced in the Win32 API as one means of synchronizing threads. Other synchronization objects include mutexes, semaphores, and critical sections. An event object is really just a Boolean variable in the operating system (a kernel object) that is either *set* or *reset*. Think of an event object as a flag that is either raised (signaled) or lowered (nonsignaled).

WIN32 EVENT OBJECTS

Event objects are created in Win32 with the CreateEvent() function and destroyed with CloseHandle(). They are set to the signaled state with the SetEvent() and PulseEvent() functions, and to the nonsignaled state with ResetEvent().

Several *wait* functions are also defined in the Win32 API, so that a thread can block and wait until an event object is signaled. Parameters accepted by the WaitForSingleObject() function are a handle to an event object and a timeout value. This function does not return until the event becomes signaled or the timeout duration has elapsed. The WaitForMultipleObjects() function accepts an array of event-object handles and a timeout value; it does not return until one or all of the objects are signaled or the timeout period has expired.

These same wait functions can also be used to poll with event objects. By specifying a timeout value of 0, you can have the functions return immediately and indicate the current state of the event objects. Nonblocking applications and threads use this method.

The threads in a multithreaded application can use event objects to communicate. For example, if an application creates a thread to read the contents of a file into a buffer, an event object can be used by the thread to signal when the operation is complete.

In the Win32 API, there are two types of event objects:

- Manual-reset event objects must be explicitly reset to the nonsignaled state with the ResetEvent() function. Wait functions don't automatically reset the object to nonsignaled.

- Auto-reset event objects are automatically reset to the nonsignaled state once they have been detected as signaled by one of the wait functions.

WINSOCK 2 EVENT OBJECTS

WinSock 2 event objects are Win32 event objects. WinSock functions — including WSACreateEvent(), WSACloseEvent(), WSASetEvent(), WSAResetEvent(), and WSAWaitForMultipleEvents() — use the similarly named Win32 functions to perform their work. (For example, WSASetEvent() uses the Win32 SetEvent() function.) The fact that WinSock 2 event objects are implemented as Win32 objects can be extremely useful in applications that must wait for both socket and nonsocket events to be signaled. For example, a WinSock 2 event object can be included in the event-handle array that is passed to WaitForMultipleObjects() along with normal Win32 event objects.

Chapter 9: Enhanced Input/Output

As you'll see in this chapter, WinSock 2 can use event objects to signal network events or the completion of I/O requests.

Creating Event Objects

The WSACreateEvent() function creates a new event object. It takes no parameters and returns a handle to the newly created object if it succeeds. WSACreateEvent() isn't likely to fail, but if it does, it returns WSA_INVALID_EVENT, and extended error information is available from WSAGetLastError(). Here's the prototype:

```
WSAEVENT WSACreateEvent(void);
```

The newly created object is a manual-reset event object, initially in the nonsignaled state. The returned handle is used as a parameter in the WSAWaitForMultipleEvents() function as well as several others. If you wish to use an auto-reset event, you can call the Win32 CreateEvent() function instead, and use the returned handle just as if it had been created with WSACreateEvent().

All event objects created with WSACreateEvent() should eventually be closed with a call to WSACloseEvent():

```
BOOL WSACloseEvent(WSAEVENT hEvent);
```

WSACloseEvent() simply accepts an event-object handle as a parameter and returns True if it succeeds. If the function fails, extended error information is available from WSAGetLastError().

Associating Network Events

The WSAEventSelect() function accepts three parameters: a socket descriptor, a handle to an event object, and an event bitmask. The function works almost exactly like WSAAsyncSelect(). It is used to associate an event object with a socket descriptor and one or more network event codes. Just like WSAAsyncSelect(), WSAEventSelect() automatically makes the socket nonblocking.

```
int WSAEventSelect(SOCKET s,
                   WSAEVENT hEventObject,
                   long lNetworkEvents
                   );
```

Parameter	Description
s	A socket descriptor identifying the socket to be associated with the event and network event codes.
hEventObject	A handle to an event object.
lNetworkEvents	A bitmask specifying one or more network event codes.

Part III: The WinSock 2.0 API

The *lNetworkEvents* parameter is used to tell WinSock which events you're interested in receiving; Table 9.1 lists all of the valid event codes. These values can be combined with the OR (|) operator to request notifications for more than one event.

TABLE 9-1 OPTIONS FOR THE WSAEventSelect() lNetworkEvents PARAMETER

Event Code	Requests Receipt of Notification at This Event
FD_ACCEPT	A connection request has been received.
FD_CLOSE	The connection was closed.
FD_CONNECT	A connection has been established.
FD_OOB	Out-of-band data has arrived.
FD_QOS	The quality of service for the socket has changed.
FD_READ	Data is available to be read.
FD_WRITE	It is safe to send data.

The following code shows how a socket and event object are created and associated with several event-notification codes:

```
//
// Create a TCP/IP stream socket,
// make it non-blocking and associate
// it with an event object and a
// set of network events.
//
SOCKET Socket;
WSAEVENT hEvent;
int nRet;

// Create the socket
Socket = socket(AF_INET, SOCK_STREAM, IPPROTO_TCP);
if (Socket == INVALID_SOCKET)
{
    // Handle error
    return;
}

// Create an event object to be used with this socket
hEvent = WSACreateEvent();
if (hEvent == WSA_INVALID_EVENT)
{
    // Handle the error
```

```
        closesocket(Socket);
        return;
}

// Make the socket non-blocking and
// associate it with network events
nRet = WSAEventSelect(Socket,
                      hEvent,
                      FD_READ|FD_WRITE|FD_CONNECT|FD_CLOSE);
if (nRet == SOCKET_ERROR)
{
    // Handle error
    closesocket(Socket);
    WSACloseEvent(hEvent);
    return;
}
```

Each time WSAEventSelect() is called for a socket, it cancels any previous WSAEventSelect() for the same socket. So, all network event codes of interest must be specified in one call. For example, the following code will not produce the expected results:

```
// This will NOT work!
WSAEventSelect(Socket, hEvent, FD_READ);
WSAEventSelect(Socket, hEvent, FD_WRITE);
```

It will work, but the socket and event will only be associated with the FD_WRITE event (the last one specified). You can't do this using a different event object, either. A socket can only be associated with one event object and one set of network event codes at one time.

The socket can be disassociated from *all* network events by calling WSAEventSelect() with the *lNetworkEvents* parameter set to 0, like this:

```
        WSAEventSelect(Socket, hEvent, 0);
```

Closing a socket cancels the association, too, and the selection of network events. However, the application must still call WSACloseEvent() to close the event object.

New sockets returned from a listening socket automatically have the same network events in effect and are associated with the same event object — again, this is just like WSAAsyncSelect(). For example, if a listening socket is associated with the event handle *hEvent* and the event codes FD_READ and FD_WRITE, then any socket returned from accept() on the listening socket will also be associated with *hEvent* and the FD_READ and FD_WRITE events. If you want the new socket to have its own event object, then you must call WSAEventSelect() with the new socket, event handle, and network event codes.

When one of the specified network events occurs for the associated socket, WinSock sets the event object to the signaled state and records the occurrence of the event in an internal network event record.

Detecting Network Events

Once a socket descriptor has been created and associated with an event object and a set of network event codes, an application can detect when a network event has occurred. This can be done by polling, or by waiting for the event object to become signaled. The WSAWaitForMultipleEvents() function can be used in either case, polling or waiting. Here is the prototype for this function:

```
DWORD WSAWaitForMultipleEvents(
                    DWORD cEvents,
                    const WSAEVENT FAR * lphEvents,
                    BOOL fWaitAll,
                    DWORD dwTimeout,
                    BOOL fAlertable
                    );
```

Parameter	Description
cEvents	Specifies the number of event handles contained in the array pointed to by *lphEvents*. The maximum number of event object handles is WSA_MAXIMUM_WAIT_EVENTS. At least one event must be specified.
lphEvents	A pointer to an array of event handles.
fWaitAll	Specifies whether the function should wait for *all* of the event handles to be signaled or just until *any one* of the handles becomes signaled. If True, the function will not return until all of the event handles are signaled at the same time. If False, the function will return when any one of the handles in the array is signaled.
dwTimeout	Specifies a timeout value in milliseconds. If this timeout period expires, the function returns even if none of the event handles contained in the array is signaled.
fAlertable	Specifies whether the function should return when the system queues an I/O completion routine for execution by the calling thread. If True, the completion routine is executed and the function returns. If False, the completion routine is not executed when the function returns. (This is discussed in more detail in the later section "Overlapped I/O.")

The most common method of using WSAWaitForMultipleEvents() is to block and wait for the event object to become signaled. The *dwTimeout* parameter can be set to 0 so the application can intermittently poll on the event object to see if the signal criteria has been met. If *dwTimeout* is set to WSA_INFINITE, the function will continue to wait until the event or events become signaled, regardless of how much time elapses.

Event objects that were created with WSACreateEvent() or with the Win32 CreateEvent() function may be used in the *lphEvents* array of WSAWaitForMultipleEvents(). Also, if you are only interested in one event, you can take an event handle created with WSACreateEvent() and use it with the Win32 WaitForSingleObject() function. WaitForSingleObject() works in much the same way as WSAWaitForMultipleEvents() — accepting an event handle and a timeout parameter — but it only accepts a single object handle rather than a pointer to an array of handles.

Determining What Occurred

The WSAEnumNetworkEvents() function is used to determine exactly which network event(s) caused the event object to become signaled.

```
int WSAEnumNetworkEvents(
                SOCKET s,
                WSAEVENT hEventObject,
                LPWSANETWORKEVENTS lpNetworkEvents
                );
```

Parameter	Description
s	A socket descriptor.
hEventObject	Optional handle to an event object. If the event object is specified (isn't NULL), then the event object is reset to the nonsignaled state.
lpNetworkEvents	A pointer to a WSANETWORKEVENTS structure that will be filled with indications of the network events that have occurred, and the error code returned for each event.

The *s* and *hEventObject* parameters are the socket and event handle that were previously associated with a set of network event codes.

The *lpNetworkEvents* parameter points to a WSANETWORKEVENTS structure:

```
typedef struct _WSANETWORKEVENTS {
       long lNetworkEvents;
           int iErrorCode[FD_MAX_EVENTS];
} WSANETWORKEVENTS, FAR * LPWSANETWORKEVENTS;
```

The *lNetworkEvents* field of this structure indicates which network events have occurred since the last call to WSAEnumNetworkEvents(), or since the call to WSAEventSelect() if this is the first call to WSAEnumNetworkEvents with this particular socket and event handle. The *lNetworkEvents* field is a bitmask containing one or more FD_X event codes. Since more than one event may have occurred, you have to check for each event code with the AND (&) operator.

The error code for any indicated event is contained in the *iErrorCode* array. There is a predefined FD_X_BIT constant defined for each network event. The following example shows how to check for the FD_CONNECT and FD_READ events and their associated error codes:

```
WSANETWORKEVENTS events;
int nRet = WSAEnumNetworkEvents(Socket,
                                hEvent,
                                &events);
if (nRet == SOCKET_ERROR)
{
    // Handle error
}
if (events.lNetworkEvents & FD_CONNECT)
{
    // FD_CONNECT event occurred.
    // Error code is in:
    // events.iErrorCode[FD_CONNECT_BIT]
}
if (events.lNetworkEvents & FD_READ)
{
    // FD_READ event occurred.
    // Error code is in:
    // events.iErrorCode[FD_READ_BIT]
}
```

WinSock keeps a list of all events that occur between calls to WSAEnumNetworkEvents(). Calling WSAEnumNetworkEvents() clears this record of the events reported by the function.

Like WSAAsyncSelect(), WSAEventSelect() will not record a second occurrence of a network event until one of the event's reenabling functions has been called. For example, once the FD_READ notification has been recorded for a socket, it won't be recorded again until recv(), recvfrom(), WSARecv(), or WSARecvFrom() has been called. These are the reenabling functions for the FD_READ event. Even if WinSock receives data again after recording the FD_READ event, the notification won't be recorded again until the application has received data. If the reenabling call to one of the receive functions does not read all of the data that WinSock has available, the FD_READ event will be immediately recorded again. So, one call to a receive function (even with a very small buffer) is sufficient for each FD_READ notification. If there is still more data to be read after the call, WinSock will record another event notification and signal the appropriate event object.

Table 9-2 lists the reenabling functions for each event code.

Chapter 9: Enhanced Input/Output   287

TABLE 9-2 REENABLING FUNCTIONS FOR ASYNCHRONOUS EVENT CODES

Event Code	Reenabling Functions
FD_ACCEPT	accept() or WSAAccept()
FD_CLOSE	None
FD_CONNECT	None
FD_OOB	recv(), recvfrom(), WSARecv(), WSARecvFrom()
FD_QOS	WSAIoctl() with SIO_GET_QOS
FD_READ	recv(), recvfrom(), WSARecv(), WSARecvFrom()
FD_WRITE	send(), sendto(), WSASend(), WSASendTo()

The GetHTTP2 Sample

Listing 9-1 contains the source code for a simple console application that can retrieve a file from an HTTP server. This program is also on the CD-ROM in the \CH09\GETHTTP2 directory. It uses the functions discussed in the foregoing section to receive asynchronous notification of network events.

The program accepts the name of a host and a filename on the command line. It looks up the address of the given host and attempts to connect to port 80 (HTTP Service). If it is able to connect, it issues a GET request for the file.

Note: This program is intended to be used as a quick-and-dirty command-line utility for retrieving files from the Web.

Listing 9-1: GETHTTP2.CPP

```
//
// GETHTTP2.cpp — Retrieve a file from a HTTP server
//
//              This version uses event objects and
//              WSASelectEvent() for asynchronous
//              notification of network events.
//

#include <stdio.h>
#include <fcntl.h>
#include <io.h>
#include <winsock2.h>
```

```c
void GetHTTP(LPCSTR lpServerName, LPCSTR lpFileName);

// Helper macro for displaying errors
#define PRINTERROR(s)   \
        fprintf(stderr,"\n%: %d\n", s, WSAGetLastError())

void main(int argc, char **argv)
{
    WORD wVersionRequested = WINSOCK_VERSION;
    WSADATA wsaData;
    int nRet;

    //
    // Check arguments
    //
    if (argc != 3)
    {
        fprintf(stderr,
            "\nSyntax: GetHTTP ServerName FullPathName\n");
        return;
    }

    //
    // Initialize WinSock.dll
    //
    nRet = WSAStartup(wVersionRequested, &wsaData);
    if (nRet)
    {
        fprintf(stderr,"\nWSAStartup(): %d\n", nRet);
        WSACleanup();
        return;
    }

    //
    // Check WinSock version
    //
    if (wsaData.wVersion != wVersionRequested)
    {
        fprintf(stderr,"\nWinSock version 1.1 not supported\n");
        WSACleanup();
        return;
    }

    //
    // Set "stdout" to binary mode
    // so that redirection will work
    // for .gif and .jpg files
    //
    _setmode(_fileno(stdout), _O_BINARY);

    //
    // Call GetHTTP() to do all the work
```

Chapter 9: Enhanced Input/Output   289

```
    //
    GetHTTP(argv[1], argv[2]);
    WSACleanup();
}

////////////////////////////////////////////////////////////////

void GetHTTP(LPCSTR lpServerName, LPCSTR lpFileName)
{
    //
    // Lookup host
    //
    LPHOSTENT lpHostEntry;
    lpHostEntry = gethostbyname(lpServerName);
    if (lpHostEntry == NULL)
    {
        PRINTERROR("gethostbyname()");
        return;
    }

    //
    // Fill in the server address structure
    //
    SOCKADDR_IN sa;
    sa.sin_family = AF_INET;
    sa.sin_addr = *((LPIN_ADDR)*lpHostEntry->h_addr_list);
    sa.sin_port = htons(80);    // Well-known HTTP port

    //
    // Create a TCP/IP stream socket
    //
    SOCKET  Socket;
    Socket = socket(AF_INET, SOCK_STREAM, IPPROTO_TCP);
    if (Socket == INVALID_SOCKET)
    {
        PRINTERROR("socket()");
        return;
    }

    //
    // Create an event object to be used with this socket
    //
    WSAEVENT hEvent;
    hEvent = WSACreateEvent();
    if (hEvent == WSA_INVALID_EVENT)
    {
        PRINTERROR("WSACreateEvent()");
        closesocket(Socket);
        return;
    }

    //
    // Make the socket non-blocking and
```

```
// associate it with network events
//
int nRet;
nRet = WSAEventSelect(Socket,
                      hEvent,
                      FD_READ|FD_CONNECT|FD_CLOSE);
if (nRet == SOCKET_ERROR)
{
    PRINTERROR("EventSelect()");
    closesocket(Socket);
    WSACloseEvent(hEvent);
    return;
}

//
// Request a connection
//
nRet = connect(Socket,
               (LPSOCKADDR)&sa,
               sizeof(SOCKADDR_IN));
if (nRet == SOCKET_ERROR)
{
    nRet = WSAGetLastError();
    if (nRet == WSAEWOULDBLOCK)
    {
        fprintf(stderr,"\nConnect would block");
    }
    else
    {
        PRINTERROR("connect()");
        closesocket(Socket);
        WSACloseEvent(hEvent);
        return;
    }
}

//
// Handle async network events
//
char szBuffer[4096];
WSANETWORKEVENTS events;
while(1)
{
    //
    // Wait for something to happen
    //
    DWORD dwRet;
    dwRet = WSAWaitForMultipleEvents(1,
                                     &hEvent,
                                     FALSE,
                                     10000,
                                     FALSE);
```

```
//
// Figure out what happened
//
nRet = WSAEnumNetworkEvents(Socket,
                            hEvent,
                            &events);
if (nRet == SOCKET_ERROR)
{
    PRINTERROR("WSAEnumNetworkEvents()");
    break;
}

//                //
// Handle events //
//                //

// Connect event?
if (events.lNetworkEvents & FD_CONNECT)
{
    fprintf(stderr,"\nFD_CONNECT: %d",
            events.iErrorCode[FD_CONNECT_BIT]);
    // Send the http request
    sprintf(szBuffer, "GET %s\n", lpFileName);
    nRet = send(Socket, szBuffer, strlen(szBuffer), 0);
    if (nRet == SOCKET_ERROR)
    {
        PRINTERROR("send()");
        break;
    }
}

// Read event?
if (events.lNetworkEvents & FD_READ)
{
    fprintf(stderr,"\nFD_READ: %d",
            events.iErrorCode[FD_READ_BIT]);
    // Read the data and write it to stdout
    nRet = recv(Socket, szBuffer, sizeof(szBuffer), 0);
    if (nRet == SOCKET_ERROR)
    {
        PRINTERROR("recv()");
        break;
    }
    fprintf(stderr,"\nRead %d bytes", nRet);
    // Write to stdout
    fwrite(szBuffer, nRet, 1, stdout);
}

// Close event?
if (events.lNetworkEvents & FD_CLOSE)
{
    fprintf(stderr,"\nFD_CLOSE: %d",
            events.iErrorCode[FD_CLOSE_BIT]);
```

```
            break;
        }

        // Write event?
        if (events.lNetworkEvents & FD_WRITE)
        {
            fprintf(stderr,"\nFD_WRITE: %d",
                    events.iErrorCode[FD_WRITE_BIT]);
        }
    }
    closesocket(Socket);
    WSACloseEvent(hEvent);
    return;
}
```

Analysis of GetHTTP2

GetHTTP2 prints the contents of the retrieved file to *stdout*. Each time the program receives an event notification, it prints a message to *stderr*. By redirecting the output from this program to a file, you can both capture the contents of the file (even a binary file) *and* see the occurrence of events.

For example, running GetHTTP2 like this:

```
gethttp2 www.idgbooks.com / > index.html
```

will retrieve the default file from www.idgbooks.com and save it into the file INDEX.HTML. GetHTTP2 sets stdout to binary mode so that image files, executables, and other binary files are correctly written to disk through redirection.

Immediately after creating the socket descriptor, the program creates an event object and associates the socket and the event object with several event notification codes. The program then requests a connection to the server and expects to receive the WSAEWOULDBLOCK error message, because the call to WSAEventSelect() made the socket nonblocking.

GetHTTP2 next enters a loop, using WSAWaitForMultipleEvents() to block until some network event occurs. The call to WSAWaitForMultipleEvents() specifies a timeout value of ten seconds (10,000 milliseconds). The program continues this loop until the FD_CLOSE event is received or some error occurs. After breaking out of the loop, the program closes the socket and the event handle.

By the way, since only one event handle is being used here, the program could have used the Win32 WaitForSingleObject() function to block on the event handle. With WSAWaitForMultipleEvents() used instead, you get to see it at work.

Note: At the end of Chapter 2, I referred to a program on the CD named GETHTTP.C — a stream, connection-oriented client utility to retrieve files from the World Wide Web. It is essentially the same program as the GetHTTP2 application you're studying here, but the Chapter 2 program uses blocking socket routines rather than asynchronous notification. You might want to compare the source code for these two programs; they do exactly the same thing in two different ways.

Overlapped I/O

Asynchronous input/output, also known as overlapped I/O, was introduced in the Win32 API to allow processes and threads to continue their work while I/O was performed in the background. Overlapped I/O functions always return immediately (they don't block) even though the I/O request may not be complete. This allows an application to initiate an I/O request, then proceed with other processing and come back later to see if the requested task completed successfully. In the Win32 environment, overlapped I/O can be used with almost any type of device that can be opened with the CreateFile() function – such as files, pipes, and mail slots.

In the Win 32 environment, overlapped I/O worked with sockets even before WinSock 2. Now, asynchronous input/output is officially part of the WinSock specification. WinSock 2 includes mechanisms specifically designed to perform overlapped I/O with sockets. The following functions support it:

- WSARecv()
- WSARecvFrom()
- WSASend()
- WSASendTo()
- WSAIoctl()

Overlapped I/O can only be performed with sockets that have the *overlapped* attribute. Sockets created with the familiar socket() function have this attribute by default. Sockets created with the new WSASocket() function must include WSA_FLAG_OVERLAPPED in the *dwFlags* parameter.

Note: A socket with the *overlapped* attribute is not the same thing as a nonblocking socket. Overlapped I/O is asynchronous; it does not block. In the context of input and output, then, the blocking mode of a socket is irrelevant if it is used exclusively with overlapped I/O. In other situations, of course, blocking mode is still important, as in connection-oriented applications that call either connect() or WSAConnect(). Both of these functions can still block for long periods of time unless used with asynchronous notification. The point is this: Don't confuse asynchronous notification with asynchronous I/O.

Another important thing to note is that overlapped I/O is *not* available for files and other devices under Windows 95. Attempts to use overlapped functions on Windows 95 result in the NOT_SUPPORTED error. Even though Windows 95 does not support overlapped I/O, the WinSock 2 overlapped mechanisms work on Windows 95 as well as Windows NT. Multithreading is used on Windows 95 to imitate the overlapped behavior available in Windows NT.

The primary purpose of overlapped I/O is to allow applications to continue processing while an I/O operation is performed in the background. However, there are other benefits: The proper use of overlapped I/O can also greatly increase throughput. This performance improvement is achieved primarily from reducing the number of times a buffer is copied during transmission. For example, normally when data arrives for a socket, the protocol stack must buffer the data internally and wait for the application to call a receive function. Then the data is copied out of the internal buffer into the application's buffer. With overlapped I/O, the WSARecv() and WSARecvFrom() functions can be used to post receive buffers before any data has arrived. Then, when data arrives for a socket, the protocol stack can copy the data directly to the application's buffers, instead of having to make an internal copy.

The same benefit of reduced buffer copies can be achieved when sending as well. When a buffer of data is sent with synchronous I/O, the protocol stack first copies the data to an internal buffer before actually transmitting the data. With overlapped I/O, multiple buffers can be posted with the WSASend() and WSASendTo() functions. The application agrees not to reuse these buffers until the I/O operation has actually completed. Because it has exclusive access to these buffers, the protocol stack is free to send the data directly from the application's buffers rather than making an internal copy.

Checking for Overlapped I/O Completion

Several mechanisms are available to help an application know when an overlapped I/O operation has completed:

- Event objects can be signaled.

- Application-defined completion functions can be called.

- In the case of Windows NT, I/O completion ports can be used.

All of the asynchronous capable I/O functions accept an optional pointer to a WSAOVERLAPPED structure (*lpOverlapped*) and an optional pointer to a completion function (*lpCompletionRoutine*). The combination of these parameters determines the completion indication mechanism that will be used.

Here is the definition of the WSAOVERLAPPED structure from WINSOCK2.H:

```
typedef struct _WSAOVERLAPPED {
    DWORD    Internal;
    DWORD    InternalHigh;
    DWORD    Offset;
    DWORD    OffsetHigh;
    WSAEVENT hEvent;
} WSAOVERLAPPED, FAR * LPWSAOVERLAPPED;
```

The WSAOVERLAPPED structure is identical to the Win32 OVERLAPPED structure that is used with files and other devices. In Win32 overlapped file I/O, the *Offset* and *OffsetHigh* fields are used to maintain a file pointer. In WinSock applications, the *hEvent* field is the only one used. It can contain an event object that will be signaled when the I/O operation has completed.

The *lpCompletionRoutine* parameter can point to a function that will be called when the I/O request has finished. This function can have any name the application chooses, but it must have the following prototype:

```
void CALLBACK CompletionFunctionName(
                              DWORD dwError,
                              DWORD cbTransferred,
                              LPWSAOVERLAPPED lpOverlapped,
                              DWORD dwFlags
                              );
```

Parameter	Description
dwError	The specific error code associated with the requested operation; it's not necessary to call WSAGetLastError().
cbTransferred	The number of bytes transferred.
lpOverlapped	A pointer to the same WSAOVERLAPPED structure that was passed in the call that initiated the I/O request.
dwFlags	Contains information about the way the transfer was processed. See Table 9-3.

CHOOSING A COMPLETION MECHANISM

As stated earlier, each of the overlapped-capable socket functions accept optional pointers to both a WSAOVERLAPPED structure and a completion function. The combination of these parameters determines the way an application is notified of I/O completion.

If the *lpOverlapped* parameter is set to NULL, the function will operate synchronously; it will block even if a pointer to a completion function is given. If this parameter is non-NULL, there are three possible means for the application to be notified of completion: event signal, completion function, or completion port.

EVENT SIGNAL   If the *hEvent* field of the *lpOverlapped* parameter isn't NULL, WinSock will signal this event object when the I/O has completed. Specific information about the results of the operation can then be retrieved with WSAGetOverlappedResult().

If an application chooses to use event signaling, the I/O operation can be started while other processing takes place. Then, at some point, the application can block and wait for the event to be signaled with WSAWaitForMultipleEvents() or with one of the Win32 wait functions. The application can also intermittently poll for completion indication, using WSAGetOverlappedResult().

COMPLETION FUNCTION If the *lpCompletionRoutine* parameter is given, then the *hEvent* field of the *lpOverlapped* parameter is ignored. When the I/O operation completes, WinSock schedules the function pointed to by *lpCompletionRoutine* to be executed the next time the application is in an alertable wait state.

Alertable wait state simply means that the application is not busy doing something else and can be notified. An application signals that it is in an alertable wait state by using WSAWaitForMultipleEvents() or any of the Win32 wait functions that accept the *fAlertable* flag as a parameter.

For example, the Win32 SleepEx() function accepts a timeout value in milliseconds and the *fAlertable* flag as parameters. If a completion function is being used, an application can call SleepEx() at regular intervals with the *dwMilliseconds* parameter set to 0 and the *fAlertable* flag set to True. During the call to SleepEx(), WinSock will know that it is safe to call the completion function because the application has signaled that it is in an alertable wait state. If any completion functions were previously queued to run, they will be executed before the call to SleepEx() returns. This strategy allows the application to perform I/O without blocking or continual polling.

If a completion function is used, then the *hEvent* field of the *lpOverlapped* parameter is ignored and the application can put this field to another use. This can be handy, since the same *lpOverlapped* parameter is passed to the completion function.

COMPLETION PORT If both the *lpCompletionRoutine* parameter and the *hEvent* field of the *lpOverlapped* parameter are NULL, then the completion port mechanism can be used. This method is only available on Windows NT and is not part of the official WinSock specification. It is mentioned here because it is the most efficient means of completion notification available to programs that will only run on NT.

OVERLAPPED I/O RETURN VALUES

Overlapped I/O functions always return immediately; they never block. The return value from an overlapped I/O function can indicate one of three situations:

- An error occurred. In this case, no further processing will take place for the request and a specific error code can be obtained through WSAGetLastError().

- The I/O operation completed during the call. In this case, the chosen completion mechanism has already occurred. If event signaling is being used, the event handle has already been signaled. If a completion routine is being used, the completion routine has already been queued to run.

- The I/O operation was initiated and will complete at a later time. Then the function will return SOCKET_ERROR, and WSAGetLastError() will be set to WSA_I/O_PENDING. This means WinSock will carry out the I/O request and indicate completion (either successfully or with an error) at a later time. Once an overlapped I/O operation has been requested, there is no way to cancel it. Closing a socket cancels all outstanding requests, but there is no way to cancel any one request without canceling them all.

THE WSAGetOverlappedResult() FUNCTION

If event signaling is being used for overlapped I/O, the results of the overlapped operation can be retrieved with WSAGetOverlappedResult(). It accepts parameters that identify both the socket and the specific overlapped operation that is pending.

An application using event signaling can determine when the event handle becomes signaled by using one of the WinSock 2 or Win32 wait functions, or it can use this WSAGetOverlappedResult() function. If the application uses one of the wait functions to determine when the operation has completed, it then calls WSAGetOverlappedResult() to obtain the results of the request. Here is the prototype for this function:

```
BOOL WSAGetOverlappedResult(
                    SOCKET s,
                    LPWSAOVERLAPPED lpOverlapped,
                    LPDWORD lpcbTransfer,
                    BOOL fWait,
                    LPDWORD lpdwFlags
                    );
```

Parameter	Description
s	A socket descriptor.
lpOverlapped	A pointer to the same WSAOVERLAPPED structure that was used in the call that initiated overlapped I/O.
lpcbTransfer	A pointer to a DWORD variable that will be set to the number of bytes transferred.
fWait	Indicates whether the function should wait until the specified overlapped I/O request has completed. If set to True, the function does not return until the operation has been completed. If set to False and the operation is still pending, the function returns False and WSAGetLastError() will indicate WSA_IO_INCOMPLETE.
pdwFlags	A pointer to a DWORD value; if this is a receive operation, this DWORD value will be set as explained later in the sections on WSARecv() and WSARecvFrom().

Note: The WSAGetOverlappedResult() function can only be used with a completion-function type of request, and with the *fWait* parameter set to False. If a completion function was specified in the call that initiated the I/O, then the contents of the *hEvent* field of the *lpOverlapped* structure may not be a valid event object. For this reason, the *fWait* parameter can't be set to True in a call specifying a pending I/O request that has a related completion function.

ORDER OF COMPLETION NOTIFICATION

Overlapped I/O can provide many benefits, and requesting overlapped I/O is simple enough. It's worth the trouble in a lot of situations. Nevertheless, using multiple buffers with overlapped I/O can be difficult to implement. What complicates matters is the fact that completion indications may not occur in the same order as their corresponding requests.

Posting multiple receive buffers can dramatically increase throughput, and WinSock will always fill the buffers in the order that they were posted. But watch out: Indications that the buffers have been filled may *not* occur sequentially. The following sequence of events is possible when using multiple buffers:

1. Post Receive buffer 1 with WSARecv().
2. Post Receive buffer 2 with WSARecv().
3. Data arrives and WinSock fills Receive buffer 1.
4. More data arrives and WinSock fills Receive buffer 2.
5. Application receives indication that Receive buffer 2 has been filled.
6. Application receives indication that Receive buffer 1 has been filled.

This sequence can make using multiple receive buffers very complex indeed. The same thing applies to multiple send buffers, though they're not as difficult to handle. WinSock will send the data buffers in the same order that they are supplied by the application, but the completion indications may occur in a different order.

Scatter and Gather

All of the socket I/O functions that support overlapped operation also accept a pointer to an array of WSABUF structures:

```
typedef struct _WSABUF {
    u_long       len;
    char FAR *   buf;
} WSABUF, FAR * LPWSABUF;
```

Each WSABUF structure contains a pointer to a buffer area, and the length of the buffer. By using an array of these structures, an application can post multiple buffers for sending or receiving in just one function call. Note that this mechanism is different from supplying multiple buffers by making multiple function calls — arrays of WSABUF structures are used for *scatter* or *gather* operations.

For example, if each data transmission contains a fixed header portion followed by data that changes each time, the static header portion can be kept in one buffer and the data in another. Both of the buffers can then be *gathered* and transmitted in the appropriate order with one function call, by posting both of the buffers in one call. When receiving data like this, the two buffers and their sizes can be specified so that incoming data is *scattered* into the appropriate places.

Note: Scatter and gather strategy doesn't work well for stream-oriented protocols, especially when receiving data. In an overlapped receive function, the I/O completion can occur before the buffers are filled. Incoming data is copied to the supplied buffers until the buffers are filled *or* until there is no more data currently available. The completion can occur regardless of whether or not the supplied buffers were filled. When used with message-oriented protocols, the buffers will contain a complete record. If the record size is known so that buffers can be created of the appropriate size, then the receive function will not complete until each buffer is filled.

For this reason, I suggest you supply multiple receive buffers with one call only when using datagram-oriented protocols that preserve record boundaries. In this situation, posting multiple buffers with one call can be used to automatically parse incoming data.

Even if you only want to pass a single buffer to one of the overlapped I/O functions, you still must wrap the buffer with a WSABUF structure. One thing to note is that the WSABUF structure itself may be constructed on the stack. The buffer referenced in the structure must remain available until the operation completes, but the WSABUF structure itself can be temporary.

Overlapped I/O Functions

Now that we've discussed in a general sense the role of overlapped I/O operations, let's look at each of overlapped I/O-capable functions.

THE WSARecv() FUNCTION

Like recv(), the WSARecv() function is used to receive incoming data. However, WSARecv() has a few important extended capabilities:

- It can be used with overlapped I/O.

- It supports the scatter mechanism by accepting multiple receive buffers.

- It both sends and receives information through the *lpFlags* parameter, which allows applications to determine if the MSG_PARTIAL flag is set.

> **About MSG_PARTIAL**
>
> In OSI and other protocols, the MSG_PARTIAL flag is used to indicate that a protocol with the XP1_MESSAGE_ORIENTED flag set in its WSAPROTOCOL_INFO structure can actually act as a byte stream. For protocols that support this flag, it indicates that the supplied receive buffer is not large enough to hold the entire record and that a partial record is being returned (message boundaries are not being preserved). The entire record can be retrieved by issuing another receive with a larger buffer.

Here is the function prototype for WSARecv() from WINSOCK2.H:

```
int WSARecv(
            SOCKET s,
            LPWSABUF lpBuffers,
            DWORD dwBufferCount,
            LPDWORD lpNumberOfBytesRecvd,
            LPDWORD lpFlags,
            LPWSAOVERLAPPED lpOverlapped,
            LPWSAOVERLAPPED_COMPLETION_ROUTINE
            lpCompletionRoutine
            );
```

Parameter	Description
s	A socket descriptor identifying a connected socket or bound connectionless socket. (The socket's local address must be known.)
lpBuffers	A pointer to an array of WSABUF structures, which in turn point to the buffers that will receive the data.
dwBufferCount	The number of WSABUF structures contained in the array pointed to by *lpBuffers*.
lpNumberOfBytesRecvd	A pointer to a DWORD variable that will indicate the number of bytes received if the function completes immediately (does not return WSA_I/O_PENDING).
lpFlags	A pointer to a DWORD variable. On input this is used to specify the MSG_PEEK or MSG_OOB flags (if wanted). On output it allows the application to receive indication of the MSG_PARTIAL flag for protocols that support it. See Table 9-3.
lpOverlapped	An optional pointer to a WSAOVERLAPPED structure. This is ignored for sockets that were created with WSASocket() without the WSA_FLAG_OVERLAPPED flag.

Parameter	Description
lpCompletionRoutine	An optional pointer to a completion function. This is ignored for sockets that were created with WSASocket() without the WSA_FLAG_OVERLAPPED flag.

For nonoverlapped sockets, the WSARecv() function acts exactly like recv() but allows the application to receive the MSG_PARTIAL flag. If data is waiting to be read, it will be copied into the supplied buffer and the function will return immediately. If there is no data waiting, the function will block and wait until data arrives. If both the *lpOverlapped* and *lpCompletionRoutine* parameters are NULL, the function blocks and waits even with overlapped sockets.

For overlapped operation, the socket descriptor must have the OVERLAPPED attribute, and the *lpOverlapped* parameter must not be NULL. If the return value is 0, that means the function completed immediately and the chosen completion indication has already occurred. (The event handle specified in the *hEvent* field of *lpOverlapped* has been signaled or the completion function has been queued.) If the return value is SOCKET_ERROR, then either a "real" error has occurred or WSAGetLastError() is set to WSA_I/O_PENDING, which signifies that the operation has been successfully started and will complete at a later time.

If the *lpCompletionRoutine* parameter is NULL and the *hEvent* field of *lpOverlapped* is a valid event object, then *hEvent* will become signaled when the operation completes. The WSAGetOverlappedResult() function can then be used to retrieve the error code and the number of bytes received.

For stream-oriented protocols, data is copied into the supplied buffers until the buffers are filled or until there is no more data currently available.

For message-oriented protocols, a message is copied into the supplied buffers. If the buffers aren't large enough to hold the message, then the first part of the message is copied into the buffers, and the function returns SOCKET_ERROR with WSAGetLastError() set to WSAEMSGSIZE. For a reliable protocol, the entire message can be retrieved by calling WSARecv() again with larger buffers. For an unreliable protocol, the message is lost.

If the completion of this function indicates that no error occurred and also that no data was transmitted when using a stream-oriented protocol, this means the connection has been closed.

RECEIVE FLAGS The *lpFlags* parameter of WSARecv() accepts the flags listed in Table 9.3. These can be combined with the OR (|) operator.

TABLE 9-3 VALUES FOR lpFlags PARAMETER OF WSARecv()

Flag	Result When Flag Is Set
MSG_PEEK	This flag can only be used with nonoverlapped sockets. It causes WSARecv() to copy available data to the buffer just as it would normally, but the data is not removed from WinSock's internal buffer. The same data can be read again with another call to WSARecv().
MSG_OOB	Receive only out-of-band (urgent) data.
MSG_PARTIAL	This message is never specified in a call to WSARecv() but may be indicated in *lpFlags* on return from the function call. It indicates that the supplied buffers were not large enough to hold the entire message and that only part of the message could be returned.

The WSARecvFrom() Function

Like recvfrom(), the WSARecvFrom() function is used to receive incoming data. However, WSARecvFrom() has the same extended capabilities as WSARecv():

- It can be used with overlapped I/O.
- It supports the scatter mechanism by accepting multiple receive buffers.
- It both sends and receives information through the *lpFlags* parameter, which allows applications to determine if the MSG_PARTIAL flag is set.

Here is the function prototype for WSARecvFrom() from WINSOCK2.H:

```
int WSARecvFrom(
            SOCKET s,
            LPWSABUF lpBuffers,
            DWORD dwBufferCount,
            LPDWORD lpNumberOfBytesRecvd,
            LPDWORD lpFlags,
            struct sockaddr FAR * lpFrom,
            LPINT lpFromlen,
            LPWSAOVERLAPPED lpOverlapped,
            LPWSAOVERLAPPED_COMPLETION_ROUTINE
            lpCompletionRoutine
            );
```

Parameter	Description
s	A socket descriptor for an *unconnected* socket.
lpBuffers	A pointer to an array of WSABUF structures, which in turn point to the buffers that will receive the data.
dwBufferCount	The number of WSABUF structures contained in the array pointed to by *lpBuffers*.
lpNumberOfBytesRecvd	A pointer to a DWORD variable that will indicate the number of bytes received if the function completes immediately (does not return WSA_I/O_PENDING).
lpFlags	A pointer to a DWORD variable. On input this is used to specify the MSG_PEEK or MSG_OOB flags (if wanted). On output it allows the application to receive indication of the MSG_PARTIAL flag for protocols that support it.
lpFrom	An optional pointer to a SOCKADDR structure that will receive the source address of the peer that sent the data.
lpFromlen	An optional pointer to an integer that specifies the size of the buffer pointed to by *lpFrom*. This is only required if *lpFrom* isn't NULL.
lpOverlapped	An optional pointer to a WSAOVERLAPPED structure. This is ignored for sockets that were created with WSASocket() without the WSA_FLAG_OVERLAPPED flag.
lpCompletionRoutine	An optional pointer to a completion function. This is ignored for sockets that were created with WSASocket() without the WSA_FLAG_OVERLAPPED flag.

WSARecvFrom() operates in much the same way as WSARecv(), but is typically only used on connectionless sockets. (For a full description of behavior, see the discussion of the WSARecv() function.) The difference in these two functions lies in the fact that WSARecvFrom() can be used to obtain the address of the peer that sent the data. On overlapped operations, these fields aren't filled in until the function completes.

The WSASend() Function

WSASend(), like its send() counterpart, is used to send outgoing data. It also has these extended capabilities:

304 Part III: The WinSock 2.0 API

- ◆ It can be used with overlapped I/O.
- ◆ It supports the gather mechanism by accepting multiple send buffers.

Here is the function prototype for WSASend() from WINSOCK2.H:

```
int WSASend(
            SOCKET s,
            LPWSABUF lpBuffers,
            DWORD dwBufferCount,
            LPDWORD lpNumberOfBytesSent,
            DWORD dwFlags,
            LPWSAOVERLAPPED lpOverlapped,
            LPWSAOVERLAPPED_COMPLETION_ROUTINE
                                                lpCompletionRoutine
           );
```

Parameter	Description
s	A socket descriptor identifying a connected socket.
lpBuffers	A pointer to an array of WSABUF structures, which in turn point to the buffers that will receive the data.
dwBufferCount	The number of WSABUF structures contained in the array pointed to by *lpBuffers*.
lpNumberOfBytesSent	A pointer to a DWORD variable that will indicate the number of bytes sent if the function completes immediately (does not return WSA_I/O_PENDING).
dwFlags	A bitmask used to affect the way the send is performed. See Table 9-4 for a list of supported flags.
lpOverlapped	An optional pointer to a WSAOVERLAPPED structure. This is ignored for sockets that were created with WSASocket() without the WSA_FLAG_OVERLAPPED flag.
lpCompletionRoutine	An optional pointer to a completion function. This is ignored for sockets that were created with WSASocket() without the WSA_FLAG_OVERLAPPED flag.

Like send(), successful completion of a WSASend() does not indicate that the data was successfully delivered. It indicates only that WinSock accepted the data and will attempt to send it to the peer system.

When used with message-oriented protocols, care must be taken not to exceed the maximum message size obtained by using getsockopt() with the SO_MAX_MSG_SIZE command. If the number of bytes to send exceeds this size,

WSASend() will return SOCKET_ERROR and WSAGetLastError() will return the WSAEMSGSIZE error.

Overlapped operation of WSASend() works as outlined earlier in this section. WSASend() returns 0 if the send operation was completed immediately. If there is an error or if the send request can't be fulfilled immediately, WSASend() returns SOCKET_ERROR. If the send request was initiated and will complete later, WSAGetLastError() will return WSA_I/O_PENDING.

The *lpFlags* parameter accepts the following values. These can be combined with the OR (|) operator.

TABLE 9-4 VALUES FOR lpFlags PARAMETER OF WSASend() AND WSASendTo()

Flag	Result When Flag Is Set
MSG_DONTROUTE	Indicates that the data should bypass the internal routing tables. This flag is only significant if the local machine is multihomed; that is, it has more than one network interface, such as a network card and a dial-up. A WinSock service provider may choose to ignore this flag.
MSG_OOB	Send data out-of-band (urgent).
MSG_PARTIAL	Indicates that the message being sent is only a partial record. This flag will be ignored by protocols that don't support MSG_PARTIAL.

The WSASendTo() Function

WSASendTo(), like its sendto() counterpart, is used to send outgoing data. It has these extended capabilities:

- It can be used with overlapped I/O.
- It supports the gather mechanism by accepting multiple send buffers.

Here is the function prototype for WSASendTo() from WINSOCK2.H:

```
int WSASendTo(
            SOCKET s,
            LPWSABUF lpBuffers,
            DWORD dwBufferCount,
            LPDWORD lpNumberOfBytesSent,
            DWORD dwFlags,
            const struct sockaddr FAR * lpTo,
```

```
                int iToLen,
                LPWSAOVERLAPPED lpOverlapped,
                LPWSAOVERLAPPED_COMPLETION_ROUTINE
                                                  lpCompletionRoutine
                );
```

Parameter	Description
s	A socket descriptor identifying a connected socket.
lpBuffers	A pointer to an array of WSABUF structures, which in turn point to the buffers that will receive the data.
dwBufferCount	The number of WSABUF structures contained in the array pointed to by *lpBuffers*.
lpNumberOfBytesSent	A pointer to a DWORD variable that will indicate the number of bytes sent if the function completes immediately (does not return WSA_I/O_PENDING).
dwFlags	A bitmask used to affect the way the send is performed. Table 9-4 lists the supported flags; these are the same flags that are accepted for WSASend().
lpTo	A pointer to a SOCKADDR structure indicating the destination address.
iToLen	An integer specifying the length of the SOCKADDR structure pointed to by *lpTo*.
lpOverlapped	An optional pointer to a WSAOVERLAPPED structure. This is ignored for sockets that were created with WSASocket() without the WSA_FLAG_OVERLAPPED flag.
lpCompletionRoutine	An optional pointer to a completion function. This is ignored for sockets that were created with WSASocket() without the WSA_FLAG_OVERLAPPED flag.

WSASendTo() operates in much the same way as WSASend(), but is typically only used on connectionless sockets. For a full description of sending behavior, see the discussion of the WSASend() function. The difference between WSASend() and WSASendTo() is that WSASendTo() requires a destination address as a parameter.

Caution: When used with message-oriented protocols, take care not to exceed the maximum message size obtained by using getsockopt() with the SO_MAX_MSG_SIZE command. If the supplied data exceeds this size, WSASendTo() will return SOCKET_ERROR and WSAGetLastError() will return the WSAEMSGSIZE error.

Overlapped operation of WSASendTo() works as outlined earlier in this section. WSASendTo() returns 0 if the send operation was completed immediately. If there is an error or if the send request can't be fulfilled immediately, WSASendTo() returns SOCKET_ERROR. If the send request was initiated and will complete later, WSAGetLastError() will return WSA_IO_PENDING.

The GetHTTP3 Sample

Listing 9-2 contains the source code for yet another example program that retrieves a file from a Web server. (Therefore, the UNIX name for this program would have been YAEPTRAFFAWS.) This program is very similar to the GetHTTP2 sample in Listing 9-1, and it performs the same work. The difference is that GetHTTP3 uses overlapped I/O.

Listing 9-2 GETHTTP3.CPP

```
//
// GetHTTP3.cpp —  Retrieve a file from a HTTP server
//
//                 This version uses overlapped I/O
//                 with a completion function.
//

#include <fcntl.h>
#include <io.h>
#include <stdio.h>
#include <winsock2.h>

void GetHTTP(LPCSTR lpServerName, LPCSTR lpFileName);

//
// Overlapped I/O completion function
//
void CALLBACK RecvComplete(DWORD dwError,
                           DWORD cbTransferred,
                           LPWSAOVERLAPPED lpOverlapped,
                           DWORD dwFlags);

// Helper macro for displaying errors
#define PRINTERROR(s)   \
        fprintf(stderr,"\n%s %d\n", s, WSAGetLastError())

#define BUFFER_SIZE 1024

//
// Structure used to pass
// additional info to the
```

Part III: The WinSock 2.0 API

```c
// completion function
//
typedef struct tagIOREQUEST
{
    WSAOVERLAPPED   over;   // Must be first
    SOCKET          Socket;
    BOOL            fFinished;
    LPBYTE          pBuffer;
} IOREQUEST, *LPIOREQUEST;


void main(int argc, char **argv)
{
    WORD wVersionRequested = WINSOCK_VERSION;
    WSADATA wsaData;
    int nRet;

    //
    // Check arguments
    //
    if (argc != 3)
    {
        fprintf(stderr,
            "\nSyntax: GetHTTP ServerName FullPathName\n");
        return;
    }

    //
    // Initialize WinSock.dll
    //
    nRet = WSAStartup(wVersionRequested, &wsaData);
    if (nRet)
    {
        fprintf(stderr, "\nWSAStartup() error (%d)\n",
                    nRet);
        WSACleanup();
        return;
    }

    //
    // Check WinSock version
    //
    if (wsaData.wVersion != wVersionRequested)
    {
        fprintf(stderr,"\nWinSock version not supported\n");
        WSACleanup();
        return;
    }

    //
    // Set "stdout" to binary mode
    // so that redirection will work
    // for binary files (.gif, .jpg, .exe, etc.)
```

```
    //
    _setmode(_fileno(stdout), _O_BINARY);

    //
    // Call GetHTTP() to do all the work
    //
    GetHTTP(argv[1], argv[2]);

    WSACleanup();
}

void GetHTTP(LPCSTR lpServerName, LPCSTR lpFileName)
{
    LPHOSTENT   lpHostEntry;
    SOCKADDR_IN saServer;
    SOCKET      Socket;
    int         nRet;

    //
    // Lookup the host address
    //
    lpHostEntry = gethostbyname(lpServerName);
    if (lpHostEntry == NULL)
    {
        PRINTERROR("socket()");
        return;
    }

    // Create a TCP/IP stream socket
    Socket = socket(AF_INET, SOCK_STREAM, IPPROTO_TCP);
    if (Socket == INVALID_SOCKET)
    {
        PRINTERROR("socket()");
        return;
    }

    //
    // Fill in the rest of the server address structure
    //
    saServer.sin_family = AF_INET;
    saServer.sin_addr = *((LPIN_ADDR)*lpHostEntry->h_addr_list);
    saServer.sin_port = htons(80);

    //
    // Connect the socket
    //
    nRet = connect(Socket,
                   (LPSOCKADDR)&saServer,
                   sizeof(SOCKADDR_IN));
    if (nRet == SOCKET_ERROR)
    {
        PRINTERROR("connect()");
```

```c
        closesocket(Socket);
        return;
    }

    //
    // Format the HTTP request
    // and send it
    //
    char szBuffer[1024];
    sprintf(szBuffer, "GET %s\n", lpFileName);
    nRet = send(Socket, szBuffer, strlen(szBuffer), 0);
    if (nRet == SOCKET_ERROR)
    {
        PRINTERROR("send()");
        closesocket(Socket);
        return;
    }

    //
    // We're connected, so we can now
    // post a receive buffer
    //

    //
    // We use a little trick here to pass additional
    // information to our completion function.
    // We append any additional info onto the end
    // of a WSAOVERLAPPED structure and pass it
    // as the lpOverlapped parameter to WSARecv()
    // When the completion function is called,
    // this additional info is then available.
    //
    BYTE aBuffer[BUFFER_SIZE];
    IOREQUEST ioRequest;
    memset(&ioRequest.over, 0, sizeof(WSAOVERLAPPED));
    ioRequest.Socket = Socket;
    ioRequest.fFinished = FALSE;
    ioRequest.pBuffer = aBuffer;

    WSABUF wsabuf;
    wsabuf.len = BUFFER_SIZE;
    wsabuf.buf = (char *)aBuffer;

    DWORD dwRecv;
    DWORD dwFlags = 0;
    nRet = WSARecv(Socket,
                   &wsabuf,
                   1,
                   &dwRecv,
                   &dwFlags,
                   (LPWSAOVERLAPPED)&ioRequest,
                   RecvComplete);
    if (nRet == SOCKET_ERROR)
```

Chapter 9: Enhanced Input/Output

```
    {
        if (WSAGetLastError() != WSA_IO_PENDING)
        {
            PRINTERROR("WSARecv()");
            closesocket(Socket);
            return;
        }
    }

    // Receive the file contents and print to stdout
    while(1)
    {
        //
        // We could do other processing here
        //

        //
        // Use the SleepEx() function to signal
        // that we are in an altertable wait state
        //
        SleepEx(0, TRUE);

        //
        // If the completion function says we're finished
        //
        if (ioRequest.fFinished)
            break;
    }
    closesocket(Socket);
}

void CALLBACK RecvComplete(DWORD dwError,
                           DWORD cbRecv,
                           LPWSAOVERLAPPED lpOver,
                           DWORD dwFlags)
{
    //
    // Check for errors
    //
    if (dwError)
    {
        fprintf(stderr,"\nRecvComplete() error: %ld",
                        dwError);
        return;
    }

    LPIOREQUEST pReq = (LPIOREQUEST)lpOver;

    //
    // If no error and no data returned,
    // then the connection has been closed.
    //
    if (cbRecv == 0)
```

```
    {
        pReq->fFinished = TRUE;
        return;
    }

    //
    // Write the received data to stdout
    //
    fwrite(pReq->pBuffer, cbRecv, 1, stdout);

    //
    // And then post the buffer to receive again
    //
    WSABUF wsabuf;
    wsabuf.len = BUFFER_SIZE;
    wsabuf.buf = (char *)pReq->pBuffer;

    DWORD dwRecv;
    dwFlags = 0;
    int nRet;
    nRet = WSARecv(pReq->Socket,
                   &wsabuf,
                   1,
                   &dwRecv,
                   &dwFlags,
                   lpOver,
                   RecvComplete);
    if (nRet == SOCKET_ERROR)
    {
        if (WSAGetLastError() != WSA_IO_PENDING)
        {
            PRINTERROR("RePost with WSARecv()");
            pReq->fFinished = TRUE;
        }
    }
}
```

Analysis of GetHTTP3

The first part of this program works just like the GetHTTP2 application. It accepts a host name and file specification from the command line, and uses this information to connect to the server and to send an HTTP GET request for the file. The I/O portion of the GetHTTP3 example, however, works much differently.

Immediately after the socket is connected, the program posts a buffer with the WSARecv() function. It requests overlapped I/O using a function for completion indication. I created the example in this way to show how completion functions are used, as well as to point out one way in which additional information can be passed to the completion function.

The program defines an IOREQUEST structure near the top of the file. The first member of this structure is a WSAOVERLAPPED structure. After this member, you can add any additional information the program needs to pass to the completion function. I have added a pointer to the receive buffer and the socket descriptor so that the completion function can repost the buffer once it reads its contents.

The Win32 SleepEx() function is used to place the program into an alertable wait state. Without this function call, the completion routine would never be invoked. Note that the program could have used a call to WSAGetOverlappedResult() to achieve the same results. I chose to use the SleepEx() function because it is simpler and to demonstrate that other Win32 functions are related to overlapped I/O. The program would actually be more efficient if it used INFINITE rather than 0 as a *dwMilliseconds* parameter to SleepEx(). Again, I made this choice only for demonstration purposes. The SleepEx() function returns very quickly – especially if the completion function isn't queued to run. Any other processing could be done, as well, in the loop with the SleepEx() call.

Determining Quality of Service

Applications that transmit and receive time-critical data, such as audio and video applications, require guarantees about the quality of communication between two or more points on a network. Other protocols and transport media, such as wireless networks, may also require special consideration. The WinSock 2 specification includes conventions that allow applications such as these, to negotiate required service levels for parameters such as bandwidth and latency.

Before an application can negotiate for a particular level of service, there must some predetermined way to describe the type or quality of service needed. WinSock 2's quality of service is based on the flow specification described in RFC 1363, "A Proposed Flow Specification." (The complete text of RFC 1363 is included on the CD; see Appendix A.)

The *flow specification* outlined in RFC 1363 describes a data structure that can be used in the negotiation to request special services from the network. The goal of RFC 1363 was to define a data structure capable of describing any flow requirement, both for guaranteed flows and applications that simply want to give hints to the network about their requirements.

QOS Data Structures

As a result of the data structure outlined in RFC 1363, the WinSock 2 group created a flow specification that allows for an indication of the network speed, its sensitivity to delay, and other characteristics. It uses what is known as a *token bucket model*. This model uses an imaginary bucket into which the network continually places tokens (or credits) at a certain rate. Each time data is transferred, the application must remove a number of tokens from the bucket equal to the size of the packet being transferred. The application must ensure that it has enough credits to handle each packet transfer.

The following FLOWSPEC data structure is defined in QOS.H. Both *uint32* and SERVICETYPE are currently defined as an unsigned long.

```
typedef struct _flowspec
{
    uint32      TokenRate;              /* In Bytes/sec */
    uint32      TokenBucketSize;        /* In Bytes */
    uint32      PeakBandwidth;          /* In Bytes/sec */
    uint32      Latency;                /* In microseconds */
    uint32      DelayVariation;         /* In microseconds */
    SERVICETYPE ServiceType;
    uint32      MaxSduSize;             /* In Bytes */
    uint32      MinimumPolicedSize;     /* In Bytes */
} FLOWSPEC, *PFLOWSPEC, FAR * LPFLOWSPEC;
```

Field	Description
TokenRate	The rate, in bytes per second, at which the token bucket is filled.
TokenBucketSize	The total volume of the imaginary token/credit bucket.
PeakBandwidth	The rate, in bytes per second, at which an application may transfer packets.
Latency	The maximum delay, in microseconds, that is to be allowed before a bit is sent and received.
DelayVariation	The difference, in microseconds, between the maximum and minimum delay allowed for each packet.
ServiceType	The level of service guarantee. Supported values for this field are listed in Table 9-5.
MaxSduSize	The maximum packet size (in bytes) that can be used.
MinimumPolicedSize	The minimum packet size that will be given the level of service requested.

Notice that the structure defines flow characteristics in a single direction. Applications that wish to negotiate flows for both sending and receiving must use two flow specifications.

The QOS structure, which is also defined in QOS.H, holds a FLOWSPEC structure for both directions as well as a pointer to a buffer containing service provider specific information.

```
typedef struct _QualityOfService
{
    FLOWSPEC    SendingFlowspec;
    FLOWSPEC    ReceivingFlowspec;
```

```
    WSABUF        ProviderSpecific; specific stuff */
} QOS, FAR * LPQOS;
```

Table 9-5 describes the values for use in the *ServiceType* field in each direction's flow specification.

TABLE 9-5 VALUES FOR ServiceType FIELD

Value	Description
SERVICETYPE_NOTRAFFIC	Indicates that there will be no data traffic in this direction.
SERVICETYPE_BESTEFFORT	Indicates that the application is giving this information as a hint to the network about its needs. No guarantee of service is given.
SERVICETYPE_CONTROLLEDLOAD	Indicates that a guaranteed level of service can be provided under "unloaded conditions." This is closely related to best-effort service. It means a high percentage of the packets transferred will receive the designated level of service.
SERVICETYPE_GUARANTEED	Indicates that the network can provide the indicated level of service regardless of other network flows.
SERVICETYPE_NETWORK_UNAVAILABLE	May be used by a service provider to indicate a loss of service or change in service level.
SERVICETYPE_GENERAL_INFORMATION	Indicates that all service types are supported for this traffic flow.
SERVICETYPE_NOCHANGE	Indicates that the flow specification contains no change from any previous negotiation.
SERVICE_IMMEDIATE_TRAFFIC_CONTROL	Used with the OR operator (|) in combination with one of the other supported flags to request that the new flow specification be used immediately.

Quality-of-Service Templates

WinSock 2 defines a number of quality-of-service templates that can be used to fill quality-of-service structures with appropriate field values for well-known media types. These templates can be requested by name with the WSAGetQOSByName() function:

```
BOOL WSAGetQOSByName(
                    SOCKET s,
                    LPWSABUF lpQOSName,
                    LPQOS lpQOS
                    );
```

WSAGetQOSByName() accepts a socket and a name, and returns a pointer to a QOS structure that contains acceptable values for a given service class or media type. If you set the *lpQOSName* parameter to NULL, some service providers will return an array of names that are supported. The application can then choose one of the names and make another call using this name to obtain a pointer to an appropriate QOS structure.

Note: The official WinSock 2 documentation for WSAGetQOSByName() will be periodically updated with a list of flow specifications and general descriptions as they become well known.

Negotiating Quality of Service

The WSAConnect() function accepts a pointer to a QOS structure that will be passed along with the connection request. If WSAConnect() completes successfully, that means the QOS request has been agreed to by the network. If the function fails and WSAGetLastError() returns the WSAEOPNOTSUPP error, it means the requested level of service could not be provided. In this situation, the application may lower the level of service requested and try again, or perhaps alert the user to the problem and exit.

Applications may also use the WSAIoctl() function with the SIO_GET_QOS and SIO_SET_QOS commands at any point during a conversation to obtain the current quality-of-service requirements or to request a change in the flow specification.

The WSAAccept() function accepts an optional pointer to a condition procedure that can be used to retrieve a QOS request from a connecting client. This condition procedure can choose to either accept or reject the connection based on requested quality of service. WSAAccept() is discussed later in this chapter in the "Exchanging Data at Connect and Disconnect" section.

There is also a new asynchronous network event code (FD_QOS) that can be used with WSAAsyncSelect() and WSAEventSelect() to ensure that the application is notified of changes in quality of service as they occur.

> **About Group Quality of Service**
>
> The original WinSock 2 specification anticipated that quality-of-service negotiation would be based on groups of sockets. As WinSock 2 neared completion, socket groups and all related functions were dropped. They are still shown in the specification documents, but are now labeled "reserved for future use." Since these group extensions aren't yet available, they aren't discussed here.

RSVP

The Internet Protocol (IP) doesn't include direct support for quality of service. However, the Resource ReSerVation Protocol (RSVP) has been developed within the IETF (Internet Engineering Task Force) to provide quality-of-service capabilities over the Internet. The protocol specification is now complete and will soon be published as an RFC.

A protocol-specific annex for the WinSock 2 specification has been developed by Microsoft and Intel; this addition describes how WinSock 2's quality of service mechanisms can be used with the RSVP protocol. See Appendix A for directions on how to find this annex and other new WinSock 2 specification documents.

Exchanging Data at Connect and Disconnect

Some service providers allow both clients and servers to exchange application-specific data when connecting and or disconnecting. Protocols that support exchange of connect data have the XP1_CONNECT_DATA flag set in the *dwServiceFlags1* field of their WSAPROTOCOL_INFO structure. Protocols that support exchange of disconnect data have the XP1_DISCONNECT_DATA flag set in this field.

At Connect

The WSAAccept() and WSAConnect() functions allow applications to exchange data as they connect. The WSASendDisconnect() and WSARecvDisconnect() functions allow applications to exchange data as they disconnect.

WSAAccept() allows the server to obtain information about the client (caller) and to accept or reject a connection request.

```
SOCKET   WSAAccept(
                SOCKET s,
                struct sockaddr FAR * addr,
```

```
                LPINT addrlen,
                LPCONDITIONPROC lpfnCondition,
                DWORD dwCallbackData
                );
```

Along with the socket and socket address parameters used with accept(), WSAAccept()accepts a pointer to a condition procedure. This condition function is defined by the application and must have the following prototype:

```
int CALLBACK ConditionFunc(
                    LPWSABUF lpCallerId,
                    LPWSABUF lpCallerData,
                    LPQOS lpSQOS,
                    LPQOS lpGQOS,
                    LPWSABUF lpCalleeId,
                    LPWSABUF lpCalleeData,
                    GROUP FAR * g,
                    DWORD dwCallbackData
                    );
```

The LPQOS parameters point to quality-of-service structures as discussed earlier. The LPWSABUF parameters allow information to be exchanged between the client and the server as the connection request is processed. The ConditionFunc() used with WSAAccept() can decide whether to accept or reject the connection request by returning CF_ACCEPT or CF_REJECT. ConditionFunc() can also return CF_DEFER to indicate that making the accept or reject decision will not happen immediately (perhaps the application will ask a user). If the function returns CF_DEFER, the service provider will do nothing with the connection request and will wait for the application to call WSAAccept() again to process the request.

The WSAConnect() function provides a means for clients to send application-specific data to the server along with a connection request, and to receive information back from the server when the request is processed. As shown in the function prototype just below, WSAConnect() also accepts pointers to WSABUF structures that can contain application specific data.

```
int WSAConnect(
            SOCKET s,
            const struct sockaddr FAR * name,
            int namelen,
            LPWSABUF lpCallerData,
            LPWSABUF lpCalleeData,
            LPQOS lpSQOS,
            LPQOS lpGQOS
            );
```

At Disconnect

The WSASendDisconnect() function can be used to simultaneously initiate a graceful close of a connection and to send application-specific data. Either end of a conversation, client or server, may initiate this process. When WSASendDisconnect()is called, the peer application is notified of the close process through receipt of an FD_CLOSE notification, or a 0 return from recv(), or a WSAEDISCON return value from WSARecv().

```
int   WSASendDisconnect(
                    SOCKET s,
                    LPWSABUF lpOutboundDisconnectData
                    );
```

When the peer realizes that a graceful close is in progress, it should then call WSARecvDisconnect() to obtain the information included in the call to WSASendDisconnect().

```
int   WSARecvDisconnect(
                    SOCKET s,
                    LPWSABUF lpOutboundDisconnectData
                    );
```

The peer can then call WSASendDisconnect() to send information back to the application that initiated the graceful close.

Multipoint and Multicast

Like broadcasting, *multipoint* and *multicast* transmission allow data to be sent to many recipients rather than just one endpoint. Instead of sending data to all nodes on a network as broadcasting does, multipoint data transmission goes to a group address. Applications that wish to receive multipoint transmissions can *join* this group address. This strategy sends the data to only the systems that wish to receive it and thereby greatly reduces network traffic.

Note: The terms *multicast* and *multipoint* mean essentially the same thing, so to simplify the text, *multipoint* is used throughout the rest of this chapter to refer to both concepts.

There are currently several different protocols and technologies that support multipoint data transmission: IP Multicast, ST-II, T.120, and ATM Point-To-Multipoint are examples. The exact processes for multipoint transmission and group address joining are performed with each of these implementations and vary considerably. WinSock 2 attempts to generalize the characteristics of all these multipoint strategies into one standard API.

> **About IP Multicast**
>
> Even though WinSock 2 introduces a new protocol-independent multipoint interface, it still supports the TCP/IP-specific multipoint mechanisms that were used in WinSock 1.1 for IP multicast. Details of this protocol-dependent interface are available in the TCP/IP section of the Windows Sockets 2 Protocol-Specific Annex document. This document can be found on the CD in the \SPECS\2 directory.

Handling Different Multipoint Strategies

WinSock 2 organizes the behavior of various multipoint strategies into two planes: the *control plane* and the *data plane*.

CONTROL PLANE

The control plane manages the way a multipoint session is established. There are two distinct methods — *rooted* and *nonrooted* — of establishing a multipoint session in the various multipoint protocols that WinSock 2 supports. In a rooted control plane, one of the session members is special; it is the root. In a nonrooted control plane, there is no special (root) member.

In a rooted control plane the special participant is called *c_root* and must be present for the duration of the session. The rest of the members of the session are known as *c_leaf*. Typically, the *c_root* member starts the multipoint session by connecting to one or more *c_leafs*. In some cases each *c_leaf* joins *c_root* after the session has been established.

In a nonrooted control plane, there is no special member. Each leaf adds itself to the session either by connecting to a special address that is always available, or by some other mechanism.

DATA PLANE

The data plane deals with the transfer of data among session participants. Like the control plane, data transfer in the data plane can be rooted or nonrooted.

In a rooted data plane, there is a special member known as *d_root*, and all of the other members are known as *d_leaf*. Data can be transferred from *d_root* to all of the *d_leaf* members or from any *d_leaf* member back to *d_root*. There is no direct communication channel between the *d_leaf* members.

In a nonrooted data plane, there is no special *d_root* member. Data is transmitted from each *d_leaf* member to every other *d_leaf* member.

Using Multipoint Protocols

Protocols that support multipoint transmission, along with their related control plane and data plane attributes, can be found by inspecting the

WSAPROTOCOL_INFO structure returned for each protocol. Protocols that support multipoint have the XP1_SUPPORT_MULTIPOINT attribute set in the *dwServiceFlags1* field. If the control plane is rooted, the protocol will also have the XP1_MULTIPOINT_CONTROL_PLANE flag set. If the data plane is rooted, the XP1_MULTIPOINT_DATA_PLANE flag will be set.

The WSASocket() function accepts special multipoint flags in the *dwFlags* parameter. These flags, listed in Table 9-6, allow a socket descriptor to be created for use with multipoint.

TABLE 9-6 MULTIPOINT FLAGS IN dwFlags PARAMETER OF WSASocket()

Flag	Results When Flag Is Set
WSA_FLAG_MULTIPOINT_C_ROOT	Specifies that the socket created will be a *c_root*. This can only be used with protocols that have the XP1_MULTIPOINT_CONTROL_PLANE flag set.
WSA_FLAG_MULTIPOINT_C_LEAF	Specifies that the socket will be a *c_leaf*. The associated protocol must have the XP1_SUPPORT_MULTIPOINT flag set.
WSA_FLAG_MULTIPOINT_D_ROOT	Specifies that the socket created will be a *d_root*. This can only be used with protocols that have the XP1_MULTIPOINT_DATA_PLANE flag set.
WSA_FLAG_MULTIPOINT_D_LEAF	Specifies that the socket will be a *d_leaf*. The associated protocol must have the XP1_SUPPORT_MULTIPOINT flag set.

The WSAJoinLeaf() Function

WSAJoinLeaf() is the only function that was added to the WinSock 2 specification to handle multipoint. It is used to join a leaf node into a session and can also exchange connect data and specify quality of service. Here is the function prototype:

```
SOCKET   WSAJoinLeaf(
                 SOCKET s,
                 const struct sockaddr FAR * name,
                 int namelen,
                 LPWSABUF lpCallerData,
                 LPWSABUF lpCalleeData,
                 LPQOS lpSQOS,
```

```
                    LPQOS lpGQOS,
                    DWORD dwFlags
                    );
```

Parameter	Description
s	A socket descriptor that was created with WSASocket() with one of the multipoint flags set.
name	The name of the peer to which the socket is to be joined.
namelen	The length in bytes of the name.
lpCallerData	A pointer to application-specific data that will be transferred to the peer during the join.
lpCalleeData	A pointer to a buffer that will receive application-specific data back from the peer when the join is complete.
lpSQOS	A pointer to the flow specifications for this socket.
lpGQOS	(Reserved for future use.)
dwFlags	Indicates whether the socket is acting as a sender, receiver, or both. The following flags are defined: JL_SENDER_ONLY JL_RECEIVER_ONLY JL_BOTH

The parameters for WSAJoinLeaf() are very similar to WSAConnect(), but you'll notice that WSAJoinLeaf() returns a socket. If no error occurs, WSAJoinLeaf() returns a new SOCKET that is a descriptor for the newly created multipoint member. If WSAJoinLeaf() fails, it returns INVALID_SOCKET and a specific error code can be found through WSAGetLastError(). If the socket passed as a parameter to WSAJoinLeaf() is using asynchronous mode, then the returned socket descriptor will not be usable until after the FD_CONNECT event notification has been received for the returned socket.

A rooted control plane can work in one of two ways: A *c_leaf* application can request admission to a multipoint session from a listening root application by calling WSAJoinLeaf(). The root application must call listen() and then accept() the leaf's request. Alternatively, the root application may call WSAJoinLeaf() to invite the leaf to join the session. In this situation, the leaf must call listen() and accept().

If the application is the *c_root*, it may call WSAJoinLeaf() multiple times to add *c_leaf* members to the session. Each WSAJoinLeaf() connection request must complete before another is started. There must never be more than one WSAJoinLeaf() connection request pending at one time.

In a nonrooted control plane, each application must call WSAJoinLeaf() to establish the multipoint session.

Getting More Information About Multipoint/Multicast

There is currently a major push to make the Internet more compatible with multipoint transmission. Information about using multipoint on the Internet is available at

`http://www.ipmulticast.com`

Summary

WinSock 2 includes several new extensions that are related to I/O. Event objects allow applications that don't have a graphical window to use asynchronous mode and can also be used to signal completion of overlapped I/O requests. Overlapped I/O allows processes and threads to continue with other processing while waiting for an I/O operation to complete. Because multiple send and receive buffers can be dedicated to data transmission, the number of buffer copies required for each transfer can be reduced, thereby increasing data throughput. When used with message-oriented protocols, scatter and gather techniques can simplify data parsing. Quality-of-service support defines a standardized means of defining network throughput capabilities and requirements.

As you've seen in Chapters 7 through 9, WinSock 2 includes a lot of new functionality. We've covered the most important new functions and data structures in detail. More information is available in the Quick Reference at the end of this book and in the WinSock 2 specification documents in the \SPECS\2 directory on the CD-ROM.

In Part IV, we'll put some of this new functionality to work by creating real-world applications. Chapter 10 develops a server application using only the functionality that is available in Version 1.1 of WinSock. Chapters 11 and 12 use many of the new features that are only available in WinSock 2.

Part IV

Applications

Chapter 10: Asynchronous Server

Chapter 11: Multithreaded Server

Chapter 12: Protocol-Independent Client and Server

Chapter 10

Asynchronous Server

IN THIS CHAPTER
In Chapter 10, we will develop an HTTP server that handles multiple simultaneous client connections by using asynchronous mode. You'll see the following tasks accomplished:

- Servicing multiple clients with asynchronous socket mode
- Implementing a simple HTTP server
- Sending large amounts of data across a network

TO BE USEFUL, MOST SERVER APPLICATIONS must be able to deal with more than one client connection at a time. If the service being performed for each client can't be completed instantaneously, the server should be able to allocate processor time and resources evenly to each client. For example, when a client requests a file from an HTTP or FTP server, the server can't simply send the entire file to one client while ignoring other clients that may be attempting to connect. If that file is large, sending it could take several minutes, and client applications and their users don't care to wait that long for a response. The server must be able to respond to incoming connections in a timely manner while the file transfer is taking place.

The two common methods used by servers to allocate processing time to clients are *asynchronous notification* and *multithreading*.

Asynchronous Mode vs. Multithreading

By using asynchronous mode (discussed in Chapter 4), a server can do a little of the work for each client as asynchronous notifications are received. The server uses the cooperative multitasking mechanism of Windows messaging to split its processing time among clients. This is the only method available to server applications that must (heaven forbid) run on 16-bit Windows. It can also be used effectively in 32-bit Windows environments.

The Win32 API supports multithreading. Rather than use asynchronous mode, servers that only need to run on Windows 95 or Windows NT can split their work

327

among multiple threads of execution. A thread can be started for each client connection, or perhaps one thread can handle sending while another handles receiving.

The best method for a particular situation depends on the hardware platform and the type of server application. Here are some of the advantages and disadvantages of each strategy:

- Asynchronous mode is very portable. It will work on any Windows platform, with any version of WinSock. Multithreading requires Windows 95 or Windows NT.

- Asynchronous mode may not distribute time evenly among clients. The amount of time spent processing any one socket message, together with the sequence of messages, may cause one client to receive less time than others. Preemptive multitasking systems schedule threads so each thread should receive roughly the same amount of processing time as other threads with the same priority.

- Multithreading can simplify server design. Even though multithreaded applications are usually thought more complex, they can actually simplify sockets code. Because each thread executes independently, blocking socket routines can be used. This allows the code to be written in a clearer, more sequential form. When using asynchronous mode, the server must somehow "remember" what is going on with each task, each time a message is received. In contrast, a thread dedicated to one client doesn't have to perform this type of housekeeping.

- Too many threads can bog down the system. A certain amount of overhead is associated with each thread. If many client threads are running at the same time, it's possible for a multithreaded server application running on a machine with only one CPU to overload the system quickly.

In this chapter, you'll study the development of a server that uses asynchronous mode. Then in Chapter 11, we'll implement an almost identical server that uses multiple threads. You'll see the difference in coding style and performance, and this comparison will help you to decide which architecture to use when writing your own server applications.

A Brief Review of the Hypertext Transfer Protocol (HTTP)

Before we can begin to write a Hypertext Transfer Protocol (HTTP) server, we must first understand the fundamentals of the conversation that takes place between an HTTP client and server. The programs we'll develop in this chapter and the next one are based on RFC 1945, "Hypertext Transfer Protocol – HTTP/1.0."

HTTP is the magic of the World Wide Web. It's the protocol used by Netscape Navigator, Microsoft Internet Explorer, and other Web browsers. Essentially, *HTTP* defines the methods an HTTP client uses to request information from an HTTP server, and the actions and responses appropriate for the server. HTTP is a connection-oriented protocol layered on top of TCP. The default port is 80, but other ports can be used.

The server passively listens on a well-known port and waits for client requests. Client applications actively seek out the server and attempt to connect. Once a connection has been established, the client application issues a simple ASCII command such as `GET /index.html`. The server responds by sending data (or possibly an error message) back to the client. The server then closes the connection.

HTTP uses a Uniform Resource Locator (URL) to specify a resource with each request. RFC 1945 defines three request methods a client can send:

GET *url*	Retrieves whatever information is identified by the resource identified by *url*. The GET command can be modified to a conditional GET if the request message includes an If-Modified-Since header field. A conditional GET method requests the identified resource be transferred only if it has been modified since the date given. The conditional GET method is intended to reduce network usage by allowing cached entities to be refreshed without requiring multiple requests or transferring unnecessary data.
HEAD *url*	Identical to GET, except the server only sends information *about* the resource rather than the resource itself. This method is often used for testing hypertext links for validity, accessibility, and recent modification.
POST *url*	Sends information to a resource rather than receiving information from a resource. This method can be used for functions such as sending data gathered in a form, posting messages to a bulletin board system, and appending records to databases.

RFC 1945 defines both a *simple* HTTP/0.9 format for requests and responses, and a *full* HTTP/1.0 format for requests and responses.

The simple format was used by Web servers and clients before Version 1.0 of HTTP was formalized and is still generally recognized. HTTP/0.9 requests are limited to only the GET method. This method includes the word GET followed by a space character, then the URL, and finally a carriage return/line feed pair. Following is an example of the data a server will receive when a client issues a simple GET request:

```
GET /index.html\r\n
```

This message says the client is requesting that the contents of the file

INDEX.HTML be sent from the server to the client. The URL (`/index.html` in this case) specifies the full path to the file.

The HTTPA Application

The application developed in this chapter — Hypertext Transfer Protocol - Asynchronous Model (HTTPA) — acts as an HTTP server. It answers requests from clients and sends back the contents of the file associated with the requested URL. It will work with virtually every Web browser client currently in use, including Netscape Navigator and Microsoft Internet Explorer.

The program is limited to the simple request-and-response format that was used in HTTP/0.9. My decision not to support the full 1.0 request-and-response was intentional. The purpose of the program in this book is not so much to support HTTP fully as it is to compare multiple-client service strategies and file-transfer performance. The If-Modified-Since request is not supported because I wanted the program to transfer a file for *each* request. This will let us more easily compare the performance of this program with the multithreaded version developed in Chapter 11.

In addition to sending files requested by clients, HTTPA also maintains statistics for the average transfer rate, the total number of connections serviced, and the total number of bytes received and sent. It also tracks the number of times a particular file has been requested by a client. Figure 10-1 shows the HTTPA server as it appeared after running for several hours, and points out the user interface elements.

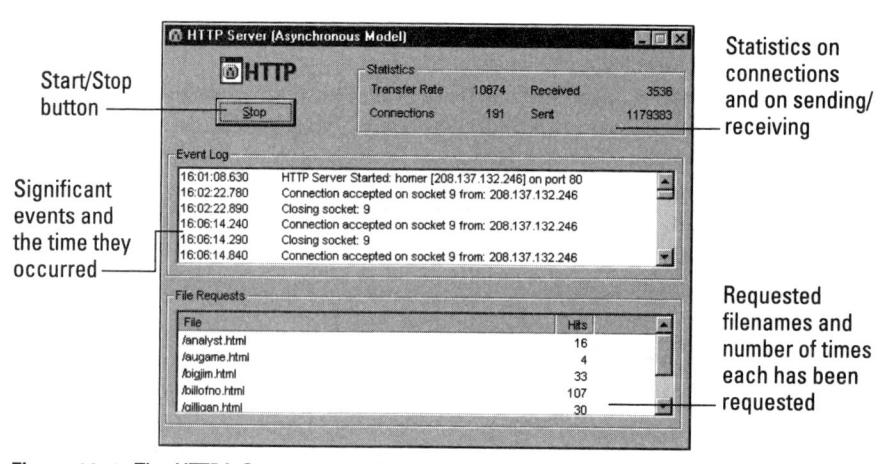

Figure 10-1: The HTTPA Server application's user interface

HTTPA uses only functions that are available in both WinSock 1.1 and 2. The program is specific to Windows 95 and Windows NT 4 only because it uses one of the new common controls: the File Requests list is a ListView control. If this

ListView control were replaced with a listbox, the program could be compiled and run on 16-bit Windows, as well.

Running HTTPA

To try the HTTPA example program, you can use the compiled executable (HTTPA.EXE) included on the CD-ROM in the \CH10 directory, or you can compile the program yourself from the source code. (The source code is also in the CD, in the same directory.) Follow these steps to run the application:

1. In the HTTP Server window, click the Start button to tell HTTPA to begin servicing HTTP clients.

2. In the Server Info dialog box (Figure 10-2), fill in the port number you want HTTPA to use. (The program defaults to port 80, the well-known port for HTTP servers.)

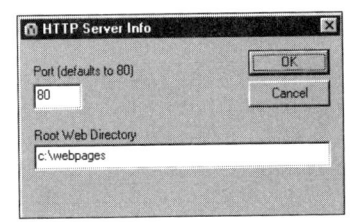

Figure 10-2: The HTTPA Server Info dialog box

3. Fill in the drive and directory where HTML files can be found. I'll refer to this as the "Root Web Directory."

    Note: You can use the \LINKS directory on the CD if you don't have other HTML files you want to use.

    Caution: HTTP clients will have read access to any files in this directory or any of its subdirectories.

4. Check to see if the application has started correctly. The Event Log list box (see Figure 10-3) should show the HTTP server started. It should also display your machine name and the port being used.

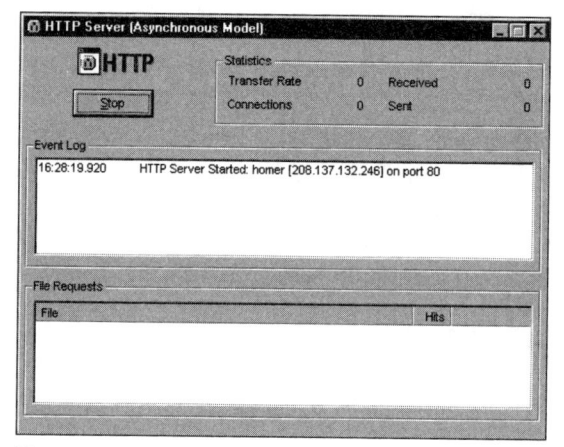

Figure 10-3: The HTTPA main window as it appears after successful startup

With the HTTP Server up and running, HTTP client applications can access your HTTP server. Clients on remote machines will be unable to access the server on your machine by name unless the name is set up either through DNS or another name resolution service (such as an entry in the client machine's *hosts* file). Your server *can*, however, be accessed by IP address without any type of name resolution entry. For example, if you are connected to the Internet or to any other TCP/IP network, remote client machines can browse your Web site by entering your full IP address, like this:

```
http://172.148.193.41
```

where 172.148.193.41 is, of course, replaced with your current IP address. If possible, HTTPA will display your current IP address in the Event Log list box when it starts up. If you aren't connected to a network, this will show up as empty brackets ([]).

You can use a Web browser or other HTTP client application on the same machine where the server is running, by specifying your local IP address just as if you were on a local machine. The client will use a different port number, so both programs can successfully run at the same IP address. On most WinSock implementations, you can run a client on the same machine as the server by specifying the *loopback* address (127.0.0.1) as the URL:

```
http://127.0.0.1
```

This tells WinSock you wish to "loop back" and connect to your own address; it will usually work even if you aren't connected to any network at all.

For example, I can start HTTPA on my machine — running the standard Microsoft WinSock — and specify port 80 and a directory where I have HTML documents stored. Then I can start Microsoft Internet Explorer, request `http://127.0.0.1`, and retrieve Web pages through HTTPA on the same machine. The File Requests ListView then shows a connection was accepted from 127.0.0.1, the names of the files requested, and the number of times each was retrieved.

Compiling HTTPA

A project file is included for HTTPA, created with Version 5 of Microsoft Visual C++, but the program should compile with any Windows-capable C compiler. If you are using a compiler other than Visual C++, compile HTTPUI.C, HTTPA.C, and REQLIST.C and link with WSOCK32.LIB (for WinSock) and COMCTL32.LIB (for the ListView common control).

HTTPA Architecture

HTTPA is not multithreaded; that is, one thread handles all client requests. Nonblocking sockets, the Windows message loop, and WinSock asynchronous notifications are used to distribute processing time between clients. As each asynchronous network event notification is received, the program does a small amount of work and then returns control to Windows and WinSock. It relies on WinSock and Windows for notification by means of a message each time some task can be performed for a client. We'll examine how this mode of operation was achieved as we work through this chapter.

The program uses a dialog box as its main window and strives to keep the user interface code separate from the WinSock code.

The source code for HTTPA is in three files on the CD in the \CH10 directory. Table 10.1 describes each source file in general; we will explore the functionality of each file more closely throughout the rest of this chapter.

TABLE 10.1 HTTPA SOURCE CODE FILES

Filename	Contents
HTTPUI.C	User interface module. WinMain, message loop, and statistics update.
HTTPA.C	WinSock HTTP server module. Dispatches WinSock asynchronous notification messages and performs all HTTP services.
REQLIST.C	Functions used to maintain a linked list of information about currently connected clients.

All of the user interface code for HTTPA is contained in the HTTPUI.C source file. The code in this file opens a dialog as a main window and processes all of the normal Windows messages associated with the user interface (such as WM_COMMAND messages). It also contains code for the Server Info dialog box that asks for the port number and Root Web directory and maintains persistent storage for these user options.

The port number and Root Web Directory designations are passed to the StartHTTP() function, along with the Windows handle and the programmer-defined message used for WinSock asynchronous notification. StartHTTP() is in the HTTPA.C source file along with all of the other WinSock code, and is discussed in a later section.

Once StartHTTP() has been called successfully, the user interface code passes WinSock asynchronous notification messages to the HandleAsyncMsg() function in the HTTPA.C source file. Functions inside HTTPA.C notify the user interface of significant events and periodically update the transfer statistics by sending a Windows message back to the user interface code.

Figure 10-4 illustrates the flow of information between the HTTPUI.C and HTTPA.C modules.

The User Interface Module: HTTPUI.C

The program begins in WinMain(), which is contained in HTTPUI.C — the user interface module. WSAStartup() is called, requesting Version 1.1 of WinSock. WinMain() then calls InitCommonControls() so the ListView common control that's used for listing file requests will work. The program then calls DialogBox() to open the main window dialog box, and enters the message loop using MainWndProc() to process messages. Listing 10-1 presents the WinMain() function.

Listing 10-1 The WinMain() Function

```c
int WINAPI WinMain(HINSTANCE hInstance,
                   HINSTANCE hPrevInstance,
                   LPSTR lpCmdLine,
                   int nCmdShow)
{
    WORD wVersionRequested = MAKEWORD(1,1);
    WSADATA wsaData;
    int nRet;

    //
    // Initialize WinSock
    //
```

Chapter 10: Asynchronous Server 335

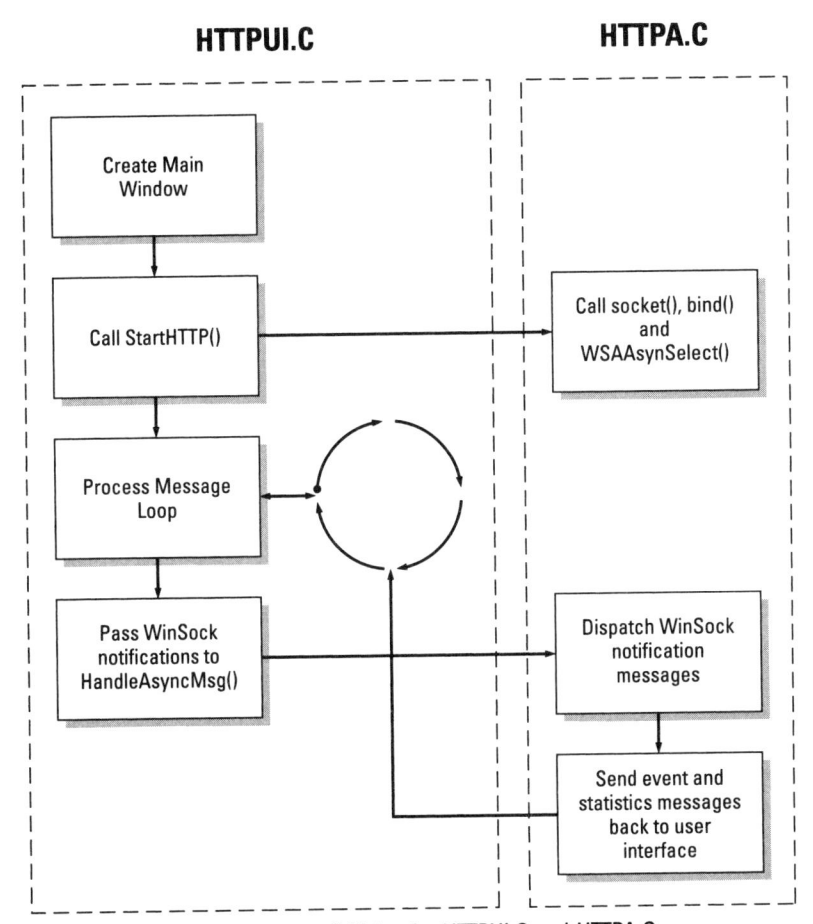

HTTPUI.C   **HTTPA.C**

Figure 10-4: Processing responsibilities for HTTPUI.C and HTTPA.C

```
nRet = WSAStartup(wVersionRequested, &wsaData);
if (nRet)
{
    MessageBox(NULL,
               "Initialize WinSock Failed",
               gszAppName,
               MB_OK);
    return 1;
}
// Check version
if (wsaData.wVersion != wVersionRequested)
{
    MessageBox(NULL,
               "Wrong WinSock Version",
               gszAppName,
               MB_OK);
```

336   Part IV: Applications

```
            return 2;
    }

    //
    // Use new common controls
    //
    InitCommonControls();

    //
    // Use a dialog as a main window
    //
    DialogBox(hInstance,
              MAKEINTRESOURCE(IDD_MAINWND),
              NULL,
              MainWndProc);

    //
    // Release WinSock
    //
    WSACleanup();
    return(0);
}
```

MainWndProc() processes all Windows messages sent to the application. It calls OnInitDialog() when the dialog box is initially opened. OnInitDialog() associates an icon with the dialog window and sets up columns in the ListView control for filename and hit count. Listing 10-2 presents OnInitDialog().

Listing 10-2 The OnInitDialog() Function

```
BOOL OnInitDialog(HWND hwnd, HWND hwndFocus, LPARAM lParam)
{
    LV_COLUMN col;
    HWND hwndList;
    TEXTMETRIC tm;

    //
    // Associate an icon with the dialog box.
    //
    SetClassLong(hwnd,
                 GCL_HICON,
                 (LONG)LoadIcon(GetWindowInstance(hwnd),
                 MAKEINTRESOURCE(IDI_APP)));

    //
    // Setup List Control
    //
    hwndList = GetDlgItem(hwnd, IDC_LIST);
    GetTextMetrics(GetDC(hwnd), &tm);

    col.mask     = LVCF_FMT|LVCF_TEXT|LVCF_WIDTH;
```

```
    col.fmt     = LVCFMT_LEFT;
    col.pszText = "File";
    col.cx      = tm.tmAveCharWidth*50;
    ListView_InsertColumn(hwndList, 0, &col);

    col.fmt     = LVCFMT_RIGHT;
    col.pszText = "Hits";
    col.cx      = tm.tmAveCharWidth*5;
    ListView_InsertColumn(hwndList, 1, &col);

    return(TRUE);
}
```

Starting and Stopping HTTP Service

The OnCommand() function (Listing 10-3) is called to handle all WM_COMMAND messages.

Listing 10-3 The OnCommand() Function

```
void OnCommand(HWND hwnd, int nId, HWND hwndCtl, UINT codeNotify)
{
    static BOOL  fStarted = FALSE;
    HWND         hwndButton;
    HTTPSERVINFO si;
    char         szRootDir[_MAX_PATH];
    int          nRet;

    switch (nId)
    {
        //
        // Start/Stop HTTP Server
        //
        case IDC_START_STOP:
            hwndButton = GetDlgItem(hwnd, IDC_START_STOP);

            if (!fStarted)
            {
                //
                // Get user preferences
                //
                nRet = DialogBox(GetWindowInstance(hwnd),
                        MAKEINTRESOURCE(IDD_SERVINFO),
                        hwnd,
                        InfoWndProc);
                if (nRet == IDOK)
                {
                    // Fill in the server info
                    si.nPort = GetProfileInt(gszAppName,
                                gszPortKey,
```

338   Part IV: Applications

```
                                0);
                GetProfileString(gszAppName,
                        gszDirKey,
                        "",
                        szRootDir,
                        sizeof(szRootDir));
                si.lpRootDir = szRootDir;
                si.hwnd      = hwnd;
                si.uMsgAsy   = UM_ASYNC;
                si.uMsgApp   = UM_HTTP;
                if (StartHTTP(&si))
                {
                    SetWindowText(hwndButton, "&Stop");
                    fStarted = TRUE;
                }
            }
        }
        else
        {
            StopHTTP();
            SetWindowText(hwndButton, "&Start");
            fStarted = FALSE;
        }
        break;

    case IDCANCEL:
        //
        // If HTTP is running, stop it
        //
        if (fStarted)
            StopHTTP();
        fStarted = FALSE;
        EndDialog(hwnd, 0);
        break;
    }
}
```

When the Start button is clicked, the OnCommand() function first checks a static Boolean variable named *fStarted* to see if HTTP service is being started or stopped. This variable is initially set to False, so the first time the button is clicked it attempts to start HTTP service.

Before calling StartHTTP() to start the service, OnCommand() gathers the user's preferences for port number and Root Web directory by opening the Server Info (IDD_SERVINFO) dialog box. InfoWndProc() handles messages for this dialog and saves the user's values in the WIN.INI file. By using the old Get/WriteProfile() functions rather than the new registry functions, InfoWndProc() maintains compatibility with 16-bit Windows.

If the Server Info dialog box is canceled, OnCommand() simply returns. If however, the Server Info dialog's OK button is clicked, however, OnCommand() fills in an HTTPSERVINFO structure. This is a required parameter to StartHTTP() and is defined in HTTPA.H. Table 10-2 describes the fields of HTTPSERVINFO.

TABLE 10-2 THE HTTPSERVINFO STRUCTURE

Type	Name	Description
HWND	*hwnd*	The handle to the window that processes the main message loop.
UINT	*uMsgAsy*	A programmer-defined message that will be used in the call to WSAAsyncSelect() to identify WinSock network event notifications. Defined as UM_ASYNC (WM_USER+1) near the top of HTTPUI.C.
UINT	*uMsgApp*	A programmer-defined message that will be used to send messages from the WinSock server module back to the user interface module. Defined as UM_HTTP (WM_USER+2) near the top of HTTPUI.C.
short	*nPort*	The port number specified by the user in the Server Info dialog box, or 0 if the server module is to use well-known port 80.
LPCSTR	*lpRootDir*	The drive and directory name specified by the user in the Server Info dialog box. This is the location where HTML files are stored.

All of this information is passed to the StartHTTP() function in HTTPA.C. You'll see how this information is used later in this chapter when we discuss the WinSock code in HTTPA.C.

If StartHTTP() returns True — indicating HTTP service was successfully started — the OnCommand() function that made the call does two things: It changes the text of the Start button to Stop, and sets the *fStarted* variable to True. If StartHTTP() returns False — indicating it could not start HTTP service — OnCommand() assumes the user has already been notified with the reason for the error.

Later, when the IDC_START_STOP button is clicked again, OnCommand() finds the *fStarted* variable is True, meaning HTTP service should be stopped rather than started. In this case it calls StopHTTP() to have the listening socket and all client sockets closed. Any clients who happen to be connected when this function is called will receive an abortive close from the server.

Relaying WinSock Event Notifications

When the main message loop receives a UM_ASYNC message, the loop dispatches the message to MainWndProc(), just as it does with all other Windows messages. MainWndProc() watches for these messages and passes them on to the HandleAsyncMsg() function in HTTPA.C, along with the WPARAM and LPARAM parameters. The user interface does no other processing of WinSock messages. Listing 10-4 presents the MainWndProc() function.

Listing 10-4 The MainWndProc() Function

```
BOOL CALLBACK MainWndProc(HWND hwnd,
                          UINT uMsg,
                          WPARAM wParam,
                          LPARAM lParam)
{
    switch (uMsg)
    {
        HANDLE_DLG_MSG(hwnd, WM_INITDIALOG, OnInitDialog);
        HANDLE_DLG_MSG(hwnd, WM_COMMAND,    OnCommand);

        //
        // Pass async messages to HTTPSERV
        //
        case UM_ASYNC:
            HandleAsyncMsg(hwnd, wParam, lParam);
            return TRUE;

        //
        // Handle messages from HTTPSERV here
        //
        case UM_HTTP:
            switch(wParam)
            {
                case HTTP_FILEOK_MSG:
                    FileRequested(hwnd, 0, (LPCSTR)lParam);
                    break;
                case HTTP_FILENOTFOUND_MSG:
                    FileRequested(hwnd, 404, (LPCSTR)lParam);
                    break;
                case HTTP_STATS_MSG:
                    Statistics(hwnd, (LPHTTPSTATS)lParam);
                    break;
                case HTTP_EVENT_MSG:
                    ShowEvent(hwnd, (LPCSTR)lParam);
                    break;
            }
            return TRUE;
    }
    return FALSE;
}
```

Receiving Event and Statistics Notification Messages

When a significant event occurs in the WinSock module, one of the functions in HTTPA.C will send a message to the application's main window along with specific information about the event. MainWndProc() watches for these UM_HTTP messages and understands four notifications that are specified in the WPARAM parameter.

Message	Description
HTTP_FILEOK_MSG	The WinSock module received a request for a file it was able to find and open successfully. The contents of the file have not yet been sent.
HTTP_FILENOTFOUND_MSG	The WinSock module received a request for a file it was *not* able to find. The connection with the client will be closed and no further processing will take place.
HTTP_STATS_MSG	A connection with a client has been completed and closed. The LPARAM parameter points to an HTTPSTATS structure that contains information about the conversation, including the number of bytes received, the number of bytes sent, and the total number of milliseconds elapsed from the time the connection was accepted until it was closed.
HTTP_EVENT_MSG	Some event of interest has occurred (an error or a normal processing message) that should be displayed to the user or logged to a file. The LPARAM parameter points to a string the user interface adds to the Event Log list box.

DISPLAYING FILE HIT COUNT

The user interface module defines three functions for handling all four of these notification messages. The FileRequested() function is called for both HTTP_FILEOK_MSG and HTTP_FILENOTFOUND_MSG. For HTTP_FILENOTFOUND_MSG, MainWndProc() passes an error code along with the filename to FileRequested(). For HTTP_FILEOK_MSG, zero is passed in the error code parameter. Listing 10-5 presents the FileRequested() function.

Listing 10-5 The FileRequested() Function
```c
void FileRequested(HWND hwnd, int nError, LPCSTR lpFileName)
{
    char szBuf[256];
    char szDisplayName[_MAX_PATH+10];
    DWORD dwHitCount;
    HWND hwndList = GetDlgItem(hwnd, IDC_LIST);
    LV_FINDINFO fi;
    LV_ITEM     lvItem;
    int nItem;

    //
    // Was the file found?
    //
    if (!nError)
        strcpy(szDisplayName, lpFileName);
    else
        wsprintf(szDisplayName,
                 "%d - %s",
                 nError,
                 lpFileName);

    //
    // See if the item is already in the list
    //
    fi.flags = LVFI_STRING;
    fi.psz   = szDisplayName;
    nItem = ListView_FindItem(hwndList, -1, &fi);

    //
    // If it is, increment the hit count
    //
    if (nItem != -1)
    {
        lvItem.mask = LVIF_TEXT;
        lvItem.iItem = nItem;
        lvItem.iSubItem = 1;
        lvItem.pszText = szBuf;
        lvItem.cchTextMax = sizeof(szBuf);
        if (ListView_GetItem(hwndList, &lvItem))
        {
            dwHitCount = atol(szBuf);
            dwHitCount++;
            wsprintf(szBuf, "%ld", dwHitCount);
            ListView_SetItem(hwndList, &lvItem);
            return;
        }
    }

    //
    // Not already in the list - add it
```

```
    //
    lvItem.mask = LVIF_TEXT;
    lvItem.iItem = 0;
    lvItem.iSubItem = 0;
    lvItem.pszText = szDisplayName;
    nItem = ListView_InsertItem(hwndList, &lvItem);
    lvItem.iItem = nItem;
    lvItem.iSubItem = 1;
    lvItem.pszText = "1";
    ListView_SetItem(hwndList, &lvItem);
}
```

The FileRequested() function accepts three parameters: a window handle, an error code, and a pointer to a filename. This information is used to build a display string. If the *nError* parameter isn't 0, the function builds a display string containing both the requested filename and the error code. If *nError* is 0, the filename alone is used for the display.

FileRequested() then checks to see if the display string is already contained in the ListView control. If it is, the hit count for the file is incremented and the function returns. If the display string isn't already in the ListView control, the hit count is set to 1 and the string is added to the list.

MAINTAINING STATISTICS

When MainWndProc() receives an HTTP_STATS_MSG indicator, it calls the Statistics() function with the LPARAM parameter cast as a pointer to an HTTPSTATS structure. HTTPSTATS is defined in HTTPA.H and contains the following fields:

Type	Name	Description
DWORD	*dwElapsedTime*	The total number of milliseconds that elapsed from the time the connection was accepted until it was closed.
DWORD	*dwRecv*	The number of bytes received in the HTTP request.
DWORD	*dwSend*	The number of bytes sent to the client (the size of the file that was requested or the size of the error message sent back for bad requests).

The Statistics() function, Listing 10-6, simply adds the contents of the HTTPSTATS structure to its accumulated totals and updates the user interface.

Listing 10-6 The Statistics() Function

```c
void Statistics(HWND hwnd, LPHTTPSTATS lpStats)
{
    static DWORD dwTransferred = 0L;
    static DWORD dwConnections = 0L;
    static DWORD dwReceived    = 0L;
    static DWORD dwRate        = 0L;
    DWORD dwX;
    char szBuf[sizeof("4294967295 ")];

    #define UPDATENUMBER(n, id) \
        wsprintf(szBuf,"%ld", n); \
        SetDlgItemText(hwnd, id, szBuf);

    dwConnections++;
    UPDATENUMBER(dwConnections, IDC_CONNECTIONS);

    //
    // Convert elapsed time to seconds
    //
    dwX = lpStats->dwElapsedTime/1000L;
    if (dwX > 1)
        dwX = (lpStats->dwSend+lpStats->dwRecv) / dwX;
    else
        dwX = (lpStats->dwSend+lpStats->dwRecv);
    if (dwRate > 0)
        dwRate = (dwRate+dwX)/2;
    else
        dwRate = dwX;

    UPDATENUMBER(dwRate, IDC_RATE);
    dwReceived += lpStats->dwRecv;
    UPDATENUMBER(dwReceived, IDC_RECEIVED);
    dwTransferred += lpStats->dwSend;
    UPDATENUMBER(dwTransferred, IDC_TRANSFERRED);
}
```

DISPLAYING EVENT MESSAGES

When MainWndProc() receives an HTTP_EVENT_MSG indicator, it calls the ShowEvent() function with the LPARAM parameter cast as a pointer to a string.

The ShowEvent() function builds a display string containing the current time and the *lpEvent* string parameter, and adds this display string to the Event Log list box. Because Windows list boxes (list boxen?) are limited to containing a certain amount of information, ShowEvent() ensures the list never contains more than 500 items. Each time a line is added, the function obtains a count of the number of items in the list box and deletes the oldest line if the count is greater than 500. Listing 10-7 presents the ShowEvent() function.

Listing 10-7 The ShowEvent() Function

```
void ShowEvent(HWND hwnd, LPCSTR lpEvent)
{
    char szBuf[284];
    SYSTEMTIME st;
    HWND hwndEvents = GetDlgItem(hwnd, IDC_EVENTLOG);

    GetLocalTime(&st);
    wsprintf(szBuf,"%02d:%02d:%02d.%03d\t%s",
            st.wHour,   st.wMinute,
            st.wSecond, st.wMilliseconds,
            lpEvent);
    ListBox_AddString(hwndEvents, szBuf);
    if (ListBox_GetCount(hwndEvents) > 500)
        ListBox_DeleteString(hwndEvents, 0);
}
```

User Interface Summary

Note: Now that you've examined all of the user interface code, notice the only WinSock functions called are WSAStartup() and WSACleanup(). Almost all the WinSock code is contained in HTTPA.C. In separating the code into two modules like this, the source code is easier to read, and you can more readily pull functions out of the WinSock module for use in your own programs.

The WinSock HTTP Server Module: HTTPA.C

The WinSock HTTP server module, HTTPA.C, contains almost all the WinSock code for the application. It contains all the functions that interact directly with client applications.

Starting HTTP Service

Processing begins in the WinSock server module (HTTPA.C) when the user interface calls the StartHTTP() function (Listing 10-8). StartHTTP() accepts a pointer to the HTTPSERVINFO structure that was discussed earlier in this chapter. This structure contains a window handle, two message identifiers, a port number, and the drive and directory where HTML files are located. The first thing this function does is store all this information in variables that are global to this module.

Listing 10-8 The StartHTTP() Function

```c
BOOL StartHTTP(LPHTTPSERVINFO lpInfo)
{
    SOCKADDR_IN     saServer;
    LPSERVENT       lpServEnt;
    DWORD           dwAddrStrLen;
    char            szBuf[256];
    char            szAddress[128];
    int             nRet;

    //
    // Save the Window handle and message
    // ID's for further use
    //
    ghwnd   = lpInfo->hwnd;
    guMsgAsy = lpInfo->uMsgAsy;
    guMsgApp = lpInfo->uMsgApp;
    if (lpInfo->lpRootDir != NULL)
        strcpy(szWebRoot, lpInfo->lpRootDir);
    else
        strcpy(szWebRoot, "/WebPages");

    //
    // Create a TCP/IP stream socket
    //
    listenSocket = socket(AF_INET,
                          SOCK_STREAM,
                          IPPROTO_TCP);
    if (listenSocket == INVALID_SOCKET)
    {
        LogWinSockError(ghwnd,
                        "Could not create listen socket",
                        WSAGetLastError());
        return FALSE;
    }

    //
    // Request async notification
    //
    nRet = WSAAsyncSelect(listenSocket,
                          ghwnd,
                          guMsgAsy,
                          FD_ACCEPT   |
                          FD_READ     |
                          FD_WRITE    |
                          FD_CLOSE);
    if (nRet == SOCKET_ERROR)
    {
        LogWinSockError(ghwnd,
                        "WSAAsyncSelect() error",
                        WSAGetLastError());
```

```c
        closesocket(listenSocket);
        return FALSE;
    }

    //
    // If a specific port number was specified
    // then use it
    //
    if (lpInfo->nPort != 0)
        saServer.sin_port = htons(lpInfo->nPort);
    else
    {
        //
        // Find a port number
        //
        lpServEnt = getservbyname("http", "tcp");
        if (lpServEnt != NULL)
            saServer.sin_port = lpServEnt->s_port;
        else
            saServer.sin_port = htons(HTTPPORT);
    }

    //
    // Fill in the rest of the address structure
    //
    saServer.sin_family = AF_INET;
    saServer.sin_addr.s_addr = INADDR_ANY;

    //
    // bind our name to the socket
    //
    nRet = bind(listenSocket,
                (LPSOCKADDR)&saServer,
                sizeof(struct sockaddr));
    if (nRet == SOCKET_ERROR)
    {
        LogWinSockError(ghwnd,
                        "bind() error",
                        WSAGetLastError());
        closesocket(listenSocket);
        return FALSE;
    }

    //
    // Set the socket to listen
    //
    nRet = listen(listenSocket, SOMAXCONN);
    if (nRet == SOCKET_ERROR)
    {
        LogWinSockError(ghwnd,
                        "listen() error",
                        WSAGetLastError());
        closesocket(listenSocket);
```

```
            return FALSE;
    }

    gethostname(szBuf, sizeof(szBuf));
    dwAddrStrLen = sizeof(szAddress);
    GetLocalAddress(szAddress, &dwAddrStrLen);
    LogEvent(ghwnd,
             "HTTP Server Started: %s [%s] on port %d",
             szBuf,
             szAddress,
             htons(saServer.sin_port));
    return TRUE;
}
```

After storing all the information from the HTTPSERVINFO structure, StartHTTP() then attempts to create the TCP/IP socket descriptor. If this succeeds, the function requests asynchronous notification for the socket using the windows handle and message passed in from the user interface module. It then names the listening socket with bind() and calls listen(), specifying it wants WinSock to queue the maximum number of pending connection requests possible.

If everything succeeds, StartHTTP() calls LogEvent() to notify the user interface that HTTP service has been started. The LogEvent() function accepts a variable number of arguments and works in much the same way as printf() or wsprintf(). It builds a string from the parameters and sends the string to the user interface module by sending the HTTP_EVENT_MSG discussed earlier. Here is the LogEvent() function:

```
void LogEvent(HWND hwnd, LPCSTR lpFormat, ...)
{
    va_list Marker;
    char szBuf[256];

    // Write text to string
    // and append to edit control
    va_start(Marker, lpFormat);
    vsprintf(szBuf, lpFormat, Marker);
    va_end(Marker);
    SendMessage(ghwnd,
                guMsgApp,
                HTTP_EVENT_MSG,
                (LPARAM)szBuf);
}
```

Obtaining the Local Address

At the end of StartHTTP(), LogEvent() is called with parameters that describe the address the host is using to listen. Then the local host name, IP address, and port number are displayed to the user. The WinSock gethostname() function is used to retrieve the local host name. The GetLocalAddress() function used to obtain the local IP address is defined near the bottom of HTTPA.C.

Listing 10-9 presents the GetLocalAddress() function.

Listing 10-9 The GetLocalAddress() Function

```
int GetLocalAddress(LPSTR lpStr, LPDWORD lpdwStrLen)
{
    struct in_addr *pinAddr;
    LPHOSTENT   lpHostEnt;
    int         nRet;
    int         nLen;

    //
    // Get our local name
    //
    nRet = gethostname(lpStr, *lpdwStrLen);
    if (nRet == SOCKET_ERROR)
    {
        lpStr[0] = '\0';
        return SOCKET_ERROR;
    }

    //
    // "Lookup" the local name
    //
    lpHostEnt = gethostbyname(lpStr);
    if (lpHostEnt == NULL)
    {
        lpStr[0] = '\0';
        return SOCKET_ERROR;
    }

    //
    // Format first address in the list
    //
    pinAddr = ((LPIN_ADDR)lpHostEnt->h_addr);
    nLen = strlen(inet_ntoa(*pinAddr));
    if ((DWORD)nLen > *lpdwStrLen)
    {
        *lpdwStrLen = nLen;
        WSASetLastError(WSAEINVAL);
        return SOCKET_ERROR;
    }

    *lpdwStrLen = nLen;
    strcpy(lpStr, inet_ntoa(*pinAddr));
    return 0;
}
```

Part IV: Applications

The Berkeley sockets API includes the gethostid() function to retrieve the local machine's IP address. Unfortunately, WinSock has no such function. In fact, the WinSock specification doesn't define any guaranteed way of obtaining the local IP address at all. This can be done in two ways; note, neither of them works on all WinSock implementations.

- One method is to use getsockname() to obtain the socket's current SOCKADDR. This only works on connected sockets.

- You can also call gethostbyname() using the string returned from gethostname() to obtain a pointer to a HOSTENT structure. This works on *most* WinSock implementations (including Microsoft's) and even works on sockets that aren't connected.

The GetLocalAddress() function in our sample HTTPA application uses the gethostbyname() method. It calls gethostname() to retrieve a string containing the local host machine's name. It then calls gethostbyname() using this string as a parameter, to get a pointer to a HOSTENT structure for the local machine. Then it uses inet_ntoa() to convert the IP address in the HOSTENT to a user-readable string.

Waiting for Event Notifications

Once StartHTTP() has successfully completed, the application does nothing but wait for a network event notification from WinSock. When the message loop in the user interface module receives a WinSock event notification message, the message and the parameters are passed to HandleAsyncMsg(). Listing 10-10 presents HandleAsyncMsc().

Listing 10-10 The HandleAsyncMsg() Function

```
void HandleAsyncMsg(HWND hwnd,
                    WPARAM wParam,
                    LPARAM lParam)
{
    int nErrorCode = WSAGETSELECTERROR(lParam);

    switch(WSAGETSELECTEVENT(lParam))
    {
        case FD_ACCEPT:
            OnAccept(hwnd, (SOCKET)wParam, nErrorCode);
            break;

        case FD_READ:
            OnRead((SOCKET)wParam, nErrorCode);
            break;

        case FD_WRITE:
```

```
                OnWrite((SOCKET)wParam, nErrorCode);
                break;

        case FD_CLOSE:
                OnClose((SOCKET)wParam, nErrorCode);
                break;
    }
}
```

HandleAsyncMsg() uses the WinSock WSAGETSELECTEVENT() macro to determine exactly what type of network event has occurred. To obtain the error code associated with the event, the WSAGETSELECTERROR() macro is used. The WPARAM parameter contains the socket descriptor on which the event occurred. HandleAsyncMsg() calls an appropriate function to handle the message passing *wParam* cast as a socket, and the error code.

Accepting Client Connections

The first event notification message received should be FD_ACCEPT, which occurs when a client requests a connection to the server. HandleAsyncMsg() calls OnAccept(), shown in Listing 10-11, to handle this event.

Listing 10-11 The OnAccept() Function

```
void OnAccept(HWND hwnd, SOCKET socket, int nErrorCode)
{
    SOCKADDR_IN SockAddr;
    LPREQUEST   lpReq;
    SOCKET      peerSocket;
    int         nRet;
    int         nLen;

    //
    // accept the new socket descriptor
    //
    nLen = sizeof(SOCKADDR_IN);
    peerSocket = accept(listenSocket,
                        (LPSOCKADDR)&SockAddr,
                        &nLen);
    if (peerSocket == SOCKET_ERROR)
    {
        nRet = WSAGetLastError();
        if (nRet != WSAEWOULDBLOCK)
        {
            //
            // Just log the error and return
            //
            LogWinSockError(ghwnd,
                            "accept() error",
```

```
                                WSAGetLastError());
            return;
        }
    }
    //
    // Make sure we get async notices for this socket
    //
    nRet = WSAAsyncSelect(peerSocket,
                          hwnd,
                          guMsgAsy,
                          FD_READ | FD_WRITE | FD_CLOSE);
    if (peerSocket == SOCKET_ERROR)
    {
        nRet = WSAGetLastError();
        //
        // Just log the error and return
        //
        LogWinSockError(ghwnd,
                        "accept() error",
                        WSAGetLastError());
        return;
    }

    //
    // Add the connection to the linked list
    //
    lpReq = AddRequest(peerSocket,
                       (LPSOCKADDR)&SockAddr,
                       nLen);
    if (lpReq == NULL)
    {
        // We're probably out of memory
        closesocket(peerSocket);
    }
    LogEvent(ghwnd,
             "Connection accepted on socket %d from: %s",
             peerSocket,
             inet_ntoa(SockAddr.sin_addr));
}
```

OnAccept() calls accept() to connect with the client and obtain the remote socket's address. If no error occurs, OnAccept() calls WSAAsyncSelect() to register the new socket for asynchronous notification. This isn't strictly necessary because the new socket is supposed to be registered already in the same way as the listening socket. Some WinSock 1.1 implementations don't reliably keep this association, however, so we do it here to ensure that we will receive notification messages for the socket.

Tracking Connections

The call to AddRequest() adds an entry for this connection in a linked list. As you'll see in the following sections, the WinSock module uses the information contained in this linked list to "remember" the stage of the conversation it is currently having with each client.

THE REQUEST STRUCTURE

Each entry in the linked list points to a REQUEST structure. This structure is defined in HTTPA.H and contains the fields listed in Table 10-3.

TABLE 10-3 REQUEST STRUCTURE FIELDS

Type	Name	Description
SOCKET	Socket	The socket descriptor that was accepted for this connection.
LPSOCKADDR	lpSockAddr	A pointer to the SOCKADDR associated with the socket.
int	nAddrLen	The length of the SOCKADDR pointed to by lpSockAddr.
int	nMethod	The method requested by the client. Only METHOD_GET is supported by this server.
DWORD	dwConnectTime	The value returned from the Win32 GetTickCount() function when the connection was added to the list (tick count when the connection was accepted).
DWORD	dwRecv	The total number of bytes received from the client on this connection.
DWORD	dwSend	The total number of bytes sent to the client on this connection.
HFILE	hFile	The handle to the file being sent to the client.
DWORD	dwFilePtr	The point in the file where the last read operation took place (explained later in "Sending the File to the Client").
struct tagREQUEST *	lpNext	A pointer to the next REQUEST structure in the linked list.

THE REQLIST.C MODULE

The AddRequest() function and all the other linked list functions can be found in REQLIST.C. These functions implement a singly linked list, like that used in many C and C++ programs. Rather than discuss these functions in detail, following is a simple summary of what each one does.

AddRequest()   AddRequest() accepts a socket, a SOCKADDR, and the length of the SOCKADDR. This function allocates memory for a REQUEST structure, fills in default values, appends the structure to the list, and returns a pointer to this new entry. The function also makes a copy of the SOCKADDR and fills in the *lpSockAddr, Socket,* and *dwConnectTime* fields in the REQUEST structure.

```
LPREQUEST AddRequest(SOCKET Socket,
                     LPSOCKADDR lpSockAddr,
                     int nAddrLen);
```

GetRequest()   This function returns a pointer to a REQUEST entry in the linked list for a given socket. It returns NULL if the socket is not in the list.

```
LPREQUEST GetRequest(SOCKET Socket);
```

GetFirstRequest()   This function returns a pointer to the first REQUEST entry in the linked list. It returns NULL if the list is empty.

```
LPREQUEST GetFirstRequest(void);
```

GetNextRequest()   This function returns a pointer to the next entry in the list after *lpThis*. It returns NULL if *lpThis* points to the last entry.

```
LPREQUEST GetNextRequest(LPREQUEST lpThis);
```

DelRequest()   This function deletes the *lpThis* entry from the list and frees the memory for the REQUEST structure.

```
void DelRequest(LPREQUEST lpThis);
```

DelAllRequests()   This function deletes all of the entries in the list and frees all memory for all REQUEST structures.

```
void DelAllRequests(void);
```

Reading the Client's Request

Let's review what we've done so far. We started HTTP service by opening a listening socket and registering for asynchronous notification. Then a REQUEST entry was added to the linked list when a connection was established with a client during FD_ACCEPT message processing.

The next message received after FD_ACCEPT will probably be FD_WRITE, to notify us it is safe to write with this socket. We'll ignore the first FD_WRITE message we receive for a new connection. Later, in the "Sending the File to the Client" section, we'll discuss how the program knows it's the first FD_WRITE message. What we're looking for at this point is a request string from the client.

Once this connection request has been accepted, we expect to receive an HTTP request such as GET url\r\n. When WinSock receives data from the client, it will post the FD_READ message. Our hard-working HandleAsyncMsg() function will call OnRead() (Listing 10-12) to handle this message.

Listing 10-12 The OnRead() Function

```
void OnRead(SOCKET socket, int nErrorCode)
{
    static BYTE     buf[2048];
    LPREQUEST       lpReq;
    int             nRet;

    //
    // Zero the buffer so the recv is null-terminated
    //
    memset(buf, 0, sizeof(buf));

    //
    // Find this socket in the linked list
    //
    lpReq = GetRequest(socket);
    if (lpReq == NULL)
    {
        //
        // Not in the list. Log the error,
        // read the data to clear the buffers
        // and close the connection
        //
        nRet = 0;
        while(nRet != SOCKET_ERROR)
            nRet = recv(socket, buf, sizeof(buf)-1, 0);
        closesocket(socket);
        return;
    }

    //
    // Recv the data
```

```
//
nRet = recv(socket, buf, sizeof(buf)-1, 0);
if (nRet == SOCKET_ERROR)
{
    if (WSAGetLastError() == WSAEWOULDBLOCK)
        return;
    LogWinSockError(ghwnd,
                    "recv()",
                    WSAGetLastError());
    CloseConnection(lpReq);
    return;
}

//
// Keep statistics
//
lpReq->dwRecv += nRet;

//
// Parse the HTTP request
//
ParseRequest(lpReq, buf);
}
```

The OnRead() function looks up the socket in the linked list and then calls recv() to read the client's request. If all goes well, OnRead() updates the *dwRecv* field in the socket's REQUEST structure to keep count of how many bytes have been received. It then calls the ParseRequest() function, shown in Listing 10-13.

Listing 10-13 The ParseRequest() Function

```
void ParseRequest(LPREQUEST lpReq, LPBYTE lpBuf)
{
    char szFileName[_MAX_PATH];
    char szSeps[] = " \n";
    char *cpToken;

    //
    // Don't let requests include ".." characters
    // in requests
    //
    if (strstr(lpBuf, "..") != NULL)
    {
        // Send "bad request" error
        SendError(lpReq, HTTP_STATUS_BADREQUEST);
        CloseConnection(lpReq);
        return;
    }

    //
    // Determine request method
```

Chapter 10: Asynchronous Server

```
    //
    cpToken = strtok(lpBuf, szSeps);
    if (!_stricmp(cpToken, "GET"))
        lpReq->nMethod = METHOD_GET;
    else
    {
        // Send "not implemented" error
        SendError(lpReq, HTTP_STATUS_NOTIMPLEMENTED);
        CloseConnection(lpReq);
        return;
    }

    //
    // Get the file name
    //
    cpToken = strtok(NULL, szSeps);
    if (cpToken == NULL)
    {
        // Send "bad request" error
        SendError(lpReq, HTTP_STATUS_BADREQUEST);
        CloseConnection(lpReq);
        return;
    }
    strcpy(szFileName, szWebRoot);
    if (strlen(cpToken) > 1)
        strcat(szFileName, cpToken);
    else
        strcat(szFileName, "/index.html");
    SendFile(lpReq, szFileName);
}
```

ParseRequest() first verifies the client's request doesn't include the previous directory (..) characters. (We don't want to allow access to files in the directory structure below the files that we, in fact, want available.) If the request contains these characters, the SendError() function sends the client a small string of HTML that says 400 Bad Request. Note, HTTP/1.0 clients and servers can send just an error code rather than an entire string of HTML. In this case, though, we're adhering only to the HTTP/0.9 standard, so we send error text back to the client.

The error codes used by HTTP servers and clients are defined in RFC 1945.

Next, ParseRequest() uses the C run-time strtok() function to break the client's request data into tokens. We're only implementing the GET method, so if any other method is attempted by the client, then the Not Implemented error is sent back to the client.

Sending the File to the Client

If the request makes it through the ParseRequest() checks, the name of the file requested is appended to the end of the directory name passed to StartHTTP(). If no

358   Part IV: Applications

full file name is given, /index.html is appended to the directory name instead. HTTP clients expect to be able to send an abbreviated request like this:

GET /

to receive the default file. In this server, /index.html is the default filename. Once the full path to the requested file has been built, ParseRequest() calls SendFile().

SendFile(), shown in Listing 10-14, does a little more of the work needed before the contents of the file are sent to the client. (We'll see in a moment why this function only performs this small amount of work rather than sending the entire file.)

Listing 10-14 The SendFile() Function

```
void SendFile(LPREQUEST lpReq, LPCSTR lpFileName)
{
    //
    // Open the file for reading
    //
    lpReq->hFile = _lopen(lpFileName,
                         OF_READ|OF_SHARE_COMPAT);
    if (lpReq->hFile == HFILE_ERROR)
    {
        SendMessage(ghwnd,
                    guMsgApp,
                    HTTP_FILENOTFOUND_MSG,
                    (LPARAM)(LPCSTR)lpFileName);
        // Send "404 Not Found" error
        SendError(lpReq, HTTP_STATUS_NOTFOUND);
        CloseConnection(lpReq);
        return;
    }

    //
    // Tell the user interface about the file hit
    // (Sending just the request portion - without
    // the root web directory portion
    //
    SendMessage(ghwnd,
                guMsgApp,
                HTTP_FILEOK_MSG,
                (LPARAM)(LPCSTR)lpFileName + strlen(szWebRoot));

    //
    // Send as much of the file as we can
    //
    lpReq->dwFilePtr = 0L;
    SendFileContents(lpReq);
}
```

SendFile() attempts to open the requested file and lets the client know if the file couldn't be opened. If the file is successfully opened, an HTTP_FILEOK_MSG is sent to the user interface so the hit count can be updated. If the file cannot be opened, the HTTP_FILENOTFOUND_MSG is sent instead. After successfully opening a file, SendFile() ensures the *dwFilePtr* field in the socket's REQUEST structure is 0 and then calls SendFileContents().

As its name implies, SendFileContents() sends the contents of the requested file to the client. It sets up a loop, in which it reads a buffer of bytes from the file and then sends the buffer to the client with the send() function. If no errors occur while reading from the file or sending to the client, then end-of-file is eventually reached and the connection and the file are closed. Listing 10-15 presents the SendFileContents() function.

Listing 10-15 The SendFileContents() Function

```
void SendFileContents(LPREQUEST lpReq)
{
    static BYTE buf[1024];
    UINT uBytes;
    BOOL fEof;
    int nBytesSent;

    fEof = FALSE;

    //
    // We may be continuing, so seek to where
    // we left off last time
    //
    if (lpReq->dwFilePtr > 0)
        _llseek(lpReq->hFile, lpReq->dwFilePtr, FILE_BEGIN);

    //
    // Send as much of the file as we can
    //
    while(1)
    {
        //
        // Read a buffer full from the file
        //
        uBytes = _lread(lpReq->hFile,
                        buf,
                        sizeof(buf));
        if (uBytes == HFILE_ERROR)
        {
            LogEvent(ghwnd,
                    "Read file error: %d",
                    GetLastError());
            // Send "500 Internal server" error
            SendError(lpReq, HTTP_STATUS_SERVERERROR);
```

```
            CloseConnection(lpReq);
            lpReq->hFile = HFILE_ERROR;
            return;
        }

        //
        // Are we at End of File?
        //
        if (uBytes < sizeof(buf))
            fEof = TRUE;

        //
        // Send this buffer to the client
        //
        nBytesSent = send(lpReq->Socket,
                          buf,
                          uBytes,
                          0);
        if (nBytesSent == SOCKET_ERROR)
        {
            if (WSAGetLastError() != WSAEWOULDBLOCK)
            {
                LogWinSockError(ghwnd,
                                "send()",
                                WSAGetLastError());
                CloseConnection(lpReq);
                lpReq->hFile = HFILE_ERROR;
                return;
            }
            nBytesSent = 0;
        }

        //
        // Keep track of what has actually been sent
        // from the file
        //
        lpReq->dwFilePtr += nBytesSent;

        //
        // And for statistics
        //
        lpReq->dwSend += nBytesSent;

        //
        // Are the protocol stack buffers full?
        //
        if (nBytesSent < (int)uBytes)
        {
            // We'll have to finish later
            return;
        }

        //
```

```
        // Are we finished?
        //
        if (fEof)
        {
            CloseConnection(lpReq);
            lpReq->hFile = HFILE_ERROR;
            return;
        }
    }
}
```

Sending Large Amounts of Data

It is reasonable to assume this process of reading from the file and repeatedly calling send() may outrun the protocol stack's ability to send the data. If this happens, send() will return SOCKET_ERROR with WSAGetLastError() set to WSAEWOULDBLOCK, or the return value will indicate something less than the requested number of bytes were actually sent.

If a send() attempt returns SOCKET_ERROR with WSAEWOULDBLOCK, or if less than the requested number of bytes were sent, SendFileContents() leaves the file open and returns. Once WinSock has had a chance to catch up and clear some of its internal buffers, it will post another FD_WRITE message for the socket.

The OnWrite() function is called whenever an FD_WRITE message is received. OnWrite() first determines whether this is the first FD_WRITE message received for the socket by checking the *hFile* member. If the request has a file open, OnWrite() calls SendFileContents() again to continue sending the file contents. Listing 10-16 presents the OnWrite() function.

Listing 10-16 The OnWrite() Function

```
void OnWrite(SOCKET socket, int nErrorCode)
{
    LPREQUEST lpReq;
    BYTE buf[1024];
    int nRet;

    lpReq = GetRequest(socket);
    if (lpReq == NULL)
    {
        //
        // Not in our list!?
        //
        nRet = 0;
        while(nRet != SOCKET_ERROR)
            nRet = recv(socket, buf, sizeof(buf)-1, 0);
        closesocket(socket);
        return;
```

Part IV: Applications

```
    }
    //
    // Is this the first FD_WRITE
    // or did we fill the protocol
    // stack buffers?
    //
    if (lpReq->hFile == HFILE_ERROR)
        return;

    //
    // Continue sending a file
    //
    SendFileContents(lpReq);
}
```

Closing the Connection

Once the entire file has been sent to the client (or an unrecoverable error occurs), the CloseConnection() function is called (Listing 10-17). This function logs the close event and closes the socket. It then computes the time elapsed since the connection was accepted and puts this value into an HTTPSTATS structure, along with the total number of bytes received and sent. Then CloseConnection() sends a pointer to this HTTPSTATS structure to the user interface, so the values of the statistics can be updated. When this has completed, the function deletes the socket's entry from the linked list by calling DelRequest().

Listing 10-17 The CloseConnection() Function

```
void CloseConnection(LPREQUEST lpReq)
{
    HTTPSTATS stats;

    LogEvent(ghwnd,
            "Closing socket: %d",
            lpReq->Socket);
    //
    // Log the event and close the socket
    //
    closesocket(lpReq->Socket);

    //
    // If the file is still open,
    // then close it
    //
    if (lpReq->hFile != HFILE_ERROR)
        _lclose(lpReq->hFile);

    //
```

```
    // Give the user interface the stats
    //
    stats.dwElapsedTime =
            (GetTickCount() - lpReq->dwConnectTime);
    stats.dwRecv = lpReq->dwRecv;
    stats.dwSend = lpReq->dwSend;
    SendMessage(ghwnd,
                guMsgApp,
                HTTP_STATS_MSG,
                (LPARAM)&stats);
    DelRequest(lpReq);
}
```

Stopping HTTP Service

The IDC_START_STOP button in HTTPA's main window enables the user to call StopHTTP() to shut down HTTP service at any time. Listing 10-18 presents the StopHTTP() function.

Note, StopHTTP() takes a brute-force approach to shutting down. It simply closes the listening socket and loops through the list of connected clients, performing abortive closes. Any client that happens to be connected and is still receiving data will lose its connection with the server; none of the remaining data will be sent. A more elaborate scheme for stopping HTTP service might be to close the listening socket and then wait for each client conversation to complete before shutting down.

Listing 10-18 The StopHTTP() Function
```
void StopHTTP()
{
    LPREQUEST lpReq;

    //
    // Close the listening socket
    //
    closesocket(listenSocket);

    //
    // Close all open connections
    //
    lpReq = GetFirstRequest();
    while(lpReq)
    {
        closesocket(lpReq->Socket);
        if (lpReq->hFile != HFILE_ERROR)
            _lclose(lpReq->hFile);
        lpReq = GetNextRequest(lpReq);
    }
```

```
//
// And clean up the linked list
// of connections
//
DelAllRequests();
LogEvent(ghwnd, "Server Stopped");
}
```

Summary

In this chapter you've seen how a server application can handle multiple client connections with just one thread. WinSock's asynchronous notification mechanism allows the server to do a small amount of processing each time a message is received, and then return and wait for another message. This approach works well with any number of simultaneous connections and is extremely portable among Windows environments.

The application in Chapter 11 creates another HTTP server — it performs exactly the same function as the one you've just finished studying, but with multiple threads. Even though they perform the same function, the WinSock module used in the next application is quite different from HTTPA.

Chapter 11

Multithreaded Server

IN THIS CHAPTER
In Chapter 11 we will develop an HTTP server that handles multiple simultaneous client connections by using multiple threads. You'll see how to set up the following:

- Servicing multiple clients with threads
- Using event objects with overlapped I/O
- Tracking client threads
- Maintaining a responsive user interface while using blocking socket routines

AS DISCUSSED IN CHAPTER 10, A SERVER APPLICATION must be able to handle more than one client connection at a time. In Chapter 10, we created an HTTP server that used WinSock asynchronous network event notification to schedule time for each client. In this chapter, you'll examine another HTTP server that performs the same duties, but this one uses multithreading to handle multiple simultaneous client connections.

Note: Before you begin working through this chapter, you should already be familiar with the HTTP protocol and a typical conversation between an HTTP client and server, or have already read at least the following sections of Chapter 10: "A Brief Review of the Hypertext Transfer Protocol" and "Running HTTPA."

The HTTPMT Application

The application developed in this chapter — Hypertext Transfer Protocol MultiThreaded Model (HTTPMT) — acts as an HTTP server. It answers requests from clients, sending back the contents of the file associated with the requested URL. HTTPMT will work with virtually every modern Web browser client, including Netscape Navigator and Microsoft Internet Explorer. The program is limited to the simple request-and-response format that was used in HTTP/0.9. (The HTTP/0.9 and HTTP/1.0 formats for requests and responses are explained in Chapter 10.)

The user interface for HTTPMT is almost identical to the HTTPA program developed in Chapter 10. Along with its duties of sending files requested by clients,

HTTPMT also maintains statistics for average transfer rate, total number of connections serviced, and the total number of bytes received and sent. It also keeps track of how many times a particular file has been requested by a client. In Figure 11-1 you can see the HTTPMT server as it appears after running for several hours and points out the user interface elements.

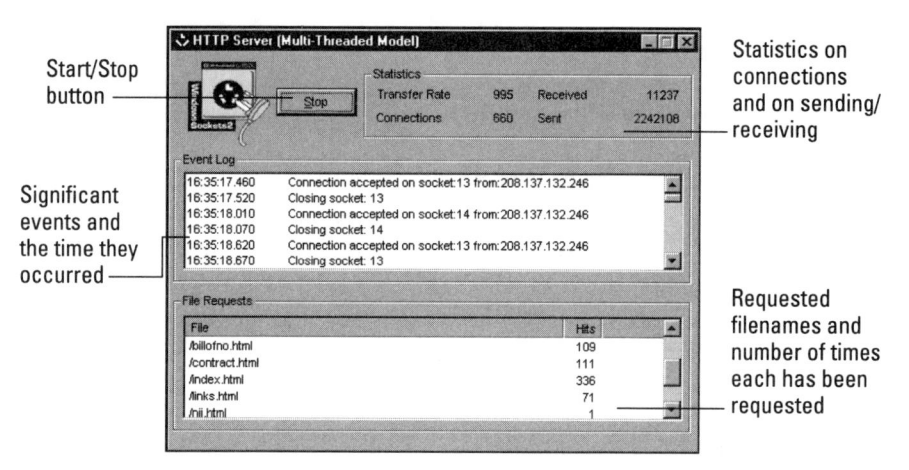

Figure 11-1: The HTTPMT Server application's user interface

HTTPMT uses event objects and overlapped I/O, which are only available in WinSock 2. This program will run only on Windows 95 or Windows NT.

Running HTTPMT

To try the HTTPMT application, you can use the compiled executable (HTTPMT.EXE) included on the CD in the \CH11 directory, or compile the program yourself from the source code. The source code, too, is in the \CH11 directory on the CD. Follow these steps to run the application:

1. In the application's main window, click the Start button to tell HTTPMT to begin servicing HTTP clients.

2. In the HTTP Server Info dialog box (Figure 11-2), fill in the port number you'd like HTTPMT to use. (The program defaults to port 80, the well-known port for HTTP servers.)

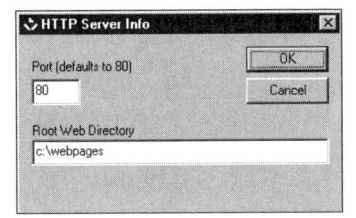

Figure 11-2: Server Info dialog box

3. Fill in the drive and directory where HTML files can be found.

   Note: You can use the \LINKS directory on the CD if you don't have other HTML files you'd like to use.

   Caution: HTTP clients will have read access to any files in this directory and any of its subdirectories.

4. Check to see if the application has started correctly. The Event Log list box (see Figure 11-3) should show that the HTTPMT server started. It should also display your machine name and the port being used.

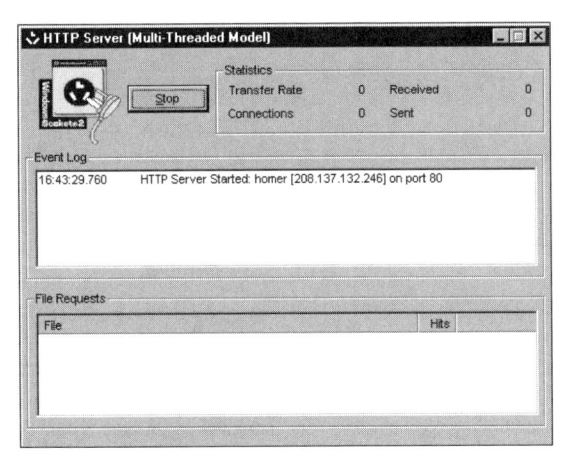

Figure 11-3: The HTTPMT main window as it appears after successful startup

If you haven't read Chapter 10, or you need more information about accessing the server from remote machines or from the local machine, see the "Running HTTPA" section of Chapter 10.

Compiling HTTPMT

A project file is included for HTTPMT, created with Version 5 of Microsoft Visual C++, but the program should compile with any 32-bit Windows-capable C compiler. If you are using a compiler other than Visual C++, compile HTTPUI.C, HTTPMT.C, and COUNTC.C and then link with WS2_32.LIB (for WinSock) and COMCTL32.LIB (for the ListView common control).

HTTPMT Architecture

HTTPMT is multithreaded. The Win32 environment creates one thread of execution when the program starts, and this thread handles the Windows message loop and the user interface. Another thread is created to listen for incoming connection requests. Then other threads are created — one for *each* currently connected client. Figure 11-4 illustrates the role of the two main source modules.

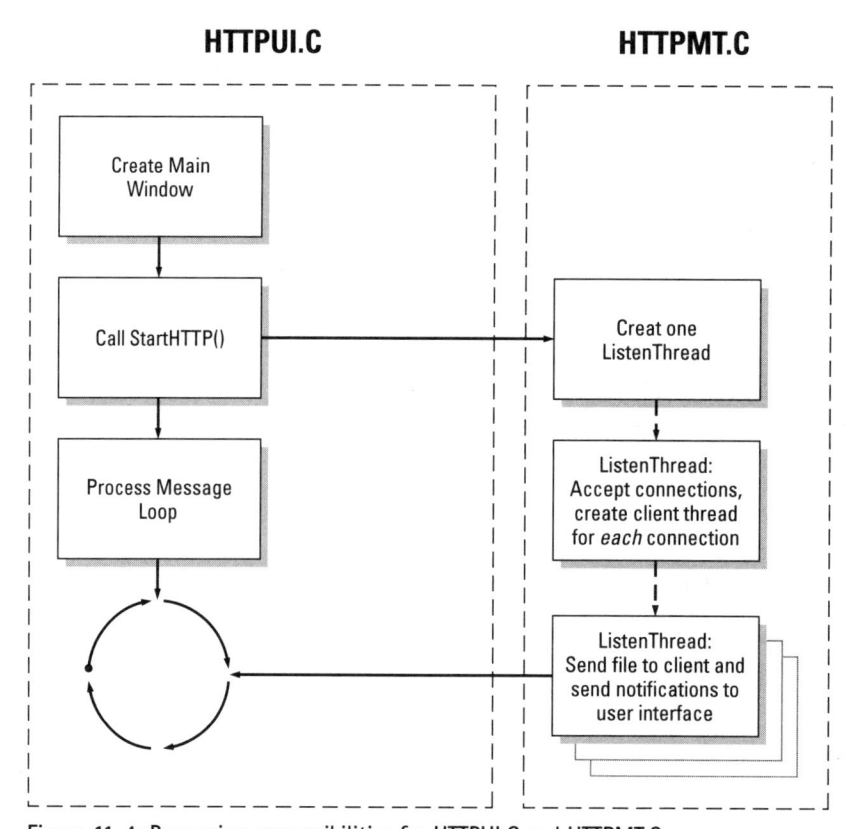

Figure 11-4: Processing responsibilities for HTTPUI.C and HTTPMT.C

Just like the sample in Chapter 10, HTTPMT uses a dialog box as its main window and strives to keep the user interface code separate from the WinSock code. The source code for HTTPMT is available on the CD in the \CH11 directory. Table 11-1 summarizes the code contained in each source file. We will examine the functionality contained in each of these files as we work through the rest of this chapter.

TABLE 11-1 HTTPMT SOURCE CODE FILES

Filename	Contents
HTTPUI.C	User interface module. WinMain(), message loop, and statistics update.
HTTPMT.C	WinSock HTTP server module. Creates threads to handle all HTTP services.
COUNTC.C	Functions used to maintain a count of currently connected clients.

The User Interface Module: HTTPUI.C

The user interface module for HTTPMT is almost identical to the interface code used in Chapter 10, with a few subtle differences:

- The WinMain() function in HTTPMT requests WinSock 2 rather than WinSock 1.1.

- The HTTPSERVINFO structure passed to StartHTTP() from OnCommand() doesn't include a programmer-defined message for asynchronous notifications. HTTPMT doesn't use asynchronous notification, so this message isn't needed.

- Because they aren't used, MainWndProc() doesn't have to dispatch asynchronous notification messages.

The rest of the user interface code is identical to the asynchronous server from Chapter 10.

The HTTPMT.C Module

The multithreaded WinSock HTTP server module — HTTPMT.C — contains almost all the WinSock code for the application. The code in this file differs dramatically from the application developed in Chapter 10.

Starting HTTP Service

Processing begins in the WinSock server module when the user interface calls the StartHTTP() function (Listing 11-1). StartHTTP() accepts a pointer to a HTTPSERV-INFO structure. This structure contains a window handle, one message identifier, a port number, and the drive and directory where HTML files are located. The first thing the function does is store all of this information in variables that are global to this module. The window handle and message are used to send information back to the user interface.

Listing 11-1 The StartHTTP() Function

```c
BOOL StartHTTP(LPHTTPSERVINFO lpInfo)
{
    SOCKADDR_IN     saServer;
    LPSERVENT       lpServEnt;
    unsigned        ThreadAddr;
    char            szBuf[256];
    char            szAddress[80];
    DWORD           dwAddrStrLen;
    int             nRet;

    //
    // Save the Window handle and message
    // ID for further use
    //
    ghwnd    = lpInfo->hwnd;
    guAppMsg = lpInfo->uMsgApp;
    if (lpInfo->lpRootDir != NULL)
        strcpy(szWebRoot, lpInfo->lpRootDir);
    else
        strcpy(szWebRoot, "/WebPages");

    //
    // Create the exit signal event object
    //
    ghExit = CreateEvent(NULL,      // Security
                         TRUE,      // Manual reset
                         FALSE,     // Initial State
                         NULL);     // Name
    if (ghExit == NULL)
        return FALSE;
```

```c
//
// Create a TCP/IP stream socket
//
listenSocket = socket(AF_INET,
                      SOCK_STREAM,
                      IPPROTO_TCP);
if (listenSocket == INVALID_SOCKET)
{
    LogWinSockError(ghwnd,
                    "Could not create listen socket",
                    WSAGetLastError());
    return FALSE;
}

//
// If a specific port number was specified
// then use it
//
if (lpInfo->nPort != 0)
    saServer.sin_port = htons(lpInfo->nPort);
else
{
    //
    // Find a port number
    //
    lpServEnt = getservbyname("http", "tcp");
    if (lpServEnt != NULL)
        saServer.sin_port = lpServEnt->s_port;
    else
        saServer.sin_port = htons(HTTPPORT);
}

//
// Fill in the rest of the address structure
//
saServer.sin_family = AF_INET;
saServer.sin_addr.s_addr = INADDR_ANY;

//
// bind our name to the socket
//
nRet = bind(listenSocket,
            (LPSOCKADDR)&saServer,
            sizeof(struct sockaddr));
if (nRet == SOCKET_ERROR)
{
    LogWinSockError(ghwnd,
                    "bind() error",
                    WSAGetLastError());
    closesocket(listenSocket);
    return FALSE;
}
```

```
//
// Set the socket to listen
//
nRet = listen(listenSocket, SOMAXCONN);
if (nRet == SOCKET_ERROR)
{
    LogWinSockError(ghwnd,
                    "listen() error",
                    WSAGetLastError());
    closesocket(listenSocket);
    return FALSE;
}

//
// Create the listening thread
//
gdwListenThread = _beginthreadex(
                    NULL,           // Security
                    0,              // Stack size
                    ListenThread,   // Function address
                    &ghExit,        // Argument
                    0,              // Init flag
                    &ThreadAddr);   // Thread address
if (!gdwListenThread)
{
    LogEvent(ghwnd,
            "Could not create listening thread: %d",
            GetLastError());
    closesocket(listenSocket);
    return FALSE;
}

//
// Display the host name and address
//
gethostname(szBuf, sizeof(szBuf));
dwAddrStrLen = sizeof(szAddress);
GetLocalAddress(szAddress, &dwAddrStrLen);
LogEvent(ghwnd,
        "HTTP Server Started: %s [%s] on port %d",
        szBuf,
        szAddress,
        htons(saServer.sin_port));

return TRUE;
}
```

After storing all of the information from the HTTPSERVINFO structure, StartHTTP() then creates an event object that will be used to signal the shutdown request when StopHTTP() is called. I'll refer to this event object as the *exit object*, and we'll see how it is used as we look at the rest of the code.

StartHTTP() next creates a socket descriptor that will be used to listen for incoming connections. It calls bind() and listen(), but leaves the socket in blocking mode. Note, *listenSocket* is declared at file scope so it is global to this module.

A new thread is then created that will start with the ListenThread() function. A pointer to the exit object is passed as a parameter. If all of this succeeds, the server's name and local address are sent to the user interface (just as they were in the asynchronous example in Chapter 10).

Waiting for Connection Requests

Once StartHTTP() has been called, the ListenThread() function (Listing 11-2) begins waiting for incoming connections.

Listing 11-2 The ListenThread() Function

```
unsigned __stdcall ListenThread(void *pVoid)
{
    SOCKET      socketClient;
    unsigned    ThreadAddr;
    DWORD       dwClientThread;
    SOCKADDR_IN SockAddr;
    LPREQUEST   lpReq;
    int         nLen;
    DWORD       dwRet;
    HANDLE      hNoClients;
    LPHANDLE    pHandle = (LPHANDLE)pVoid;

    //
    // Initialize client thread count to 0
    //
    hNoClients = InitClientCount();

    //
    // Loop forever accepting connections
    //
    while(1)
    {
        //
        // Block on accept()
        //
        nLen = sizeof(SOCKADDR_IN);
        socketClient = accept(listenSocket,
                              (LPSOCKADDR)&SockAddr,
                              &nLen);
        if (socketClient == INVALID_SOCKET)
        {
            //
            // StopHTTP() closes the listening socket
            // when it wants this thread to stop.
            break;
```

```c
    }
    //
    // We have a connection
    //
    LogEvent(ghwnd,
            "Connection accepted on socket:%d from:%s",
            socketClient,
            inet_ntoa(SockAddr.sin_addr));

    //
    // Allocate parms for client and fill in defaults
    //
    lpReq = malloc(sizeof(REQUEST));
    if (lpReq == NULL)
    {
        LogEvent(ghwnd,
                "No memory for client request");
        continue;
    }
    lpReq->hExit   = *pHandle;
    lpReq->Socket  = socketClient;
    lpReq->dwConnectTime = GetTickCount();
    lpReq->hFile = INVALID_HANDLE_VALUE;
    lpReq->dwRecv = 0;;
    lpReq->dwSend = 0;


    //
    // Start a client thread to handle this request
    //
    dwClientThread = _beginthreadex(
                        NULL,           // Security
                        0,              // Stack size
                        ClientThread,   // Thread function
                        lpReq,          // Argument
                        0,              // Init flag
                        &ThreadAddr);   // Thread address
    if (!dwClientThread)
    {
        LogEvent(ghwnd, "Couldn't start client thread");
    }
    //
    // We won't be using client thread handles,
    // so we close them when they are created.
    // The thread will continue to execute.
    //
    CloseHandle((HANDLE)dwClientThread);
}

//
// Wait for exit event
//
```

```
    WaitForSingleObject((HANDLE)*pHandle, INFINITE);

    //
    // Wait for ALL clients to exit
    //
    dwRet = WaitForSingleObject(hNoClients, 5000);
    if (dwRet == WAIT_TIMEOUT)
    {
        LogEvent(ghwnd,
            "One or more client threads did not exit");
    }
    DeleteClientCount();
    return 0;
}
```

Because we're using a separate thread to wait for connections, we don't have to worry about blocking the message loop. The ListenThread() function sets up an endless loop and blocks on the call to accept(). It waits there until the call to accept() completes — either with a connection request from a client or until some error occurs. Later, when StopHTTP() is called, it will close *listenSocket*, causing this call to accept() to fail with the WSAENOTSOCK error. The ListenThread() function uses this as a signal to break out of its loop and returns.

If accept() completes successfully, returning a new socket connection to a client, ListenThread() first allocates a REQUEST structure (similar to the one used in the asynchronous example). This structure is then filled with the exit object handle, the newly connected socket descriptor, and the current tick count.

Next, a new thread is created that will start at the ClientThread() function. The REQUEST structure is passed as a parameter to ClientThread(). The handle returned from _beginthreadex() is closed, and then the loop goes back to wait for accept() to complete again.

ListenThread() doesn't keep the new thread's handle and will, therefore, have no way of knowing when the thread completes. ListenThread() doesn't care when the thread completes — its job is to accept connections and create new threads to handle them. Later, however, when StopHTTP() is called, ListenThread() will want to know if all its client threads have completed.

Synchronizing Client Threads

The functions contained in COUNTC.C provide a means of tracking the number of client threads that are currently running. These functions update a client count variable (which is protected by a critical section) and signal an event object when the count is 0.

You can see in Listing 11-2 that before ListenThread() begins its loop, it calls InitClientCount():

```
HANDLE InitClientCount(void)
{
```

376   Part IV: Applications

```
    gdwClientCount = 0;

    InitializeCriticalSection(&gcriticalClients);
    //
    // Create the "no clients" signal event object
    //
    ghNoClients = CreateEvent(NULL,      // Security
                              TRUE,      // Manual reset
                              TRUE,      // Initial State
                              NULL);     // Name
    return ghNoClients;
}
```

This function sets a variable (declared at file scope in COUNTC.C) to 0, initializes a critical section object and returns a handle to an event object that it creates. ListenThread() will later use this event object handle to determine if all of the client threads have terminated. Once all of the client threads have terminated, ListenThread() will call the DeleteClientCount() function to delete the critical section and close the event handle. Here is DeleteClientCount():

```
void DeleteClientCount(void)
{
    DeleteCriticalSection(&gcriticalClients);
    CloseHandle(ghNoClients);
}
```

Each time a client thread is started, it calls IncrementClientCount() to have itself counted as a currently running thread. IncrementClientCount() enters the critical section, adds 1 to the total number of running clients, and ensures that the *ghNoClients* event object is nonsignaled. Here's IncrementClientCount():

```
void IncrementClientCount(void)
{
    EnterCriticalSection(&gcriticalClients);
    gdwClientCount++;
    LeaveCriticalSection(&gcriticalClients);
    ResetEvent(ghNoClients);
}
```

Just before a client thread exits, it calls DecrementClientCount() to subtract 1 from the total number of client threads variable. If this operation puts the number at 0, the DecrementClientCount() function signals the *ghNoClients* event object, as follows:

```
void DecrementClientCount(void)
{
 EnterCriticalSection(&gcriticalClients);
 if (gdwClientCount > 0)
```

```
        gdwClientCount--;
    LeaveCriticalSection(&gcriticalClients);
    if (gdwClientCount < 1)
        SetEvent(ghNoClients);
}
```

All the client threads watch for the exit event object, created in StartHTTP(). If it becomes signaled, the threads exit. So, signaling the exit object causes all the clients to exit, and waiting on the *ghNoClients* event signals when all client threads have stopped. This is exactly what takes place when StopHTTP() is called.

```
void StopHTTP()
{
    int nRet;

    //
    // Signal the exit event
    //
    SetEvent(ghExit);

    //
    // Close the listening socket
    //
    nRet = closesocket(listenSocket);

    //
    // And wait for the listen thread to stop
    //
    nRet = WaitForSingleObject((HANDLE)gdwListenThread, 10000);
    if (nRet == WAIT_TIMEOUT)
        LogEvent(ghwnd, "TIMEOUT waiting for ListenThread");

    CloseHandle((HANDLE)gdwListenThread);
    CloseHandle(ghExit);
    LogEvent(ghwnd, "Server Stopped");
}
```

StopHTTP() first signals the exit object and closes the listening socket. This causes ListenThread() to break out of its accept() loop. ListenThread() then waits for the "no more clients" event object to become signaled, and then returns. StopHTTP() waits for ListenThread() to terminate before returning.

Communicating with the Client

Now that we've seen how client threads are started and stopped, let's look at what they do while they're running. When ListenThread() accepts a connection, it calls _beginthreadex() to create a new thread for handling the conversation with the client. This thread begins executing at the ClientThread() function (Listing 11-3).

Listing 11-3 The ClientThread() Function

```
unsigned __stdcall ClientThread(void *pVoid)
{
    int nRet;
    BYTE buf[1024];
    LPREQUEST lpReq = (LPREQUEST)pVoid;

    //
    // Count this client
    //
    IncrementClientCount();

    //
    // Recv the request data
    //
    if (!RecvRequest(lpReq, buf, sizeof(buf)))
    {
        CloseConnection(lpReq);
        free(lpReq);
        DecrementClientCount();
        return 0;
    }

    //
    // Parse the request info
    //
    nRet = ParseRequest(lpReq, buf);
    if (nRet)
    {
        SendError(lpReq, nRet);
        CloseConnection(lpReq);
        free(lpReq);
        DecrementClientCount();
        return 0;
    }

    //
    // Send the file to the client
    //
    SendFile(lpReq);

    //
    // Clean up
    CloseConnection(lpReq);
    free(pVoid);

    //
    // Subtract this client
    //
    DecrementClientCount();
    return 0;
}
```

As discussed earlier, ClientThread() begins by calling IncrementClientCount(), to add 1 to the count of currently running client threads. It then calls RecvRequest() to get the client's request string, and then calls ParseRequest() to break out the HTTP method and filename. If both of those calls succeed, ClientThread() calls SendFile() to send the file to the client; then it closes the connection and calls DecrementClientCount() before it terminates.

This is straightforward code, especially when compared to the asynchronous example in the previous chapter. The function goes sequentially down the list of tasks it has to perform. No need exists for a linked list of connections or any "where were we?" housekeeping.

Note, substantial drawbacks exist to this method, however. As mentioned earlier, threads aren't free. System overhead is associated with every new thread. So if the server receives a lot of clients simultaneously (many more than the number of CPUs in the machine), the system will become bogged down with context switching. I can only recommend this method for servers that won't receive a lot of simultaneous connections. Servers that must handle a large number of simultaneous connections should use the asynchronous model described in Chapter 10, or — better yet — should only run on Windows NT, where I/O completion ports can be used.

Using Overlapped I/O with Event Objects

In the earlier section on StopHTTP(), I mentioned each client thread watches for the exit event object to become signaled. In the ClientThread() function, however, there isn't any code to do that — because the functions that actually perform I/O do the watching for this event object to become signaled. If the exit event object is signaled, these I/O functions will return before they have completed all of their duties.

The ClientThread() function calls two functions that transmit data with WinSock: RecvRequest() and SendFile(). Both of these functions use blocking socket routines to transmit data, and they both use overlapped I/O with event objects so they can watch for the exit signal.

Receiving the Client's Request

When ClientThread() starts, it calls IncrementClientCount() and then RecvRequest() to retrieve the request string from the client. Note, WinSock hasn't told us any data is waiting — all we know at this point is a client has requested a connection. We're assuming the client is going to send us a request, because that's what HTTP clients are supposed to do. The RecvRequest() function is presented in Listing 11-4.

Listing 11-4 The RecvRequest() Function

```
BOOL RecvRequest(LPREQUEST lpReq, LPBYTE pBuf, DWORD dwBufSize)
{
    WSABUF          wsabuf;
    WSAOVERLAPPED   over;
    DWORD           dwRecv;
    DWORD           dwFlags;
    DWORD           dwRet;
    HANDLE          hEvents[2];
    BOOL            fPending;
    int             nRet;

    //
    // Zero the buffer so the recv is null-terminated
    //
    memset(pBuf, 0, dwBufSize);

    //
    // Setup the WSABUF and WSAOVERLAPPED structures
    //
    wsabuf.buf  = pBuf;
    wsabuf.len  = dwBufSize;
    over.hEvent = WSACreateEvent();

    dwFlags = 0;
    fPending = FALSE;
    nRet = WSARecv(lpReq->Socket,   // Socket
                   &wsabuf,          // WSABUF
                   1,                // Number of buffers
                   &dwRecv,          // Bytes received
                   &dwFlags,         // Flags
                   &over,            // WSAOVERLAPPED
                   NULL);            // Completion function
    if (nRet != 0)
    {
        if (WSAGetLastError() != WSA_IO_PENDING)
        {
            LogWinSockError(ghwnd,
                            "WSARecv()",
                            WSAGetLastError());
            CloseHandle(over.hEvent);
            return FALSE;
        }
        else
            fPending = TRUE;
    }

    //
    // If the I/O isn't finished...
    //
    if (fPending)
```

```
    {
        //
        // Wait for the request to complete or the exit event
        //
        hEvents[0] = over.hEvent;
        hEvents[1] = lpReq->hExit;
        dwRet = WaitForMultipleObjects(2,
                                       hEvents,
                                       FALSE,
                                       INFINITE);
        //
        // Was the recv event signaled?
        //
        if (dwRet != 0)
        {
            CloseHandle(over.hEvent);
            return FALSE;
        }
        if (!WSAGetOverlappedResult(lpReq->Socket,
                                    &over,
                                    &dwRecv,
                                    FALSE,
                                    &dwFlags))
            CloseHandle(over.hEvent);
            return FALSE;
    }

    //
    // Recv event is complete - keep statistics
    //
    lpReq->dwRecv += dwRecv;
    CloseHandle(over.hEvent);
    return TRUE;
}
```

RecvRequest() begins by setting up a WSAOVERLAPPED structure to use with WSARecv(). A new event object is created with WSACreateEvent(), and then WSARecv() is called with a pointer to the WSAOVERLAPPED structure and the *lpCompletionRoutine* parameter set to NULL.

RecvRequest() checks the return value from WSARecv() to see if the function completed immediately. If the client has already sent the request, WSARecv() will get the data and return 0. If no error occurred and WSARecv() didn't complete immediately, the *fPending* flag is set to True.

If the I/O hasn't yet completed, RecvRequest() fills an event object array with both the overlapped I/O event object and the exit event object. It then uses the Win32 WaitForMultipleObjects() function to wait until one of the objects becomes signaled. The thread goes to sleep at this point and does nothing until either the overlapped I/O operation completes or StopHTTP() is called.

When WaitForMultipleObjects() completes, RecvRequest() checks to see which event object was signaled. If it wasn't the overlapped I/O event object (0 in the event array), then RecvRequest() assumes the exit event object has been signaled and it returns without waiting for the I/O event to complete. If the I/O event object was the one that was signaled, WSAGetOverlappedResult() is called to obtain the results of the WSARecv() operation.

Sending the File to the Client

Once RecvRequest() has completed, the ClientThread() function calls ParseRequest() to retrieve the HTTP method and requested file name. If this succeeds, ClientThread() calls SendFile(), shown in Listing 11-5, to send the file to the client.

Listing 11-5 The SendFile() Function
```
void SendFile(LPREQUEST lpReq)
{
    //
    // Open the file for reading
    //
    lpReq->hFile = CreateFile(lpReq->szFileName,
                              GENERIC_READ,
                              FILE_SHARE_READ,
                              NULL,
                              OPEN_EXISTING,
                              FILE_ATTRIBUTE_NORMAL,
                              NULL);
    if (lpReq->hFile == INVALID_HANDLE_VALUE)
    {
        SendMessage(ghwnd,
                    guAppMsg,
                    HTTP_FILENOTFOUND_MSG,
                    (LPARAM)(LPCSTR)lpReq->szFileName);
        // Send "404 Not Found" error
        SendError(lpReq, HTTP_STATUS_NOTFOUND);
        return;
    }

    //
    // Tell the user interface about the file hit
    // (Sending just the request portion — without
    // the root web directory portion
    //
    SendMessage(ghwnd,
                guAppMsg,
                HTTP_FILEOK_MSG,
                (LPARAM)(LPCSTR)
                    &lpReq->szFileName[strlen(szWebRoot)]);
    //
    // Send the file contents to the client
    //
    SendFileContents(lpReq);
```

Chapter 11: Multithreaded Server

```
    //
    // Close the file
    //
    if (CloseHandle(lpReq->hFile))
        lpReq->hFile = INVALID_HANDLE_VALUE;
    else
        LogEvent(ghwnd,
                 "Error closing file: %d",
                 GetLastError());
}
```

SendFile() attempts to open the requested file and updates the user interface with the results — sending HTTP_FILENOTFOUND_MSG or HTTP_FILEOK_MSG. It then calls SendFileContents() to do all the work of sending the file's data to the client. When SendFileContents() completes, it closes the file and returns. SendFileContents() is presented in Listing 11-6.

Listing 11-6 The SendFileContents() Function

```
void SendFileContents(LPREQUEST lpReq)
{
    static BYTE buf[1024];
    DWORD  dwRead;
    BOOL   fRet;

    //
    // Read and send data until EOF
    //
    while(1)
    {
        //
        // Read a buffer full from the file
        //
        fRet = ReadFile(lpReq->hFile,
                        buf,
                        sizeof(buf),
                        &dwRead,
                        NULL);
        if (!fRet)
        {
            // Send "404 Not Found" error
            SendError(lpReq, HTTP_STATUS_SERVERERROR);
            break;
        }

        if (dwRead == 0)
            break;

        //
        // Send this buffer to the client
```

Part IV: Applications

```
        //
        if (!SendBuffer(lpReq, buf, dwRead))
            break;

        //
        // Add for statistics
        //
        lpReq->dwSend += dwRead;
    }
}
```

In Chapter 10's asynchronous example, SendFileContents() had to be capable of being called multiple times and "remembering" its place in file transfer with each client. In this version of a server, however, SendFileContents() simply enters a loop, reading a buffer from the file and then transmitting it to the client. The function continues in this loop until all the data from the file has been transmitted or some error occurs. As each buffer is read from the file, the SendBuffer() function is called (Listing 11-7) to actually transmit the data.

Listing 11-7 The SendBuffer() Function

```
BOOL SendBuffer(LPREQUEST lpReq, LPBYTE pBuf, DWORD dwBufSize)
{
    WSABUF            wsabuf;
    WSAOVERLAPPED     over;
    DWORD             dwRecv;
    DWORD             dwFlags;
    DWORD             dwRet;
    HANDLE            hEvents[2];
    BOOL              fPending;
    int               nRet;

    //
    // Setup the WSABUF and WSAOVERLAPPED structures
    //
    wsabuf.buf = pBuf;
    wsabuf.len = dwBufSize;
    over.hEvent = WSACreateEvent();

    fPending = FALSE;
    nRet = WSASend(lpReq->Socket,    // Socket
                   &wsabuf,           // WSABUF
                   1,                 // Number of buffers
                   &dwRecv,           // Bytes received
                   0,                 // Flags
                   &over,             // WSAOVERLAPPED
                   NULL);             // Completion function
    if (nRet != 0)
    {
        if (WSAGetLastError() == WSA_IO_PENDING)
```

Chapter 11: Multithreaded Server

```
            fPending = TRUE;
        else
        {
            LogWinSockError(ghwnd,
                            "WSASend()",
                            WSAGetLastError());
            CloseHandle(over.hEvent);
            return FALSE;
        }
    }

    //
    // If the I/O isn't finished...
    //
    if (fPending)
    {
        //
        // Wait for the request to complete
        // or the exit event to be signaled
        //
        hEvents[0] = over.hEvent;
        hEvents[1] = lpReq->hExit;
        dwRet = WaitForMultipleObjects(2,
                                       hEvents,
                                       FALSE,
                                       INFINITE);
        //
        // Was the recv event signaled?
        //
        if (dwRet != 0)
        {
            CloseHandle(over.hEvent);
            return FALSE;
        }

        //
        // Get I/O result
        //
        if (!WSAGetOverlappedResult(lpReq->Socket,
                                    &over,
                                    &dwRecv,
                                    FALSE,
                                    &dwFlags))
        {
            LogWinSockError(ghwnd,
                            "WSAGetOverlappedResult()",
                            WSAGetLastError());
            CloseHandle(over.hEvent);
            return FALSE;
```

```
        }
    }

    CloseHandle(over.hEvent);
    return TRUE;
}
```

The SendBuffer() function uses overlapped I/O with an event object in much the same way that RecvRequest() did. SendBuffer() begins by filling a WSAOVERLAPPED structure with a pointer to the buffer and an event handle that it creates. SendBuffer() then calls WSASend(), requesting event-object notification for completion. If the I/O operation doesn't complete immediately, SendBuffer() calls WaitForMultipleObjects() to wait on both the I/O event object and the exit event object. If the exit event object is signaled, SendBuffer() returns False, indicating it didn't complete the I/O. If the I/O operation completed, SendBuffer() uses WSAGetOverlappedResult() to determine what happened.

Extending the HTTP Example Servers

Both the HTTP servers presented here in Part IV (HTTPA and HTTPMT) work as they are, but they can be extended to become full-featured HTTP servers. Following are some suggestions of what you might want to add to these example programs.

HTTP/1.0

Both of the server examples are limited to the HTTP/0.9 simple request-and-response format. The ParseRequest() function in both examples could be easily extended to accept the HTTP/1.0 full request and to support other HTTP methods. Use of the HTTP/1.0 If-Modified-Since field could *greatly* reduce the amount of work the server has to perform, by letting clients know a particular file hasn't been modified since it was last retrieved.

Common Gateway Interface

If the HTTP/1.0 full request were implemented, a CGI interface could be added to these servers. CGI would allow the servers to work with forms, on-line databases, and other types of dynamic Web pages.

Allowing Clients to Complete

In Chapter 10, I discussed the concept that a server such as this might want to shut down and stop accepting new clients, but let all the currently connected clients finish before stopping operation altogether. HTTPMT could easily be modified to behave in this way. If StopHTTP() simply didn't signal the exit event object and only closed the listening socket, then new connections wouldn't be accepted; the currently connected clients, however, would be allowed to finish. One line would have to be removed from ListenThread() to make this work. Near the end of the ListenThread() function, it waits for the exit object to be signaled, as follows:

```
//
// Wait for exit event
//
WaitForSingleObject((HANDLE)*pHandle, INFINITE);
```

If StopHTTP() didn't signal the exit event object and this line were removed from ListenThread(), then ListenThread() would simply stop accepting new connections and wait for all of the currently connected clients to complete before it returned.

Summary

The WinSock code in this version of our HTTP server is much simpler. Because a thread is used to handle each client connection, blocking socket routines can be used without interfering with the operation of the rest of the program. Remember, this type of multithreaded server doesn't scale well. If a large number of clients are simultaneously connected, the system can easily become bogged down with context switching. Servers that must handle a large number of simultaneous connections should use Windows NT and I/O completion ports instead.

Even with this limitation, the mechanism used in this multithreaded example can be used *very* successfully in client applications. A client application would probably not need more than one or two threads to handle data transfer and could greatly simplify its WinSock code by using blocking functions.

Chapter 12

Protocol-Independent Client and Server

IN THIS CHAPTER
In this chapter we will develop connectionless client and server programs that are independent of both protocol and WinSock version. The following topics are discussed:

- Using WinSock 2 protocol independence
- Explicitly linking to WinSock
- Using datagram sockets
- Handling Unicode with WinSock

BY NOW YOU'RE FAMILIAR with the many new capabilities WinSock 2 provides to application developers. One of the primary reasons you'd want to use WinSock 2 is for its protocol independence. As you've seen in action, WinSock 2 applications can discover transport protocols at run-time and select those that are appropriate for the application's needs. This is an extremely important feature and over time will be more and more valued by developers and their customers alike.

In this chapter you'll see the development of simple ECHO client and server programs that are protocol independent. They will generally follow the guidelines for a datagram ECHO service as outlined in RFC 862, "Echo Protocol." RFC 862 defines both a TCP-based, connection-oriented ECHO service, and a connectionless UDP service. Both of these perform the same simple task: an ECHO server simply sends any data that it receives back to the source. An ECHO client sends data to an ECHO server and usually records the amount of time it took for the data to make the round trip. Some sort of check on the received data is also performed by the client, to ensure that it wasn't corrupted during transmission.

The programs in this chapter will implement a connectionless, protocol-independent ECHO service. We'll select protocols at run-time that support connectionless operation.

Linking to WinSock at Run-Time

Windows 95 has a firm grasp on the desktop market and there are a lot of Windows 95 machines out there to support. Because it is so new, WinSock 2 isn't yet widely installed on Windows 95 machines. No doubt this will change very soon — but we have to write programs that work *now*, not soon.

One strategy for WinSock application development today is to use WinSock 2 if it is available on the user's machine, and fall back to WinSock 1.1 if it's not. In order for this strategy to work, the application must link to WinSock at run-time rather than compile time. Any program that is statically linked to WS2_32.LIB will not execute on a machine that only has WinSock 1.1 installed. Likewise, any program that is statically linked to WSOCK32.LIB can't use any of the new functionality in WinSock 2.

As well as being protocol independent, the programs developed in this chapter are also WinSock version independent. Both the client and the server dynamically link to WinSock at run-time. If WS2_32.DLL is available, the programs will use the WinSock 2 WSAEnumProtocols() function to find and use all installed connectionless protocols. If WinSock 2 is not available, the programs fall back to WinSock 1.1 and work on the assumption that UDP is available.

The Socket Adapter Library

On the CD (in the \CH12 directory), you'll find a library of routines I developed that greatly ease the tasks involved in explicitly linking to WinSock. I call this the Socket Adapter Library. By using the routines in this library, an application can use WinSock 2 functionality if it's available and fall back to WinSock 1.1 if it's not. This library contains the files listed in Table 12-1.

TABLE 12-1 SOCKET ADAPTER LIBRARY

Filename	Description
DWINSOCK.C	Functions for dynamically linking to WinSock, and WinSock 2 emulation functions for use with WinSock 1.1.
DWINSOCK.H	Function prototypes and definitions for DWINSOCK.C.
DWNSOCK1.H	Macros to aid in mapping the functions that are available in both WinSock 1.1 and 2.
DWNSOCK2.H	Macros to aid in mapping the functions that are available only in WinSock 2.

Using the Socket Adapter Library

Dynamic linking (also called *explicit linking*) requires that the application call the LoadLibrary() function and *explicitly* name the DLL. The application then acquires a pointer to the functions it is interested in calling, by using GetProcAddress(). When the application no longer requires the services of the DLL, it must call FreeLibrary() to unload the DLL. Since the program calls functions in the DLL through a function pointer, the compiler does not generate external references. So there is no need to link with an import library when using explicit dynamic linking. For example, the following sequence would be used to load the WinSock 2 DLL at run-time:

```
//
// Explicitly link to WinSock 2 and call WSAStartup()
//
typedef int (WSAAPI * LPFN_WSASTARTUP)(WORD, LPWSADATA);
LPFN_WSASTARTUP p_WSAStartup;
HANDLE hndlWinSock;

//
// Load WinSock 2 DLL
//
hndlWinSock = LoadLibrary("WS2_32.DLL");
if (hndlWinSock == NULL)
{
    // WinSock 2 not available
    return ERROR;
}

//
// Map pointer to WSAStartup() procedure address
//
p_WSAStartup = (LPFN_WSASTARTUP)GetProcAddress(hndlWinSock,
                                                "WSAStartup");
if (!p_WSAStartup)
{
    // Error getting WSAStartup address
    FreeLibrary(hndlWinSock);
    return ERROR;
}

//
// Call WSAStartup
//
WORD    wVersionRequested = MAKEWORD(2,2);
WSADATA wsaData;
int     nRet;
nRet = p_WSAStartup(wVersionRequested, &wsaData);
.
.
.
```

The procedure for loading the DLL is straightforward, but it can lead to a lot of work if you want to map to more than a few functions. To do this cleanly, a new type must be created for each function, which includes the function's parameter list. That's what this line (from the preceding example) does:

```
typedef int (WSAAPI * LPFN_WSASTARTUP)(WORD, LPWSADATA);
```

This type definition is used to declare an appropriate function pointer as well as a cast in the call to GetProcAddress(). Luckily for us, the good folks who created the WINSOCK2.H header already did all that work for us. If you define INCL_WINSOCK_API_TYPEDEFS before you include WINSOCK2.H, it will generate all of the needed type definitions.

Note: Luckily for me, I read Matt Pietrek's article in the September 1997 issue of *Microsoft Systems Journal* (see Appendix D) that describes a slick way of performing all of this drudgery. Because the WINSOCK2.H file includes all of the needed type definitions, I was able to extend on Matt's idea and make a clean, easy-to-use library to explicitly link to WinSock.

Declaring Function Pointers

The file DWINSOCK.C declares a pointer for all of the WinSock 2 functions at file scope. It does this with only three lines of code:

```
#define DWINSOCK_GLOBAL
#include "dwnsock1.inc"
#include "dwnsock2.inc"
```

Both the includes, DWINSOCK1.INC and DWINSOCK2.INC, define a macro named DYNAMICWINSOCK() that accepts two arguments. In addition, both includes contain a list of calls to this macro — one call for each WinSock function — using the function name and function pointer type as parameters. Here is a portion of DWNSOCK1.INC, which shows the macro definitions and calls for the first four functions:

```
#ifdef DWINSOCK_GLOBAL
  #undef DYNAMICWINSOCK
  #define DYNAMICWINSOCK(name, ptr) ptr p_##name
#endif

#ifdef DWINSOCK_EXTERN
  #undef DYNAMICWINSOCK
  #define DYNAMICWINSOCK(name, ptr) extern ptr p_##name
#endif

#ifdef DWINSOCK_GETPROCADDRESS
  #undef DYNAMICWINSOCK
  #define DYNAMICWINSOCK(name, ptr) \
```

```
                    p_##name = (ptr)GetProcAddress(hndlWinSock, #name);\
                    if (p_##name == NULL) fOK = FALSE
#endif

//
// Function available in both versions
//
DYNAMICWINSOCK(accept, LPFN_ACCEPT);
DYNAMICWINSOCK(bind, LPFN_BIND);
DYNAMICWINSOCK(closesocket, LPFN_CLOSESOCKET);
DYNAMICWINSOCK(connect, LPFN_CONNECT);
    .
    .
    .
```

The DYNAMICWINSOCK() macro is redefined based on which of three constants is defined. These constants are described in the following paragraphs.

DWINSOCK_GLOBAL If DWINSOCK_GLOBAL is defined before including the DWNSOCK.INC files, the DYNAMICWINSOCK macro is defined to declare each function pointer as a global variable. The token pasting operator (##) is used to simply declare each function pointer. Here is one example of how the macro would expand:

```
LPFN_WSASTARTUP p_WSAStartup;
```

By defining DWINSOCK_GLOBAL and including both of the DWNSOCK.INC files, an application declares a function pointer for every function in WinSock.

DWINSOCK_EXTERN If DWINSOCK_EXTERN is defined before including the DWNSOCK.INC files, the DYNAMICWINSOCK macro is defined to declare each function pointer as an external variable (extern). Here's how the macro would expand for WSAStart():

```
extern LPFN_WSASTARTUP p_WSAStartup;
```

In an application made up of several source modules, the DWINSOCK.C file can be used to declare the global function pointers, and every other source module can declare external linkage to them by defining DWINSOCK_EXTERN and including the two DWNSOCK.INC files.

DWINSOCK_GETPROCADDRESS When DWINSOCK_GETPROCADDRESS is defined, it causes the DYNAMICWINSOCK macro to be defined as a call to GetProcAddress(). The macro uses the token pasting operator (##) and the stringizing operator (#) to build an appropriate call. Here's how the macro would expand for WSAStartup():

```
p_WSAStartup = (LPFN_WSASTARTUP)GetProcAddress(hndlWinSock,
                                               "WSAStartup");
if (p_WSAStartup == NULL) fOK = FALSE;
```

Note that this version of the macro relies on a Boolean variable named *fOK*. We'll see how this is used in the next section.

Loading WinSock

To use the Socket Adapter Library, your application must compile and link with the DWINSOCK.C module. DWINSOCK.C defines DWINSOCK_GLOBAL and includes the two DWNSOCK.INC files. This declares a function pointer for all of the WinSock functions at file scope.

DWINSOCK.C also contains several other functions that make using the library more convenient. All of the functions contained in DWINSOCK.C are prefixed with the letters *DWS*, which is a TLA (Three Letter Acronym) for Dynamic WinSock. Rather than calling WSAStartup(), the first WinSock call in your application *must* be to DWSInitWinSock(), presented in Listing 12-1.

Listing 12-1 The DWSInitWinSock() Function

```
int DWSInitWinSock(void)
{
    WORD wVersionRequested;
    BOOL f2Loaded = TRUE;
    WSADATA wsaData;
    int nRet;

    //
    // Attempt to dynamically load WS2_32.DLL
    //
    hndlWinSock = LoadLibrary("WS2_32.DLL");
    if (hndlWinSock == NULL)
    {
        //
        // Couldn't load WinSock 2, try 1.1
        //
        f2Loaded = FALSE;
        hndlWinSock = LoadLibrary("WSOCK32.DLL");
        if (hndlWinSock == NULL)
            return 0;
    }

    //
    // Use GetProcAddress to initialize
    // the function pointers
    //
    if (!MapFunctionPointers(f2Loaded))
        return 0;

    //
    // If WinSock 2 was loaded, ask for 2.2 otherwise 1.1
    //
```

Chapter 12: Protocol-Independent Client and Server

```
    if (f2Loaded)
        wVersionRequested = MAKEWORD(2,2);
    else
        wVersionRequested = MAKEWORD(1,1);

    //
    // Call WSAStartup()
    //
    nRet = p_WSAStartup(wVersionRequested, &wsaData);
    if (nRet)
    {
        FreeLibrary(hndlWinSock);
        return 0;
    }

    if (wVersionRequested != wsaData.wVersion)
    {
        FreeLibrary(hndlWinSock);
        return 0;
    }

    // Save Max UDP for use with 1.1
    nMaxUdp = wsaData.iMaxUdpDg;

    //
    // Return 1 or 2
    //
    nVersion = f2Loaded ? 2 : 1;
    return(nVersion);
}
```

DWSInitWinSock() first attempts to load WS2_32.DLL using LoadLibrary(). If this call fails, the variable *f2Loaded* is set to False to indicate that WinSock 2 couldn't be loaded. DWSInitWinSock() then attempts to load WSOCK32.DLL. If this library isn't available either, the function returns 0 to indicate that no WinSock was available.

If either of the LoadLibrary() calls succeeds, then DWSInitWinSock() calls a function that is for its internal use only: MapFunctionPointers(). (Because this function isn't meant to be used outside of DWINSOCK.C, it doesn't have the DWS prefix.) MapFunctionPointers() is in Listing 12-2.

Listing 12-2 The MapFunctionPointers() Function

```
BOOL MapFunctionPointers(BOOL fMapVersion2)
{
    //
    // This variable must be declared
    // with this name in order to use
    // #define DWINSOCK_GETPROCADDRESS
    //
```

```
    BOOL fOK = TRUE;

    //
    // GetProcAddress for functions
    // available in both 1.1 and 2
    //
    #define DWINSOCK_GETPROCADDRESS
    #include "dwnsock1.inc"

    //
    // If that went OK, and we're supposed
    // to map version 2, then do GetProcAddress
    // for functions only available in WinSock 2
    //
    if (fOK && fMapVersion2)
    {
        #include "dwnsock2.inc"
    }
    return fOK;
}
```

MapFunctionPointers() declares the Boolean variable *fOK*, needed by the DWINSOCK_GETPROCADDRESS version of the DYNAMICWINSOCK() macro. MapFunctionPointers() always attempts to map the functions listed in DWNSOCK1.INC, which are the functions that are available in both WinSock 1.1 and 2. MapFunctionPointers() accepts one parameter that indicates whether or not it should attempt to map the functions in DWNSOCK2.INC. The functions listed in this file are only available in WinSock 2 and can only be mapped if WS2_32.DLL was successfully loaded.

Note: Even if WSOCK32.DLL was loaded, the MapFunctionPointers() process doesn't map pointers to the following functions:

WSACancelBlockingCall()	WSAIsBlocking()
WSASetBlockingHook()	WSAUnhookBlockingHook()

These functions were dropped from the WinSock specification in WinSock 2, and their use is discouraged. (See the "Pseudoblocking" section of Chapter 7 for details.)

If MapFunctionPointers() succeeds, DWSInitWinSock() then calls WSAStartup() through the function pointer p_WSAStartup() and requests either WinSock 1.1 or 2.2, depending on which library was loaded. DWSInitWinSock() then returns either 1 or 2 to the caller to indicate the major version number of WinSock that was loaded.

Once DWSInitWinSock() has successfully completed, the function pointers can be used to call WinSock functions. In fact, *all* WinSock calls in the application *must* be made through these function pointers so that the program does not have to be statically linked to either WSOCK32.LIB or WS2_32.LIB.

Unloading WinSock

Before it exits, a program that uses the Socket Adapter Library should call DWSFreeWinSock(). DWSFreeWinSock() simply calls WSACleanup() and unloads the DLL. Here is the DWSFreeWinSock() function:

```
BOOL DWSFreeWinSock(void)
{
    if (p_WSACleanup != NULL)
        p_WSACleanup();
    nVersion = 0;
    return(FreeLibrary(hndlWinSock));
}
```

Socket Adapter Library Summary

To make life a little easier in an application that doesn't always have access to WinSock 2, the DWINSOCK.C file includes a few utility functions. A summary of these is listed here.

DWSVersion()   DWSVersion() returns the major version number of the previously loaded WinSock library. It returns 1 if WinSock 1.1 was loaded, or 2 if WinSock 2 was loaded. This function should be used to determine when it is safe to call a WinSock 2 function.

```
int   DWSVersion(void);
```

DWSMaxMsgSize()   In WinSock 1.1, the maximum message size that can be used with a datagram socket is retrieved from WSADATA during the call to WSAStartup(). In WinSock 2, however, the protocol-specific maximum message size is discovered using getsockopt() with the SO_MAX_MSG_SIZE command. DWSMaxMsgSize() accepts a socket and returns the appropriate maximum message size regardless of which version of WinSock is loaded. It uses the value previously saved from WSADATA if WinSock 1.1 was loaded, or calls getsockopt() if WinSock 2 is available.

```
int   DWSMaxMsgSize(SOCKET socket);
```

DWSAddressToString() DWSAddressToString() provides a version-independent means of converting a SOCKADDR to a human-readable string. This function uses WSAAddressToString() to convert the address if WinSock 2 is available, and inet_ntoa() if it isn't.

```
int  DWSAddressToString(LPSOCKADDR pAddr, DWORD dwAddrLen,
                        LPSTR lpAddrStr, LPDWORD pdwStrLen);
```

Parameter	Description
pAddr	A pointer to a SOCKADDR to translate into a string.
dwAddrLen	The size in bytes of the SOCKADDR.
lpAddrStr	A buffer that will receive the translated string.
pdwStrLen	The length of the *lpAddrStr* buffer on input. On output, the length of the string actually copied into the *lpAddrStr* buffer.

DWSEnumProtocols() If WinSock 2 is available, DWSEnumProtocols() just passes its call along to WSAEnumProtocols(). If only WinSock 1.1 is available, DWSEnumProtocols() returns a "fake" WSAPROTOCOL_INFO buffer containing workable descriptions of TCP and UDP. This function differs from WSAEnumProtocols() only in that it always returns all available protocols; it doesn't support the protocol restriction array. Other than that, it works exactly like WSAEnumProtocols().

```
int  DWSEnumProtocols(LPWSAPROTOCOL_INFO lpProtocolBuffer,
                      LPDWORD pdwBufLen);
```

DWSSelectProtocols() DWSSelectProtocols() works exactly like the SelectProtocols() function described in Chapter 7. Rather than calling WSAEnumProtocols directly, it relies on DWSEnumProtocols() to provide information if WinSock 2 isn't available. It accepts two sets of flags that describe the characteristics of desirable protocols, and fills the *lpProtocolBuffer* with information about all matching transports.

```
int  DWSSelectProtocols(DWORD dwSetFlags,
                        DWORD dwNotSetFlags,
                        LPWSAPROTOCOL_INFO lpProtocolBuffer,
                        LPDWORD lpdwBufferLength);
```

Parameter	Description
dwSetFlags	A bitmask specifying values that must be set in the protocol's WSAPROTOCOL_INFO.dwServiceFlags1 field. Only protocols that have these flags set will be returned.
dwNotSetFlags	A bitmask specifying values that must *not* be set in the protocol's WSAPROTOCOL_INFO.dwServiceFlags1 field. Only protocols that do *not* have these flags set will be returned.
lpProtocolBuffer	This is the buffer to be filled with WSAPROTOCOL_INFO structures.
lpdwBufferLength	On input, indicates the size in bytes of the buffer pointed to by the *lpProtocolBuffer* parameter. On output, indicates the minimum size the buffer must be to retrieve all of the requested information.

DWSDnsOnly() If WinSock 2 can't be loaded, then the WSAEnumNameSpaceProviders() function can't be used. DWSDnsOnly() returns True if only WinSock 1.1 could be loaded, or if WinSock 2 was loaded but there's only a DNS name space provider available.

```
BOOL DWSDnsOnly(void);
```

Note: I use this function to find out if anything is to be gained by using the service registration and resolution (RNR) functions. If DWSDnsOnly() returns True, I don't bother to use any of the RNR functions.

UNICODE SUPPORT

The Socket Adapter library provides some support for Unicode. The DWINSOCK.H header defines generic names for the pointers to the WinSock 2 functions that have both ANSI and "wide" versions. Here's an example from DWINSOCK.H:

```
#ifdef UNICODE
  #define p_WSAAddressToString p_WSAAddressToStringW
#else
  #define p_WSAAddressToString p_WSAAddressToStringA
#endif
```

The example programs in this chapter, as well as the functions in DWINSOCK.C, are all aware of Unicode and use the TCHAR.H approach to building applications that can be compiled for either ANSI or Unicode.

Adding the Socket Adapter Library to Your Applications

Follow these steps to add the Socket Adapter library to your applications:

1. Compile and link DWINSOCK.C with your application.

   Note: Do *not* link to either WS2_32.LIB or WSOCK32.LIB.

2. Declare DWINSOCK_EXTERN, and include the DWNSOCK.INC files in each source file where you want to call WinSock functions.

   ```
   #define DWINSOCK_EXTERN
   #include "dwnsock1.inc"
   #include "dwnsock2.inc"
   ```

3. Call DWSInitWinSock() *before* using any of the function pointers, and check the return value!

4. Use DWSVersion() to determine if it is safe to use WinSock 2.

   ```
   if (DWSVersion() == 0)
       // WinSock isn't loaded
       return;
   if (DWSVersion() == 2)
       // Safe to use WinSock 2 functions
   else
       // Only WinSock 1.1 available
   ```

5. Make all calls to WinSock functions in your program through the function pointers. For example, use p_socket() rather than socket() and p_connect() rather than connect().

6. Call DWSFreeWinSock() before your application exits.

The Socket Adapter ECHO Client

The ECHO client application developed in this chapter sends a buffer of data to an ECHO server application and records the round-trip time for the data to be returned. It also confirms that the data received back from the server is identical to the data buffer that was sent.

The ECHO client program uses the functions found in DWINSOCK.C to dynamically link to WinSock as discussed earlier in this chapter. If only WinSock 1.1 is available, the program uses UDP. If WinSock 2 is available, the client can use any connectionless, message-oriented protocol that is installed on the local machine. For the AF_INET family, it searches for hosts by name and expects to find them on well-known ECHO port 7. If WinSock 2 is loaded, the WinSock 2 WSALookupService() functions are used with a predefined GUID to locate servers.

The complete source code for the ECHO client application is in the \CH12\CLIENT directory on the CD. All of the WinSock and user interface code is contained in the ECHOCLNT.C source file.

The Client's User Interface

The ECHO client displays a dialog box as its main window. Figure 12-1 shows the ECHO client running on a machine with WinSock 2 installed.

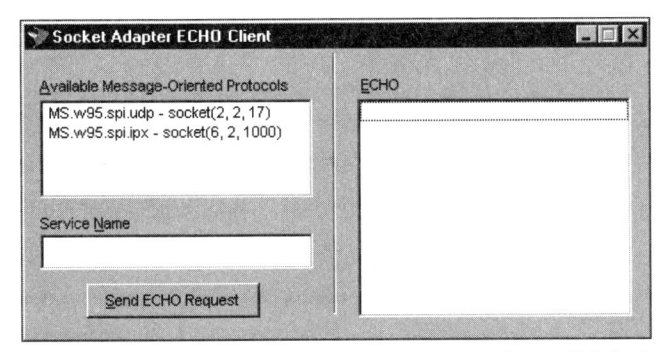

Figure 12-1: The Socket Adapter ECHO client running on WinSock 2

This dialog box displays a list of all of the installed protocols that are available for this application (that is, all of the connectionless, message-oriented protocols). To operate the Socket Adapter ECHO client, the user selects a protocol from the Available...list box, enters a host or service name in the Service Name text box, and then clicks the Send ECHO Request button. Each ECHO request that is sent out is labeled with a unique sequence number. When the ECHO is received back from the server, the sequence number and the elapsed time are listed in the large list box on the right.

Linking to WinSock

The ECHO client makes all of its WinSock calls through the function pointers mapped in DWINSOCK.C. The ECHOCLNT.C source file declares all of these function pointers as external by defining DWINSOCK_EXTERN and including the DWNSOCK.INC files as discussed earlier.

```
//
// Pull in global function pointers as extern
//
#define DWINSOCK_EXTERN
#include "..\dwnsock1.inc"
#include "..\dwnsock2.inc"
```

In WinMain(), Listing 12-3, the client calls DWSInitWinSock() and checks the return value to ensure that a WinSock library was loaded. Just before exiting, the program calls DWSFreeWinSock() to unload WinSock.

Listing 12-3 The WinMain() Function

```
int WINAPI WinMain(HINSTANCE hInstance,
                   HINSTANCE hPrevInstance,
                   LPSTR lpCmdLine,
                   int nCmdShow)
{
    int nVersion;

    //
    // Dynamically link to newest available WinSock
    //
    nVersion = DWSInitWinSock();
    if (!nVersion)
    {
        MessageBox(NULL,
                   _TEXT("No WinSock Available"),
                   gszAppName,
                   MB_OK);
        return 0;
    }

    //
    // Use a dialog as a main window
    //
    DialogBox(hInstance,
              MAKEINTRESOURCE(IDD_MAINWND),
              NULL,
              MainWndProc);

    //
    // Free dynamically linked WinSock DLL
    //
    DWSFreeWinSock();
    return(0);
}
```

Selecting Transport Protocols

In MainWndProc(), the client calls OnInitDialog() to handle the WM_INITDIALOG message. OnInitDialog(), shown in Listing 12-4, checks to see what version of WinSock was loaded by calling DWSVersion(), and decides which icon to associate with the main dialog window. It then calls FillSocketChoices().

Chapter 12: Protocol-Independent Client and Server 403

Listing 12-4 The OnInitDialog() Function

```
BOOL OnInitDialog(HWND hwnd, HWND hwndFocus, LPARAM lParam)
{
    ghwnd = hwnd;
    //
    // Associate an icon with the dialog box.
    //
    if (DWSVersion() == 1)
        SetClassLong(hwnd,
                     GCL_HICON,
                     (LONG)LoadIcon(GetWindowInstance(hwnd),
                     MAKEINTRESOURCE(IDI_ICON1)));
    else
        SetClassLong(hwnd,
                     GCL_HICON,
                     (LONG)LoadIcon(GetWindowInstance(hwnd),
                     MAKEINTRESOURCE(IDI_ICON2)));

    FillSocketChoices(hwnd);
    return(TRUE);
}
```

FillSocketChoices(), presented in Listing 12-5, calls DWSSelectProtocols() to find all of the connectionless, message-oriented protocols. It allocates a buffer large enough to hold one socket descriptor for each returned protocol; then it loops through the list of returned protocols, opening a socket for each one. It uses the information from the WSAPROTOCOL_INFO buffer to find appropriate parameters for the call to socket() — using the p_socket function pointer. If the socket descriptor is successfully created, FillSocketChoices() requests asynchronous notification for the socket and adds a description for this entry to the list box.

Listing 12-5 The FillSocketChoices() Function

```
void FillSocketChoices(HWND hwnd)
{
    LPWSAPROTOCOL_INFO  pInfo;
    SOCKET              *pSock;
    HWND                hwndList;
    DWORD               dwNeededLen;
    TCHAR               szBuf[256];
    int                 nCount;
    int                 nRet;

    //
    // Determine size for protocol buffer
    //
    dwNeededLen = 0;
    nRet = DWSSelectProtocols(XP1_CONNECTIONLESS |
```

Part IV: Applications

```
                            XP1_MESSAGE_ORIENTED,
                            0,
                            NULL,
                            &dwNeededLen);
if (nRet == SOCKET_ERROR)
{
    if (p_WSAGetLastError() != WSAENOBUFS)
    {
        ShowWinSockError(hwnd,
                    _TEXT("EnumProtocols 1"),
                    p_WSAGetLastError());
        return;
    }
}

//
// Allocate the buffer
//
gpProtocolBuf = malloc(dwNeededLen);
if (gpProtocolBuf == NULL)
{
    MessageBox(hwnd,
            _TEXT("Insufficient memory"),
            gszAppName, MB_OK);
    return;
}

//
// Make the "real" call
//
nRet = DWSSelectProtocols(XP1_CONNECTIONLESS |
                            XP1_MESSAGE_ORIENTED,
                            0,
                            (LPWSAPROTOCOL_INFO)gpProtocolBuf,
                            &dwNeededLen);
if (nRet == SOCKET_ERROR)
{
    ShowWinSockError(hwnd,
                _TEXT("EnumProtocols 2"),
                p_WSAGetLastError());
    return;
}

//
// Allocate a buffer for socket descriptors
//
gpSockets = malloc(sizeof(SOCKET)*nRet);
if (gpSockets == NULL)
{
    MessageBox(hwnd,
            _TEXT("Insufficient memory"),
            gszAppName, MB_OK);
    return;
```

```
    }

    //
    // Loop through the returned protocols
    // creating socket descriptors and adding
    // descriptions to the listbox.
    //
    hwndList   = GetDlgItem(hwnd, IDC_SOCKETS);
    pInfo      = (LPWSAPROTOCOL_INFO)gpProtocolBuf;
    pSock      = (SOCKET *)gpSockets;
    gNbrSockets= nRet;
    for(nCount = 0; nCount < gNbrSockets; nCount++)
    {
        *pSock = p_socket(pInfo->iAddressFamily,
                          pInfo->iSocketType,
                          pInfo->iProtocol);
        if (*pSock == INVALID_SOCKET)
        {
            ShowWinSockError(hwnd,
                            _TEXT("socket()"),
                            p_WSAGetLastError());
            gNbrSockets = nCount-1;
            return;
        }
        //
        // Request async notification
        //
        nRet = p_WSAAsyncSelect(*pSock,
                                hwnd,
                                UM_ASYNC,
                                FD_READ);
        if (nRet == SOCKET_ERROR)
        {
            ShowWinSockError(hwnd,
                            _TEXT("WSAAsyncSelect()"),
                            p_WSAGetLastError());
            return;
        }
        wsprintf(szBuf,
                _TEXT(" %s - socket(%d, %d, %d)"),
                pInfo->szProtocol,
                pInfo->iAddressFamily,
                pInfo->iSocketType,
                pInfo->iProtocol);
        ListBox_AddString(hwndList, szBuf);
        pInfo++;
        pSock++;
    }
}
```

Sending an ECHO Request

When the user clicks the Send ECHO Request button, the OnCommand() function calls SendEcho(). This function, shown in Listing 12-6, begins by ensuring that the user has selected a protocol from the list. It also requires that the user enter a host name if the selected protocol belongs to the AF_INET address family. We'll see the reason for this restriction in a moment. SendEcho() then calls FindEchoServer() to locate the server's address, fills an ECHOREQ data structure, and then sends the ECHO request with the p_sendto() function pointer.

Listing 12-6 The SendEcho() Function

```
void SendEcho(HWND hwnd)
{
    LPWSAPROTOCOL_INFO  lpInfo;
    TCHAR       szHostName[256];
    ECHOREQ     echoReq;
    SOCKET      *pSock;
    SOCKADDR    saHost;
    HWND        hwndList;
    HWND        hwndEdit;
    int         nIndex;
    int         nRet;

    //
    // Get protocol selection and
    // associated socket descriptor
    //
    hwndList = GetDlgItem(hwnd, IDC_SOCKETS);
    nIndex = ListBox_GetCurSel(hwndList);
    if (nIndex == LB_ERR)
    {
        MessageBox(hwnd,
                _TEXT("Please select a socket"),
                gszAppName, MB_OK);
        return;
    }
    if (nIndex > gNbrSockets)
    {
        MessageBox(hwnd,
                _TEXT("Internal error"),
                gszAppName, MB_OK);
        return;
    }

    lpInfo = (LPWSAPROTOCOL_INFO)gpProtocolBuf;
    lpInfo += nIndex;
    pSock = (SOCKET *)gpSockets;
    pSock += nIndex;
```

```c
    hwndEdit = GetDlgItem(hwnd, IDC_HOSTNAME);
    GetWindowText(hwndEdit, szHostName,
                  sizeof(szHostName) / sizeof(TCHAR));
    //
    // AF_INET family MUST have a host name
    //
    if (lpInfo->iAddressFamily == AF_INET)
    {
        if (!_tcslen(szHostName))
        {
            MessageBox(hwnd,
                       _TEXT("AF_INET Family requires a host name"),
                       _TEXT("Pleae enter a host name"),
                       MB_OK);
            SetFocus(hwndEdit);
            return;
        }
    }

    //
    // Find the host for this address family
    //
    if (!FindEchoServer(*pSock,
                        lpInfo,
                        &saHost,
                        sizeof(SOCKADDR),
                        szHostName))
    {
        MessageBox(hwnd,
                   _TEXT("Host not found for this socket"),
                   gszAppName, MB_OK);
        return;
    }

    //
    // Send an ECHO request
    //
    FillEchoRequest(&echoReq);
    nRet = p_sendto(*pSock,
                    (char *)&echoReq,
                    sizeof(ECHOREQ),
                    0,
                    &saHost,
                    sizeof(SOCKADDR));
    if (nRet == SOCKET_ERROR)
        ShowWinSockError(hwnd,
                         _TEXT("sendto()"),
                         p_WSAGetLastError());
}
```

Finding a Server

The SendEcho() function requires that the user supply a host name for sockets using the AF_INET address family. The reason for this can be found in the FindEchoServer() function. FindEchoServer() calls DWSVersion() to determine which version of WinSock was loaded.

- ◆ If only WinSock 1.1 functionality is available, FindEchoServer() uses the WinSock 1.1 database functions to resolve the host name or address and to find the ECHO port. This is one reason to require a host name for AF_INET sockets, but there is still another.

- ◆ If WinSock 2 is available, FindEchoServer() uses the new WSALookupServiceX() functions to find a service. For the AF_INET family, FindEchoServer() uses the special, predefined SVCID_ECHO_UDP GUID; for other protocols, the function uses its own GUID that is defined in AEGUID.H. This is the other reason to require a host name for AF_INET sockets.

The ECHO client program assumes that AF_INET sockets will search for a host using DNS. For other address families, the program hopes that a dynamic name space is being used and that the server developed later in this chapter is already registered. If the server has already registered for service on a dynamic name space using the service's GUID, then a name may not be necessary to find the service. If the user chooses a socket that does not belong to the AF_INET family, and the ECHO server developed in this chapter isn't registered on a dynamic or persistent name space, then the function will fail and the user will be notified that no host could be found.

Listing 12-7 presents the FindEchoServer() function.

Listing 12-7 The FindEchoServer() Function

```
BOOL FindEchoServer(SOCKET socket,
                    LPWSAPROTOCOL_INFO pInfo,
                    LPSOCKADDR pAddr,
                    int nAddrLen,
                    LPTSTR lpHostName)
{
    char            szHostName[256];
    WSAQUERYSET     qs;
    LPHOSTENT       lpHost;
    LPSERVENT       lpServ;
    LPSOCKADDR_IN   pInAddr;
    IN_ADDR         iaHost;
    DWORD           dwFlags;
    int             nRet;
    HANDLE          hLookup;
```

Chapter 12: Protocol-Independent Client and Server 409

```c
    BYTE            bufResult[2048];
    DWORD           dwLen;
    LPWSAQUERYSET   pqs;
    LPCSADDR_INFO   pcsa;
    GUID guidEchoUdp = SVCID_ECHO_UDP;

    //
    // If we're using WinSock 1.1 use the old functions
    //
    if (DWSVersion() == 1)
    {
        pInAddr = (LPSOCKADDR_IN)pAddr;

        //
        // If Unicode, convert lpHostName
        //
        #ifdef UNICODE
            WideCharToMultiByte(CP_ACP,
                                0,
                                lpHostName,
                                -1,
                                szHostName,
                                sizeof(szHostName),
                                NULL,
                                NULL);

        #else
            strcpy(szHostName, lpHostName);
        #endif
        //
        // Name might actually be an address
        // Use inet_addr to check
        //
        iaHost.s_addr = p_inet_addr(szHostName);
        if (iaHost.s_addr == INADDR_NONE)
        {
            // Wasn't an IP address string, assume it is a name
            lpHost= p_gethostbyname(szHostName);
        }
        else
        {
            // It was a valid IP address string
            lpHost = p_gethostbyaddr((const char *)&iaHost,
                                    sizeof(struct in_addr),
                                    AF_INET);
        }
        if (lpHost == NULL)
            return FALSE;
        //
        // Find the port
        //
        lpServ = p_getservbyname("echo", "udp");
        if (lpServ == NULL)
```

```c
            pInAddr->sin_port = p_htons(7);
        else
            pInAddr->sin_port = lpServ->s_port;
        pInAddr->sin_family = AF_INET;
        pInAddr->sin_addr = *((LPIN_ADDR)*lpHost->h_addr_list);
        return TRUE;
    }

    //
    // Workaround for IPX until SAP/NDS provider is released
    //
    if (pInfo->iAddressFamily == AF_IPX && DWSDnsOnly())
    {
        // Asumme IPX address as "NetworkNumber.NodeNumber"
        return(FillIpx((LPSOCKADDR_IPX)pAddr,
                        nAddrLen,
                        lpHostName));
    }


    //
    // Must be WinSock 2 - Use new service resolution functions
    //

    memset(&qs, 0, sizeof(WSAQUERYSET));
    qs.dwSize                  = sizeof(WSAQUERYSET);
    qs.lpszServiceInstanceName = lpHostName;
    qs.dwNameSpace             = NS_ALL;

    //
    // If it's an Internet address, assume DNS (non-dynamic)
    // Use special GUID for ECHO on UDP
    //
    // Otherwise, use our GUID from ..\aeguid.h
    //
    if (pInfo->iAddressFamily == AF_INET)
        qs.lpServiceClassId = &guidEchoUdp;
    else
        qs.lpServiceClassId = &guidAdapterEcho;

    //
    // Begin lookup
    //
    dwFlags = LUP_RETURN_NAME|LUP_RETURN_ADDR;
    nRet = p_WSALookupServiceBegin(&qs,
                                    dwFlags,
                                    &hLookup);
    if (nRet == SOCKET_ERROR)
    {
        ShowWinSockError(ghwnd,
                        _TEXT("LookupServiceBegin()"),
                        p_WSAGetLastError());
        return FALSE;
```

```
    }

    //
    // Use the first one found
    //
    dwFlags = LUP_RETURN_NAME|LUP_RETURN_ADDR;
    dwLen = sizeof(bufResult);
    nRet = p_WSALookupServiceNext(hLookup,
                                  dwFlags,
                                  &dwLen,
                                  (LPWSAQUERYSET)bufResult);
    if (nRet == SOCKET_ERROR)
    {
        nRet = p_WSAGetLastError();
        if (nRet != WSAENOMORE && nRet != WSA_E_NO_MORE)
            ShowWinSockError(ghwnd,
                        _TEXT("LookupServiceNext()"),
                        p_WSAGetLastError());
        p_WSALookupServiceEnd(hLookup);
        return FALSE;
    }

    //
    // Cast the result to a WSAQUERYSET pointer
    //
    pqs = (LPWSAQUERYSET)bufResult;

    //
    // Cast the lpcsaBuffer to a CSADDR_INFO pointer
    //
    pcsa = pqs->lpcsaBuffer;

    //
    // Check the length
    //
    if (pcsa->RemoteAddr.iSockaddrLength > nAddrLen)
    {
        MessageBox(NULL,
                   _TEXT("SOCKADDR too large"),
                   gszAppName, MB_OK);
        p_WSALookupServiceEnd(hLookup);
        return FALSE;
    }

    //
    // Copy the SOCKADDR
    //
    memcpy(pAddr,
           pcsa->RemoteAddr.lpSockaddr,
           pcsa->RemoteAddr.iSockaddrLength);
    p_WSALookupServiceEnd(hLookup);
    return TRUE;
}
```

> ### IPX Workaround
>
> As of this writing, Novell's SAP and NDS name space providers still aren't publicly available. Because Netware is so prevalent and because IPX (if it's available) will be chosen for use by these programs, I decided to add a special case for the AF_IPX address family.
>
> If the selected socket uses the AF_IPX address family and DWSDnsOnly() returns True, indicating that DNS is the only available name space provider, then the ECHO client program assumes the Service Name box will contain the server's network address and node number.
>
> For example, the machine with which I tested was node 000086095938 on network 0026d105. I was able to reach the server from the client by specifying this address for Service Name:
>
> 0026d105.000086095938
>
> This workaround is only necessary until the WinSock 2 SAP and NDS name space providers are released.

Receiving an ECHO Response

When the client receives an ECHO response, WinSock will generate an FD_READ notification. The HandleAsyncMsg() function will then call RecvEcho(), shown in Listing 12-8. This function receives the incoming data with p_recvfrom() and checks the contents to ensure that the data received is the same data sent. It also computes the time elapsed since the ECHO request was sent and adds a description to the ECHO list box.

Listing 12-8 The RecvEcho() Function

```
void RecvEcho(HWND hwnd, SOCKET socket, int nErrorCode)
{
    char        szBuf[256];
    HWND        hwndList;
    ECHOREQ     echoReq;
    SOCKADDR    saFrom;
    DWORD       dwElapsed;
    int         nFromLen;
    int         nCount;
    int         nRet;

    //
    // Receive the data from the server
    //
    nRet = p_recvfrom(socket,
```

```
                            (char *)&echoReq,
                            sizeof(echoReq),
                            0,
                            &saFrom,
                            &nFromLen);
    if (nRet == SOCKET_ERROR)
    {
        ShowWinSockError(hwnd,
                        _TEXT("recvfrom()"),
                        p_WSAGetLastError());
        return;
    }

    //
    // Check the request
    //
    for (nCount = 0; nCount < ECHODATASIZE; nCount++)
    {
        if (echoReq.nData[nCount] != nCount)
        {
            MessageBox(NULL,
                    _TEXT("Received ECHO is corrupted"),
                    gszAppName,
                    MB_OK);
            return;
        }
    }

    //
    // Add it to the ECHO listbox
    //
    hwndList = GetDlgItem(hwnd, IDC_ECHOS);
    dwElapsed = (GetTickCount() - echoReq.dwSentTime);

    wsprintf(szBuf,
            _TEXT("Seq: %ld Elapsed: %ld"),
            echoReq.dwSeq, dwElapsed);
    ListBox_AddString(hwndList, szBuf);
    return;
}
```

That's it for the ECHO client. The program strives to be as protocol dependent as it can be. It makes concessions for AF_INET protocols because it assumes they will be implemented on a host-centric rather than a service-centric name space.

The Socket Adapter ECHO Server

The ECHO server developed in this section dynamically links to WinSock just as the client does. If WinSock 2 is available, it searches for acceptable transport protocols and opens a listening socket for each; if only WinSock 1.1 is available, only a UDP socket is opened. The server simply waits for incoming datagrams and echoes them back to the sender. The server maintains statistics for the total number of datagrams received and a per-protocol total, as well.

The complete source code for the ECHO server application can be found in the \CH12\SERVER directory on the CD. The server uses asynchronous notification and is constructed much like the asynchronous server developed in Chapter 10. Almost all of the WinSock code is in ECHOSERV.C, and the user interface code is in ECHOUI.C.

The Server's User Interface

Like the client program, the ECHO server displays a dialog box for its main window (see Figure 12-2). The dialog maintains an Event Log that shows significant events as they occur. It also displays statistics for the total number of datagrams received and the total number of datagrams received through each protocol. The example in Figure 12-2 shows that the server started and is using WinSock 2, and is listening with two different sockets – one on UPD and another on Novell's IPX.

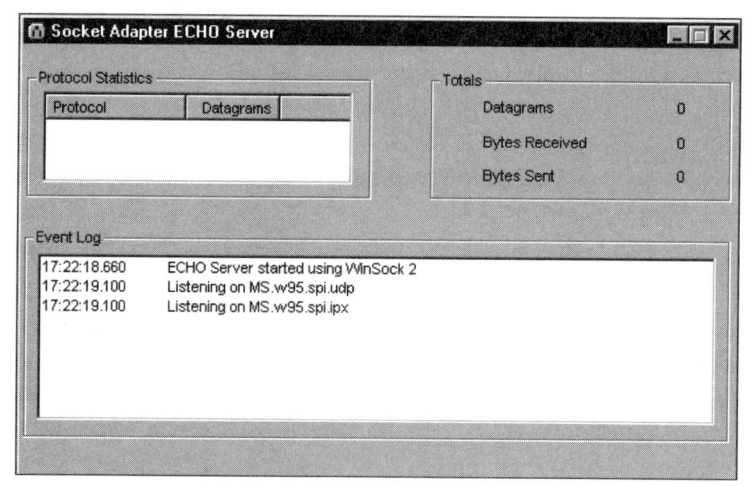

Figure 12-2: The Socket Adapter ECHO server running on WinSock 2

WinMain() calls DWSInitWinSock() when starting and DWSFreeWinSock() before exiting. No user parameters are required to start the server, so the OnInitDialog() function calls StartServer() as soon as the main window opens. The MainWndProc() passes WinSock asynchronous notification messages to a HandleAsyncMsg() function in the WinSock module. The WinSock module passes Windows messages back to the user interface whenever the statistics need to be updated or when a significant event has occurred.

The WinSock Module

Almost all of the WinSock code for the server is kept in ECHOSERV.C. Processing begins when the user interface calls StartServer(), which accepts a window handle that it uses with WSAAsyncSelect() as well as to send messages back to the user interface module. StartServer() also accepts two message IDs:

- The *uAsyMsg* parameter is used with WSAAsyncSelect() to register for asynchronous notification. The user interface module will dispatch all these messages to the HandleAsyncMsg() function in ECHOSERV.C.

- The *uAppMsg* parameter is used when the WinSock module wants to send messages back to the user interface.

Listing 12-9 presents the StartServer() function.

Listing 12-9 The StartServer() Function

```
BOOL StartServer(HWND hwnd, UINT uAsyMsg, UINT uAppMsg)
{
    LPSOCKETENTRY   lpEntry;
    TCHAR           szAddrStr[256];
    DWORD           dwStrLen;
    int             nRet;

    //
    // Save HWND and message for later use
    //
    ghwnd    = hwnd;
    guAsyMsg = uAsyMsg;
    guAppMsg = uAppMsg;

    LogEvent(hwnd, _TEXT("ECHO Server starting using WinSock %d"),
             DWSVersion());

    //
    // If there are Name Space providers other than
    // DNS, then install service class if not already installed
    //
    if (!DWSDnsOnly())
        InstallClass();

    //
    // Open a listening socket for each appropriate protocol
    //
    if (!OpenListeners(hwnd, uAsyMsg))
        return FALSE;

    //
    // If there are Name Space providers other than
```

Part IV: Applications

```
    // DNS, then advertise that we're starting
    //
    if (!DWSDnsOnly())
        SetEchoService(RNRSERVICE_REGISTER);

    //
    // Add listening socket descriptions to the listbox
    //
    lpEntry = GetFirstSocketEntry();
    dwStrLen = sizeof(szAddrStr) / sizeof(TCHAR);
    while(lpEntry != NULL)
    {
        nRet = DWSAddressToString(lpEntry->lpSockAddr,
                                  lpEntry->Info.iMaxSockAddr,
                                  szAddrStr,
                                  &dwStrLen);
        LogEvent(ghwnd, _TEXT("Listening on %s at %s"),
                 lpEntry->Info.szProtocol,
                 szAddrStr);
        lpEntry = GetNextSocketEntry(lpEntry);
    }
    return TRUE;
}
```

Once the window handle and message identifiers have been saved, StartServer() calls DWSDnsOnly() to determine if name spaces other than DNS are available. This function returns True if only WinSock 1.1 is available or if DNS was the only name space found with WSAEnumNameSpaceProviders(). If a name space other than DNS is available, the server ensures that its service class has been installed. We'll talk more about that later, in the section "Registering the Service."

OPENING LISTENING SOCKETS

StartServer() then calls OpenListeners(), which attempts to open a socket for each connectionless, message-oriented protocol installed on the machine. OpenListeners()then checks once again to see if name spaces other than DNS are available. If they are, then the function calls SetEchoService() to advertise the server's availability. The call to OpenListeners() built a linked list of socket descriptors containing an entry for each socket that was opened. StartServer traverses this linked list, adding descriptions of the listening sockets to the user interface's event log.

Listing 12-10 The OpenListeners() Function

```
BOOL OpenListeners(HWND hwnd, UINT uAsyMsg)
{
    LPSOCKETENTRY       lpEntry;
    LPWSAPROTOCOL_INFO  pInfo;
    LPBYTE              pProtocolBuf = NULL;
```

Chapter 12: Protocol-Independent Client and Server   417

```
    SOCKET              socket;
    TCHAR               szBuf[256];
    DWORD               dwNeededLen;
    int                 nCount;
    int                 nSockets;
    int                 nRet;

    //
    // Find all connectionless, message-oriented protocols
    // First, determine size for protocol buffer
    //
    dwNeededLen = 0;
    nRet = DWSSelectProtocols(XP1_CONNECTIONLESS |
                              XP1_MESSAGE_ORIENTED,
                              0,
                              NULL,
                              &dwNeededLen);
    if (nRet == SOCKET_ERROR)
    {
        if (p_WSAGetLastError() != WSAENOBUFS)
        {
            LogWinSockError(hwnd,
                            _TEXT("EnumProtocols 1"),
                            p_WSAGetLastError());
            return FALSE;
        }
    }

    //
    // Allocate the buffer
    //
    pProtocolBuf = malloc(dwNeededLen);
    if (pProtocolBuf == NULL)
    {
        MessageBox(hwnd,
                   _TEXT("Insufficient memory"),
                   _TEXT("OpenListeners()"),
                   MB_OK);
        return FALSE;
    }

    //
    // Make the "real" call
    //
    nRet = DWSSelectProtocols(XP1_CONNECTIONLESS |
                              XP1_MESSAGE_ORIENTED,
                              0,
                              (LPWSAPROTOCOL_INFO)pProtocolBuf,
                              &dwNeededLen);
    if (nRet == SOCKET_ERROR)
    {
        LogWinSockError(hwnd,
                        _TEXT("EnumProtocols 2"),
```

```
                            p_WSAGetLastError());
    return FALSE;
}

//
// Loop through the returned protocols
// creating socket descriptors and adding
// descriptions to the linked list
//
pInfo    = (LPWSAPROTOCOL_INFO)pProtocolBuf;
nSockets = nRet;
for(nCount = 0; nCount < nSockets; nCount++)
{
    socket = p_socket(pInfo->iAddressFamily,
                      pInfo->iSocketType,
                      pInfo->iProtocol);
    if (socket == INVALID_SOCKET)
    {
        wsprintf(szBuf,
                 _TEXT("socket() failed on %s"),
                 pInfo->szProtocol);
        LogWinSockError(hwnd,
                        szBuf,
                        p_WSAGetLastError());
        continue;
    }

    //
    // Add the socket to our list
    //
    lpEntry = AddSocketEntry(socket, pInfo);
    if (lpEntry == NULL)
    {
        MessageBox(hwnd,
                   _TEXT("Error adding socket to list"),
                   _TEXT("OpenListeners()"),
                   MB_OK);
        return FALSE;
    }

    //
    // Request async notification
    //
    nRet = p_WSAAsyncSelect(lpEntry->Socket,
                            ghwnd,
                            uAsyMsg,
                            FD_READ);
    if (nRet == SOCKET_ERROR)
    {
        wsprintf(szBuf,
                 _TEXT("WSAAsyncSelect() on %s"),
                 pInfo->szProtocol);
        LogWinSockError(hwnd, szBuf, p_WSAGetLastError());
```

Chapter 12: Protocol-Independent Client and Server 419

```
            p_closesocket(lpEntry->Socket);
            DelSocketEntry(lpEntry);
            continue;
        }


        //
        // Fill our local address so that we can bind()
        //
        if (!FillLocalAddress(lpEntry->Socket,
                              lpEntry->lpSockAddr,
                              pInfo))
        {
            LogEvent(hwnd,
                    _TEXT("Could not fill local address for %s"),
                    pInfo->szProtocol);
            p_closesocket(lpEntry->Socket);
            DelSocketEntry(lpEntry);
            continue;

        }

        //
        // bind local name to the socket
        //
        nRet = p_bind(lpEntry->Socket,
                      lpEntry->lpSockAddr,
                      lpEntry->Info.iMaxSockAddr);
        if (nRet == SOCKET_ERROR)
        {
            wsprintf(szBuf,
                    _TEXT("bind() error on %s"),
                    lpEntry->Info.szProtocol);
            LogWinSockError(ghwnd,
                            szBuf,
                            p_WSAGetLastError());
            p_closesocket(lpEntry->Socket);
            DelSocketEntry(lpEntry);
            return FALSE;
        }
        pInfo++;
    }
    //
    // Any sockets in the list?
    //
    lpEntry = GetFirstSocketEntry();
    if (lpEntry == NULL)
        return FALSE;
    else
        return TRUE;
}
```

420   Part IV: Applications

OpenListeners() begins by calling DWSSelectProtocols() to search for all available, connectionless, message-oriented protocols. If WinSock 2 was loaded, this function will use WSAEnumProtocols() in its search. If WinSock 2 couldn't be loaded, DWSSelectProtocols() will return only UDP, since that's the only officially supported WinSock 1.1 protocol that meets our criteria.

OpenListeners() then loops through each of the returned protocols and attempts to open a socket, using parameters from the individual protocol's WSAPROTOCOL_INFO entry. If this succeeds, OpenListeners() requests asynchronous notification for the socket and adds it to the linked list. It then calls FillLocalAddress() to initialize the SOCKADDR structure so that bind() can be called.

FILLING THE LOCAL ADDRESS

The FillLocalAddress() function attempts to initialize specific portions of a SOCKADDR so that it will bind() to an appropriate address. It looks for known address family identifiers in the *iAddressFamily* field of the protocol's WSAPROTOCOL_INFO structure. It then casts the generic SOCKADDR to a fully detailed SOCKADDR that is associated with the socket's address family, and fills in the specifics of the requested address. Listing 12-11 presents the FillLocalAddress() function.

Listing 12-11 The FillLocalAddress() Function

```
BOOL FillLocalAddress(SOCKET socket,
                      LPSOCKADDR lpAddr,
                      LPWSAPROTOCOL_INFO lpInfo)
{
    LPSERVENT        lpServEnt;
    LPSOCKADDR_IN    pInAddr;
    LPSOCKADDR_IPX   pIpxAddr;

    //
    // Fill in local address based on address family
    //
    switch (lpInfo->iAddressFamily)
    {
        case AF_INET:
            pInAddr = (LPSOCKADDR_IN)lpAddr;
            pInAddr->sin_family = AF_INET;
            pInAddr->sin_addr.s_addr = INADDR_ANY;
            //
            // Find a port number
            //
            lpServEnt = p_getservbyname("echo", "udp");
            if (lpServEnt != NULL)
                pInAddr->sin_port = lpServEnt->s_port;
            else
                // Default to well-known UDP ECHO port
                pInAddr->sin_port = p_htons(AE_UPDPORT);
            return TRUE;
```

```
            case AF_IPX:
                pIpxAddr = (LPSOCKADDR_IPX)lpAddr;
                memset(pIpxAddr->sa_netnum, 0,
                        sizeof(pIpxAddr->sa_netnum));
                memset(pIpxAddr->sa_nodenum, 0,
                        sizeof(pIpxAddr->sa_nodenum));
                pIpxAddr->sa_family = AF_IPX;
                pIpxAddr->sa_socket = p_htons(AE_IPXPORT);
                return TRUE;

            //
            // Fill in known values for other
            // address families here.
            //

            default:
                memset(lpAddr, 0, lpInfo->iMaxSockAddr);
                lpAddr->sa_family = lpInfo->iAddressFamily;
                return TRUE;
        }
        return FALSE;
}
```

The WinSock specification says that before calling bind(), a SOCKADDR can have only its address family field filled in, and the data portion set to ADDR_ANY (which is 0). This is acceptable for clients that don't have to designate anything in particular in their address. It's not sufficient, however, for servers that need to be specific about portions of their address — such as the UDP port number in this case. For this reason, a server must have some prior knowledge of the address families that it is going to support. In the FillLocalAddress() function in Listing 12-11, it is assumed that you have TCP/IP installed on your machine, so the specifics for the AF_INET family are filled in and the others are blank.

Other address families will still successfully bind(), but they accept whatever address WinSock gives them. This, too, may be okay for address families that are supported by dynamic name spaces. The reason for being specific about the server's address is only to allow clients to find the server. All of the listening sockets should have been opened before calling WSASetService(), so a server could just accept any available address from WinSock and then rely on dynamic or persistent name spaces to tell clients about the current address. Which brings us around again to the subject of service registration.

REGISTERING THE SERVICE

StartServer() checked to see if name spaces other than DNS were available, and if there were, it called InstallClass(). This function is included in the source here as a demonstration of one strategy. Alternatively, the steps performed by InstallClass() could be included in a separate installation program for the server and perhaps even for a client.

Part IV: Applications

If WinSock 2 is available, then the InstallClass() function will use the WSAGetServiceClassNameByClassId() function to determine if the service class has already been installed for this server. If it's not able to get the service class name, then this WSAGet... function assumes that the service class hasn't been installed. In that case it uses WSAInstallServiceClass() to install name-space-specific parameters for the service. This again points out that even though clients can operate almost completely without prior knowledge of any particular transport protocol, servers can't — they must know some details of their address strategy.

Listing 12-12 presents the InstallClass() function. I've filled in some parameters for DNS and SAP name spaces here as an example.

Note: As this book goes to press, the SAP name space provider hasn't been released — so I haven't been able to test this code. Watch Novell's Web site (www.novell.com) for further information.

Listing 12-12 The InstallClass() Function

```
void InstallClass(void)
{
    WSASERVICECLASSINFO sci;
    TCHAR               szBuf[256];
    DWORD               dwLen;
    WSANSCLASSINFO      nsciArray[4];
    DWORD               dwZero = 0;
    DWORD               dwPort;
    DWORD               dwSapId = AE_SAPID;
    LPSERVENT           lpServEnt;
    int                 nRet;

    //
    // If we're using WinSock 1.1,
    // we can't do this
    //
    if (DWSVersion() == 1)
        return;

    //
    // Has the class already been installed?
    //
    dwLen = sizeof(szBuf) / sizeof(TCHAR);
    nRet = p_WSAGetServiceClassNameByClassId(&guidAdapterEcho,
                                             szBuf,
                                             &dwLen);
    if (nRet != SOCKET_ERROR)
        return;

    //
    // Check for specific error
    //
    if (p_WSAGetLastError() != WSASERVICE_NOT_FOUND)
```

```
    {
        LogWinSockError(ghwnd,
                        _TEXT("Error retrieving class name"),
                        p_WSAGetLastError());
        //return;
    }


    //
    // Service class not found, install it
    //

    //
    // Fill in service class info
    //
    sci.lpServiceClassId = &guidAdapterEcho;
    sci.lpszServiceClassName = AE_SERVICECLASSNAME;
    sci.dwCount = 4;
    sci.lpClassInfos = nsciArray;

    //
    // DNS setup
    //

    // Connectionless
    nsciArray[0].lpszName = SERVICE_TYPE_VALUE_CONN;
    nsciArray[0].dwNameSpace = NS_DNS;
    nsciArray[0].dwValueType = REG_DWORD;
    nsciArray[0].dwValueSize = sizeof(DWORD);
    nsciArray[0].lpValue     = &dwZero;

    // Port number
    lpServEnt = p_getservbyname("echo", "udp");
    if (lpServEnt != NULL)
        dwPort = p_ntohs(lpServEnt->s_port);
    else
        dwPort = AE_UPDPORT;
    nsciArray[1].lpszName = SERVICE_TYPE_VALUE_UDPPORT;
    nsciArray[1].dwNameSpace = NS_DNS;
    nsciArray[1].dwValueType = REG_DWORD;
    nsciArray[1].dwValueSize = sizeof(DWORD);
    nsciArray[1].lpValue     = &dwPort;


    //
    // Novell SAP setup
    //

    // Connectionless
    nsciArray[2].lpszName = SERVICE_TYPE_VALUE_CONN;
    nsciArray[2].dwNameSpace = NS_SAP;
    nsciArray[2].dwValueType = REG_DWORD;
    nsciArray[2].dwValueSize = sizeof(DWORD);
```

Part IV: Applications

```
            nsciArray[2].lpValue      = &dwZero;
            // SAP ID
            nsciArray[3].lpszName = SERVICE_TYPE_VALUE_SAPID;
            nsciArray[3].dwNameSpace = NS_SAP;
            nsciArray[3].dwValueType = REG_DWORD;
            nsciArray[3].dwValueSize = sizeof(DWORD);
            nsciArray[3].lpValue      = &dwSapId;

            //
            // Add parameters for other name spaces here
            //

            //
            // Install the new class
            //
            nRet = p_WSAInstallServiceClass(&sci);
            if (nRet == SOCKET_ERROR)
            {
                LogWinSockError(ghwnd,
                                _TEXT("Could not install service class"),
                                p_WSAGetLastError());
            }
      }
```

If a name space other than DNS is available, StartServer() calls SetEchoService() *after* the listening sockets have been opened. This function fills in a WSAQUERY-SET structure and then loops through the linked list of listening sockets, building a CSADDR_INFO structure for each one. All of this address information is then registered with the WSASetService() function. Using code such as this in SetEchoService(), a server with access to a dynamic name space can advertise the exact address where it can be found. Clients can then find the server using only a GUID and service name. Listing 12-13 presents the SetEchoService() function.

Listing 12-13 The SetEchoService() Function

```
void SetEchoService(WSAESETSERVICEOP essOp)
{
      LPBYTE              lpcsaBuffer;
      LPBYTE              lpAddrBuffer;
      LPSOCKETENTRY       lpEntry;
      LPCSADDR_INFO       lpCsa;
      LPSOCKADDR          lpAddr;
      WSAQUERYSET         qs;
      WSAVERSION          Version;
      int                 nNbrAddresses;
      int                 nTotalAddrSize;
      int                 nRet;

      //
      // If we're using WinSock 1.1,
```

```
    // we can't do this
    //
    if (DWSVersion() == 1)
        return;

    //
    // If we don't have any sockets,
    // we don't have anything to advertise
    //
    lpEntry = GetFirstSocketEntry();
    if (lpEntry == NULL)
        return;

    //
    // Count the number of addresses we
    // have available and the total space
    // needed to hold all SOCKADDRs
    //
    nNbrAddresses = 0;
    nTotalAddrSize = 0;
    while(lpEntry != NULL)
    {
        nNbrAddresses++;
        nTotalAddrSize += lpEntry->Info.iMaxSockAddr;
        lpEntry = GetNextSocketEntry(lpEntry);
    }

    //
    // Allocate a buffer for the CSADDR_INFO structures
    //
    lpcsaBuffer = malloc(sizeof(CSADDR_INFO)*nNbrAddresses);
    if (lpcsaBuffer == NULL)
    {
        LogEvent(ghwnd,
                _TEXT("Advertise(): No memory for CSADDR_INFO"));
        return;
    }
    lpCsa = (LPCSADDR_INFO)lpcsaBuffer;

    //
    // Allocate a buffer for a copy of all the SOCKADDRs
    //
    lpAddrBuffer = malloc(nTotalAddrSize);
    if (lpAddrBuffer == NULL)
    {
        LogEvent(ghwnd,
                _TEXT("Advertise(): No memory for SOCKADDRs"));
        free(lpcsaBuffer);
        return;
    }
    lpAddr = (LPSOCKADDR)lpAddrBuffer;

    //
```

```
    // Loop through our addresses, filling
    // in the CSADDR_INFO structures
    //
    lpEntry = GetFirstSocketEntry();
    while(lpEntry != NULL)
    {
        lpCsa->iProtocol   = lpEntry->Info.iProtocol;
        lpCsa->iSocketType = lpEntry->Info.iSocketType;

        // Copy the SOCKADDR
        memcpy(lpAddr,
               lpEntry->lpSockAddr,
               lpEntry->Info.iMaxSockAddr);

        lpCsa->LocalAddr.iSockaddrLength =
                        lpEntry->Info.iMaxSockAddr;
        lpCsa->RemoteAddr.iSockaddrLength =
                        lpEntry->Info.iMaxSockAddr;

        lpCsa->LocalAddr.lpSockaddr  = lpAddr;
        lpCsa->RemoteAddr.lpSockaddr = lpAddr;

        //
        // Move to next entries in buffers
        //
        lpAddr += lpEntry->Info.iMaxSockAddr;
        lpCsa++;
        lpEntry = GetNextSocketEntry(lpEntry);
    }

    //
    // Register service for availability
    //
    memset(&qs, 0, sizeof(WSAQUERYSET));
    qs.dwSize                = sizeof(WSAQUERYSET);
    qs.lpszServiceInstanceName = AE_INSTANCENAME;
    qs.lpServiceClassId      = &guidAdapterEcho;
    qs.lpVersion             = &Version;
            Version.dwVersion = 1;
            //Version.ecHow   = COMP_NOTLESS;
    qs.dwNameSpace           = NS_ALL;
    qs.dwNumberOfCsAddrs     = nNbrAddresses;
    qs.lpcsaBuffer           = (LPCSADDR_INFO)lpcsaBuffer;

    nRet = p_WSASetService(&qs,
                           essOp,
                           SERVICE_MULTIPLE);
    if (nRet == SOCKET_ERROR)
    {
        nRet = p_WSAGetLastError();
        LogWinSockError(ghwnd,
                        _TEXT("SetService()"),
                        p_WSAGetLastError());
```

```
    }
    free(lpcsaBuffer);
    free(lpAddrBuffer);
}
```

Receiving an ECHO Request

When data arrives for one of the listening sockets, WinSock posts an FD_READ notification. The MainWndProc() in the user interface module forwards this message to HandleAsyncMsg(), which in turn calls RecvAndEcho().

RecvAndEcho(), shown in Listing 12-14, receives the data and the source address in a call to p_recvfrom(). It then simply sends the received data back to the client with p_sendto(). Once the data has been echoed back to the client, RecvAndEcho() updates the user interface with statistics information and an event log entry showing the sending entity's address.

Listing 12-14 The RecvAndEcho() Function

```
void RecvAndEcho(SOCKET socket, int nErrorCode)
{
    LPSOCKETENTRY   lpEntry;
    BYTE            buf[2048];
    TCHAR           szAddrStr[256];
    DWORD           dwStrLen;
    int             nAddrLen;
    int             nBytes;
    int             nRet;
    STATS           stats;

    //
    // Retrieve the SOCKETENTRY
    //
    lpEntry = GetSocketEntry(socket);
    if (lpEntry == NULL)
    {
        LogEvent(ghwnd,
                 _TEXT("RecvAndEcho(): Entry not found for %d"),
                 socket);
        return;
    }

    //
    // Receive the data from the client
    //
    nAddrLen = lpEntry->Info.iMaxSockAddr;
    nRet = p_recvfrom(socket,
                     buf,
                     sizeof(buf),
                     0,
```

```
                        lpEntry->lpSockAddr,
                        &nAddrLen);
    if (nRet == SOCKET_ERROR)
    {
        LogWinSockError(ghwnd,
                        _TEXT("recvfrom() error"),
                        p_WSAGetLastError());
        return;
    }

    nBytes = nRet;

    //
    // Echo the same data back
    //
    nRet = p_sendto(socket,
                    buf,
                    nBytes,
                    0,
                    lpEntry->lpSockAddr,
                    nAddrLen);
    if (nRet == SOCKET_ERROR)
    {
        LogWinSockError(ghwnd,
                        _TEXT("sendto() error"),
                        p_WSAGetLastError());
        return;
    }

    //
    // Convert the address to a display string
    //
    dwStrLen = sizeof(szAddrStr) / sizeof(TCHAR);
    nRet = DWSAddressToString(lpEntry->lpSockAddr,
                              nAddrLen,
                              szAddrStr,
                              &dwStrLen);
    if (nRet == SOCKET_ERROR)
    {
        LogWinSockError(ghwnd,
                        _TEXT("AddressToString()"),
                        p_WSAGetLastError());
    }
    LogEvent(ghwnd,
             _TEXT("%d bytes echoed to %s using %s"),
             nBytes,
             szAddrStr,
             lpEntry->Info.szProtocol);
    //
    // Update the statistics
    //
    stats.dwDatagrams = 1;
    stats.dwRecv      = nBytes;
```

```
    stats.dwSend      = nBytes;
    stats.pInfo       = &lpEntry->Info;
    SendMessage(ghwnd,
                guAppMsg,
                ECHO_STATS_MSG,
                (LPARAM)&stats);
}
```

Summary

In this chapter we created a client application and a server application that are both protocol independent and WinSock version independent.

By using explicit, dynamic linking, we were able to construct applications that would use WinSock 2 when available, yet would not fail when the Version 2 functionality was not present. The Socket Adapter Library developed in this chapter can be used to allow applications to take advantage of protocol independence and overlapped I/O when it is available, and quietly revert to WinSock 1.1 functionality when it's not.

You have seen that client applications can operate with almost no prior knowledge of transport protocols; servers must, nevertheless, know some specifics of different address families. Remember, some of the code presented here for service registration and name resolution is for example purposes only. As the WinSock 2 specification matures and more vendors make WinSock 2 products available, these service registration and resolution functions will become even more useful.

WinSock 2 is quickly gaining momentum and will almost assuredly become *the* API to use for any type of network programming in Windows. We finally have one API that can be used on virtually any type of network. Several major vendors are busy right now making products for WinSock 2. Watch my Web site (www.sockaddr.com) for updates. I'll be posting new information there as it becomes available.

Quick Reference to WinSock Functions, Structures, and Errors

This Quick Reference provides a comprehensive listing of all functions, data structures, and error codes in both WinSock Versions 1.1 and 2.2.

Function Reference

The following function reference isn't meant as a replacement for the WinSock specification, which provides the most comprehensive and detailed information you will need to use the WinSock functions. This list tells you which WinSock versions support each function, and the minimum amount of information needed to construct a function call: a one-line description, a list of parameters, and a description of the return values.

accept   1.1   2.2

Accepts a connection request on a listening socket.

```
SOCKET WSAAPI accept(
    SOCKET s,
    struct sockaddr FAR * addr,
    int FAR * addrlen
);
```

PARAMETERS

s	Socket descriptor for a listening socket.
addr	An optional pointer to a buffer that receives the address of the client requesting the connection.
addrlen	An optional pointer to an integer containing the length of the address pointed to by *addr*.

431

RETURN VALUES
A new SOCKET that is connected to the peer or INVALID_SOCKET.

bind   1.1   2.2

Associates a local address with a socket.

```
int WSAAPI bind(
    SOCKET s,
    const struct sockaddr FAR * name,
    int namelen
);
```

PARAMETERS

s   A socket descriptor for an unbound socket.

name   A pointer to an initialized SOCKADDR structure to assign the socket.

namelen   The length of the SOCKADDR structure pointed to by *name*.

RETURN VALUES
0 or SOCKET_ERROR.

closesocket   1.1   2.2

Closes a socket.

```
int WSAAPI closesocket(
    SOCKET s
);
```

PARAMETERS

s   The socket descriptor to close.

RETURN VALUES
0 or SOCKET_ERROR

connect   1.1   2.2

Establishes a connection to a specified socket.

```
int WSAAPI connect(
    SOCKET s,
    const struct sockaddr FAR * name,
    int namelen
);
```

PARAMETERS

s A socket descriptor for an unconnected socket.

name A pointer to a SOCKADDR structure that contains address information for the peer socket.

namelen The length of the SOCKADDR pointed to by *name*.

RETURN VALUES
0 or SOCKET_ERROR

gethostbyaddr   1.1   2.2

Returns a HOSTENT structure for the given address.

```
struct hostent FAR * WSAAPI gethostbyaddr(
    const char FAR * addr,
    int len,
    int type
);
```

PARAMETERS

addr A pointer to an address in network byte order.

len The length of the address pointed to by *addr*.

type An integer identifying the type of address pointed to by *addr*. AF_INET, AF_IPX, and so forth.

RETURN VALUES
A pointer to a HOSTENT structure or NULL.

gethostbyname 1.1 2.2

Returns a HOSTENT structure for the given host name.

```
struct hostent FAR * WSAAPI gethostbyname(
    const char FAR * name
};
```

PARAMETERS

name   A pointer to a null-terminated character array that identifies the host.

RETURN VALUES
A pointer to a HOSTENT structure or NULL.

gethostname 1.1 2.2

Returns the name of the local machine.

```
int WSAAPI gethostname(
    char FAR * name,
    int namelen
};
```

PARAMETERS

name   A pointer to a buffer that will receive the host name.

namelen   The length of the buffer pointed to by *name*.

RETURN VALUES
0 or SOCKET_ERROR

getpeername 1.1 2.2

Retrieves the address of the peer to which a socket is connected.

```
int WSAAPI getpeername(
    SOCKET s,
    struct sockaddr FAR * name,
    int FAR * namelen
);
```

PARAMETERS

s A socket descriptor for a connected socket.

name A pointer to a buffer that will receive a SOCKADDR structure.

namelen The length of buffer pointed to by *name*.

RETURN VALUES
0 or SOCKET_ERROR

getprotobyname 1.1 2.2

Returns a PROTOENT structure for a given protocol name.

```
struct protoent FAR * WSAAPI getprotobyname(
    const char FAR * name
);
```

PARAMETERS

name A pointer to a null-terminated character array that identifies a protocol.

RETURN VALUES
A pointer to a PROTOENT structure or NULL.

getprotobynumber 1.1   2.2

Returns a PROTOENT structure for a given protocol number.

```
struct protoent FAR * WSAAPI getprotobynumber(
    int number
);
```

PARAMETERS

number   A protocol number in host byte order. IPPROTO_IP, IPPROTO_ICMP, NSPROTO_IPX, and so forth.

RETURN VALUES
A pointer to a PROTOENT structure or NULL.

getservbyname 1.1   2.2

Returns a SERVENT structure for the given service name and protocol.

```
struct servent FAR * WSAAPI getservbyname(
    const char FAR * name,
    const char FAR * proto
);
```

PARAMETERS

name   A pointer to a null-terminated character array that identifies the service.

proto   An optional pointer to a null-terminated character array that identifies a protocol. If this parameter is NULL, the function returns the first entry that matches the *name* parameter only.

RETURN VALUES
A pointer to a SERVENT structure or NULL.

getservbyport   1.1   2.2

Returns a SERVENT structure for a given port number and protocol.

```
struct servent FAR * WSAAPI getservbyport(
    int port,
    const char FAR * proto
);
```

PARAMETERS

port   A port number in network byte order.

proto   An optional pointer to a null-terminated character array that identifies a protocol. If this parameter is NULL, the function returns the first entry that matches the *port* parameter.

RETURN VALUES
A pointer to a SERVENT structure or NULL.

getsockname   1.1   2.2

Returns a SOCKADDR containing the local address of the given socket.

```
int WSAAPI getsockname(
    SOCKET s,
    struct sockaddr FAR * name,
    int FAR * namelen
);
```

PARAMETERS

s   A socket descriptor for a bound socket.

name   A pointer to a buffer that will receive the SOCKADDR structure.

namelen   The length of the buffer pointed to by *name*.

RETURN VALUES
0 or SOCKET_ERROR

getsockopt   1.1   2.2

Returns the value for a given socket option.

```
int WSAAPI getsockopt(
    SOCKET s,
    int level,
    int optname,
    char FAR * optval,
    int FAR * optlen
};
```

PARAMETERS

s	A socket descriptor.
level	The level at which the option is defined. SOL_SOCKET or IPPROTO_TCP.
optname	The socket option name (see Table QR-1).
optval	A pointer to a buffer that will receive the option information.
optlen	The length of the buffer pointed to by *optval*.

RETURN VALUES
0 or SOCKET_ERROR

TABLE QR-1 SOCKET OPTIONS USED WITH getsockopt()

Option Name	Data Type	Description	1.1	2.2
Level = SO_SOCKET:				
PVD_CONFIG	Service Provider Dependent	Points to a service provider specific data structure.		•
SO_ACCEPTCONN	BOOL	Will socket accept() a connection? (Has listen() been called?)	•	•
SO_BROADCAST	BOOL	Should the socket be allowed to send broadcast messages?	•	•

Option Name	Data Type	Description	1.1	2.2
SO_DEBUG (optional)	BOOL	Is debug output enabled?	Optional	•
SO_DONTLINGER	BOOL	Should the socket block while waiting for closesocket() to complete?	•	•
SO_DONTROUTE	BOOL	Should WinSock bypass the protocol routing mechanisms?	•	•
SO_ERROR	int	Retrieve and then clear the error status for the socket.	•	•
SO_KEEPALIVE	BOOL	Should WinSock send "keepalive" requests for the socket?	•	•
SO_LINGER	struct linger	Should the socket block while waiting for closesocket() to complete? And if so, for how long?	•	•
SO_MAX_MSG_SIZE	unsigned int	Maximum outbound datagram size. Only valid for message-oriented sockets. (No way to determine maximum inbound size.)		•
SO_OOBINLINE	BOOL	Receive out-of-band data for the socket in the normal data stream?	•	•
SO_PROTOCOL_INFO	WSAPROTOCOL_INFO	Information about the protocol in use with this socket.		•
SO_RCVBUF	int	Size of the buffer used for receiving data.	Optional	•

(continued)

Option Name	Data Type	Description	1.1	2.2
SO_REUSEADDR	BOOL	Should other sockets be allowed to use this socket's address?	•	•
SO_SNDBUF	int	Size of buffer used for sending data.	Optional	•
SO_TYPE	int	Retrieve the socket type. (SOCK_STREAM, SOCK_DGRAM, and so forth.)	•	•
Level = IPPROTO_TCP:				
TCP_NODELAY	BOOL	Use Nagle algorithm for send coalescing?	•	•

htonl   1.1   2.2

Converts an unsigned long integer to TCP/IP network byte order.

```
u_long WSAAPI htonl(
    u_long hostlong
);
```

PARAMETERS

hostlong   A 32-bit integer in host byte order.

RETURN VALUES
The *hostlong* parameter converted to TCP/IP (big-endian) byte order.

htons   1.1   2.2

Converts an unsigned short integer to TCP/IP network byte order.

```
u_short WSAAPI htons(
    u_short hostshort
);
```

PARAMETERS

hostshort   A 16-bit integer in host byte order.

RETURN VALUES
The *hostshort* value converted to TCP/IP (big-endian) network byte order.

inet_addr   1.1   2.2

Converts an IPv4 address in dot-quad notation to an unsigned long.

```
unsigned long WSAAPI inet_addr(
    const char FAR * cp
);
```

PARAMETERS

cp   A pointer to a null-terminated character array containing the string representation of the address.

RETURN VALUES
The converted address or INADDR_NONE.

inet_ntoa   1.1   2.2

Converts an in_addr structure to a human-readable string.

```
char FAR * WSAAPI inet_ntoa(
    struct in_addr in
);
```

PARAMETERS

in   A pointer to an *in_addr* structure containing an IPv4 address.

RETURN VALUES
A pointer to a static character string or NULL.

ioctlsocket   1.1   2.2

Controls the I/O mode of a socket.

```
int WSAAPI ioctlsocket(
    SOCKET s,
    long cmd,
    u_long FAR * argp
};
```

PARAMETERS

s	A socket descriptor.
cmd	One of the predefined command codes in Tables QR-2 and QR-3.
argp	A pointer to the parameter to be used for the command.

RETURN VALUES
0 or SOCKET_ERROR

TABLE QR-2   COMMANDS AVAILABLE IN VERSION 1.1 AND 2.2

FIONBIO	Enable or disable nonblocking mode. If *argp* points to 1, nonblocking mode is enabled. If *argp* points to 0, nonblocking mode is disabled.
FIONREAD	Returns the amount of data waiting to be read on the socket. On stream-oriented sockets, *argp* will be set to number of bytes waiting. On message-oriented sockets, *argp* will be set to the size of the first datagram queued to be read.
SIOCATMARK	Determines if all available out-of-band data has been read.

TABLE QR-3 COMMANDS AVAILABLE IN VERSION 2.2 ONLY

SIO_ASSOCIATE_HANDLE	Associates a socket with the handle of a companion interface.
SIO_ENABLE_CIRCULAR_QUEUEING	Indicates to the underlying message-oriented service provider that a newly arrived message should never be dropped because of a buffer queue overflow.
SIO_FIND_ROUTE	Requests that the route to the remote address be discovered.
SIO_FLUSH	Discards current contents of the sending queue associated with a socket.
SIO_GET_BROADCAST_ADDRESS	Fills a buffer with a sockaddr struct containing a suitable broadcast address for use with sendto() or WSASendTo().
SIO_GET_EXTENSION_FUNCTION_POINTER	Retrieves a pointer to a vendor-specific extension function.
SIO_GET_QOS	Retrieves current flow specifications for the socket.
SIO_MULTIPOINT_LOOKBACK	Controls whether data sent in a multipoint session will also be received by the same socket on the local host.
SIO_MULTICAST_SCOPE	Specifies the scope over which multicast transmissions will occur.
SIO_SET_QOS	Establishes new flow specifications for the socket.
SIO_TRANSLATE_HANDLE	Obtains a corresponding handle for a socket that is valid in the context of a companion interface. (This is protocol specific.)

listen 1.1 2.2

Places a socket into passive, listening mode and establishes the size of the pending connection queue.

```
int WSAAPI listen(
    SOCKET s,
    int backlog
);
```

PARAMETERS

s A descriptor for a bound unconnected socket.

backlog Maximum number of incoming connection requests for WinSock to queue before automatically returning the WSAECONNREFUSED error to unanswered connection request. Usually specified by using the predefined SOMAXCONN value.

RETURN VALUES
0 or SOCKET_ERROR

ntohl 1.1 2.2

Converts an unsigned long integer to host byte order.

```
u_long WSAAPI ntohl(
    u_long netlong
);
```

PARAMETERS

netlong A 32-bit integer in TCP/IP (big-endian) byte order.

RETURN VALUES
The *netlong* value converted to host byte order.

ntohs   1.1   2.2

Converts a short integer to host byte order.

```
u_short WSAAPI ntohs(
    u_short netshort
);
```

PARAMETERS

netshort   A 16-bit integer in TCP/IP (big-endian) byte order.

RETURN VALUES
The *netshort* value converted to host byte order.

recv   1.1   2.2

Receives data on a connected socket.

```
int WSAAPI recv(
    SOCKET s,
    char FAR * buf,
    int len,
    int flags
);
```

PARAMETERS

s   A descriptor for a connected socket.

buf   A pointer to a buffer that will receive the data.

len   The length of the buffer pointed to by *buf*.

flags   One of the predefined options (Table QR-4) or 0.

RETURN VALUES
0 or SOCKET_ERROR

Table QR-4 recv() FLAGS

MSG_PEEK	Receive waiting data, but do not remove it from the socket's queue. The same data will be retrieved again in the next call to recv().
MSG_OOB	Receive out-of-band data.

recvfrom   1.1   2.2

Receives data and the sender's address.

```
int WSAAPI recvfrom(
    SOCKET s,
    char FAR * buf,
    int len,
    int flags,
    struct sockaddr FAR * from,
    int FAR * fromlen
);
```

PARAMETERS

s	A descriptor for a bound socket.
buf	A pointer to a buffer that will receive the data.
len	The length of the buffer pointed to by *buf*.
flags	One of several predefined options (see Table QR-4) or 0.
from	An optional pointer to a buffer that will receive the sender's address.
fromlen	The length of the buffer pointed to by *from*.

RETURN VALUES
0 or SOCKET_ERROR

select   1.1   2.2

Determines the status of one or more sockets.

```
int WSAAPI select(
    int nfds,
    fd_set FAR * readfds,
    fd_set FAR * writefds,
    fd_set FAR *exceptfds,
    const struct timeval FAR * timeout
};
```

PARAMETERS

nfds	Ignored; provided only for compatibility with BSD sockets.
readfds	An optional pointer to an *fd_set* of sockets to be checked for readability.
writefds	An optional pointer to an *fd_set* of sockets to be checked for writeability.
exceptfds	An optional pointer to an *fd_set* of sockets to be checked for errors.
timeout	An optional pointer to a TIMEVAL structure defining the maximum time for select() to block. If NULL, select() blocks until an event occurs.

RETURN VALUES

The total number of descriptors that meet the specified criteria, or 0 if the timeout value expired, or SOCKET_ERROR.

send   1.1   2.2

Sends data on a connected socket.

```
int WSAAPI send(
    SOCKET s,
    const char FAR * buf,
    int len,
    int flags
};
```

PARAMETERS

s	A descriptor for a connected socket.
buf	A pointer to a buffer that contains the data to be sent.
len	The length of the data in *buf*.
flags	One of the predefined options in Table QR-5, or 0.

RETURN VALUES
0 or SOCKET_ERROR

TABLE QR-5 send() FLAGS

MSG_DONTROUTE	Bypass the standard internal routing tables.
MSG_OOB	Send data out-of-band.

sendto   1.1   2.2

Sends data to the specified address.

```
int WSAAPI sendto(
    SOCKET s,
    const char FAR * buf,
    int len,
    int flags,
    const struct sockaddr FAR * to,
    int tolen
};
```

PARAMETERS

s	A socket descriptor.
buf	A pointer to a buffer that contains the data to be sent.
len	The length of the data in *buf*.
flags	One of the predefined options in Table QR-5, or 0.
to	A pointer to a SOCKADDR structure that has been initialized with the recipient's address.
tolen	The length of the SOCKADDR structure pointed to by *to*.

RETURN VALUES
0 or SOCKET_ERROR

setsockopt   1.1   2.2

Sets the value for a given socket option.

```
int WSAAPI setsockopt(
    SOCKET s,
    int level,
    int optname,
    const char FAR * optval,
    int optlen
);
```

PARAMETERS

s	The socket descriptor for which you want to change an option value.
level	The protocol level to which the option belongs.
optname	The option to set (from Table QR-6).
optval	A pointer to a buffer containing the new value for the option. The appropriate size for this buffer depends on the option being set.
optlen	The length of the buffer referenced by *optval*.

RETURN VALUES
0 or SOCKET_ERROR

TABLE QR-6 SOCKET OPTIONS USED WITH setsockopt()

Option Name	Data Type	Description	1.1	2.2
Level = SO_SOCKET:				
PVD_CONFIG	Service provider dependent	A service provider specific data structure.	•	
SO_BROADCAST	BOOL	Should the socket be allowed to send broadcast messages?	•	•
SO_DEBUG (optional)	BOOL	Is debug output enabled?	Optional	•

(continued)

TABLE QR-6 (CONTINUED)

Option Name	Data Type	Description	1.1	2.2
SO_DONTLINGER	BOOL	Should the socket block while waiting for closesocket() to complete?	•	•
SO_DONTROUTE	BOOL	Should WinSock bypass the protocol routing mechanisms?	•	•
SO_KEEPALIVE	BOOL	Should WinSock send "keepalive" requests for the socket?	•	•
SO_LINGER	struct linger	Should the socket block while waiting for closesocket() to complete? And if so, for how long?	•	•
SO_OOBINLINE	BOOL	Receive out-of-band data for the socket in the normal data stream?	•	•
SO_RCVBUF	int	Size of the buffer used for receiving data.	Optional	•
SO_REUSEADDR	BOOL	Should other sockets be allowed to use this socket's address?	•	•
SO_SNDBUF	int	Set the size of buffer used for sending data.	Optional	•
SO_TYPE	int	Retrieve the socket type. (SOCK_STREAM, SOCK_DGRAM, and so forth.)	•	•

(continued)

TABLE QR-6 (CONTINUED)

Level = IPPROTO_TCP:

TCP_NODELAY	Use the Nagle algorithm for send coalescing?	•	•

shutdown   1.1   2.2

Disables sending or receiving on a socket or both.

```
int WSAAPI shutdown(
    SOCKET s,
    int how
);
```

PARAMETERS

s   A socket descriptor.

how   Operation to perform:
                SD_SEND: Disable sending.
                SD_RECEIVE: Disable receiving.
                SD_BOTH: Disable both.

RETURN VALUES
0 or SOCKET_ERROR

socket   1.1   2.2

Creates a socket descriptor.

```
SOCKET WSAAPI socket(
    int af,
    int type,
    int protocol
);
```

PARAMETERS

af   Address family. AF_INET, AF_IPX, and so forth.

type	Socket type. SOCK_STREAM, SOCK_DGRAM, and so forth.
protocol	Protocol. IPPROTO_TCP, NSPROTO_IPX, and so forth.

RETURN VALUES
Socket descriptor or INVALID_SOCKET.

WSAAccept   2.2

Accepts a connection request on a listening socket. Optionally, allows an application-defined procedure to determine if a new connection request will be accepted or denied based on the caller information passed in as parameters. May also be used to provide QOS flowspecs or transfer connection data.

```
SOCKET WSAAPI WSAAccept(
    SOCKET s,
    struct sockaddr FAR * addr,
    LPINT addrlen,
    LPCONDITIONPROC lpfnCondition,
    DWORD dwCallbackData
};
```

PARAMETERS

s	Socket descriptor for a listening socket.
*struct sockaddr FAR * addr,*	An optional pointer to a buffer that receives the address of the client requesting the connection.
addrlen	An optional pointer to an integer that specifies the length of the buffer pointed to by *addr*.
lpfnCondition	An optional pointer to an application-defined acceptance function.
dwCallbackData	The application-specific data passed back to the application as the value of the *dwCallbackData* parameter of the condition function.

RETURN VALUES
A socket descriptor or INVALID_SOCKET.

WSAAddressToString   2.2

Converts a SOCKADDR structure to a human-readable form as appropriate for the SOCKADDR's address family.

```
INT WSAAPI WSAAddressToString(
    LPSOCKADDR          lpsaAddress,
    DWORD               dwAddressLength,
    LPWSAPROTOCOL_INFO  lpProtocolInfo,
    LPSTR               lpszAddressString,
    LPDWORD             lpdwAddressStringLength
};
```

PARAMETERS

lpsaAddress	A pointer to a SOCKADDR structure containing the address to be converted.
dwAddressLength	The length of the SOCKADDR structure pointed to by *lpsaAddress*.
lpProtocolInfo	An optional pointer to a WSAPROTOCOL_INFO structure designating the protocol and provider to be used for translating the address. If this is NULL, the first provider that supports the SOCKADDR's *sa_family* will be used.
lpszAddressString	A pointer to a buffer that will receive the translated address.
lpdwAddressStringLength	On input, a pointer to a 32-bit integer indicating the size of the *lpszAddressString* parameter. On output, the number of characters copied into the buffer.

RETURN VALUES
0 or SOCKET_ERROR

WSAAsyncGetHostByAddr   1.1   2.2

Asynchronously retrieves a HOSTENT structure and all of its related information for a given address.

```
HANDLE WSAAPI WSAAsyncGetHostByAddr(
    HWND hWnd,
    u_int wMsg,
    const char FAR * addr,
    int len,
    int type,
    char FAR * buf,
    int buflen
};
```

PARAMETERS

hWnd The handle of the window that will receive a message when the asynchronous request has completed.

wMsg The user-defined message that will be posted to the window.

addr A pointer to an address in network byte order.

len The length of the address pointed to by *addr*.

type The type of address. AF_INET, AF_IPX, and so forth.

buf A pointer to a buffer that will receive the *hostent* data. Note that this must be larger than the size of a *hostent* structure. On successful completion, this buffer will contain not only a *hostent* structure but all of the strings referenced in the *hostent* structure as well. Ensure that this buffer is at least MAXGETHOSTSTRUCT bytes long.

buflen The size of data area pointed to by the *buf* parameter above (must be MAXGETHOSTSTRUCT or larger).

RETURN VALUES
A nonzero handle if the process was successfully initiated, or 0 if an error occurred.

WSAAsyncGetHostByName   1.1   2.2

Asynchronously retrieves a HOSTENT structure and all of its related information for a given name.

```
HANDLE WSAAPI WSAAsyncGetHostByName(
    HWND hWnd,
    u_int wMsg,
    const char FAR * name,
    char FAR * buf,
    int buflen
};
```

PARAMETERS

hWnd The handle of the window that will receive a message when the asynchronous request has completed.

wMsg The user-defined message that will be posted to the window.

name A pointer to a null-terminated character string containing the name of the host.

buf	A pointer to a buffer that will receive the *hostent* data. Note, this must be larger than the size of a *hostent* structure. On successful completion, this buffer will contain not only a *hostent* structure but all of the strings referenced in the *hostent* structure as well. Ensure that this buffer is at least MAXGETHOSTSTRUCT bytes long.
buflen	The size of data area pointed to by the *buf* parameter above. (Must be MAXGETHOSTSTRUCT or larger.)

RETURN VALUES
A nonzero handle if the process was successfully initiated, or 0 if an error occurred.

WSAAsyncGetProtoByName   1.1   2.2

Asynchronously retrieves a PROTOENT structure and all of its related information for a given name.

```
HANDLE WSAAPI WSAAsyncGetProtoByName(
    HWND hWnd,
    u_int wMsg,
    const char FAR * name,
    char FAR * buf,
    int buflen
};
```

PARAMETERS

hWnd	The handle of the window that will receive a message when the asynchronous request has completed.
wMsg	The user-defined message that will be posted to the window.
name	A pointer to a null-terminated character string containing the name of the protocol to be resolved.
buf	A pointer to a buffer that will receive the *protoent* data. Note, this must be larger than the size of a *protoent* structure. On successful completion, this buffer will contain not only a *protoent* structure but all of the strings referenced in the *protoent* structure as well. Ensure that this buffer is at least MAXGETHOSTSTRUCT bytes long.
buflen	The size of data area pointed to by *buf*. (Must be MAXGETHOSTSTRUCT or larger.)

RETURN VALUES
A nonzero handle if the process was successfully initiated, or 0 if an error occurred.

WSAAsyncGetProtoByNumber   1.1   2.2

Asynchronously retrieves a PROTOENT structure and all of its related information for a given protocol number.

```
HANDLE WSAAPI WSAAsyncGetProtoByNumber(
    HWND hWnd,
    u_int wMsg,
    int number,
    char FAR * buf,
    int buflen
};
```

PARAMETERS

hWnd   The handle of the window that will receive a message when the asynchronous request has completed.

wMsg   The user-defined message that will be posted to the window.

number   The protocol number to be resolved.

buf   A pointer to a buffer that will receive the *protoent* data. Note, this must be larger than the size of a *protoent* structure. On successful completion, this buffer will contain not only a *protoent* structure but all of the strings referenced in the *protoent* structure as well. Ensure that this buffer is at least MAXGETHOSTSTRUCT bytes long.

buflen   The size of data area pointed to by the *buf* parameter above. (Must be MAXGETHOSTSTRUCT or larger.)

RETURN VALUES
A nonzero handle if the process was successfully initiated, or 0 if an error occurred.

WSAAsyncGetServByName   1.1   2.2

Asynchronously retrieves a SERVENT structure and all of its related information for a given service name.

```
HANDLE WSAAPI WSAAsyncGetServByName(
    HWND hWnd,
    u_int wMsg,
    const char FAR * name,
    const char FAR * proto,
    char FAR * buf,
    int buflen
};
```

PARAMETERS

hWnd	The handle of the window that will receive a message when the asynchronous request has completed.
wMsg	The user-defined message that will be posted to the window.
name	A pointer to a null-terminated character array containing a service name.
proto	An optional pointer to a null-terminated character array containing a protocol name. If this parameter is NULL, WSAAsyncGetServByName() returns the first service matching name. If it isn't NULL, WSAAsyncGetServByName() attempts to match both *name* and *proto*.
buf	A pointer to a buffer that will receive the servent data. Note, this must be larger than the size of a *servent* structure. On successful completion, this buffer will contain not only a *servent* structure but all of the strings referenced in the *servent* structure as well. Ensure that this buffer is at least MAXGETHOSTSTRUCT bytes long.
buflen	The size of data area pointed to by the *buf* parameter above. (Must be MAXGETHOSTSTRUCT or larger.)

RETURN VALUES
A nonzero handle if the process was successfully initiated, or 0 if an error occurred.

WSAAsyncGetServByPort   1.1   2.2

Asynchronously retrieves a SERVENT structure and all of its related information for a given port number.

```
HANDLE WSAAPI WSAAsyncGetServByPort(
    HWND hWnd,
    u_int wMsg,
    int port,
```

```
    const char FAR * proto,
    char FAR * buf,
    int buflen
};
```

PARAMETERS

hWnd	The handle of the window that will receive a message when the asynchronous request has completed.
wMsg	The user-defined message that will be posted to the window.
port	A port number in network byte order.
proto	An optional pointer to a null-terminated character array containing a protocol name. If this parameter is NULL, WSAAsyncGetServByName() returns the first service matching port. If it isn't NULL, WSAAsyncGetServByName() attempts to match both the *port* and *proto*.
buf	A pointer to the data area to receive the servent data. Note, this must be larger than the size of a *servent* structure. On successful completion, this buffer will contain not only a *servent* structure but all of the strings referenced in the *servent* structure as well. Ensure that this buffer is at least MAXGETHOSTSTRUCT bytes long.
buflen	The size of data area pointed to by the *buf* parameter above. (Must be MAXGETHOSTSTRUCT or larger.)

RETURN VALUES
A nonzero handle if the process was successfully initiated, or 0 if an error occurred.

WSAAsyncSelect   1.1   2.2

Requests asynchronous notification of network events for a given socket. Makes the socket nonblocking.

```
int WSAAPI WSAAsyncSelect(
    SOCKET s,
    HWND hWnd,
    u_int wMsg,
    long lEvent
};
```

PARAMETERS

s   Socket descriptor.

hWnd   Handle to window that will receive asynchronous notifications.

wMsg   A user-defined message that will be received when a network event occurs.

lEvent   A bitmask specifying the combination of network events in which the application is interested. (See Table QR-7.)

RETURN VALUES
0 or SOCKET_ERROR

TABLE QR-7   WSAAsyncSelect() EVENT CODES

Event Code	Requests Receipt of Notification When...	1.1	2.2
FD_ACCEPT	A connection request has been received.	•	•
FD_CLOSE	The connection was closed.	•	•
FD_CONNECT	A connection has been established.	•	•
FD_OOB	Out-of-band data has arrived.	•	•
FD_QOS	The quality of service for the socket has changed.		•
FD_READ	Data is available to be read.	•	•
FD_WRITE	It is safe to send data.	•	•

WSACancelAsyncRequest   1.1   2.2

Cancels an incomplete asynchronous database operation.

```
int WSAAPI WSACancelAsyncRequest(
    HANDLE hAsyncTaskHandle
);
```

PARAMETERS

hAsyncTaskHandle   A handle that was returned from one of the WSAAsyncGetXByY() functions.

RETURN VALUES
0 or SOCKET_ERROR

WSACancelBlockingCall   1.1

Cancels a blocking call that is in progress.

```
int WSAAPI WSACancelBlockingCall(void);
```

RETURN VALUES
0 or SOCKET_ERROR

WSACleanup   1.1   2.2

Frees process resources and stops use of WinSock.

```
int WSAAPI WSACleanup(void);
```

RETURN VALUES
0 or SOCKET_ERROR

WSACloseEvent   2.2

Closes an event object.

```
BOOL WSAAPI WSACloseEvent(
    WSAEVENT hEvent
);
```

PARAMETERS

hEvent   A handle to an open event object.

RETURN VALUES
True if successful; False if not.

WSAConnect 2.2

Establishes a connection with a specified socket. Can optionally exchange QOS flowspecs and/or connect data.

```
int WSAAPI WSAConnect(
    SOCKET s,
    const struct sockaddr FAR * name,
    int namelen,
    LPWSABUF lpCallerData,
    LPWSABUF lpCalleeData,
    LPQOS lpSQOS,
    LPQOS lpGQOS
};
```

PARAMETERS

s	A descriptor for an unconnected socket.
name	A pointer to a SOCKADDR structure that contains address information for the peer socket.
namelen	The length of the SOCKADDR pointed to by *name*.
lpCallerData	An optional pointer to application-defined data that is passed to the host.
lpCalleeData	An optional pointer to application-defined data that is returned from the host.
lpSQOS	An optional pointer to two flowspecs; one for each direction.
LPQOS lpGQOS	Reserved for future use.

RETURN VALUES
0 or SOCKET_ERROR

WSACreateEvent 2.2

Creates a new event object.

```
WSAEVENT WSAAPI WSACreateEvent(void);
```

RETURN VALUES
An event handle or WSA_INVALID_EVENT.

WSADuplicateSocket 2.2

Returns a WSAPROTOCOL_INFO structure that can be used with WSASocket() to create a duplicate descriptor for the given socket.

```
int WSAAPI WSADuplicateSocket(
    SOCKET s,
    DWORD dwProcessId,
    LPWSAPROTOCOL_INFOA lpProtocolInfo
};
```

PARAMETERS

s	The socket descriptor to duplicate.
dwProcessId	The ID of the process that will use the duplicated descriptor.
lpProtocolInfo	A pointer to a buffer that will receive the WSAPROTOCOL_INFO structure.

RETURN VALUES
0 or SOCKET_ERROR

WSAEnumNameSpaceProviders 2.2

Retrieves an array of WSANAMESPACE_INFO structures, one for each installed name space provider.

```
INT WSAAPI WSAEnumNameSpaceProviders(
    LPDWORD              lpdwBufferLength,
    LPWSANAMESPACE_INFOA lpnspBuffer
};
```

PARAMETERS

lpdwBufferLength	On input, the size of the buffer pointed to by *lpnspBuffer*. On output, if the function fails with WSAEFAULT, the minimum size required to hold all of the information.

lpnspBuffer   A pointer to a buffer that will receive the name space information.

RETURN VALUES
0 or SOCKET_ERROR

WSAEnumNetworkEvents   2.2

Determines which network events have occurred on the given socket since the last call to this function and clears the internal event record.

```
int WSAAPI WSAEnumNetworkEvents(
    SOCKET s,
    WSAEVENT hEventObject,
    LPWSANETWORKEVENTS lpNetworkEvents
);
```

PARAMETERS

s   The socket descriptor.

hEventObject   An optional handle to an event object that will be reset before the function returns.

lpNetworkEvents   A pointer to a WSANETWORKEVENTS structure that will receive event notifications and associated error codes.

RETURN VALUES
0 or SOCKET_ERROR

WSAEnumProtocols   2.2

Retrieves an array of WSAPROTOCOL_INFO structures, one for each installed protocol or protocol chain that meets the specified criteria.

```
int WSAAPI WSAEnumProtocols(
    LPINT lpiProtocols,
    LPWSAPROTOCOL_INFOA lpProtocolBuffer,
    LPDWORD lpdwBufferLength
);
```

PARAMETERS

lpiProtocols	An optional pointer to null-terminated array of integers that restricts the enumeration to the protocols listed in the array.
lpProtocolBuffer	A pointer to a buffer that will receive the array of WSAPROTOCOL_INFO structures.
lpdwBufferLength	On input, the length of the buffer pointed to by *lpProtocolBuffer*. On output, if the function fails with WSAENOBUFS, the minimum buffer size required to retrieve all of the requested information.

RETURN VALUES
0 or SOCKET_ERROR

WSAEventSelect 2.2

Associates a socket and event object with a set of network event notifications. Makes the socket nonblocking.

```
int WSAAPI WSAEventSelect(
    SOCKET s,
    WSAEVENT hEventObject,
    long lNetworkEvents
};
```

PARAMETERS

s	A socket descriptor.
hEventObject	An event object handle.
lNetworkEvents	A bitmask specifying the combination of network events in which the application is interested. (See Table QR-8.)

RETURN VALUES
0 or SOCKET_ERROR

TABLE QR-8 EVENT CODES USED WITH WSAEventSelect()

Event Code	Requests Receipt of Notification When...
FD_ACCEPT	A connection request has been received.
FD_CLOSE	The connection was closed.
FD_CONNECT	A connection has been established.
FD_OOB	Out-of-band data has arrived.
FD_QOS	The quality of service for the socket has changed.
FD_READ	Data is available to be read.
FD_WRITE	It is safe to send data.

WSAGetLastError 1.1 2.2

Retrieves the error code associated with the last WinSock function call that failed.

```
int WSAAPI WSAGetLastError(void);
```

RETURN VALUES
The specific error code for the last operation that failed in this process.

WSAGetOverlappedResult 2.2

Returns the completion results for the specified overlapped operation.

```
BOOL WSAAPI WSAGetOverlappedResult(
    SOCKET s,
    LPWSAOVERLAPPED lpOverlapped,
    LPDWORD lpcbTransfer,
    BOOL fWait,
    LPDWORD lpdwFlags
);
```

PARAMETERS

s	A socket descriptor that was used earlier to initiate an overlapped operation.
lpOverlapped	A pointer to a WSAOVERLAPPED structure that was used earlier to initiate an overlapped operation.
lpcbTransfer	A pointer to a 32-bit integer that will receive the number of bytes transferred during the overlapped operation.
fWait	If True, indicates that the function should wait until the pending operation has completed. If False, and the operation is not yet complete, the function sets the last error to WSA_IO_INCOMPLETE. This flag can only be used if the overlapped operation is using event object notification.
lpdwFlags	A pointer to a 32-bit integer that will receive the flags that would have been received with WSARecv() for WSARecvFrom().

RETURN VALUES

True if the overlapped operation completed successfully; False if the operation is not yet complete or the overlapped operation incurred an error.

WSAGetQOSByName 2.2

Retrieves a QOS structure for a named template, or enumerates all available template names.

```
BOOL WSAAPI WSAGetQOSByName(
    SOCKET s,
    LPWSABUF lpQOSName,
    LPQOS lpQOS
};
```

PARAMETERS

s	A socket descriptor.
lpQOSName	A pointer to a WSABUF structure that identifies the template name. If the *buf* field in the WSABUF is NULL, on return the *buf* field is filled with a double-null-terminated array of null-terminated template names.
lpQOS	A pointer to a QOS structure that will receive the values associated with the named template.

RETURN VALUES
True if successful; False if an error occurred.

WSAGetServiceClassInfo 2.2

Retrieves the service class information retained by the specified name space provider for the given service class.

```
INT WSAAPI WSAGetServiceClassInfo(
    LPGUID  lpProviderId,
    LPGUID  lpServiceClassId,
    LPDWORD lpdwBufSize,
    LPWSASERVICECLASSINFOA lpServiceClassInfo
};
```

PARAMETERS

lpProviderId   A pointer to a GUID that specifies the name space provider.

lpServiceClassId A pointer to a GUID that specifies the service class.

lpdwBufSize   On input, the number of bytes in the buffer pointed to by *lpServiceClassInfo*. On output, if the function fails with WSAEFAULT, the minimum number of bytes required to return all of the requested information.

lpServiceClassInfo A pointer to a buffer that will receive the service class information.

RETURN VALUES
0 or SOCKET_ERROR

WSAGetServiceClassNameByClassId 2.2

Retrieves the name of the specified service class.

```
INT WSAAPI WSAGetServiceClassNameByClassId(
    LPGUID  lpServiceClassId,
    LPSTR   lpszServiceClassName,
    LPDWORD lpdwBufferLength
};
```

PARAMETERS

lpServiceClassId A pointer to a GUID that identifies the service.

lpszServiceClassName A pointer to a buffer that will receive the service class name.

lpdwBufferLength On input, the length of the buffer pointed to by *lpszServiceClassName*. On output, the number of characters copied into the buffer.

RETURN VALUES
0 or SOCKET_ERROR

WSAHtonl   2.2

Converts a 32-bit integer to network order as appropriate for the specified socket.

```
int WSAAPI WSAHtonl(
    SOCKET s,
    u_long hostlong,
    u_long FAR * lpnetlong
};
```

PARAMETERS

s   A socket descriptor.

hostlong A 32-bit integer in host byte order.

lpnetlong A pointer to a 32-bit integer that will receive the converted value.

RETURN VALUES
0 or SOCKET_ERROR

WSAHtons   2.2

Converts a 16-bit integer to network byte order as appropriate for the specified socket.

```
int WSAAPI WSAHtons(
    SOCKET s,
    u_short hostshort,
    u_short FAR * lpnetshort
};
```

PARAMETERS

s A socket descriptor.

hostshort A 16-bit integer in host byte order.

lpnetshort A pointer to a 16-bit integer that will receive the converted value.

RETURN VALUES
0 or SOCKET_ERROR

WSAInstallServiceClass 2.2

Registers service class information within one or more name spaces.

```
INT WSAAPI WSAInstallServiceClass(
    LPWSASERVICECLASSINFOA   lpServiceClassInfo
};
```

PARAMETERS

lpServiceClassInfo A pointer to an initialized WSASERVICECLASSINFO structure.

RETURN VALUES
0 or SOCKET_ERROR

WSAIoctl 2.2

Controls the I/O mode of a socket.

```
int WSAAPI WSAIoctl(
    SOCKET s,
    DWORD dwIoControlCode,
    LPVOID lpvInBuffer,
    DWORD cbInBuffer,
    LPVOID lpvOutBuffer,
    DWORD cbOutBuffer,
    LPDWORD lpcbBytesReturned,
    LPWSAOVERLAPPED lpOverlapped,
    LPWSAOVERLAPPED_COMPLETION_ROUTINE lpCompletionRoutine
};
```

PARAMETERS

s	A socket descriptor.
dwIoControlCode,	One of the predefined command codes in Tables QR-2 and QR-3.
lpvInBuffer	A pointer to the input buffer.
cbInBuffer	The size of the buffer pointed to by *lpvInBuffer*.
lpvOutBuffer	A pointer to the output buffer.
cbOutBuffer	The size of the buffer pointed to by *lpvOutBuffer*.
lpcbBytesReturned	A pointer to a 32-bit integer that will receive the number of bytes output.
lpOverlapped	An optional pointer to a WSAOVERLAPPED structure.
CompletionRoutine	An optional pointer to a completion function.

RETURN VALUES
0 or SOCKET_ERROR

WSAIsBlocking   1.1

Determines if a blocking call is currently in progress.

```
BOOL WSAAPI WSAIsBlocking(void);
```

RETURN VALUES
True if a blocking function is currently processing; False if not.

WSAJoinLeaf 2.2

Joins a leaf node into a multipoint session. Can optionally be used to exchange connect data and QOS flowspecs.

```
SOCKET WSAAPI WSAJoinLeaf(
    SOCKET s,
    const struct sockaddr FAR * name,
    int namelen,
    LPWSABUF lpCallerData,
    LPWSABUF lpCalleeData,
    LPQOS lpSQOS,
    LPQOS lpGQOS,
    DWORD dwFlags
};
```

PARAMETERS

s	A descriptor for a multipoint socket.
name	A pointer to a SOCKADDR structure indicating the address of the peer to which the socket is to be joined.
namelen	The length of the buffer pointed to by *name*.
lpCallerData	An optional pointer to application-defined data that will be sent to the peer.
lpCalleeData	An optional pointer to application-defined data that will be returned from the peer.
lpSQOS	An optional pointer to two flowspecs, one for each direction.
lpGQOS	Reserved for future use.
dwFlags	Flags that indicate whether the socket is acting as a sender, receiver, or both. JL_SENDER_ONLY, JL_RECEIVER_ONLY, or JL_BOTH.

RETURN VALUES
A socket descriptor or INVALID_SOCKET.

WSALookupServiceBegin 2.2

Initiates a service lookup session.

```
INT WSAAPI WSALookupServiceBegin(
    LPWSAQUERYSETA  lpqsRestrictions,
    DWORD           dwControlFlags,
    LPHANDLE        lphLookup
};
```

PARAMETERS

lpqsRestrictions	A pointer to a WSAQUERYSET structure used to define the search.
dwControlFlags	Controls the depth of the search. (See Table QR-9.)
lphLookup	A pointer to a handle that can be used with WSALookupServiceNext().

RETURN VALUES
0 or SOCKET_ERROR

TABLE QR-9 WSALookupServiceBegin() CONTROL FLAGS

LUP_DEEP	Query deep as opposed to just the first level. This flag and the next two container flags are related to hierarchical name spaces such as NDS and X.500.
LUP_CONTAINERS	Return containers only
LUP_NOCONTAINERS	Do not return any containers
LUP_FLUSHCACHE	Some name space providers cache previously returned information. This flag causes the provider to ignore the cache and to perform the full query again.
LUP_NEAREST	If possible, return results in the order of distance. The measure of distance is provider specific.
LUP_RES_SERVICE	This indicates whether the prime response is in the RemoteAddr or LocalAddr portion of the returned CSADDR_INFO structure. The other part should be usable in either case.
LUP_RETURN_ALIAS	Requests all available alias information be returned as well as the primary information.
LUP_RETURN_NAME	Requests that the resulting WSAQUERYSET contain the service or host name in the *lpszServiceInstanceName* field.

LUP_RETURN_TYPE	Requests that the resulting WSAQUERYSET contain the service class type in the *lpServiceClassId* field.
LUP_RETURN_VERSION	Requests that the resulting WSAQUERYSET contain the service's version in the *lpVersion* field.
LUP_RETURN_COMMENT	Requests that the resulting WSAQUERYSET contain the service's comment in the *lpszComment* field.
LUP_RETURN_QUERY_STRING	Requests that the unparsed remainder of the service instance name be returned in the resulting WSAQUERYSET *lpszQueryString* field.
LUP_RETURN_ADDR	Requests that the resulting WSAQUERYSET contain the service's addresses and protocol information in the *lpcsaBuffer* field.
LUP_RETURN_BLOB	Requests that the resulting WSAQUERYSET contain the service's name space specific data in the *lpBlob* field. On TCP/IP requests, an example of this would be a HOSTENT or SERVENT structure.
LUP_RETURN_ALL	Requests that all of the information be retrieved.

WSALookupServiceEnd 2.2

Terminates a lookup service session.

```
INT WSAAPI WSALookupServiceEnd(
    HANDLE  hLookup
);
```

PARAMETERS

hLookup   A handle returned from WSALookupServiceBegin().

RETURN VALUES
0 or SOCKET_ERROR

WSALookupServiceNext 2.2

Continues a service lookup session started by WSALookupServiceBegin().

```
INT WSAAPI WSALookupServiceNext(
    HANDLE          hLookup,
    DWORD           dwControlFlags,
    LPDWORD         lpdwBufferLength,
    LPWSAQUERYSETA  lpqsResults
};
```

PARAMETERS

hLookup	The handle returned from the previous call to WSALookupServiceBegin().
dwControlFlags	A bitmask that controls provider behavior. The value LUP_FLUSHPREVIOUS or any of the *dwControlFlags* values discussed in the WSALookupServiceBegin() section may be used here.
lpdwBufferLength	On input, a pointer to a 32-bit integer indicating the size of the *lpqsResults* buffer. On output, if the function fails with WSAEFAULT, the minimum buffer size needed to hold all of the information.
lpqsResults	A pointer to a buffer that will receive the resulting WSAQUERYSET structure and related information.

RETURN VALUES
0 or SOCKET_ERROR

WSANtohl 2.2

Converts a 32-bit integer to host byte order as appropriate for the specified socket.

```
int WSAAPI WSANtohl(
    SOCKET s,
    u_long netlong,
    u_long FAR * lphostlong
};
```

PARAMETERS

s	A socket descriptor.
netlong	A 32-bit integer in network byte order.
lphostlong	A pointer to a 32-bit integer that will receive the converted value.

RETURN VALUES
0 or SOCKET_ERROR

WSANtohs 2.2

Converts a 16-bit integer to host order as appropriate for the specified socket.

```
int WSAAPI WSANtohs(
    SOCKET s,
    u_short netshort,
    u_short FAR * lphostshort
};
```

PARAMETERS

s	A socket descriptor.
netshort	A 16-bit integer in network byte order.
lphostshort	A pointer to a 16-bit integer that will receive the converted value.

RETURN VALUES
0 or SOCKET_ERROR

WSARecv 2.2

Receives data on a connected socket.

```
int WSAAPI WSARecv(
    SOCKET s,
    LPWSABUF lpBuffers,
    DWORD dwBufferCount,
```

```
    LPDWORD lpNumberOfBytesRecvd,
    LPDWORD lpFlags,
    LPWSAOVERLAPPED lpOverlapped,
    LPWSAOVERLAPPED_COMPLETION_ROUTINE lpCompletionRoutine
};
```

PARAMETERS

s	A socket descriptor identifying a connected socket.
lpBuffers	A pointer to an array of WSABUF structures, which in turn point to the buffers that will receive the data.
dwBufferCount	The number of WSABUF structures contained in the array pointed to by *lpBuffers*.
lpNumberOfBytesRecvd	A pointer to a 32-bit integer that will receive the number of bytes received if the function completes immediately.
lpFlags	A pointer to a 32-bit integer. On input this is used to specify the MSG_PEEK or MSG_OOB flags. On output it allows the application to receive indication of the MSG_PARTIAL flag for protocols that support it.
lpOverlapped	An optional pointer to a WSAOVERLAPPED structure. This is ignored for sockets that were created with WSASocket() without the WSA_FLAG_OVERLAPPED flag.
lpCompletionRoutine	An optional pointer to a completion function. This is ignored for sockets that were created with WSASocket() without the WSA_FLAG_OVERLAPPED flag.

RETURN VALUES

0 if the function completes immediately with no errors, or SOCKET_ERROR if an error occurred or the operation is pending.

WSARecvDisconnect 2.2

Disables receives on a socket and retrieves disconnect data.

```
int WSAAPI WSARecvDisconnect(
    SOCKET s,
    LPWSABUF lpInboundDisconnectData
};
```

PARAMETERS

s
A socket descriptor.

lpInboundDisconnectData
A pointer to a buffer that will receive the application-defined disconnect data.

RETURN VALUES
0 or SOCKET_ERROR

WSARecvFrom 2.2

Receives data and the sender's address.

```
int WSAAPI WSARecvFrom(
    SOCKET s,
    LPWSABUF lpBuffers,
    DWORD dwBufferCount,
    LPDWORD lpNumberOfBytesRecvd,
    LPDWORD lpFlags,
    struct sockaddr FAR * lpFrom,
    LPINT lpFromlen,
    LPWSAOVERLAPPED lpOverlapped,
    LPWSAOVERLAPPED_COMPLETION_ROUTINE lpCompletionRoutine
    );
```

PARAMETERS

s
A socket descriptor for an *unconnected* socket.

lpBuffers
A pointer to an array of WSABUF structures, which in turn point to the buffers that will receive the data.

dwBufferCount
The number of WSABUF structures contained in the array pointed to by *lpBuffers*.

lpNumberOfBytesRecvd
A pointer to a 32-bit integer that will indicate the number of bytes received if the function completes immediately.

lpFlags
A pointer to a 32-bit integer. On input this is used to specify the MSG_PEEK or MSG_OOB flags (if wanted). On output it allows the application to receive indication of the MSG_PARTIAL flag for protocols that support it.

(continued)

lpFrom	An optional pointer to a SOCKADDR structure that will receive the source address of the peer that sent the data.
lpFromlen	An optional pointer to an integer that specifies the size of the buffer pointed to by *lpFrom*. Only required if *lpFrom* isn't NULL.
lpOverlapped	An optional pointer to a WSAOVERLAPPED structure. Ignored for sockets that were created with WSASocket() without the WSA_FLAG_OVERLAPPED flag.
lpCompletionRoutine	An optional pointer to a completion function. Ignored for sockets that were created with WSASocket() without the WSA_FLAG_OVERLAPPED flag.

RETURN VALUES
0 if the function completes immediately with no errors, or SOCKET_ERROR if an error occurred or the operation is pending.

WSARemoveServiceClass 2.2

Removes service class information for the specified service.

```
INT WSAAPI WSARemoveServiceClass(
    LPGUID   lpServiceClassId
);
```

PARAMETERS

lpServiceClassId   A pointer to a GUID that identifies the service.

RETURN VALUES
0 or SOCKET_ERROR

WSAResetEvent 2.2

Sets an event object to the nonsignaled state.

```
BOOL WSAAPI WSAResetEvent(
    WSAEVENT hEvent
);
```

PARAMETERS

hEvent   A handle to an event object.

RETURN VALUES
True if the function succeeds; False if not.

WSASend   2.2

Sends data on a connected socket.

```
int WSAAPI WSASend(
    SOCKET s,
    LPWSABUF lpBuffers,
    DWORD dwBufferCount,
    LPDWORD lpNumberOfBytesSent,
    DWORD dwFlags,
    LPWSAOVERLAPPED lpOverlapped,
    LPWSAOVERLAPPED_COMPLETION_ROUTINE lpCompletionRoutine
);
```

PARAMETERS

s	A descriptor for a connected socket.
lpBuffers	A pointer to an array of WSABUF structures, which in turn point to the buffers that will receive the data.
dwBufferCount	The number of WSABUF structures contained in the array pointed to by *lpBuffers*.
lpNumberOfBytesSent	A pointer to a 32-bit integer that will receive the number of bytes sent if the function completes immediately.
dwFlags	A bitmask used to affect the way the send is performed.
lpOverlapped	An optional pointer to a WSAOVERLAPPED structure. This is ignored for sockets that were created with WSASocket() without the WSA_FLAG_OVERLAPPED flag.

(continued)

lpCompletionRoutine   An optional pointer to a completion function. This is ignored for sockets that were created with WSASocket() without the WSA_FLAG_OVERLAPPED flag.

RETURN VALUES
0 if the function completes immediately with no errors, or SOCKET_ERROR if an error occurred or the operation is pending.

WSASendDisconnect   2.2

Initiates shutdown of a connection and sends disconnect data.

```
int WSAAPI WSASendDisconnect(
    SOCKET s,
    LPWSABUF lpOutboundDisconnectData
);
```

PARAMETERS

s   A socket descriptor.

lpOutboundDisconnectData   A pointer to a WSABUF structure that in turn points to application-defined disconnect data.

RETURN VALUES
0 or SOCKET_ERROR

WSASendTo   2.2

Sends data to the specified address.

```
int WSAAPI WSASendTo(
    SOCKET s,
    LPWSABUF lpBuffers,
    DWORD dwBufferCount,
    LPDWORD lpNumberOfBytesSent,
    DWORD dwFlags,
    const struct sockaddr FAR * lpTo,
```

```
    int iToLen,
    LPWSAOVERLAPPED lpOverlapped,
    LPWSAOVERLAPPED_COMPLETION_ROUTINE lpCompletionRoutine
};
```

PARAMETERS

s	A socket descriptor.
lpBuffers	A pointer to an array of WSABUF structures, which in turn point to the buffers that will receive the data.
dwBufferCount	The number of WSABUF structures contained in the array pointed to by *lpBuffers*.
lpNumberOfBytesSent	A pointer to a DWORD variable that will indicate the number of bytes sent if the function completes immediately.
dwFlags	A bitmask used to affect the way the send is performed.
lpTo	A pointer to a SOCKADDR structure indicating the destination address.
iToLen	An integer specifying the length of the SOCKADDR structure pointed to by *lpTo*.
lpOverlapped	An optional pointer to a WSAOVERLAPPED structure. Ignored for sockets that were created with WSASocket() without the WSA_FLAG_OVERLAPPED flag.
lpCompletionRoutine	An optional pointer to a completion function. Ignored for sockets that were created with WSASocket() without the WSA_FLAG_OVERLAPPED flag.

RETURN VALUES

0 if the function completes immediately with no errors, or SOCKET_ERROR if an error occurred or the operation is pending.

WSASetBlockingHook   1.1

Install an application-defined blocking hook function.

```
FARPROC WSAAPI WSASetBlockingHook(
    FARPROC lpBlockFunc
};
```

PARAMETERS

lpBlockFunc   A pointer to the application-defined function.

RETURN VALUES
A pointer to the previously installed blocking hook function or NULL.

WSASetEvent   2.2

Sets an event object to the signaled state.

```
BOOL WSAAPI WSASetEvent(
    WSAEVENT hEvent
);
```

PARAMETERS

hEvent   An event object handle.

RETURN VALUES
True if the function succeeds; False if it doesn't.

WSASetLastError   1.1   2.2

Sets the error code that will be retrieved in a subsequent call to WSAGetLastError().

```
void WSAAPI WSASetLastError(
    int iError
);
```

PARAMETERS

iError   The error code.

WSASetService   2.2

Registers or deregisters service availability within one or more name spaces.

```
INT WSAAPI WSASetService(
    LPWSAQUERYSETA lpqsRegInfo,
    WSAESETSERVICEOP essoperation,
    DWORD dwControlFlags
);
```

PARAMETERS

lpqsRegInfo	A pointer to an initialized WSAQUERYSET structure.
essOperation	One of the operation codes in Table QR-10.
dwControlFlags	The meaning of *dwControlFlags* is dependent on the value of *essOperation* field.

RETURN VALUES
0 or SOCKET_ERROR

TABLE QR-10 essOperation CODES

Flags	Service Already Exists	Service Does Not Exist
RNRSERVICE_REGISTER:		
NONE	Completely overwrite the object and only use the addresses in the accompanying CSADDR_INFO structures.	Create a new object, using the addresses listed in the CSADDR_INFO structures.
SERVICE_MULTIPLE	Update the object, adding the addresses listed in the CSADDR_INFO structures to the already installed list.	Create a new object, using the addresses listed in the CSADDR_INFO structures.

(continued)

Table QR-10 (CONTINUED)

Flags	Service Already Exists	Service Does Not Exist
RNRSERVICE_DEREGISTER:		
NONE	Remove all addresses, but don't remove object from name space.	SOCKET_ERROR. WSAGetLastError() equals WSASERVICE_NOT_FOUND
SERVICE_MULTIPLE	Remove the specified addresses and only deregister the service if no addresses remain.	SOCKET_ERROR. WSAGetLastError() equals WSASERVICE_NOT_FOUND
RNRSERVICE_DELETE:		
NONE	Remove the object from the name space.	SOCKET_ERROR. WSAGetLastError() equals WSASERVICE_NOT_FOUND
SERVICE_MULTIPLE	Remove the specified addresses and only remove the object if no addresses remain.	SOCKET_ERROR. WSAGetLastError() equals WSASERVICE_NOT_FOUND

WSASocket   2.2

Creates a socket descriptor.

```
SOCKET WSAAPI WSASocket(
    int af,
    int type,
    int protocol,
    LPWSAPROTOCOL_INFOA lpProtocolInfo,
    GROUP g,
    DWORD dwFlags
};
```

PARAMETERS

af   Address family. AF_INET, AF_IPX, and so forth, or FROM_PROTOCOL_INFO.

type	Socket type. SOCK_STREAM, SOCK_DGRAM, and so forth, or FROM_PROTOCOL_INFO.
protocol	Protocol. IPPROTO_TCP, NSPROTO_IPX, and so forth, or FROM_PROTOCOL_INFO.
lpProtocolInfo	An optional pointer to a WSAPROTOCOL_INFO structure indicating a desired protocol. If this parameter is NULL, the first three parameters are used to create the socket.
g	Reserved for future use.
dwFlags	Socket attribute specification (see Table QR-11).

RETURN VALUES
A socket descriptor or INVALID_SOCKET.

TABLE QR-11 dwFlags VALUES

WSA_FLAG_OVERLAPPED	Creates a socket that may be used with overlapped operations.
WSA_FLAG_MULTIPOINT_C_ROOT	The socket will be a c_root in a multipoint session.
WSA_FLAG_MULTIPOINT_C_LEAF	The socket will be a c_leaf in a multipoint session.
WSA_FLAG_MULTIPOINT_D_ROOT	The socket will be a d_root in a multipoint session.
WSA_FLAG_MULTIPOINT_D_LEAF	The socket will be a d_leaf in a multipoint session.

WSAStartup   1.1   2.2

Initializes use of WinSock by a process.

```
int WSAAPI WSAStartup(
    WORD wVersionRequested,
    LPWSADATA lpWSAData
};
```

PARAMETERS

wVersionRequested	The version of WinSock that the application would like to use.
lpWSAData	A pointer to a WSADATA structure.

RETURN VALUES
0 or a specific error code. Do not call WSAGetLastError().

WSAStringToAddress 2.2

Fills a SOCKADDR structure with values converted from a human-readable string.

```
INT WSAAPI WSAStringToAddress(
    LPSTR              AddressString,
    INT                AddressFamily,
    LPWSAPROTOCOL_INFO lpProtocolInfo,
    LPSOCKADDR         lpAddress,
    LPINT              lpAddressLength
};
```

PARAMETERS

AddressString	A pointer to a null-terminated character array containing the address.
AddressFamily	The address family to which the address belongs.
lpProtocolInfo	An optional pointer to a WSAPROTOCOL_INFO structure indicating the service provider to be used for the conversion.
lpAddress	A pointer to a SOCKADDR structure that will receive the converted address.
lpAddressLength	The length of the SOCKADDR structure pointed to by *lpAddress*.

RETURN VALUES
0 or SOCKET_ERROR

WSAUnhookBlockingHook   1.1

Restores the default blocking hook function.

```
int WSAAPI WSAUnhookBlockingHook(void);
```

RETURN VALUES
0 or SOCKET_ERROR

WSAWaitForMultipleEvents   2.2

Waits for an event object to become signaled or for a timeout period to elapse. Places the process in an alertable wait state.

```
DWORD WSAAPI WSAWaitForMultipleEvents(
    DWORD cEvents,
    const WSAEVENT FAR * lphEvents,
    BOOL fWaitAll,
    DWORD dwTimeout,
    BOOL fAlertable
);
```

PARAMETERS

cEvents	Specifies the number of event handles contained in the array pointed to by *lphEvents*. The maximum number of event object handles is WSA_MAXIMUM_WAIT_EVENTS. At least one event must be specified.
lphEvents	A pointer to an array of event handles.
fWaitAll	Specifies whether the function should wait for *all* of the event handles to be signaled or just until *any one* of the handles becomes signaled. If True, the function will not return until all of the event handles are signaled at the same time. If False, the function will return when any one of the handles in the array is signaled.
dwTimeout	Specifies a timeout value in milliseconds or WSA_INFINITE. If the timeout period expires, the function returns even if none of the event handles contained in the array is signaled.
fAlertable	Specifies whether the function should return when the system queues an I/O completion routine for execution by the calling thread. If True, the completion routine is executed and the function returns. If False, the completion routine is not executed when the function returns.

RETURN VALUES
WSA_WAIT_FAILED if the function fails. WSA_WAIT_TIMEOUT if the timeout interval elapsed. WAIT_IO_COMPLETION if one or more completion routines are queued for execution. An index value indicating which event object became signaled; WSA_WAIT_EVENT_0 to (WSA_WAIT_EVENT_0 + cEvents.

Data Structures

This reference shows the fields contained in each of the WinSock defined data structures along with their data type and a brief description.

AFPROTOCOLS

```
typedef struct _AFPROTOCOLS {
    INT iAddressFamily;
    INT iProtocol;
} AFPROTOCOLS, *PAFPROTOCOLS, *LPAFPROTOCOLS;
```

iAddressFamily	Address family designation. AF_INET, AF_IPX, and so forth.
iProtocol	Protocol designation. IPPROTO_TCP, NSPROTO_IPX, and so forth.

timeval

```
struct timeval {
        long    tv_sec;
        long    tv_usec;
};
```

tv_sec	Number of seconds.
tv_usec	Number of microseconds.

CSADDR_INFO

```
typedef struct _CSADDR_INFO {
    SOCKET_ADDRESS LocalAddr ;
    SOCKET_ADDRESS RemoteAddr ;
    INT iSocketType ;
```

Quick Reference 489

```
    INT iProtocol ;
} CSADDR_INFO;
```

LocalAddr	A SOCKET_ADDRESS structure that contains a pointer to a SOCKADDR structure (*lpSockAddr*) and the length of the SOCKADDR (*iSockaddrLength*).
RemoteAddr	A SOCKET_ADDRESS structure that contains a pointer to a SOCKADDR structure (*lpSockAddr*) and the length of the SOCKADDR (*iSockaddrLength*).
iSocketType	An integer that can be used for the socket type parameter in a call to socket() or WSASocket().
iProtocol	An integer that can be used for the protocol parameter in a call to socket() or WSASocket()

FLOWSPEC

```
typedef struct _flowspec
{
    uint32       TokenRate;
    uint32       TokenBucketSize;
    uint32       PeakBandwidth;
    uint32       Latency;
    uint32       DelayVariation;
    SERVICETYPE  ServiceType;
    uint32       MaxSduSize;
    uint32       MinimumPolicedSize;
} FLOWSPEC, *PFLOWSPEC, FAR * LPFLOWSPEC;
```

TokenRate	The rate, in bytes per second, at which the token bucket is filled.
TokenBucketSize	The total volume of the imaginary token/credit bucket.
PeakBandwidth	The rate, in bytes per second, at which an application may transfer packets.
Latency	The maximum delay, in microseconds, that is to be allowed in the time a bit is sent and received.
DelayVariation	The difference, in microseconds, between the maximum and minimum delay allowed for each packet.

(continued)

ServiceType The level of service guarantee.

MaxSduSize The maximum packet size (in bytes) that can be used.

MinimumPolicedSize The minimum packet size that will be given the level of service requested.

HOSTENT

```
struct  hostent {
        char    FAR * h_name;
        char    FAR * FAR * h_aliases;
        short   h_addrtype;
        short   h_length;
        char    FAR * FAR * h_addr_list;
};
```

h_name A null-terminated ASCII string containing the official name of the host.

h_aliases A null-terminated array of null-terminated ASCII strings containing host alias names. This may not contain any entries.

h_addrtype Specifies the type of address being returned. For a standard version 1.1 WinSock this value is always AF_INET (Address Family Internet). It could be AF_IPX, AF_OSI, AF_APPLETALK, or some other value in other WinSock implementations.

h_length The length in bytes of each address contained in the following *h_addr_list* field. This value relates to the type of address specified in *h_addrtype*. If *h_addrtype* is AF_INET, this value will be 4 (32-bit IP address).

h_addr_list A null-terminated array of pointers to network addresses. This list usually contains only one address. If it contains more than one, it usually means that the host has several different network interfaces.

linger

```
struct  linger {
        u_short l_onoff;
        u_short l_linger;
};
```

Quick Reference

l_onoff   Indicates whether linger is on (True) or off (False).

l_linger   Timeout value in seconds.

protoent

```
struct  protoent {
        char    FAR * p_name;
        char    FAR * FAR * p_aliases;
        short   p_proto;
};
```

p_name   Official name of the protocol. These are always in lowercase. (ip, icmp, tcp, and so forth)

p_aliases   A null-terminated array of null-terminated ASCII strings containing alternate protocol names.

p_proto   The protocol number in host byte order.

QOS

```
typedef struct _QualityOfService
{
    FLOWSPEC    SendingFlowspec;
    FLOWSPEC    ReceivingFlowspec;
    WSABUF      ProviderSpecific; specific stuff */
} QOS, FAR * LPQOS;
```

SendingFlowspec   A FLOWSPEC structure describing the quality of service for the sending direction.

ReceivingFlowspec   A FLOWSPEC structure describing the quality of service for the receiving direction.

ProviderSpecific   A WSABUF structure pointing to a buffer that contains provider-specific information.

servent

```
struct  servent {
        char    FAR * s_name;
        char    FAR * FAR * s_aliases;
        short   s_port;
        char    FAR * s_proto;
};
```

s_name	Official name of the service. These are always lowercase (ftp, http, and so forth).
s_aliases	A null-terminated array of null-terminated ASCII strings containing host alternate service names.
s_port	Port number in network order.
s_proto	Null-terminated ASCII string containing the name of the protocol associated with this service name and port.

sockaddr

```
struct sockaddr {
        u_short sa_family;
        char    sa_data[14];
};
```

sa_family	Address family.
sa_data	Protocol-specific data.

sockaddr_in

```
struct sockaddr_in {
        short   sin_family;
        u_short sin_port;
        struct  in_addr sin_addr;
        char    sin_zero[8];
};
```

sin_family	Address family (AF_INET).
sin_port	Port number in network order.
in_addr	Structure that holds the 32-bit address and makes portions available by name.

SOCKET_ADDRESS

```
typedef struct _SOCKET_ADDRESS {
    LPSOCKADDR lpSockaddr ;
    INT iSockaddrLength ;
} SOCKET_ADDRESS, *PSOCKET_ADDRESS, FAR * LPSOCKET_ADDRESS ;
```

lpSockAddr	A pointer to a SOCKADDR structure.
iSockaddrLength	The length of the SOCKADDR pointed to by *lpSockAddr*.

WSABUF

```
typedef struct _WSABUF {
    u_long     len;
    char FAR * buf;
} WSABUF, FAR * LPWSABUF;
```

len	The length in bytes of the buffer pointed to by *buf*.
buf	A pointer to a buffer.

WSAData

```
typedef struct WSAData {
        WORD            wVersion;
        WORD            wHighVersion;
        char            szDescription[WSADESCRIPTION_LEN+1];
        char            szSystemStatus[WSASYS_STATUS_LEN+1];
        unsigned short  iMaxSockets;
        unsigned short  iMaxUdpDg;
        char FAR *      lpVendorInfo;
} WSADATA;
```

wVersion	The version of the WinSock API that the DLL expects the calling application to use. This is usually the same as the *wVersionRequired* parameter passed to WSAStartup().
wHighVersion	The highest version of WinSock that this DLL can support. Normally, this is the same as the *wVersion* member, but it can be higher. For example, if you request version 1.1 from a WinSock 2 DLL, on return, *wVersion* will be 1.1 and *wHighVersion* will be 2.0.
szDescription	A null-terminated ASCII string (up to 256 characters long) containing a text description of the WinSock DLL and vendor. Each vendor is free to use this field as desired; there is no predefined format.
szSystemStatus	A null-terminated ASCII string (up to 128 characters long) containing a text description of the WinSock DLL's current status or configuration information. Each vendor is free to use this field for whatever is thought necessary. There is no formal format.
iMaxSockets	The maximum number of sockets available to the calling application at the time of the call to WSAStartup().
iMaxUdpDg	The size in bytes of the largest UDP datagram that an application may send or receive. Note: In WinSock 2 this value should not be used. An application should instead retrieve the size for a specific protocol by using getsockopt() with the SO_MAX_MSG_SIZE option.
lpVendorInfo	A pointer to a buffer containing vendor-specific information. The format of the buffer pointed to by *lpVendorInfo* is completely up to the implementer. Its contents are not defined in the WinSock specification. Note: In WinSock 2 this value should not be used. An application should instead retrieve the vendor-specific information from a protocol by using getsockopt() with the PVD_CONFIG option.

WSANAMESPACE_INFO

```
typedef struct _WSANAMESPACE_INFO {
    GUID            NSProviderId;
    DWORD           dwNameSpace;
    BOOL            fActive;
    DWORD           dwVersion;
    LPSTR           lpszIdentifier;
} WSANAMESPACE_INFOA;
```

NSProviderId	The GUID that has been assigned to this particular name-space provider vendor.
dwNameSpace	Identifies the type of name space. Acceptable values are found in WINSOCK2.H (NS_DNS, NS_SAP, NS_X500, and so forth).
fActive	If True, indicates that this provider is active. If False, the provider is inactive and is not accessible.
dwVersion	Version number.
lpszIdentifier	Pointer to a character array containing a description or name of the name space.

WSANETWORKEVENTS

```
typedef struct _WSANETWORKEVENTS {
      long lNetworkEvents;
      int iErrorCode[FD_MAX_EVENTS];
} WSANETWORKEVENTS, FAR * LPWSANETWORKEVENTS;
```

lNetworkEvents	A bitmask containing the FD_*xxx* events that occurred.
iErrorCode	Array of error codes associated with each event. Use the predefined offsets to index each error code: FD_ACCEPT_BIT FD_CLOSE_BIT FD_CONNECT_BIT FD_OOB_BIT FD_QOS_BIT FD_READ_BIT FD_WRITE_BIT

WSANSCLASSINFO

```
typedef struct _WSANSCLASSINFO
{
    LPSTR   lpszName;
    DWORD   dwNameSpace;
    DWORD   dwValueType;
    DWORD   dwValueSize;
    LPVOID  lpValue;
}WSANSCLASSINFO;
```

lpszName	A pointer to a null-terminated character array specifying the item name. Commonly used names can be found in NSAPI.H (SERVICE_TYPE_VALUE_CONN, SERVICE_TYPE_VALUE_TCPPORT, and so forth).
dwNameSpace	A name space identifier. NS_DNS, NS_SAP, and so forth.
dwValueType	Defines the data type. Commonly used values can be found in WINNT.H (REG_DWORD, REG_SZ, and so forth).
dwValueSize	The size of the value in bytes; `sizeof(DWORD)` for example.
lpValue	A pointer to the value itself.

WSAOVERLAPPED

```
typedef struct _WSAOVERLAPPED {
    DWORD    Internal;
    DWORD    InternalHigh;
    DWORD    Offset;
    DWORD    OffsetHigh;
    WSAEVENT hEvent;
} WSAOVERLAPPED, FAR * LPWSAOVERLAPPED;
```

Internal	Reserved; not used by WinSock.
InternalHigh	Reserved; not used by WinSock.
Offset	Reserved; not used by WinSock.
OffsetHigh	Reserved; not used by WinSock.
hEvent	An event handle if the overlapped function is to use event notification. Or can be used to hold application-defined information if a completion function is being used.

WSAPROTOCOLCHAIN

```
typedef struct _WSAPROTOCOLCHAIN {
    int ChainLen;
    DWORD ChainEntries[MAX_PROTOCOL_CHAIN];
} WSAPROTOCOLCHAIN, FAR * LPWSAPROTOCOLCHAIN;
```

ChainLen	The length of the chain: 0 = Layered protocol 1 = Base protocol > 1 = Protocol chain
ChainEntries	A list of catalog entry IDs.

WSAPROTOCOL_INFO

```
typedef struct _WSAPROTOCOL_INFO {
    DWORD dwServiceFlags1;
    DWORD dwServiceFlags2;
    DWORD dwServiceFlags3;
    DWORD dwServiceFlags4;
    DWORD dwProviderFlags;
    GUID ProviderId;
    DWORD dwCatalogEntryId;
    WSAPROTOCOLCHAIN ProtocolChain;
    int iVersion;
    int iAddressFamily;
    int iMaxSockAddr;
    int iMinSockAddr;
    int iSocketType;
    int iProtocol;
    int iProtocolMaxOffset;
    int iNetworkByteOrder;
    int iSecurityScheme;
    DWORD dwMessageSize;
    DWORD dwProviderReserved;
    WCHAR szProtocol[WSAPROTOCOL_LEN+1];
} WSAPROTOCOL_INFO, FAR * LPWSAPROTOCOL_INFO
```

dwServiceFlags1	A bitmask describing the services provided by the protocol. Possible flags are listed in Table QR-12.
dwServiceFlags2 *dwServiceFlags3* *dwServiceFlags4*	Reserved for future use.
dwProviderFlags	A bitmask describing more information about the protocol and its corresponding catalog entry. Possible values are listed in Table QR-13.

(continued)

ProviderId	A globally unique identifier assigned to the provider. May be useful for distinguishing between several service providers that provide the same protocol.
dwCatalogEntryId	A unique identifier assigned by the WS2_32.DLL for each WSAPROTOCOL_INFO structure.
ProtocolChain	A structure that indicates whether this entry represents a base protocol, a layered protocol, or a protocol chain and, in the case of a chain, holds information about the chain's protocol layers:
ProtocolChain.ChainLen = 0	Layered protocol. Because layered protocols aren't directly usable by an application, this should never be returned.
ProtocolChain.ChainLen = 1	Base protocol.
ProtocolChain.ChainLen > 1	Protocol chain.
ProtocolChain.ChainEntries[ ]	This array contains information about each layered protocol and the base protocol that make up the chain.
iVersion	Protocol version identifier.
iAddressFamily	The address family this protocol uses. Can be used as the address family parameter in a call to socket() or WSASocket(). Can also be used to determine the exact structure of a SOCKADDR to be used with the protocol.
iMaxSockAddr	The maximum size in bytes of an address used with this protocol.
iMinSockAddr	The minimum size in bytes of an address used with this protocol.
iSocketType	The value to use as the socket type parameter in a call to socket() or WSASocket() in order to open a socket for this protocol.
iProtocol	The value to use as the protocol parameter in a call to socket() or WSASocket() in order to open a socket for this protocol.
iProtocolMaxOffset	The maximum value that may be added to *iProtocol* when supplying a value for the protocol parameter to socket() and WSASocket(). Not all protocols allow a range of values. When this is the case *iProtocolMaxOffset* will be zero.

iNetworkByteOrder	The network byte order used by the protocol. WINSOCK2.H defines two constants to be used with this field: BIGENDIAN and LITTLEENDIAN.
iSecurityScheme	Indicates the type of security scheme employed (if any). WINSOCK2.H currently only defines SECURITY_PROTOCOL_NONE to indicate that the protocol does not provide any type of security. Other values would be provided by the service provider vendor. For example, SSL-enabled transports would have the value SECURITY_PROTOCOL_SSL here.
dwMessageSize	The maximum message size supported by the protocol or one of the following special values:
	0 – The protocol is stream oriented and the concept of message size is not relevant.
	0x1 – The maximum message size depends on the underlying network MTU (Maximum Transmission Unit) and cannot be determined until the socket is bound. Bind the socket and then use SO_MAX_MSG_SIZ with getsockopt() to retrieve the value.
	0xFFFFFFFF – The protocol is message oriented, but there is no maximum limit to the size of messages that may be transmitted.
dwProviderReserved	Reserved for use by service providers.
szProtocol	An array of up to 255 characters containing the name of the protocol. For example, "MS.w95.spi.tcp," Microsoft's Windows 95 TCP service provider.

TABLE QR-12 dwServiceFlags1 VALUES

XP1_CONNECTIONLESS	If set, this indicates that the protocol is connectionless. If not set, the protocol is connection oriented.
XP1_GUARANTEED_DELIVERY	The protocol guarantees delivery of all data sent. (It is a "reliable" protocol.)

(continued)

XP1_GUARANTEED_ORDER	The protocol guarantees that *if data is delivered*, it will arrive in the order in which it was sent and that it will not be duplicated.
XP1_MESSAGE_ORIENTED	The protocol preserves message boundaries.
XP1_PSEUDO_STREAM	A special type of message-oriented protocol that does not preserve message boundaries on data being received.
XP1_GRACEFUL_CLOSE	If set, the protocol supports graceful close. If not set, only abortive closes are performed.
XP1_EXPEDITED_DATA	The protocol supports expedited (OOB) data.
XP1_CONNECT_DATA	The protocol supports connect data.
XP1_DISCONNECT_DATA	The protocol supports disconnect data.
XP1_SUPPORT_BROADCAST	The protocol supports a broadcast mechanism.
XP1_SUPPORT_MULTIPOINT	The protocol supports a multipoint or multicast mechanism.
XP1_QOS_SUPPORTED	The protocol supports quality-of-service requests.
XP1_UNI_SEND	The protocol is unidirectional in the send() direction.
XP1_UNI_RECV	The protocol is unidirectional in the recv() direction.
XP1_IFS_HANDLES	The socket descriptors returned by the provider are operating system Installable File System (IFS) handles.
XP1_PARTIAL_MESSAGE	The MSG_PARTIAL flag is supported in WSASend() and WSASendTo().

TABLE QR-13 dwProviderFlags VALUES

PFL_MULTIPLE_PROTOCOL_ENTRIES	Indicates this is one of two or more entries for this protocol from this provider. Protocols that can be configured to exhibit different behaviors will have this value set. For example, SPX can be used as a message-oriented protocol or a pseudostream. Pseudostream operation is message-oriented on sends and stream-oriented on receives.

(continued)

Table QR-13 (CONTINUED)

PFL_RECOMMENDED_PROTO_ENTRY	Indicates this is the recommended catalog entry to use for this protocol. This is only applicable if the protocol is capable of implementing multiple behaviors as noted above.
PFL_HIDDEN	Set by a service provider to indicate this protocol should not be returned in the result buffer generated by WSAEnumProtocols(). Obviously, a WinSock 2 application should never see an entry with this bit set.
PFL_MATCHES_PROTOCOL_ZERO	Indicates a value of zero in the protocol parameter of socket() or WSASocket() matches this protocol entry.

WSAQUERYSET

```
typedef struct _WSAQuerySet
{
    DWORD            dwSize;
    LPWSTR           lpszServiceInstanceName;
    LPGUID           lpServiceClassId;
    LPWSAVERSION     lpVersion;
    LPWSTR           lpszComment;
    DWORD            dwNameSpace;
    LPGUID           lpNSProviderId;
    LPWSTR           lpszContext;
    DWORD            dwNumberOfProtocols;
    LPAFPROTOCOLS    lpafpProtocols;
    LPWSTR           lpszQueryString;
    DWORD            dwNumberOfCsAddrs;
    LPCSADDR_INFO    lpcsaBuffer;
    DWORD            dwOutputFlags;
    LPBLOB           lpBlob;
} WSAQUERYSET;
```

DURING REGISTRATION

Field	Meaning (During Registration)
dwSize	Must be set to sizeof(WSAQUERYSET). This is a versioning mechanism.
dwOutputflags	Not applicable to registration.
lpszServiceInstanceName	Pointer to a character array containing the service name.
lpServiceClassId	A pointer to the GUID for the previously installed service class.
lpVersion	An optional pointer to a WSAVERSION structure containing a DWORD version number. Clients can select among instances of a service by comparing this version number (if supplied).
lpszComment	An optional pointer to a character array containing a comment; may be anything the service wants.
dwNameSpace1	Identifier of a single name-space in which to register, or NS_ALL to register in all available name spaces. The combination of this field and the next field (*lpNSProviderId*) determines which name space providers the service uses. If the *lpNSProviderId* field isn't NULL, then this field is ignored.
lpNSProviderId	An optional pointer to a GUID for a specific name-space provider. If this field isn't NULL, then the *dwNameSpace1* field is ignored.
lpszContext	Not applicable to registration.
dwNumberOfProtocols	Not applicable to registration.
lpafpProtocols	Not applicable to registration.
lpszQueryString	Not applicable to registration.
dwNumberOfCsAddrs	The number of elements in the array of CSADDRO_INFO structures referenced by *lpcsaBuffer*.
lpcsaBuffer	A pointer to an array of CSADDR_INFO structures that contain the protocol and address information for the socket on which the service is listening.
lpBlob	An optional pointer to a provider-specific structure.

DURING RESOLUTION

Field	Meaning (During Resolution)
dwSize	Must be set to `sizeof(WSAQUERYSET)`. This is a versioning mechanism.
dwOutputflags	Not applicable to queries.
lpszServiceInstanceName	Optional pointer to a character array containing the service name. Some name spaces support wildcarding in order to find all instances of a given service class, but the mechanisms for doing this are not well documented. For Novell's SAP and NDS name spaces, NULL matches all names.
lpServiceClassId	A pointer to a GUID indicating a service class that was either previously installed with WSAInstallServiceClass() or preassigned by the name space for a well-known service. This field (and any other field not marked as optional) is required.
lpVersion	An optional pointer to a WSAVERSION structure containing a DWORD version number (*lpVersion>dwVersion*) and a comparison operation code (*lpVersion->ecHow*). If *ecHow* is set to COMP_EQUALS, only services that exactly match the given version number are returned. If *ecHow* is set to COMP_NOTLESS, only services with a version number equal to or greater than the given version number are returned.
lpszComment	Not applicable to queries.
dwNameSpace1	Identifier of a single name-space in which to search, or NS_ALL to search in all available name spaces. The combination of this field and the next field (*lpNSProviderId*) determines which name space providers are searched. If the *lpNSProviderId* field isn't NULL, then this field is ignored. This field relates to the WSANAMESPACE_INFO.*dwNameSpace* field returned from WSAEnumNameSpaceProviders().
lpNSProviderId	An optional pointer to a GUID for a specific name-space provider. If this field isn't NULL, then the *dwNameSpace1* field is ignored. This value is the same as the WSANAMESPACE_INFO.*NSProviderId* returned from WSAEnumNameSpaceProviders().

(continued)

lpszContext	An optional pointer to a character string that indicates the starting point of the query in a hierarchical name space. This field is used with name spaces such as NDS and X.500, which are organized in a directory tree structure. The following values apply: NULL or blank ("") starts at the default context. "\" starts the search at the top of the name space. Any other value starts the search at the designated point.
dwNumberOfProtocols	Number of elements contained in the optional *lpafpProtocols* constraint array. This may be 0.
lpafpProtocols	An optional pointer to an array of AFPROTOCOLS structures, which constrain the search to services that use one of the designated protocols.
lpszQueryString	An optional pointer to a character array that specifies additional query information. This is only used with name spaces (such as whois++) that support simple text queries.
dwNumberOfCsAddrs	Not applicable to queries.
lpcsaBuffer	Not applicable to queries.
lpBlob	An optional pointer to a provider-specific structure.

WSASERVICECLASSINFO

```
typedef struct _WSASERVICECLASSINFO
{
    LPGUID              lpServiceClassId;
    LPSTR               lpszServiceClassName;
    DWORD               dwCount;
    LPWSANSCLASSINFOA   lpClassInfos;
}WSASERVICECLASSINFO;
```

lpServiceClassId	The GUID for this class. May be generated with UUIDGEN.EXE for new services, or one of the predefined GUIDs for use with well-known services listed in SVCGUID.H.
lpszServiceClassName	A pointer to a null-terminated character array containing the service class name.

dwCount	The number of WSANSCLASSINFO structures pointed to by *lpClassInfos*.
lpClassInfos	A pointer to one or more WSANSCLASSINFO structures.

WSAVERSION

```
typedef struct _WSAVersion
{
    DWORD           dwVersion;
    WSAECOMPARATOR  ecHow;
}WSAVERSION, *PWSAVERSION, *LPWSAVERSION;
```

dwVersion	Version number.
ecHow	Comparison operation code: *ecHow* = COMP_EQUALS. Version number must match query exactly. *ecHow* = COMP_NOTLESS. Version number must be equal to or greater than the given version number.

Error Reference

This error reference lists the manifest constants used to define the WinSock error codes. The numeric list contains the actual number currently assigned to these constants.

Note: The number used to represent a particular error could change at some point in the future. All WinSock error numbers are currently defined as a value added to WSABASEERR. We assume here that WSABASEERR is defined as 10000. This is the current value assigned to WSABASEERR in both WINSOCK.H and WINSOCK2.H.

The errors are listed in numeric order in the following table, which can be used as a cross-reference. Following the table is an alphabetical list by symbolic (manifest) constant name.

Errors in Numeric Order

Error Code	Symbolic Constant	Error Code	Symbolic Constant
10004	WSAEINTR	10056	WSAEISCONN
10009	WSAEBADF	10057	WSAENOTCONN
10013	WSAEACCES	10058	WSAESHUTDOWN
10014	WSAEFAULT	10059	WSAETOOMANYREFS
10022	WSAEINVAL	10060	WSAETIMEDOUT
10024	WSAEMFILE	10061	WSAECONNREFUSED
10035	WSAEWOULDBLOCK	10062	WSAELOOP
10036	WSAEINPROGRESS	10063	WSAENAMETOOLONG
10037	WSAEALREADY	10064	WSAEHOSTDOWN
10038	WSAENOTSOCK	10065	WSAEHOSTUNREACH
10039	WSAEDESTADDRREQ	10066	WSAENOTEMPTY
10040	WSAEMSGSIZE	10067	WSAEPROCLIM
10041	WSAEPROTOTYPE	10068	WSAEUSERS
10042	WSAENOPROTOOPT	10069	WSAEDQUOT
10043	WSAEPROTONOSUPPORT	10070	WSAESTALE
10044	WSAESOCKTNOSUPPORT	10071	WSAEREMOTE
10045	WSAEOPNOTSUPP	10091	WSASYSNOTREADY
10046	WSAEPFNOSUPPORT	10092	WSAVERNOTSUPPORTED
10047	WSAEAFNOSUPPORT	10093	WSANOTINITIALISED
10048	WSAEADDRINUSE	10101	WSAEDISCON
10049	WSAEADDRNOTAVAIL	10102	WSAENOMORE
10050	WSAENETDOWN	10103	WSAECANCELLED
10051	WSAENETUNREACH	10104	WSAEINVALIDPROCTABLE
10052	WSAENETRESET	10105	WSAEINVALIDPROVIDER
10053	WSAECONNABORTED	10106	WSAEPROVIDERFAILEDINIT
10054	WSAECONNRESET	10107	WSASYSCALLFAILURE
10055	WSAENOBUFS	10108	WSASERVICE_NOT_FOUND

Error Code	Symbolic Constant	Error Code	Symbolic Constant
10109	WSATYPE_NOT_FOUND	11001	WSAHOST_NOT_FOUND
10110	WSA_E_NO_MORE	11002	WSATRY_AGAIN
10111	WSA_E_CANCELLED	11003	WSANO_RECOVERY
10112	WSAEREFUSED	11004	WSANO_DATA

Alphabetical Error Descriptions

WSAEACCES – Access denied.
Some attempt was made to access a service for which the process or socket does not have sufficient privileges:

- Set by connect() and WSAConnect() when attempting to connect a socket with a broadcast address without first setting the socket's SO_BROADCAST option to True. Returned from sendto() when trying to send to a broadcast address without first setting the socket's SO_BROADCAST option to True.

- Set by WSAAccept() when a attempting to connect to a request that has timed out or been withdrawn.

- Set by WSAGetServiceClassInfo(), WSAInstallServiceClass(), WSARemoveServiceClass(), and WSASetService when the calling process does not have sufficient privileges to access or alter the information.

WSAEADDRINUSE – Address already in use.
An attempt was made to use an address that some other socket is already using. A socket cannot use the same local address as another socket unless the socket's SO_REUSEADDR option has been set to True.

WSAEADDRNOTAVAIL – Invalid address.
Some portion of an address isn't valid – for example, when attempting to connect or send to a remote address that has not been initialized.

WSAEAFNOSUPPORT – Address family not supported by protocol family.
An attempt was made to use an address that is not compatible with the protocol family – for example, calling socket() with incompatible parameters. Sockets are associated with a particular protocol when they are created. SOCKADDR structures are associated with a particular address family by the *sa_family* field. Therefore, any function that accepts both a socket and an address could return this error, since the socket (protocol) may not be compatible with the SOCKADDR (address family).

WSAEALREADY – Operation already in progress.
This code is used in several situations:

- It can mean that an attempt to cancel an asynchronous operation failed because the operation has already been canceled.

- On WinSock 2, it can be caused by attempting to connect again on a nonblocking socket that is already attempting to connect. This situation can be caused by two or more calls to WSAConnect(), connect(), or WSAJoinLeaf().

- WSAInstallServiceClass() sets this error to indicate that the service class has already been installed.

WSAEBADF – Bad file descriptor.
Not officially assigned to any error in the WinSock specification. May be used by some providers as an equivalent for WSAENOTSOCK.

WSAECANCELLED – Canceled.
See WSA_E_CANCELLED. Conflicting constants are defined in WinSock 2 for WSAECANCELLED (10103) and WSA_E_CANCELLED (10111). WSAECANCELLED will be removed in a future specification, but applications should continue to watch for this constant since it may still be in use by some service providers.

WSAECONNABORTED – Software caused connection abort.
An established connection was lost due to a timeout or some other error.

WSAECONNREFUSED – Connection refused.
The peer machine actively refused a connection request.

WSAECONNRESET – Connection reset by peer.
An established connection was closed by the peer system.

WSAEDESTADDRREQ – Destination address required.
A socket operation was attempted without a proper destination address. Typically caused by using an invalid address with connect() or sendto().

WSAEDISCON – Graceful shutdown in progress.
An established connection is being closed by the peer system.

WSAEDQUOT – Disk quota.
Provided for compatibility with BSD sockets. Not officially assigned to any error in the WinSock specification.

WSAEFAULT – Bad address.
A buffer parameter addresses an area that is not a valid part of the process's address space, or a buffer is too small.

WSAEHOSTDOWN – Host is down.
Not officially assigned to any error in the WinSock specification. See WSAETIMEDOUT.

WSAEHOSTUNREACH – No route to host.
An operation was attempted to an unreachable host. See WSAENETUNREACH.

WSAEINPROGRESS – Blocking operation already in progress.
A blocking operation is currently in progress or the service provider is still processing a callback function. WinSock only allows one blocking operation to be in progress per process or thread. If any other WinSock function call is made while a blocking operation is still in progress, it receives this error code.

WSAEINTR - Function call interrupted.
A blocking WinSock 1.1 call was canceled with WSACancelBlockingCall().

WSAEINVAL – Invalid argument.
A parameter passed to a WinSock function is invalid for any one of several reasons. For example:

- Calling accept() without calling listen()
- Calling bind() for a socket that is already bound
- Attempting to connect with a listening socket
- A flag or other input parameter contains an invalid value

WSAEINVALIDPROCTABLE – Invalid procedure table from service provider.
Defined in WINSOCK2.H, but not officially assigned to any error in the WinSock specification.

WSAEINVALIDPROVIDER – Invalid service provider version number.
Defined in WINSOCK2.H, but not officially assigned to any error in the WinSock specification.

WSAEISCONN – Socket is already connected.
An attempt was made to use an already connected socket in an illogical manner. For example:

- Calling connect(), listen(), or bind() on a connected socket
- Using sendto() with a connected socket

WSAELOOP – Loop.
Provided for compatibility with BSD sockets. Not officially assigned to any error in the WinSock specification.

WSAEMFILE – Too many open sockets.
There are no more socket descriptors available.

WSAEMSGSIZE – Message too long.
A message sent on a message-oriented socket was larger than the maximum size supported by the underlying protocol; or the buffer supplied to a receive operation with a message-oriented socket was not large enough to hold the entire message.

WSAENAMETOOLONG – Name too long.
Provided for compatibility with BSD sockets. Not officially assigned to any error in the WinSock specification.

WSAENETDOWN – Network is down.
The network subsystem failed.

WSAENETRESET – Network dropped connection on reset.
A connection was closed as the result of a failure detected by the "keep-alive" mechanism.

WSAENETUNREACH – Network is unreachable.
The network can't be reached or a host can't be found. Equivalent to WSAEHOSTUNREACH.

WSAENOBUFS – No buffer space available.
WinSock can't allocate buffer space for some operation, or the buffer parameter passed to a function is too small to hold all of the requested information.

WSAENOMORE – No more data available.
See WSA_E_NO_MORE. Conflicting constants are defined in WinSock 2 for WSAENOMORE (10102) and WSA_E_NO_MORE (10110), but applications should continue to watch for this constant since it may still be in use by some service providers.

WSAENOPROTOOPT – Bad protocol option.
The specified socket option or ioctl command is not recognized or not supported in the given context; or some other operation was attempted that isn't supported by the protocol. Examples:

- Some socket options are only supported on certain types of sockets. (SO_BROADCAST isn't supported on stream sockets, for example.)
- Connect and disconnect data aren't supported by all protocols.

WSAENOTCONN — Socket is not connected.
An operation was attempted that requires a connected socket. For example, send(), recv(), and getpeername() all require a connected socket.

WSAENOTEMPTY — Directory not empty.
Provided for compatibility with BSD sockets. Not officially assigned to any error in the WinSock specification.

WSAENOTSOCK — Specified socket is invalid.
An operation was attempted specifying an invalid value for a socket parameter.

WSAEOPNOTSUPP — Operation not supported.
An operation was attempted that is not supported by the socket type or protocol. For example:

- Attempting to send or receive OOB data on a socket that does not support it.
- Attempting to use accept() with a connectionless-oriented socket.
- Calling WSACancelBlockingCall() from WinSock 2.

WSAEPFNOSUPPORT — Protocol family not supported.
The specified protocol family isn't supported or hasn't been configured.

WSAEPROCLIM — Too many processes.
The limit on the number of processes that WinSock can handle simultaneously has been reached. WSAStartup() may return this error.

WSAEPROTONOSUPPORT — Protocol not supported.
The specified protocol is not supported or the attempted operation isn't supported by a protocol. For example, specifying a SOCK_DGRAM with a stream protocol or attempting to use *lpCallerData* with a protocol that doesn't support it.

WSAEPROTOTYPE — Wrong protocol type for socket.
The protocol type specified in a call to socket() or WSASocket() doesn't match the requested socket type. For example, trying to create a stream socket descriptor for a message-oriented protocol.

WSAEPROVIDERFAILEDINIT — Unable to initialize a service provider.
Defined in WINSOCK2.H, but not officially assigned to any error in the WinSock specification.

WSAEREFUSED — Refused.
Defined in WINSOCK2.H, but not officially assigned to any error in the WinSock specification.

WSAEREMOTE — Remote.
Provided for compatibility with BSD sockets. Not officially assigned to any error in the WinSock specification.

WSAESHUTDOWN — Cannot send after socket shutdown.
A send or receive operation was attempted on a socket that had already been shut down, disallowing the send or receive operation or both.

WSAESOCKTNOSUPPORT — Socket type not supported.
The specified socket type is not supported; for example, when attempting to use SOCK_RAW in an implementation that does not support raw sockets.

WSAESTALE — Stale.
Provided for compatibility with BSD sockets. Not officially assigned to any error in the WinSock specification.

WSAETIMEDOUT — Connection timed out.
An operation failed because the peer system didn't respond within an allotted amount of time. Returned from connect() when a connection attempt fails or when the underlying protocol determines that a connected peer is no longer responding.

WSAETOOMANYREFS — Too many references.
Provided for compatibility with BSD sockets. Not officially assigned to any error in the WinSock specification.

WSAEUSERS — Too many users.
Provided for compatibility with BSD sockets. Not officially assigned to any error in the WinSock specification.

WSAEWOULDBLOCK — Operation would block.
The socket being used has been set to nonblocking and the requested operation has been started but has not yet completed.

WSAHOST_NOT_FOUND — Host not found.
The name-resolution service could not find the given host. This may also be returned for protocol and service queries.

WSANOTINITIALISED – Successful WSAStartup() not yet performed.
An attempt was made to use a WinSock function without first calling WSAStartup().

WSANO_DATA – Valid name no data record of requested type.
The host, protocol, or service name was valid but was not found during a query operation. Or, the name was found but no data was available. For example, this is returned if a call to WSALookupServiceX() specifies LUP_CONTAINER and the underlying name space does not support containers.

WSANO_RECOVERY – Nonrecoverable error.
A nonrecoverable error occurred. When used with a database lookup, this indicates that the name-resolution service was not available.

WSASERVICE_NOT_FOUND – Service not found.
No such service is known. The service cannot be found in the specified name space. Returned from the WSALookupServiceBegin(), WSALookupServiceNext(), and WSASetService() functions.

WSASYSCALLFAILURE – System call failure.
Returned as an indication that a system call that never fails has in fact failed (hey, it happens...). The example given in the WinSock specification is the WaitForMultipleObjects() function.

WSASYSNOTREADY – Network subsystem is unavailable.
Returned by WSAStartup() to indicate that the network system is unstable or isn't configured properly.

WSATRY_AGAIN – Nonauthoritative host not found.
In general, a WinSock application should interpret WSAHOST_NOT_FOUND and WSANO_DATA as indicating that the key (name, address, and so forth) was not found. WSATRY_AGAIN and WSANO_RECOVERY suggest that the name service itself is nonoperational.

WSATYPE_NOT_FOUND – Type not found.
The specified class was not found in a call to WSAGetServiceClassInfo() or WSARemoveServiceClass().

WSAVERNOTSUPPORTED – WINSOCK.DLL version out of range.
Returned by WSAStartup() to indicate that the requested WinSock version isn't supported by the current WinSock implementation.

WSA_E_CANCELLED – Lookup canceled.
A call to WSALookupServiceEnd() was made before a call to WSALookupServiceNext() was still processing; the lookup was canceled.

WSA_E_NO_MORE – No more data available.
Used with WSALookupServiceNext() to indicate that more information is available.

Appendix A
What's on the CD-ROM

The accompanying CD-ROM contains all of the sample programs developed in the chapter text. It also contains the official WinSock specification documents for both Version 1.1 and 2, and a complete set of Request For Comments (RFC) documents.

A Setup program is included on the CD-ROM that will install some or all of these files automatically. The files may also be read directly from the CD using File Manager or Windows Explorer.

Installation Instructions

The setup program (SETUP.EXE) is stored in the root directory of the CD-ROM. This program requires Windows 3.1 or higher, or Windows 95 or Windows NT. Here are the steps to run the Setup program:

1. Insert the CD-ROM into the CD drive.
2. Run SETUP.EXE and follow the instructions.

With this Setup program you can select from several installation options:

- Install everything.
- Install only the sample programs.
- Install only the WinSock 1.1 specification documents.
- Install only the WinSock 2 specification documents.
- Install any combination of specification documents and sample programs.

It is not necessary to restart your computer when the Setup program finishes.

Changing the Windows Read-Only Attribute

You may not be able to access files on the CD-ROM after you copy the files to your computer. Once you've copied or moved the entire contents of the CD to your hard disk or another storage medium (such as a Zip disk), you may get the following error message when you attempt to open a file with its associated application:

```
[Application] is unable to open the [file].
Please make sure the drive and file are writable.
```

Windows sees all files on a CD-ROM drive as read-only. This makes sense, normally, because a CD-ROM is a read-only medium — that is, you can't write data back to it. However, when you copy a file from a CD to your hard disk or to a Zip disk, Windows doesn't automatically change the file attribute from read-only to writeable. Most installation software takes care of this for you, but in this case, because the files are intended to be manually copied to your disk, you have to change the file attribute yourself. Luckily, it's easy:

1. Open the Start menu, select Programs, and select Windows Explorer.
2. Highlight the filename(s) on the hard disk or Zip disk.
3. Right-click the highlighted filename(s), and select Properties from the pop-up menu.
4. Uncheck the Read-only option.
5. Click the OK button.

You will now be able to use the file(s) with the specific application, and without getting that annoying error message.

Contents of the CD-ROM

The CD-ROM uses standard 8.3 DOS filenames for all files (it doesn't support long filenames). Holding to this format enables the files to be read with earlier versions of Windows as well as from MS-DOS.

The sample programs are organized into folders/directories designating the chapter in which they were referenced. The WinSock specifications and the RFC documents also have their own directories. There's also a directory that contains links to additional WinSock-related resources.

The following table describes the directories and files on the CD-ROM:

Directory\Program	Contents
\ (root)	SETUP.EXE program and associated files. Also contains a README.TXT file with the latest information.
\SPECS	Official WinSock specification documents.
\SPECS\1.1	WinSock specification for Version 1.1.
\SPECS\2	WinSock specification documents for Version 2.

About the Official WinSock Specifications

The WinSock specification documents are distributed in Microsoft Word format. If you do not have Microsoft Word, you can obtain the free Microsoft Word Viewer program from `http://www.microsoft.com` so you can view and print these files.

WinSock Specification Disclaimer and License

The official WinSock Specification documents contain the following disclaimer and license:

- This specification is provided "as is" with no warranties whatsoever, including any warranty of merchantability, fitness for any particular purpose, or any warranty otherwise arising out of any proposal, specification or sample.

- A license is hereby granted to reproduce this specification, but only in its entirety and without modification. No other license, express or implied, by estoppel or otherwise, to any other intellectual property rights is granted herein.

- Intel, Microsoft, Stardust, and the other companies whose contributions are acknowledged below disclaim all liability, including liability for infringement of any proprietary rights, relating to implementation of information in this specification. Said companies do not warrant or represent that such implementation(s) will not infringe such rights.

- Third-party trademarks are the property of their respective owners.

Additional Information Sources

Directory\Program	Contents
\LINKS	HTML file (INDEX.HTM) with links to additional WinSock-related information available via the Internet.
\RFC	A complete set of RFC documents. An index with links to each RFC text file is provided in HTML format (INDEX.HTM).

Sample Programs Used in This Book

Directory	Contents
\CH02	Sample programs from Chapter 2.
\CH02\	MAKEWORD.H contains the MAKEWORD macro for use with 16-bit Windows.
\CH02\DataGram	Very simple console datagram client and server applications.
\CH02\GetHTTP	Console utility to retrieve files from a Web server.
\CH02\HostInfo	Console utility used to retrieve host information.
\CH02\Stream	Simple console stream client and server applications.
\CH02\WSVer	WinSock version negotiation sample.
\CH04	CheckMail sample TCP/IP client application that checks for the incoming e-mail.
\CH05\Ping	Ping program using ICMP and RAW Sockets.
\CH05\PingI	Ping program using the proprietary Microsoft ICMP API.
\CH06\SendMail	TCP/IP client application that uses the Microsoft CSocket class to send e-mail.
\CH06\WSTerm	TCP/IP client application that uses the Microsoft CAsyncSocket class to create a general-purpose terminal utility.
\CH07\EnumProt	Sample program that displays all installed protocols and protocol chains along with detailed information about each protocol.

Directory	Contents
\CH07\SelProto	General-purpose protocol selection function and example program.
\CH08\Services	MFC sample program that uses WinSock 2 Name Resolution API to display information for given host names and services.
\CH09\GetHTTP2	Console utility that retrieves a file from an HTTP server and uses event objects and WSASelectEvent() for asynchronous notification.
\CH09\GetHTTP3	Console utility that retrieves a file from an HTTP server and uses WinSock 2 overlapped I/O functions.
\CH10	Sample application that uses a single thread and asynchronous notification to create an HTTP server capable of handling many simultaneous client connections. The is the preferred way to handle multiple simultaneous connections.
\CH11	Sample application that uses multithreading and blocking socket routines to create an HTTP server capable of handling multiple simultaneous client connections.
\CH12	Socket Adapter Library. Source code and associated files that enables a program to select either WinSock 1.1 or WinSock 2 at run time using explicit linking.
\CH12\CLIENT	WinSock version-independent datagram ECHO client. If WinSock 2 is available, the program is also protocol independent.
\CH12\SERVER	WinSock version-independent datagram ECHO server. If WinSock 2 is available, the program is also protocol independent.

Appendix B

Related Win32 Functions

The Win32 API contains a number of functions that are of interest to anyone developing WinSock applications.

RAS (Remote Access Service) Functions

The *Remote Access Service* (RAS) API enables applications to programmatically perform tasks that are available through dial-up networking, including

- ◆ Display of predefined dialog boxes that help the user create or edit an entry in the phone book file.
- ◆ Establish or terminate a connection with a remote machine.
- ◆ Determine the status of an existing RAS connection.
- ◆ On Version 4 of Windows NT, support RAS server administration and third-party extensions to RAS server security and connection management.

RAS Functions Available on Windows NT and 95

Only part of the RAS API is implemented on Windows 95. Table B-1 lists all of the RAS functions available on both Windows NT and Windows 95. There are many more RAS functions available on Windows NT. All of these functions begin with the letters *Ras*, so they are easy to find in the Win32 documentation.

Programs that use these functions must include RAS.H and link with RAS-API32.LIB.

TABLE B-1 RAS FUNCTIONS IN BOTH NT AND 95

RAS Function	Description
RasCreatePhonebookEntry()	Displays a dialog box with which the user can create a new phone book entry.
RasDial()	Attempts to establish a connection with a remote machine.
RasDialFunc()	Used to display the ongoing progress of a connection process. This function can be application defined, or a predefined function from the RAS library.
RasDialFunc1()	An extended version of the application-defined or library-defined RasDialFunc function. Receives a handle to the RAS connection and an extended error code.
RasEditPhonebookEntry()	Displays a dialog box with which the user can edit an existing phone book entry.
RasEnumConnections()	Returns a list of all active RAS connections.
RasEnumEntries()	Returns a list of all entry names contained in a remote access phone book.
RasGetConnectStatus()	Returns information about the status of a specified remote connection. The required RASCONN handle can be obtained from a call to RasDial() or RasEnumConnections().
RasGetEntryDialParams()	Retrieves the connection information saved by the last successful call to RasDial() or RasSetEntryDialParams() for a specified phone book entry.
RasGetErrorString()	Returns an error message string or a specified RAS error return code.
RasGetProjectionInfo()	Returns information related to the protocol used to establish the connection (PPP, SLIP, AMB, etc.).
RasHangUp()	Terminates an RAS connection.
RasSetEntryDialParams()	Changes the connection information saved by the last successful call to the RasDial() or RasSetEntryDialParams() for a specified phone book entry.

Service Control Manager Interface

Windows NT supports an application known as a *service* that conforms to a specially defined user interface. This interface allows a service to be manipulated by the *Service Control Manager* (SCM).

By using the SCM, a user can start and stop the service application through the Services control panel applet. Applications that conform to the SCM interface can be started automatically when the machine is started or by other Win32 applications. These applications can even be started when no user is logged on to the system.

Windows NT Service Control Interface

The SCM interface is explained in detail in Microsoft's Win32 API documentation. It consists of the following functions:

ChangeServiceConfig()	CloseServiceHandle()
ControlService()	CreateService()
DeleteService()	EnumDependentServices()
EnumServicesStatus()	GetServiceDisplayName()
GetServiceKeyName()	Handler()
LockServiceDatabase()	NotifyBootConfigStatus()
OpenSCManager()	OpenService()
QueryServiceConfig()	QueryServiceLockStatus()
QueryServiceObjectSecurity()	QueryServiceStatus()
RegisterServiceCtrlHandler()	ServiceMain()
SetServiceBits()	SetServiceObjectSecurity()
SetServiceStatus()	StartService()
StartServiceCtrlDispatcher()	UnlockServiceDatabase()

Windows 95 Service Control Interface

Windows 95 doesn't support the NT service control interface. At this time, only one function is available on Windows 95 that provides similar services. The RegisterServiceProcess() function is used to register or unregister a service process

524 WinSock 2.0

on Windows 95. A service process registered with this function continues to run after the user logs off. RegisterServiceProcess() returns 1 to indicate success or 0 if it fails.

```
DWORD RegisterServiceProcess(
      DWORD dwProcessId,
      DWORD dwType
);
```

Parameter	Description
dwProcessId	Specifies the process identifier of the process to register as a service. Use NULL to register the current process.
dwType	Specifies whether the service is to be registered or unregistered. This parameter can be one of the following values:
	RSP_SIMPLE_SERVICE - Registers the process as a service.
	RSP_UNREGISTER_SERVICE - Unregisters the process as a service.

Appendix C

Additional Resources

The following are what I believe are the best sources of information about WinSock and WinSock programming.

WinSock 2

Windows Sockets 2 for Windows 95 Software Development Kit. The final release of the binary components of WinSock 2 for Windows 95, and the newest development files for both Windows 95 and Windows NT 4. Released June 10, 1997.

http://www.microsoft.com/win32dev/netwrk/winsock2/ws295sdk.html

Microsoft Development Kits Support Home Page. Latest information and updates for the WinSock 2 SDK. From here you can also select the Knowledge Base tab and type in **Windows Sockets** or **WinSock** as a search phrase to find Knowledge Base Articles.

http://www.microsoft.com/win32devsupport/

Stardust Technologies Inc. Always has the latest information about WinSock and related topics. This is *the* source for WinSock information.

http://www.winsock.com/

WinSock Development Information Page. Bob Quinn's WinSock page. Lots of great advice, sample code, and links to other resources. Bob chairs the WinSock 2 Editorial Review Board and is *very* knowledgeable about WinSock.

http://www.sockets.com/

Novell. Lots of great online information about Novell's family of protocols and networking products. Keep an eye on this site – Novell is very serious about WinSock 2.

http://www.novell.com/

Intel's WinSock 2 Page. Intel was heavily involved in the creation of WinSock 2 and provided many valuable resources to keep the project going. This is another good resource for the latest WinSock 2 specifications.

http://developer.intel.com/ial/winsock2/index.htm

Network Multimedia

ReSerVation Protocol RSVP. Quality of Service for the Internet.

http://www.isi.edu/div7/rsvp/rsvp.html

Intel's RSVP Page

http://developer.intel.com/ial/rsvp/TECHBAK.HTM

The IP Multicast Initiative. Everything you need to know about IP multicast.

http://www.ipmulticast.com

MBONE Information

http://www.lbl.gov/WWW-Info/MBONE.html

MBONE: Multicasting Tomorrow's Internet. A great resource for more information on the MBONE.

http://www.northcoast.com/savetz/mbone/toc.html

MBONE FAQ. Frequently Asked Questions (FAQ) on the Multicast Backbone (MBONE).

http://www.mediadesign.co.at/newmedia/more/mbone-faq.html

Real Time Protocol (RTP). Real time on the Internet.

http://www.cs.columbia.edu/~hgs/rtp/

Web Development

IP Next Generation (IPng - IPv6). Stretching IP addresses.

http://playground.sun.com/ipng/

W3C: World Wide Web Consortium. Information related to HTML, HTTP, and other World Wide Web matters. Led by the creator of the Web, Tim Berners-Lee.

http://www.w3.org

The Common Gateway Interface (CGI)

http://hoohoo.ncsa.uiuc.edu/cgi/

Fast CGI

http://www.fastcgi.com/

Internet Standards

Internet Engineering Task Force (IETF)

http://www.ietf.org/

IETF RFC Search. Search for RFC documents by keyword or RFC number.

http://ds.internic.net/ds/dspg1intdoc.html

Internet Assigned Numbers Authority (IANA). The official keepers of "well-known" port numbers.

http://www.iana.org/iana/

Internet Research Task Force (IRTF)

http://www.irtf.org/irtf/

Internet Architecture Board (IAB)

http://www.iab.org/iab/

Internet Society

http://info.isoc.org

Internet Network Information Center

http://www.internic.net/

Security

Internet Security (SSL)

http://home.netscape.com/newsref/std/SSL.html

Secure Electronic Transaction (SET)

http://www.visa.com/cgi-bin/vee/sf/standard.html?2+0

Intel's Common Data Security Architecture

http://www.intel.com/ial/security/index.htm

WinSock Development Tools

Win-Tech. Socket Spy WinSock Trace Utility.

http://www.win-tech.com

Systems, Software, Technology Inc. WinSock and database "Spy" tools.

http://www.sstinc.com

WinSock Shareware

SIMTEL

http://www.coast.net/SimTel/win3/winsock.html

The Consummate WinSock Apps List

http://cws.wilmington.net/

The Ultimate Collection of WinSock Software

http://www.tucows.com

Trumpet WinSock

http://www.trumpet.com.au

Mailing Lists

WinSock2 List. Send e-mail to

majordomo@mailbag.intel.com

with "subscribe winsock-2" in the body of the message.

Winsock 2 Hypermail Archives

http://www.stardust.com/hypermail/ws2arc.html

WinSock 2 Mailing List by thread

http://www.stardust.com/hypermail/winsock2/

winsock-hackers. Subscribe by mailing to

majordomo@mailbag.intel.com

with "subscribe winsock-hackers" in the body of the message.

USENET Newsgroups

alt.winsock

alt.winsock.programming

comp.os.ms-windows.networking.tcp-ip:

comp.os.ms-windows.networking.windows:

comp.os.ms-windows.programmer.networks

comp.os.ms-windows.programmer.tools.winsock

comp.os.ms-windows.programmer.win32

Appendix D

Bibliography

Windows Sockets 2 Application Programming Interface Revision 2.2.1, May 2, 1997.

Windows Sockets 2 Application Programming Interface Revision 2.2.1, May 10, 1996.

Windows Sockets Version 1.1, An Open Interface for Network Programming under Microsoft Windows Version 1.1, January 20, 1993.

Windows Sockets 2 Service Provider Interface Revision 2.2.1, May 2, 1997.

Windows Sockets 2 Protocol-Specific Annex Revision 2.0.3, May 10, 1996.

WinSock 2 Debug and Trace Facilities

WinSock2 Generic QOS Mapping (Draft) Version 2.6, March 31,1997.

"How to Configure a Time-Out on a CSocket Operation." In Microsoft Knowledge Base [database online]. Article ID: Q138692, July 2, 1997, Microsoft Corporation, Redmond, WA.

Wingo, Scot and Justin Rudd. "Microsoft Visual C++/Microsoft Foundation Classes (MFC) Frequently Asked Questions, Version 5.0." May 15, 1997. Available from http://www.stingsoft.com/mfc_faq/.

Pietrek, Matt. "WinInet Utility." *Microsoft Systems Journal* (September, 1997).

Postel, J. "RFC 768, User Datagram Protocol." August 28, 1980.[1]

Postel, J. "RFC 792, Internet Control Message Protocol." September 1, 1981.[1]

Postel, J. "RFC 793, Transmission Control Protocol." September 1, 1981.[1]

Postel, J. "RFC 821, Simple Mail Transfer Protocol." August 1, 1982.[1]

Postel, J. "RFC 862, Echo Protocol." May 1983.[1]

Postel, J. "RFC 867, Daytime Protocol." May 1, 1983.[1]

Nagel, J. "RFC 896, Congestion Control in IP/TCP Internetworks." January 6, 1984.[1]

Postel, J. and J. Reynolds. "RFC 959, File Transfer Protocol." October 1, 1985.[1]

Kantor, B. and P. Lapsley. "RFC 977, Network News Transfer Protocol: A Proposed Standard for the Stream-Based Transmission of News." February 1, 1986.[1]

Postel, J. and J. Reynolds. "RFC 1010, Assigned Numbers." May 1, 1987.[1]

Mockapetris, P. "RFC 1034, Domain names - Concepts and Facilities." November 1, 1987.[1]

Mockapetris, P. "RFC 1035, Domain names - Implementation and Specification." January 1, 1987.[1]

Postel, J. and J. Reynolds. "RFC 1060, Assigned Numbers." March 20, 1990.[1]

Braden, R. "RFC 1122, Requirements for Internet Hosts - Communication Layers." October 1, 1989.[1]

Partridge, C. "RFC 1363, A Proposed Flow Specification." September 10, 1992.[1]

Myers, J. and M. Rose. "RFC 1725, Post Office Protocol - Version 3." November 23, 1994.[1]

Berners-Lee, T, L. Masinter, and M. McCahill. "RFC 1738, Uniform Resource Locators (URL)." December 20, 1994.[1]

Postel, J. "RFC 1880, Internet Official Protocol Standards." November 29, 1995.[1]

Berners-Lee, T., R. Fielding, and H. Nielsen. "RFC 1945, Hypertext Transfer Protocol - HTTP/1.0." May 17, 1996.[1]

Cohen, D. "IEN 137, On Holy Wars And A Plea For Peace." April 1, 1980.[1]

---

[1] All of these RFCs are available from http://www.isi.edu/rfc-editor/rfc-sources.html and on the accompanying CD-ROM.

Index

A

accept() function, 25, 48-49
Accept()
    as a parameter, 176-177
    function prototype for, 176
addresses, Internet, 9-10
advertising service availability, 253-260
AFXSOCK.H, 168-169
AfxSocketInit() function, calling, 169
application pairs, 24
AppWizard, Visual C++, 168-169
ARTICLE command (NNTP), 20
Asia Pacific Network Information Center (APNIC), 11
asynchronous database functions, 74
    categories, 94-95
    contents of returned hostent structure, 96-104
    contents of servent structure, 105-110
    host name and address resolution, 96
    protocol name and number resolution, 110-114
    service name and port resolution, 104-110
    WSACancelAsyncRequest() function, 114
asynchronous event notification
    associating network events, 281-283
    creating event objects, 281
    detecting network events, 284-285
    determining what occured, 285-287
    event objects, 279-280
    reenabling functions, *287*
    WinSock 2 event objects, 280-281
    Win32 event objects, 280
asynchronous events
    reenabling functions, 87-89
    responding to, 129
asynchronous messages
    canceling, 93
    handling, 73-74, 85-87
asynchronous mode, 71, 83
    cancelling messages, 93
    handling event messages, 85-87
    network event triggers, 89-93
    reenabling functions, 87-89
    requesting events, 84-85
    using, 83-130
asynchronous notification, WinSock 1.1 applications, 71-72
asynchronous server, 327-364
    asynchronous mode vs. multithreading, 327-328
    displaying event messages, 344-345
    displaying file hit count, 341-343
    maintaining statistics, 343-344
    receiving event and statistics notification messages, 341-345
    relaying WinSock event notifications, 340
    user interface summary, 345

B

base protocol, WinSock 2.0, 223-224
Berkeley API
    vs. WinSock, 58
    WinSock extensions to, 7-8
Berkeley sockets model, 7-8
Berkeley UNIX Software Distribution, 7
big-endian processors, 39-40
bind() function, 25, 47, 104
blocking and event-driven applications, 61
blocking functions, 64-65
blocking hook functions, 67-68
blocking mode, 63-68
blocking sockets, 63-64
broadcast addresses, 137-138

C

callback functions, asynchronous, 170-171
CArchive objects
    limitations of, 193-194
    using with CSocket, 192-193
CAsyncSocket class, 167
    advantages of, 170
    callback functions, 170-171
    deriving a new class that inherits from, 171-172
    using, 169-172
    using an object derived from, 172-178
CAsyncSocket-derived object
    construction of, 173-174
    using, 172-178
catenet model, 8-9
CheckMail sample application, 115-130

535

closing the connection, 130
compiling the sample program, 115-116
maintaining application state, 129-130
parsing the data, 129
responding to asynchronous events, 129
running the sample, 117
source code for, 117-128
using database functions, 128-129
circuit switching, 9
client, communicating with, 377-379
client/server
    model, 8
    program flow, 23-26
client socket, connecting to a server, 174-175
client threads, synchronizing, 375-377
ClientThread() function, 378-379
closesocket() function, 26
    closing connectionless sockets with, 54
Cohen, Danny, 40
.com (commercial) domain name, 10
connect() function, 26, 43, 104
    function prototypes for, 174-175
    return value, 175
connectionless applications, 24, 26, 27
connectionless sending and receiving, 52-53
connectionless sockets, closing, 54
connection-oriented applications, 24-26
connection-oriented protocol. *See* Transmission Control Protocol (TCP)
connection-oriented sending and receiving, 50-52
connection-oriented sockets, closing, 54-55
connection setup and teardown, in WinSock 2.0, 210
control plane, multipoint strategy, 320
cooperative multitasking, Windows programs, 62
COUNTC.C file, 375-377
CSADDR_INFO structure, 253-254
CSocket class, 167
    CArchive limitations, 193-194
    deriving a new class from, 194
    services provided by, 191
    synchronous/asynchronous socket, 191-192
    using, 191-194
    using an Archive with, 192-193
CSocketX class, 194-197
    using timeouts on Send() and Receive(), 197-198

CString objects, using with Send() and Receive(), 199
CTermView::OnSocketClose() function, 190
CTermView::OnSocketConnect() function, 189-190
CTermView::OnSocketReceive() function, 190
CWD command (FTP), 19

D

data
    exchanging at connect and disconnect, 317-319
    sending and receiving, 49-53
DATA command (SMTP), 21
database functions, asynchronous mode, 93-114
    categories, 94-95
    contents of the returned hostent structure, 96-104
    contents of the servent structure, 105-110
    host name and address resolution, 96
    protocol name and number resolution, 110-114
    service name and port resolution, 104-110
    WSACancelAsyncRequest() function, 114
datagram. *See* IP datagram
datagram ECHO service, RFC, 389
datagram sockets, record boundaries on, 53
data plane, multipoint strategy, 320
Daytime protocol, 18
DELE *argument* command (POP), 21
Department of Defense (DOD) network model, Internet protocols, 14
DLL (dynamic link library), 4
domain name system (DNS), 10-11
domain names, 10-11
dot-notation, 9-10
dotted-quad-notation form. *See* dot-notation
dwControlFlags parameter, 266-267
DWSAddressToString() utility, 398
DWSDnsOnly() utility, 399
DWSEnumProtocols() utility, 398
DWSFreeWinSock() function, 397
DWSInitWinSock() function, 394-395
DWSMaxMsgSize() utility, 397
DWSSelectProtocols() utility, 398-399
DWSVersion() utility, 397
dynamic link library (DLL), 4
dynamic linking, 391-392
dynamic name spaces, 248

Index 537

E

ECHO client program
   development of, 389
   finding a server, 408-411
   IPX workaround, 412
   linking to WinSock, 401-402
   receiving an ECHO response, 412-413
   selecting transport protocols, 402-405
   sending an ECHO request, 406-407
   user interface, 401
echo function, ICMP, 16
echo port, 45, 400
ECHO protocol, RFC, 389
ECHO request, sending, 406-407
ECHO response, receiving, 412-413
ECHO server program
   filling the local address, 420-421
   opening listening sockets, 416-420
   receiving an ECHO request, 427-429
   registering the service, 421-427
   user interface, 414
   WinSock module, 415-415
ECHO service, connectionless protocol-independent, 389
.edu (educational) domain name, 10
endpoints, 7
EnumProto application, 232-241
error messaging, ICMP, 16
error values, 32
event-driven applications, 61
event objects
   use of in WinSock 2.0, 210
   using overlapped I/O with, 379-386
explicit linking, 391-392

F

File Transfer Protocol. *See* FTP
FillLocalAddress() function, 420-421
FillSocketChoices() function, 403-405
FindEchoServer() function, 408-411
FIONBIO command, 146-147
FIONREAD command, 147
FTP (File Transfer Protocol), 18-19
   commands, 19
   RFC for, 12
function pointers, declaring, 392-394

G

GET command (HTTP), 19
gethostbyaddr() function, 32, 33-34
gethostbyname() function, 32, 33, 96-97
gethostbyX() functions, 26
GetHTTP3 source code, 307-312
   analysis of, 312-313
GetHTTP2 source code, 287-292
   analysis of, 292
GetHTTP.c client utility, 56
getprotobyname() function, 112
getprotobynumber() function, 113
getservbyname() function, 45-47, 105-106
getservbyport(), function prototype for, 108-109
getsockopt() function, 133-134
getXbyY functions, 247
.gov (governmental) domain name, 10
GROUP command (NNTP), 20
GUIDs, 249-250
   macros, 276-277
   preassigned for well-known services, 250
   special query-related, 267-268

H

Hall, Martin, 5
HEAD command (HTTP), 19
HELP command (NNTP), 20
HIBYTE macro, 30
Hitchhiker's Guide to the Internet, RFC for, 12
host name and address resolution, contents of the returned hostent structure, 96-97
host names, 10
host resolution, database functions, 94-104
Host To Host layer, 15
hostent (Host Entry) structure, 32
   members, 33
hosts and services, finding, 263-277
HTML (HyperText Markup Language) documents, retrieving, 19
HTTP (HyperText Transfer Protocol), 13, 19-20
   review of, 328-330
HTTP example servers, extending to make full-featured servers, 386-387
HTTP service, starting and stopping, 337-339
HTTP server, developing multithreaded, 365-387
HTTPA application
   architecture, 333-334
   closing the connection, 362-363

compiling, 333
reading the client's request, 355-357
REQLIST.C module, 354
running, 331-333
sending the file to the client, 357-361
sending large amounts of data, 361-362
source code files, 333
stopping HTTP service, 363-364
user interface, 330
user interface module (HTTPUI.C), 334-337
HTTPA.C
   accepting client connections, 351-352
   obtaining local address, 348-350
   request structure, 353
   request structure fields, 353
   starting HTTP service, 345-348
   tracking connections, 353-354
   waiting for event notifications, 350-351
HTTPMT application, 365-368
   compiling, 368
   running, 366-367
   source code files, 369
   user interface, 366, 369
HTTMT architecture, 368-369
HTTPMT.C server module
   communicating with the client, 377-379
   processing responsibilities, 368
   receiving the client's request, 379-382
   sending the file to the client, 382-386
   starting service, 370-373
   synchronizing client threads, 375-377
   using overlapped I/O with event objects, 379-386
   waiting for connection requests, 373-375
HTTPSERVINFO structure, 339
HTTPUI.C (user interface module), 334-337
   processing responsibilities, 368
HyperText Markup Language (HTML) documents, retreiving, 19
HyperText Transfer Protocol (HTTP), 19-20
   asynchronous model (HTTPA), 330
   commands, 19-20
Hypertext Transfer Protocol MultiThreaded Model. See HTTPMT application

I

ICMP. *See* Internet Control Message protocol (ICMP)

in_addr structure, 38-39
input/output, enhanced, 279-323
InstallClass() function, 422-424
.int (international) domain name, 10
Internet
   addresses, 9-10
   byte order, 40
   domain name server (DNS), 10-11
   structure of, 8-21
Internet Assigned Numbers Authority (IANA), 45
   assignment of protocol numbers by, 110
Internet Control Message protocol (ICMP), 16
Internet Engineering Task Force (IETF), 12
Internet layer, 14
Internet Network Information Center (InterNIC), 11
Internet Protocol, 15-16
   RFC for, 12
Internet Protocol Suite, 13-14
InterNIC, 11
INVALID_SOCKET descriptor, 42
I/O, use of overlapped in WinSock 2, 210, 293-307
ioctlsocket() function, 68-69, 146-148
IP address, 9-10
   relating domain names to, 11
IP datagram, 9
IP multicast, 162
   about, 320
   broadcast addresses, 138

L

layered protocol, WinSock 2.0, 224
LIST command
   FTP, 19
   NNTP, 20
listen() function, 25, 47-48
ListenThread() function, 373-376
little-endian format, 39, 40
LOBYTE macro, 30
local broadcast addresses, 138
Lookup Services dialog, 277

M

MAIL FROM: command (SMTP), 21
MAKEWORD macro, 28
MapFunctionPointers() function, 395-397

Index

message-driven architecture, Windows, 61-62
MFC applications, adding WinSock support to, 168-169
MFC socket classes, 165-168
.mil (military) domain name, 10
Microsoft Foundation Classes (MFC). See MFC applications; MFC socket classes
Microsoft Foundation Class Library, 165-167
Microsoft-specific extensions, 160
    performance improvement, 161-162
    support for additional transport protocols, 160-161
Microsoft's proprietary ICMP API, using to write a Ping utility, 155-160
MKD command (FTP), 19
Mosaic, 6
MSG_PARTIAL flag, 300
multicast, 162
    support in WinSock 2.0, 210
multiple protocol support, WinSock 2.0, 209
multipoint functions, support for in WinSock 2.0, 210
multipoint transmission, 319-323
    getting more information about, 323
    handling different strategies, 320
    using protocols, 320-321
multithreaded server, 365-387

N

Nagle algorithm, 145
name registration, 247
name resolution, 32-39, 247, 260
    protocol-independent in WinSock 2, 210
    utility functions, 272-276
name servers, 11
name space, 222
name space providers, WinSock 2.0, 222-223
name spaces
    enumerating available, 260-263
    types of, 248
net-directed broadcast addresses, 138
Network Access layer, 14
network byte order, 39-40
network event triggers, asynchronous mode, 89-93
network management utility, 16
Network News Transport Protocol. See NNTP

NNTP (Network News Transport Protocol), commands, 20
NNTP server, sample WSTerm session with, 178
nonblocking mode, 68-71
    determining when an operation is complete, 69-71
Novell's Service Advertising Protocol (SAP), 247
NT services, 75

O

object destruction, 177
OnInitDialog() function, 403
OnMessagePending() function, 194
OpenListeners() function, 416-420
.org (organization) domain name, 10
OSI (Open Systems Interconnection), 5, 14
    MSG_PARTIAL in, 300
out-of-band data, 16
overlapped I/O, 293-307
    checking for completion, 294-295
    choosing a completion mechanism, 295-296
    functions, 77, 299-307
    order of completion notification, 298
    return values, 296-297
    scatter and gather, 77-78, 298-299
    using, 76-77

P

packet switching, 9
packets, 9
PASS argument command (POP), 20
PeekMessage() loop, 65-66
persistent name spaces, 248
Ping, 16
    history, 150
    utility, writing, 149-155
PING.C program, 150-155
PINGI.C program, 157-160
polling method, 69-70
POP (Post Office Protocol), commands, 20-21
POP3 conversation, 116
port, finding correct, 45
port numbers. See service port numbers
POST command (HTTP), 19-20
Post Office Protocol (POP), commands, 20-21
p_proto field in host byte order, 111

Process layer, 15
process protocols, 18-20
programming
    general guidelines for application strategy, 78-80
    with WinSock, 57-80
protocol chain, WinSock 2.0, 224
protocol files, typical entries from, 95
protocol independence, for client and server programs, 389
protocol information, finding in WinSock 2.0, 225-232
protocol layers, 14-15
protocol resolution, database functions, 94-95, 110-114
protocol support, multiple in WinSock 2.0, 209
protocol types, WinSock 2.0, 223-224
protoent structure, the, 111
provider flags values, in dwProviderFlags field, 232
PumpMessages() bug, in earlier versions of MFC, 198

Q

quality of service
    data structures, 313-315
    determining, 313-317
    group, 317
    negotiating, 316
    ResourceReSerVation Protocol (RSVP), 317
    ServiceType field values, 315
    templates, 316
QUIT
    POP command, 21
    SMTP command, 21

R

RCPT TO: command (SMTP), 21
receiving and sending data, 49-53
recv() function, 26, 51-52
RecvAndEcho() function, 427-429
recvfrom() function, 26, 53
RecvRequest() function, 380-382
reenabling functions, 87-89, 287
reentrant messages, handling, 65-67
registering a service, 249-260
registration service, domain names, 11

Request For Comments documents (RFCs), 12
Réseaux IP Européens (RIPE), 11
Resource ReSerVationProtocol (RSVP), 317
RETR command (FTP), 19
RETR argument command (POP), 20
return values, WinSock, 32
RFCs (Request For Comments documents), 12. See also Appendix A
    Assigned Numbers, 250
    datagram ECHO service, 389
    Daytime protocol, 18
    Domain Name System, 11
    ECHO protocol, 389
    File Transfer Protocol (FTP), 12, 19
    The Hitchhiker's Guide to the Internet, 12
    HTTP, 19, 328-330
    ICMP, 16
    Internet Protocol, The, 12
    keep-alive option, 140-141
    NNTP, 20
    POP version 3, 21
    service port numbers, 13
    SMTP, 21, 204
    TCP, 17
    TELNET and TELNET options, 21
    UDP, 18
    URLs, 13
RMD command (FTP), 19
RNR functions. See registering a service; service resolution
RSVP. See Resource ReSerVationProtocol

S

sample programs. See Appendix A
SAP. See Novell's Service Advertising Protocol (SAP)
scatter/gather, use of in WinSock 2.0, 210
select() method, 69-71
SelectProtocols() function, 241-245
send() function, 26, 49-51
SendBuffer() function, 384-386
SendEcho() function, 406-407
SendFile() function, 382-383
SendFileContents() function, 383-384
sending and receiving data, 49-53
SendMail application
    implementing a simple SMTP client, 199
    main window, 200
SendMailMessage() function, 200-203

Index 541

sendto() function, 26, 52, 104
servent (service entry) structure, 46-47
    contents of, 105
server role, 47-49
service class, 249
    registering, 251-253
service class schema, 249
service name and port resolution, 104-110
    function sets for, 104
service port numbers, 12-13
Service Provider Interface (SPI), 59-61
service provider library, supplied by stack vendors, 60
service registration and resolution (RNR) functions. See registering a service; service resolution
service resolution, database functions, 94, 104-110
Services file, typical entries from, 95
Services utility, 277-278
server
    closing the connection, 190
    connecting a client socket to, 174-175
    connecting to, 189-190
    conversation with, 190
server socket, listening for clients with, 175-177
service flags, in dwServiceFlags1 field, 231
service provider order utility, WinSock 2.0, 222
service providers, WinSock 2.0, 221-222
Services utility, 277-278
SetEchoService() function, 424-427
setsockopt() function, 134-135
shutdown() function, closing connection-oriented sockets with, 54-55
Simple Mail Transfer Protocol (SMTP)
    commands, 21
    talking, 203-204
SIOCATMARK command, 147-148
SMTP (Simple Mail Transfer Protocol)
    commands, 21
    talking, 203-204
SO_ACCEPTCONN option, 136-137
SO_BROADCAST option, 137-138
SO_DEBUG option, 138-139
SO_DONTLINGER option, 139
SO_DONTROUTE option, 139
SO_ERROR option, 140
SO_KEEPALIVE option, 140-141
SO_LINGER option, 141-142

SO_OOBINLINE option, 142-143
SO_RCVBUF option, 143
SO_REUSEADDR option, 143
SO_SNDBUF option, 144
SO_TYPE option, 144
SOCK_DGRAM socket type, 41-42
SOCK_RAW type parameter, 149
SOCK_STREAM socket type, 41-42
Socket Adapter Library, 390
    adding to your applications, 400
    declaring function pointers, 392-394
    loading WinSock's, 394-397
    Unicode support, 399
    unloading WinSock's, 397
    using, 391-400
    utility functions, 397-399
sockaddr structure, 43-45
socket addresses, reusing, 144
socket control, 145-148
SOCKET_ERROR message, 50-51, 77
socket() function, 25, 41
socket options
    descriptions, 136-145
    getting, 136
    optional, 132-133
    setting, 135-136
sockets
    closing, 54-55
    connecting, 42
    control, 145-148
    creating, 25, 41-42
    descriptors, 42
    information needed before connecting to server, 42-49
    naming, 25
    programming with, 23-56
    raw, 148
    support for shared in WinSock 2.0, 210
    type and protocol, 41-42
sockets model, Berkeley, 7
sockets paridigm, 7-8
source code interface, WinSock as, 8
SPI (Service Provider Interface), 59
Stardust Technologies, testing of WinSock applications by, 131
StartHTTP() function, 370-373
StartServer() function, 415-416
STAT command (POP), 20
static name spaces, 248
STOR command (FTP), 19

542　WinSock 2.0

Stream client and server applications, examples, 56. *See also* Appendix A
stream sockets, record boundaries on, 52
subdomains, 10

T

TCP (Transmission Control Protocol), 17
TCP client utility. *See* WSTerm (WinSock Terminal)
TCP_NODELAY option, 145
TCP/IP, 16
　　network programming, 8
TELNET protocol, 21
top-level domain, 10
Transmission Control Protocol (TCP), 17
transport protocols, selecting, 402-405
troubleshooting, using ICMP, 16

U

UDP/IP, 16
Unicode characters, WinSock 2, 217
Unicode support, WinSock 2, 217
URLs (Uniform Resource Locators), 13
USER argument command (POP), 20
User Datagram Protocol (UDP), 18
Usenet news messages, reading, 20

V

version negotiation, 30-32
virtual circuit, 17

W

well-known services, Internet, 12-13
wide characters. *See* Unicode characters
Windows
　　handling reentrant messages, 65-67
　　message-driven architecture, 61-62
Windows C++ class libraries, 166
Windows Open Services Architecture (WOSA), WinSock as a part of, 6
Windows Sockets (WinSock) API. *See also* WinSock
　　vs. Berkeley sockets API, 58
WinInet classes, 167-168
WinMain() function, 402
WinSock
　　acceptance of, 6
　　adding support for to MFC applications, 168-169
　　blocking functions, 64-65
　　blocking sockets, 63-64
　　defined, 4-5
　　extensions, 62-63
　　files and platforms for the three distributions, 7
　　general guidelines for your application strategy, 78-80
　　initializing, 27-32
　　introduction to, 3-22
　　official specification documents for, 7
　　optional features, 131-163
　　programming fundamentals, 26
　　programming with, 57-80
　　requirements for using, 6-7
　　return values, 32
　　socket options, 132-
WinSock Group, formation of, 5, 6
WinSock HTTP server module, 345-364
WINSOCK.DLL, 131
WinSock 1.0, 58
WinSock 1.1
　　key features of, 58-59
　　MFC socket classes, 165-205
　　porting to WinSock 2, 217-221
　　Windows-specific functions added in, 62-63
WinSock Terminal. *See* WSTerm (WinSock Terminal)
WINSOCK2.H, 217
WinSock 2.0, 3, 5, 59-61
　　binary compatibility with WinSock 1.1, 218-219
　　concepts, 221-232
　　connection setup and teardown, 213
　　enhanced input/output, 212-213
　　EnumProto application, 232-241
　　event notification, 213-214
　　introduction to, 209-246
　　linking to at run-time, 390
　　multicast and multipoint, 213
　　multiple protocol support, 211
　　name space providers, 222-223
　　new features in, 209-217
　　new I/O control codes, 215-216
　　new socket options, 215
　　other frequently requested extensions, 215
　　porting from 1.1 to, 217-221
　　protocol-independent name resolution, 211-212

Index 543

protocol types, 223-224
quality of service, 214
selecting protocols, 241-245
service (server application), 223
service provider order utility, 222
service providers, 221-222
source compatibility with WinSock 1.1, 219-221
specification status, 216-217
WINSOCK2.H, 217
Winsock version independence, of application, 389, 390
Win32 event objects, 75
World Wide Web
　retrieving files from, 56
　WinSock part in growth of, 6
WSA (Windows Sockets API). *See* WinSock
WSA_IO_PENDING error code, 77
WSAAccept() function, 317-318
WSAAddressToString() function, 272-273
WSAAsyncGetHostByAddr() function, 102-104
WSAAsyncGetHostByName() function, 98-101
WSAAsyncGetProtoByName() function, 112-113
WSAAsyncGetProtoByNumber() function, 113-114
WSAAsyncGetServByName() function, 106-108
WSAAsyncGetServByPort() function, 109-110
WSAAsyncSelect() function, 72-74, 84-93
　canceling asynchronous messages, 93
　handling event messages, 85-87
　network event triggers, 89-93
　options for the event parameter, 85
　reenabling functions, 87-89, 89
　requesting asynchronous events, 84-85
WSACancelAsyncRequest() function, 74
　function prototype for, 114
WSACancelBlockingCall() function, 66-67
WSACleanup() function, 27
WSAConnect() function, 317-318
WSADATA structure, 28-30
　members, 29
　Windows 95/WinSock 1.1, 30
WSAECONNREFUSED error, 48
WSAEINPROGRESS error code, 67
WSAEINTR error, 67
WSAENOTINITIALISED error, 28
WSAEnumNameSpaceProviders() function, 260-263
WSAEnumProtocols() function, Winsock 2, 225-227

WSAEventSelect() function, 76
WSAEWOULDBLOCK error code, 68
WSAGETASYNCERROR macro, 99-100
WSAGetLastError(), 27
WSAGetOverlappedResult() function, 297-298
WSAGetServiceClassInfo() function, 275-276
WSAGetServiceClassNameByClassId() function, 274-275
WSAInstallServiceClass() function, 251-253
WSAIsBlocking() function, 66-67
WSAJoinLeaf() function, 321-323
WSALookupService() functions, 263-272
WSALookupServiceBegin() function, 263-264, 266-268
WSALookupServiceNext() function, 263, 268-272
WSALookupServiceEnd() function, 263
WSANSCLASSINFO structure, WinSock 2, 250-251
WSAPROTOCOL_INFO structure, WinSock 2, 227-228
　fields of, 228-230
　provider flags values in dwProviderFlags field, 232
　service flags values in dwServiceFlags1 field, 231
WSAQUERYSET structure
　fields when registering a service, 255-256
　lpcsaBuffer field in, 256
　using during registration, 254-255
WSARecv() function, 77, 299-302
WSARecvDisconnect() function, 317-318
WSARecvFrom() function, 77, 302-303
WSASend() function, 77, 303-305
WSASendDisconnect() function, 317-319
WSASendTo() function, 77, 305-307
WSASERVICECLASSINFO structure, 249-250
WSASetBlockingHook() function, 67-68
WSASetService() function, 257-260
WSAStartup() function, 27
WSAStringToAddress() function, 273-274
WSAUnhookBlockingHook(), 67-68
WSTerm (WinSock Terminal) application, 178-191
　building, 179
　Connect dialog box, 189
　CTermSocket class, 179-181
　CTermView class, 181-189
　limitations, 191
WSVer application, 32

IDG BOOKS WORLDWIDE, INC. END-USER LICENSE AGREEMENT

READ THIS. You should carefully read these terms and conditions before opening the software packet(s) included with this book ("Book"). This is a license agreement ("Agreement") between you and IDG Books Worldwide, Inc. ("IDGB"). By opening the accompanying software packet(s), you acknowledge that you have read and accept the following terms and conditions. If you do not agree and do not want to be bound by such terms and conditions, promptly return the Book and the unopened software packet(s) to the place you obtained them for a full refund.

1. **License Grant.** IDGB grants to you (either an individual or entity) a nonexclusive license to use one copy of the enclosed software program(s) (collectively, the "Software") solely for your own personal or business purposes on a single computer (whether a standard computer or a workstation component of a multiuser network). The Software is in use on a computer when it is loaded into temporary memory (RAM) or installed into permanent memory (hard disk, CD-ROM, or other storage device). IDGB reserves all rights not expressly granted herein.

2. **Ownership.** IDGB is the owner of all right, title, and interest, including copyright, in and to the compilation of the Software recorded on the disk(s) or CD-ROM ("Software Media"). Copyright to the individual programs recorded on the Software Media is owned by the author or other authorized copyright owner of each program. Ownership of the Software and all proprietary rights relating thereto remain with IDGB and its licensers.

3. **Restrictions On Use and Transfer.**

(a) You may only (i) make one copy of the Software for backup or archival purposes, or (ii) transfer the Software to a single hard disk, provided that you keep the original for backup or archival purposes. You may not (i) rent or lease the Software, (ii) copy or reproduce the Software through a LAN or other network system or through any computer subscriber system or bulletin-board system, or (iii) modify, adapt, or create derivative works based on the Software.

(b) You may not reverse engineer, decompile, or disassemble the Software. You may transfer the Software and user documentation on a permanent basis, provided that the transferee agrees to accept the terms and conditions of this Agreement and you retain no copies. If the Software is an update or has been updated, any transfer must include the most recent update and all prior versions.

4. **Restrictions On Use of Individual Programs.** You must follow the individual requirements and restrictions detailed for each individual program in Appendix A of this Book. These limitations are also contained in the individual license agreements recorded on the Software Media. These limitations may include a requirement that after using the program for a specified period of time, the user must pay a registration fee or discontinue use. By opening the Software packet(s), you will be agreeing to abide by the licenses and restrictions for these individual programs that are detailed in Appendix A and on the Software Media. None of the material on this Software Media or listed in this Book may ever be redistributed, in original or modified form, for commercial purposes.

5. **Limited Warranty.**

(a) IDGB warrants that the Software and Software Media are free from defects in materials and workmanship under normal use for a period of sixty (60) days from the date of purchase of this Book. If IDGB receives notification within the warranty period of defects in materials or workmanship, IDGB will replace the defective Software Media.

(b) IDGB AND THE AUTHOR OF THE BOOK DISCLAIM ALL OTHER WARRANTIES, EXPRESS OR IMPLIED, INCLUDING WITHOUT LIMITATION IMPLIED WARRANTIES OF MERCHANTABILITY AND FITNESS FOR A PARTICULAR PURPOSE, WITH RESPECT TO THE SOFTWARE, THE PROGRAMS, THE SOURCE CODE CONTAINED THEREIN, AND/OR THE TECHNIQUES DESCRIBED IN THIS BOOK. IDGB DOES NOT WARRANT THAT THE FUNCTIONS CONTAINED IN THE SOFTWARE WILL MEET YOUR REQUIREMENTS OR THAT THE OPERATION OF THE SOFTWARE WILL BE ERROR FREE.

(c) This limited warranty gives you specific legal rights, and you may have other rights that vary from jurisdiction to jurisdiction.

6. **Remedies.**

(a) IDGB's entire liability and your exclusive remedy for defects in materials and workmanship shall be limited to replacement of the Software Media, which may be returned to IDGB with a copy of your receipt at the following address: Software Media Fulfillment Department, Attn.: *WinSock 2.0*, IDG Books Worldwide, Inc., 7260 Shadeland Station, Ste. 100, Indianapolis, IN 46256, or call 1-800-762-2974. Please allow three to four weeks for delivery. This Limited Warranty is void if failure of the Software Media has resulted from accident, abuse, or misapplication. Any replacement Software Media will be warranted for the remainder of the original warranty period or thirty (30) days, whichever is longer.

(b) In no event shall IDGB or the author be liable for any damages whatsoever (including without limitation damages for loss of business profits, business interruption, loss of business information, or any other pecuniary loss) arising from the use of or inability to use the Book or the Software, even if IDGB has been advised of the possibility of such damages.

(c) Because some jurisdictions do not allow the exclusion or limitation of liability for consequential or incidental damages, the above limitation or exclusion may not apply to you.

7. **U.S. Government Restricted Rights.** Use, duplication, or disclosure of the Software by the U.S. Government is subject to restrictions stated in paragraph (c)(1)(ii) of the Rights in Technical Data and Computer Software clause of DFARS 252.227-7013, and in subparagraphs (a) through (d) of the Commercial Computer–Restricted Rights clause at FAR 52.227-19, and in similar clauses in the NASA FAR supplement, when applicable.

8. **General.** This Agreement constitutes the entire understanding of the parties and revokes and supersedes all prior agreements, oral or written, between them and may not be modified or amended except in a writing signed by both parties hereto that specifically refers to this Agreement. This Agreement shall take precedence over any other documents that may be in conflict herewith. If any one or more provisions contained in this Agreement are held by any court or tribunal to be invalid, illegal, or otherwise unenforceable, each and every other provision shall remain in full force and effect.

my2cents.idgbooks.com

Register This Book — And Win!

Visit **http://my2cents.idgbooks.com** to register this book and we'll automatically enter you in our monthly prize giveaway. It's also your opportunity to give us feedback: let us know what you thought of this book and how you would like to see other topics covered.

Discover IDG Books Online!

The IDG Books Online Web site is your online resource for tackling technology — at home and at the office.

Ten Productive and Career-Enhancing Things You Can Do at www.idgbooks.com

1. Nab source code for your own programming projects.
2. Download software.
3. Read Web exclusives: special articles and book excerpts by IDG Books Worldwide authors.
4. Take advantage of resources to help you advance your career as a Novell or Microsoft professional.
5. Buy IDG Books Worldwide titles or find a convenient bookstore that carries them.
6. Register your book and win a prize.
7. Chat live online with authors.
8. Sign up for regular e-mail updates about our latest books.
9. Suggest a book you'd like to read or write.
10. Give us your 2¢ about our books and about our Web site.

Not on the Web yet? It's easy to get started with *Discover the Internet,* at local retailers everywhere.

CD-ROM Installation Instructions

The setup program (SETUP.EXE) is stored in the root directory of the CD-ROM. This program requires Windows 3.1 or higher, or Windows 95 or Windows NT. Here are the steps to run the Setup program:

1. Insert the CD-ROM into the CD drive.
2. Run SETUP.EXE and follow the instructions.

With this Setup program you can select from several installation options:

- Install everything.
- Install only the sample programs.
- Install only the WinSock 1.1 specification documents.
- Install only the WinSock 2 specification documents.
- Install any combination of specification documents and sample programs.

It is not necessary to restart your computer when the Setup program finishes.